MW01088253

Guaranteed Pure

Guaranteed Pure

The Moody Bible Institute,
Business, and the Making of
Modern Evangelicalism

TIMOTHY E. W. GLOEGE

The University of
North Carolina Press
CHAPEL HILL

© 2015 The University of North Carolina Press
All rights reserved
Set in Calluna
by codeMantra

The paper in this book meets the guidelines for permanence and durability of the Committee on Production Guidelines for Book Longevity of the Council on Library Resources.

The University of North Carolina Press has been a member of the Green Press Initiative since 2003.

Cover illustration: A. F. Gaylord, business manager of the Moody Bible Institute, June 1927. Courtesy of the Moody Bible Institute Archives.

Complete cataloging information can be obtained online at the Library of Congress catalog website.

ISBN 978-1-4696-2101-2 (cloth: alk. paper)

ISBN 978-1-4696-3343-5 (pbk.: alk. paper)

ISBN 978-1-4696-2102-9 (ebook)

For Lillian and Eleanor

Contents

Illustrations

Acknowledgments

A decade of work has created many debts for me to gratefully acknowledge. The history department at the University of Notre Dame provided many mentors. As my advisor both in graduate school and after, George Marsden has modeled immense patience, thoughtfulness, and generosity that have been equal to his scholarly accomplishments. I benefited greatly from Gail Bederman's exemplary work in cultural history and her mentorship during a two-year postdoctoral fellowship. John McGreevy asks among the best (and most difficult) questions of anyone I know. My work is much better for seeking to answer them as a result. Doris Bergen modeled how to write religious history that engages wider cultural trends. Her perspective, grounded in the European context, brought a broader perspective into my work. Thanks also to Walter Nugent, David Waldstreicher, Scott Appleby, James Turner, Kathleen Sprows Cummings, Ted Beatty, Fr. Thomas Blantz C.S.C, Catherine Schlegel, and Tom Slaughter for their important contributions to my development as a historian.

I have benefited greatly from several sources of institutional support. A Charlotte W. Newcombe Fellowship from the Woodrow Wilson National Fellowship Foundation in 2006–7 allowed me to devote my final year of graduate school exclusively to writing. The University of Notre Dame supported my research in Chicago and Los Angeles through a Zahm Travel Grant. An Edward Sorin Postdoctoral Fellowship provided resources to do additional research and time to sketch out this book's initial framework. An invitation to give a paper at Biola University in 2003 allowed me to make an investigatory examination of its archival resources and introduced me to members of the Torrey family. I give my sincere thanks to all of these organizations.

Of the many people that contributed to the development of this book, three fellow travelers in the history of fundamentalism require special note. Matthew Sutton was an early advocate of this project. His close reading of my manuscript improved both its ideas and its prose. The influence of his work on fundamentalism will be evident in these pages. The same can be said of Kathryn Lofton. She, too, gave generously of her time and offered critical interventions that helped expand my horizons and clarify several still-nascent ideas. She has proven repeatedly that kindness and brilliance are not mutually exclusive qualities. Her belief in the project helped shore up my waning confidence at a critical juncture. Brendan Pietsch's late interventions during my final revisions were immensely helpful. I deeply appreciate his wit, insight, crystal-clear thinking, and the generosity with which he gave of his time and expertise.

I appreciate the many people at the University of North Carolina Press who made this book possible. Special thanks to Elaine Maisner for believing in this project and allowing me the time to develop it fully. Thanks also to Alison Shay and Caitlin Bell-Butterfield for guiding me through the publishing process, and to Jay Mazzocchi for his many improvements to the manuscript.

I am grateful to many archives, both public and private. Thanks to the Minnesota Historical Society in St. Paul, Minnesota, and the Kautz Family YMCA Archives at the University of Minnesota in Minneapolis. Chicago offers many wonderful resources for historians, including the Chicago Historical Society, Newberry Library, the University of Illinois at Chicago Library, and the great collection of historical newspapers at the Herold Washington Library Center.

It speaks to the maturity and stability of an institution when it gives access to its historical records. I am immensely grateful to the Moody Bible Institute (MBI) in Chicago for its openness. In addition to the standard materials housed in the archives, I was also given access to trustee and executive committee minutes and other corporate documents hitherto unexamined by historians. These were once housed in the MBI administrative offices, but they can now be found in the archives. Particular thanks to Tim Ostrander, Robert Gunter, and Michael J. Easley for granting this access and to Cassandrea Blakey for assistance with the materials. At the archives, thanks are due to the late Wally Osborne, Joe Cataio, Nikki Tochalauski, and especially Allana Coxwell Pierce for going above and beyond on several occasions.

At Biola, thanks to Fred Sanders for his initial invitation to give a paper at Biola, for his insights into Reuben A. Torrey, and for an advanced preview to the ongoing digitization project of the *King's Business*. Sue Whitehead reworked her busy schedule to allow me extra time in the archives and graciously allowed me to use digital photography to accommodate my limited stay in Los Angeles. Additional thanks to Carri Javier and Flo Ebeling for spending several afternoons and evenings in the archives extending my access even further. It was with Flo that I discovered a cache of misfiled and forgotten letters for the Testimony Publishing Company—the organization responsible for *The Fundamentals*. These documents provided an unprecedented inside look at their creation. Greg Vaughan and family, and Gary and Jen Hartenburg, offered much-appreciated hospitality in Los Angeles. I am also indebted to Darren Dochuk for research tips, sharing travel costs, and many interesting and helpful discussions. Bill Svelmoe helped with introductions and other important matters.

Some of my sources were culled from locations other than archives, forcing me to impose on the goodwill of individuals. The kindness, trust, and cooperation of the Torrey family was essential. Particular thanks to Slade Johnson for bearing with my constant pestering for sources and for putting me in contact with other family members. Lyn Newbrander offered the use of her extensive, previously unexamined collection of Torrey family correspondence, books, photographs, and ephemera. This gave me access to essential materials from Torrey's ministry in Garrettsville and Minneapolis, including an original diary from 1889 that was significantly altered when it was later published by MBI. I hope I repaid her trust by leaving the documents in better condition than I found them. Although this project did not turn into a biography of Reuben Torrey, as I had originally anticipated, I hope the book will help humanize this complex but often-caricatured figure. Archival descriptions of Torrey's warm and affectionate private life came alive in my interactions with his descendants. They also modeled the continuing relevance of Torrey's theology for many evangelicals today.

The final revisions of the book would have been impossible without two institutions in Grand Rapids. The excellent library at Calvin College more often than not had the obscure book in religious history that I needed to see. I am also deeply grateful to the Grand Rapids Public Library. Without the support of its interlibrary loan service, the ability for independent scholars like myself to continue our work would be impossible.

Three venues where some of these ideas were formally presented require special mention. The Colloquium on Religion in American History at the University of Notre Dame provided a space in which to discuss several aspects of this project in development. Thanks to George Marsden for originally organizing it and to the many participants for their thoughtful input. In 2011 the Heidelberg Center for American Studies at the University of Heidelberg hosted a conference titled "Religion and the Marketplace in the United States" that was seminal to solidifying the key ideas of the book. Thanks especially to Detlef Junker and Phil Goff for organizing it and to all the scholars who offered encouragement and insights, especially R. Laurence Moore, Mark Valeri, Grant Wacker, Matt Hedstrom, Uta Balbier, Barry Hankins, Hilde Lovdal, and Daniel Silliman. Finally, Kathryn Lofton organized a workshop for scholars of fundamentalism at Yale University in 2013. Thanks to Seth Dowland and Mike Hamilton for their helpful comments on my work, and also to the other participants, including Dan Vaca, David Watt, Mary Beth Mathews, Kati Curts, and Emily Johnson. Others have given helpful input and encouragement at various venues, including the late Sarah Hammond, Peggy Bendroth, Pamela Walker Laird, David Sicilia, Michael Flamm, John Hardin, Peter Williams, Jeanne Kilde, and Robyn Muncy.

Many informal academic conversations have been immensely helpful. One of my most important conversation partners is Heath Carter, who, despite studying very different historical subjects than me, wrestles with similar big questions. My work is all the better for my looking at this story through the eyes of his working-class subjects. My understanding of how evangelicalism operates was initially spurred by several conversations with Bryan Bademan. Thanks are also due to Joe Creech, Darren Dochuk, Chris Cantwell, Phil Sinitiere, Erik Peterson, Darren Grem, Laura Rominger Porter, Raully Donahue, David Swartz, and Cris Mihut. Thanks also to Ed Blum, Anita Talsma Gaul, Andrea Turpin, John Haas, Margaret Abruzzo, Micaela Larkin, Sarah Miglio, and Angel Cortes.

I am indebted to the comments and critiques of those who read complete drafts of this book, often in very rough form. In addition to Lofton, Sutton, and Pietsch, Lisa Workman Gloege read the entire manuscript with an economist's eye and a copyeditor's pen. Mark Noll generously read some early work on this topic and provided essential input. Thanks also to the many others who, at various stages, have read parts of this work: Kathryn Long, Edith Blumhofer, George Marsden, Sean McCloud, Kristin Kobes Du Mez, Tommy Kidd, David Swartz, Kathleen Sprows Cummings, Elizabeth Hoffman Ransford, John Turner, Tom Rzeznik, Matt Grow, and Tammy Van Dyken. Their insights in each case helped tremendously.

Grand Rapids has provided me with access to a wonderful intellectual community, academically affiliated and otherwise. In addition to some already listed, I am grateful for conversations and interactions with James K. A. Smith, Mike Wassenaar, and Steve Staggs. Adding friendship to insightful conversation are Ryan Genzink, Jen Vander Heide, Lisa Cockrel, and Meg Jenista. To the Fletters, Willinks, Monsmas, and Arnoys-LaGrands: you make me feel like I have family in town. This book would not have been completed without the help of the Sparrows, especially Lori and Monika, and also the good folks at Rowsters and Kava House. Thanks to the Meanwhile and Brewery Vivant for hosting after-hours conversations.

This book is dedicated to Lillian and Eleanor, who have lived with this project for as long as they have existed. Thanks for sitting on my lap each morning to help me remember what is truly important. Lisa has lived with this project for as long as me and has sacrificed more than anyone to let me finish it. I am forever grateful to have you as my partner in everything I do.

Guaranteed Pure

Introduction

The face of modern marketing in the early twentieth century belonged to an old-fashioned Quaker. Consumers across the United States could purchase Quaker pharmaceuticals, lace curtains, and men's negligee shirts. They were wooed with ads wryly depicting "Quaker Maids" sailing the high seas atop bottles of rye whiskey.[1] But all other efforts paled in comparison to the Quaker Oats Company. A sophisticated pioneer of promotion, it had spent millions of dollars since the mid-1880s to make its smiling Quaker trademark synonymous with breakfast food, guaranteed pure.

Members of the Society of Friends, the real Quakers, were not flattered by the attention. In 1916 they sought legal protection by a bill that outlawed using religious names "for the Purposes of Trade and Commerce." The Federal Council of Churches (FCC), an ecumenical group representing most major Protestant denominations, also threw its support behind the measure. Together they argued that the commercial use of denominational names stole goodwill from their religious owners. Surely the country's moral guardians deserved the same basic protections that secular businesses enjoyed.

Not surprisingly, the corporate attorneys for Quaker Oats vehemently disagreed. Legal precedents were clear that any word, sacred or not, could be used for commercial ends. Thus, they argued, the bill was an outrageous government overreach, confiscating a private asset—their thirty-year-old trademark—over the hurt feelings of a small sect. These business arguments held sway in the hearings that followed. "My sympathies are with the religious institution," Representative John M. Nelson insisted only halfway through the proceedings, but "under the Constitution we can not take away property rights."[2] The measure died quietly in committee.

In Chicago, Henry Parsons Crowell celebrated the outcome. As the long-standing president of Quaker Oats and a major shareholder, the bill's demise preserved his substantial financial interests. Yet whatever his material interests and disregard for denominational sentiment, Crowell was no enemy of religion. For the previous decade, he had quietly worked to advance a particular type of evangelical Protestantism soon christened "fundamentalism." He had already developed an institutional headquarters for this religious work at the Moody Bible Institute in Chicago. More recently, he and his allies had organized a full frontal attack against liberal Christianity in a publication called *The Fundamentals: A Testimony to the Truth*. These projects drew from Crowell's business techniques and raised the hackles of denominationally based conservatives and liberals like the current president of the FCC, Shailer Mathews. How fitting, then, that these parties faced each other again over a bill seeking special protection for denominations. In more ways than one, Crowell's religious and business interests were thoroughly intertwined.

THIS BOOK EXPLAINS HOW a faith like Crowell's developed during the previous forty years and came to thrive in the twentieth century and beyond. Between the Civil War and World War I, a group of "corporate evangelicals" created a new form of "old-time religion" that was not only compatible with modern consumer capitalism but also uniquely dependent on it. Leaders of this network, spanning two generations, included key participants in the fundamentalist movement. Some, like Crowell, were pioneering innovators in business. Others worked as professionals before entering into full-time religious work. Still others were ministers who exchanged their seminary training for a faith more relevant to their parishioners' workaday lives. Whatever their background, they all held the same ideological convictions. All embraced the individualistic religious assumptions of what we call evangelicalism. They held a set of ideas about self and society that were common in business. And all assumed an instrumental approach to knowledge that was born of engineering, law, and business. These ideological strands formed a "corporate evangelical" framework, a mutually reinforcing model of reality. The world worked consistently, they believed, stretching from shop floor to prayer closet, from legal library to Bible study, from the drafting table to a defense of their faith. God created this "natural order," chose to operate by its principles, and promised spiritual and material success to believers who did likewise.

There are many points of entry to this corporate evangelical network, but the story that follows focuses on one of its key institutions, the Moody

Bible Institute (MBI) in Chicago. MBI was founded by the salesman-turned-revivalist Dwight L. Moody, the most important evangelical of the late nineteenth century. He ingeniously weaved disparate ideas drawn from business and religion into a compelling, if unstable, form of evangelical Protestantism. It took America by storm in the 1870s. MBI, founded in 1889, was the culmination of Moody's efforts to train others in spreading this message by whatever means possible, a task he called "Christian work." Amid labor unrest, he and leading business figures in Chicago envisioned MBI producing an army of Christian workers that would convert the working classes and restore social stability. The Reverend Reuben A. Torrey, a Yale-educated banker's son, took the lead in developing a new theory and practice of Christian work at MBI. He combined metaphors of industrial work with expectations of God's miraculous intervention in everyday life.

After Moody's death in 1899, a second generation of evangelicals led by Crowell transformed MBI in significant ways. They shifted focus from converting the working classes to influencing middle-class Protestantism and swapped their overarching metaphor of industrial work with modern consumption. They implemented corporate-inspired changes in organization and governance to ensure a consistent message. In the 1910s, this "business basis" made MBI a central hub for the nascent fundamentalist movement. Nearly every publication, organization, and conference that contributed to the nationwide movement had direct connections to MBI, its personnel, or their close allies. This dominance helped spread its corporate and consumer orientation throughout the network. Most self-described conservative evangelicals today, the spiritual progeny of these early fundamentalists, still embrace those assumptions.

Fundamentalism is often described in terms of manifestos and theological propositions. Yet at MBI at least, the life force of the movement was its corporate evangelical framework, which operated at a more foundational level. It functioned as a set of unexamined first principles—as common sense. Once developed, these principles became for conservative evangelicalism what the rules of grammar are to a conversation: something *used* rather than analyzed. The analogy of language is particularly appropriate here, for corporate evangelicalism was embodied primarily in an interlocking set of metaphors. More than simply illustrating particular ideas, metaphors can also shape how we think about them.[3] Analogies drawn from business and business-aligned professions radically altered carefully crafted theologies of God and humanity that had been developed over hundreds of years. According to these unexamined assumptions, society was an aggregate of rational individuals who approached their decisions identically in both the marketplace and a religious context. God operated by a similar logic: creating as an engineer designs, communicating like a lawyer, and brokering relationships by contract. They linked "truth" to "purity," so that correct belief came not by scientific discovery but by legal interrogation, not by fearlessly challenging received wisdom but by rigorous processes of industrial quality control. These and other starting principles united theology and political economy into a consistent system.

Corporate evangelicals certainly were not the first Protestants to apply business ideas to their faith, but their appropriation differed in two respects. First, their economic context was different. The consumer-oriented ideas and practices from which they borrowed had developed between 1880 and 1910. These new economic realities, related to both work and consumption, coursed through already established metaphorical links, infusing their religious analogs with new meaning.

Corporate evangelicals also differed from past Protestants in the *degree* to which they relied on business ideas to understand their faith. Historically, other cultural inputs were equally important in shaping religious belief and practice. Denominational theological traditions, the natural sciences, philosophy, and other domains of knowledge formed a web of ideas, exerting varying levels of influence. Corporate evangelicals, in contrast, largely abandoned their unquestioned allegiance to a particular denominational tradition and typically exchanged the formal study of theology for a practical faith. At the same time, a large-scale revolution in scientific understanding, inspired by Darwin, had begun challenging the centrality of individual choice in shaping the world. Instead, many scientists posited, a combination of environmental factors and inborn traits were the primary drivers of development. They also embraced a new understanding of scientific knowledge, displacing direct observation and certitude for more speculative inquiries, statistical populations, and answers for which incertitude or a margin of error was never completely eliminated. Especially as these ideas spread beyond biology and into the social sciences and humanities, corporate evangelicals became alienated from academic inquiry. Instead, they became increasingly dependent on cultural arenas in which individual choices still mattered and certitude was the goal.

In the world of modern consumer-oriented business, the act of human choosing, if anything, had become even more important. For professionals in business, law, and engineering, the individual still mattered, direct observation was venerated, certain knowledge was pursued, and precise one-to-one correlations and easily quantified results were the rule. Thus evangelicals found an ideological haven in an alternate science of humanity that relied on a cluster of ideas orbiting business. It is the bifurcated nature of modernity that helps to explain many curious paradoxes of American society after the Civil War, including the persistent complaint by cultural critics that the "American Character" is simultaneously too individualistic and too conformist.[4] In this divided modernity, conservative evangelicals found space not merely to survive, but also to thrive.[5]

Thus what follows is more than a story of a single institution or religious movement. It is also a wider investigation into the intersection of religion and class in America during the birth of modern consumer capitalism. It traces the changing locus of religious authority from corporate bodies (churches) affiliated with denominations that functioned largely on democratic principles to a radically individualistic basis of religious authority, with believers loosely corralled by religious organizations structured like corporations. This shift to a consumer orientation is often associated with self-consciously liberal religious actors. Yet, I will argue, these dynamics were pioneered by the forebears of today's conservative evangelicals. Understanding how this might be the case requires a critical reexamination of how we define evangelicalism and its opposite, conceptualize "liberal" and "conservative" religion, and understand the dynamic relationships between religion, class, and social power. In the section that follows, I will offer a brief overview of a new framework for understanding a broader history of American Protestantism. Then I will sketch out the story of corporate evangelicalism told in this book in a little more detail, positioning it within this broader historical dynamic I describe.

SINCE THE EIGHTEENTH CENTURY, Protestantism in the United States has been shaped by two competing impulses. A "churchly" orientation was the older of the two and structured the first European settlements in North America. Churchly Protestants assumed that an authentic faith required sincere and active membership in a particular church and that religious authority, though rooted in the Bible, was exercised by that institution. This meant that biblical interpretation should be governed from the past through theological tradition and in the present by ordained clergy. Finally, it meant that the vitality of religious faith was judged primarily in reference to the condition of the institutional church and the community it fostered.

A church was absolutely essential to the preservation of religion and, like government, was a necessary part of the social order.

Churchly assumptions were held almost universally by "respectable" Protestants—those wielding significant social and cultural power—but this began to change after the rise of an intellectual movement called the Enlightenment. Enlightenment thinkers were deeply suspicious of tradition, aristocratic privilege, and the intrinsic authority of religious and political institutions. Instead, they encouraged individuals to think for themselves, to test long-standing assumptions using reason and empirical observations. They valorized the individual and in some cases began to conceptualize society as a collection of persons rather than an organic unity. Enlightenment thought led some advocates to reject religion altogether, but others used these ideas to create new religious forms. An "evangelical" orientation was one such hybrid of Protestantism and Enlightenment thought.

Evangelical Protestants challenged three important aspects of a churchly orientation. First, they shifted the primary locus of authentic faith from the communal context of church membership to an individual's personal relationship with God. Second, they rejected the authority of church and tradition. Instead, evangelicals asserted that God's will was revealed to believers directly. God spoke primarily through a believer's personal reading of the Bible, but communication might also come through thoughts impressed on the mind, unusual coincidences, and other nonverbal cues. These divine messages might be misinterpreted, they acknowledged. But this potential problem was addressed by a third conviction: authentic faith always produced empirically measurable outcomes. These "godly fruits" were essential to confirming the validity of their faith and the accuracy of their interpretation of God's revelation. Outcomes could include new converts to the faith, social reform, spiritual renewal, and, for some, even miracles.

I have described evangelicalism and churchly Protestantism in propositional terms, but it is important to remember that these were *orientations*, not formal creeds. They comprised a set of starting assumptions that shaped religious belief and practice at a basic level. Thus, evangelicalism could be embraced by conservatives to defend long-standing points of belief and practice, and by liberals to modify them. It was embraced both by social elites in their defense of the existing social order and by radicals seeking to overturn it. Churchly and evangelical orientations fall on a continuum, and because of their malleability, these commitments were never entirely stable. Institutions, groups, and individuals might shift to accommodate new circumstances. And some believers might combine aspects of both orientations as needs arose.

The ebb and flow of evangelical and churchly orientations have been a driving force in the history of American Protestantism. A religious movement called the Great Awakening marked the first manifestation of the evangelical orientation in the 1730s and 1740s. Initially, elites used evangelical assumptions to "revive" and reorient flagging religious adherence. But when evangelical radicals challenged the religious and social order, elite revivalists reversed course and united with the churchly traditionalists they once opposed.[6]

The same oscillation between churchly and evangelical dominance continued in the following century. An evangelical orientation produced new forms of individualistic belief and practice that seemed fresh and relevant, spurring revivals. It diminished the importance of denominational identities, allowing elites to create an informal, but still powerful, Protestant establishment that shaped law and policy.[7] But over time, the same evangelical principles also generated threats to the social order: slave rebellions, radical abolitionist movements, and utopian communities that undermined traditional concepts of gender, sexual practice, and family organization.[8] Thus a generation of evangelical expansion during the first third of the nineteenth century was followed by a churchly reversal among "respectable" Protestants that lasted through the Civil War. They emphasized church membership, denominational identity, theological systems, and religious nurture rooted in the nuclear family.[9]

The rise of modern evangelicalism after the Civil War, related in the pages that follow, was a new historical development, but it also represented another cyclical ascendance of the evangelical orientation. It came amid a crisis within churchly Protestantism, spurred by the carnage of the Civil War, new scientific and philosophical ideas, and a growing "urban crisis" that left many "respectable" Protestants demoralized and overwhelmed.[10] Evangelicalism offered compelling solutions to the problems of the day. For urban churches, a personal relationship to God offered a new avenue to authentic faith for the masses. A "plain" reading of the Bible, inspired by a "realist" approach to texts, reinvigorated a holy book weighed down by overly cautious interpretive strategies and tired denominational orthodoxies. Best of all, evangelicalism encouraged believers to expect empirical results from their faith: saved souls and reform of a society that seemed to be teetering on the edge of collapse under the social, political, and economic crises of the Gilded Age.

The reinvigorated evangelical orientation that emerged in the Gilded Age, what I call "evangelical realism," was embraced by a diverse group of Protestants that included future fundamentalists, liberal modernists, and participants in the early twentieth-century Pentecostal movement. It cleared away the theological deadwood, opening the possibility for believers to create new patterns of belief and practice, unencumbered by tradition.

One part of the broader coalition of evangelical realists, the corporate evangelicals of this story, was particularly inspired by ideas related to the emerging industrial economy, especially to metaphors associated with work. They self-consciously appropriated the title "Christian worker" to define their particular God-given calling. Leading the charge was Dwight L. Moody. He saw strong resonances between evangelism and his background in sales and set about applying "secular" methods to religious ends. As a celebrity revivalist in the 1870s, he helped spread these ideas across the country. Business elites, attracted by Moody's business-inflected religion, also believed he held the solution to easing the growing labor unrest and restoring social order. The collaboration of Moody and business elites was institutionalized in the Moody Bible Institute. MBI was funded by Chicago businessmen like Cyrus McCormick Jr. and developed in tandem with Reuben A. Torrey. They promised to unleash an army of trained Christian workers to convert the masses of Chicago.

But as with past evangelical resurgences, disorder was not far behind. Torrey brought his own vision of a Christian worker to MBI, including God's miraculous intervention as a possible "empirical" result of authentic faith. His realism ironically produced an enchanted world. When "radical evangelicals" used Moody's plain reading of the Bible and Torrey's miracle-tinged faith to their own revolutionary ends, it brought the entire evangelical project into question. Growing concerns over radical evangelicalism touched MBI directly in a controversy at the turn of the century over faith healing and the use of modern medicine. When Moody suddenly died in the midst of this crisis, it signaled the end of an era.

Faced with evangelical-inspired disorder, "respectable" Protestants historically retrenched themselves behind churchly norms: a firewall of tradition, historic creeds, and denominational authority. But at the turn of the twentieth century, the traditional cycle was disrupted by two alternative solutions. Liberal Protestants forged a self-consciously "modernist" Protestantism, using insights drawn from the social sciences. Rooted in established denominations, they embraced tradition critically, acknowledging that all beliefs developed over time and would continue to evolve in the future. They placed special emphasis on the social dimension of Christianity—both "corporate" sins, like economic systems that did not align with Jesus's ethics, and the environmental causes of "personal" sins. They embraced professional expertise and insisted on a scientific interpretation of the Bible that discounted many of its miracles and a belief in God's disruptive intervention in the present. Though these liberals also made peace with modern consumer culture, it was always in tension with their commitment to modern science.

Corporate evangelicals at MBI developed a second solution to evangelical disorder. Leveraging the metaphorical connections to business forged by Moody, new leadership headed by Crowell set about making evangelicalism safe for middle-class consumption. Crowell's theological engineer in these matters was a genteel Reformed Episcopal minister from Boston named James M. Gray. They shifted MBI's focus from converting the industrial working classes and creating Christian workers to influencing middle-class Protestantism and developing careful and savvy consumers of pure religion. They minimized God's miraculous intervention in the present using an esoteric interpretive system called dispensationalism that was inspired by legal and engineering principles. Similarly, Gray's understanding of a personal relationship to God was stripped of its disruptive potential and brokered by the same techniques that advertisers used to generate ostensible relationships between consumers and corporations. By exploiting techniques developed to control a rambunctious marketplace, they fabricated a "respectable" evangelicalism that was compatible with professional middle-class norms in a modern consumer culture.

Thus liberal modernism and corporate evangelicalism constituted two equally modern, but fundamentally incompatible, alternatives to churchly retrenchment. And since both groups aspired to speak for "respectable" Protestantism, conflict was inevitable. Corporate evangelicals fired the first volley in 1909. Working with a California oilman named Lyman Stewart, Crowell and other MBI administrators helped publish a twelve-volume theological manifesto titled *The Fundamentals*. In addition to challenging the validity of modernist biblical interpretation, it had a second, more ambitious, end: to create a generic, nonsectarian, "conservative" Protestantism free of denominational control. They promoted this new theological standard using techniques that Crowell had used to give Quaker Oats its historic patina. And like a modern promotional campaign, they distributed the publication free of charge to every Protestant minister and religious professional in the country they could find. *The Fundamentals* created an imagined community of Protestants from across the country that united as self-identified "fundamentalists." In the following decade, they rallied to the defense of this new form of "old-time religion."

As the theological battle became heated during World War I, modernists noted the populist elements the movement had attracted and painted fundamentalism as a source of religious and social disorder. Saddled by associations to allies it was unable to control, MBI backed away from the fundamentalist label in the early 1920s and laid claim to the less-controversial term "evangelical." But despite the change in name, corporate evangelicals continued their disruptive strategy. They used modern promotional techniques to bypass the authority of traditional religious institutions, transforming denominational affiliation into an identity signaling mere stylistic preference. On matters of "orthodoxy," they positioned conservative evangelicalism as the only alternative to modernism and made MBI's founder, Dwight L. Moody, the face of this evangelical orthodoxy.

The lasting significance of *The Fundamentals* project laid in its methods, not its contents. It pioneered a means of creating an evangelical "orthodoxy" out of an ever-shifting bricolage of beliefs and practices, each of varying historical significance and some entirely novel. Unencumbered by an overarching logic, the fragments that constituted conservative evangelicalism faded in and out to accommodate contemporaneous circumstances. *The Fundamentals* thus pointed the way forward for modern conservative evangelicalism by modeling the methodology for creating, and constantly recreating, whatever "orthodoxy" the present moment required.

Corporate evangelicals helped to reorient Protestantism for the modern age. Notwithstanding small pockets of traditional denominationalists,[11] most Protestants today identify primarily as being either "conservative" or "liberal." By disconnecting a modern middle-class identity from its traditional basis in church membership, corporate fundamentalists ironically provided a means for still-respectable middle-class professionals to slip outside the orbit of organized religion entirely, facilitating a wider secular turn in American society.

Thus the fusion of business ideas and conservative evangelicalism strengthened the cultural position of both. It provided evangelical conservatives with a means of relating to the wider culture despite being out of step with modern scientific understandings of humanity. This reliance on the novel ideas and methods intrinsic to consumer capitalism in turn helped naturalize them. Anyone accepting that fundamentalism represented traditional "old-time religion," whether embracing or opposing it, inevitably concluded that its complementary economic assumptions—some of which were radical departures from traditional economic morality—were simply part of the natural order. But thus entwined, conservative evangelicals effectively hobbled their ability to offer systematic critiques of capitalism once offered by self-identified conservatives of an earlier era.

GUARANTEED PURE TELLS THE story of corporate evangelicalism in two parts. The first part focuses on the rise of post–Civil War evangelicalism and the crisis that ensued. Chapter 1 traces the early life of Moody, the rise of evangelical realism, and his role in developing modern evangelicalism through ideas of Christian work. Chapter 2 charts rising labor unrest and its role in the development of the Moody Bible Institute. Chapter 3 examines Torrey's early life, his ideas about "power for service," and the ways they developed during his tenure at MBI. Finally, chapter 4 traces the developing crisis of evangelical realism in the 1890s caused by radical evangelicals, the scandal at MBI involving the faith healer John Alexander Dowie, and new strategies of interpreting the Bible developed to counter that challenge.

The second part of the book traces the transformation of corporate evangelicalism after 1900 and its development into the conservative evangelicalism that exists today. Chapter 5 charts Crowell's early life and work, his efforts to put MBI on a "business basis," and his first attempt to influence middle-class Protestantism. Chapter 6 charts the key pivot by corporate evangelicals at MBI from religious identities rooted in Christian work to consumer identities branded as "pure religion." Chapter 7 tells the story of the creation of *The Fundamentals*, the conflict and contingencies that shaped the project, and the methodology for creating an ad hoc "orthodoxy" that resulted. Chapter 8 follows the resulting conflict between fundamentalists and modernists that arose in the 1910s and the rise and fall of the fundamentalist coalition in the 1920s. An epilogue traces the role of MBI in the continuing developments of modern conservative evangelicalism to the present.

A FEW MATTERS OF definition require attention. Economic class plays a central role in my analysis of religion and social power. I will not go into detail about my particular model of what "class" is and does.[12] Let it suffice to say that, like E. P. Thompson, I consider class as something that *happens* rather than *is*. It is rooted primarily in economic conditions rather than mere social preferences, yet it is also an ideological system of power, like race, gender, and (I would argue) religion. As such, it has wide-ranging effects on noneconomic arenas of experience while also being affected by them. This is particularly evident in the class conflict within the middle classes between Populist insurgents and the professional classes aligned with elites.[13]

Race and gender considerations are interwoven throughout the work,[14] but as a book about a corporately structured, professional middle-class coalition of conservative evangelicals, its subjects are disproportionately white males. I introduce other voices when possible, but my contributions to this line of research will remain suggestive. Much more can be done to relate the racial and gendered dimensions of modern consumption to modern evangelicalism.[15]

My use of the term "evangelical" will reflect the complex and shifting patterns I already have outlined, but I should note that this is a departure from prevailing scholarly and religious definitions, which rely almost exclusively on evangelicals' self-perception. The standard academic definition, formulated by historian David Bebbington, outlines four distinguishing marks of evangelical religion: a belief in conversion, a "particular regard for the Bible," "activism" (the expression of one's faith through effort), and a particular stress on Jesus's sacrificial death.[16] This is a helpful encapsulation of conservative evangelical self-understanding, but it also perpetuates their theological judgments. That is to say, the implication of this definition is that nonevangelicals treat the Bible carelessly, reject conversion, fail to act on their faith, and largely disregard the death of Jesus (this notwithstanding the crucifixes that adorn every Catholic sanctuary). It fails to account for the ways that churchly Protestants, both conservative and liberal, differentiate themselves from evangelicals. For these, the salient differences relate to evangelicalism's intrinsic individualism, its naïve faith in a "plain" interpretation of the Bible (or, alternatively, its dispensational framework), and its excessive focus on quantifiable and empirical "results" of faith to the exclusion of other means of evaluation. While I hope evangelicals might see themselves in my definition, I believe that there is a need to balance their self-perception with interrogations of the label by outsiders. By questioning current assumptions about evangelicalism, I hope to sketch a new map of American Protestantism—and even American religion—that better accounts for both similarities and differences between groups that are often glossed over.

For the sake of clarity, let me explicitly reject the practices of equating "evangelical" with "conservative Protestant" and positing "liberal" as its opposite. An adherent's attitude toward the development of religious belief and practice over time—the crux of the matter when determining a conservative or liberal orientation—is logically (and practically) independent from whether a believer understands his or her faith as either an individualistic and quantitative project or a communal and qualitative project. Such conflation obscures the evangelical ethos of spiritual seekers like Oprah Winfrey, for example.[17] Widening the definition of evangelical helps explain how ideas once intrinsic to individualistic forms of liberal belief and practice are later adopted by individualistic conservatives. To be sure, conservative evangelicals have aspired to create a "conservative Protestantism" in their own image, but conservative churchly forms still persist. The degree to which conservative evangelicals have succeeded in making themselves the public face of conservative Protestantism has been a remarkable rhetorical achievement—but it was precisely that.

Although a transdenominational conservative Protestantism does not really exist, there is a "conservative evangelicalism" that can be defined in general terms. Briefly, conservative evangelicals emphasize that their individualistic relationship to God is with a person, generally a "he." Their individualistic, "plain" interpretation of the Bible is superintended by dispensational assumptions that keep the most radical implications of the Bible in check, even if they do not consciously ascribe to every nuance of the esoteric system. And generally, they consider social reform a fruit secondary to evangelism.

My use of the term "fundamentalist" refers simply to members of that coalition of conservative evangelicals who rallied around this label in the early 1910s and 1920s. There has never been a consistent creedal definition of fundamentalism, nor a group that has consistently chosen to identify by that name. Once seen by conservative evangelicals as a broadly appealing brand, over time it was claimed by an ever-shrinking group with a variety of motivations. Opponents have consistently used the term as a slur.

THIS BOOK THUS ATTEMPTS to explain the continuing vibrancy of conservative evangelicalism and its ideological and political allegiances to modern consumer capitalism, despite theological features that might appear esoteric and "antimodern" to the uninitiated. It finds that, notwithstanding points of continuity, the early fundamentalist movement represented a marked departure from key assumptions of nineteenth-century Protestantism. I will not claim that all self-identified fundamentalists were "champions of capitalism" or hailed from the professional middle classes. Neither do I assert that MBI alone perfectly captured what was an impossibly diverse coalition of people who claimed that label in the 1910s and 1920s, nor that connections to modern consumer capitalism explain all aspects of conservative evangelicalism.[18] But I do claim that the core leadership of the early fundamentalist movement—those who controlled its key institutions, funded its endeavors, and helped define precisely what those "fundamentals" were—was profoundly influenced by modern business. They were decidedly urban and ideologically aligned with the professional and elite bourgeoisie. They were early adopters of modern corporate organization and marketing strategies for religious ends. But even more, they accepted consumer identities and techniques that were deeply troubling to their Populist and liberal cousins. Their role as purveyors of a conservative, traditional "old-time religion" augured the broad and rapid acceptance of consumer culture in the early twentieth century and has made them powerful social actors today.

PART ONE

Christian Workers

ONE

Christian Work

As the United States teetered on the brink of dissolution in September 1860, the minister and abolitionist editor Thomas M. Eddy was busy addressing another crisis. Eddy had been part of a massive migration that had created his adopted city of Chicago virtually ex nihilo. A fourfold population increase in the last decade had strained housing, sanitation, and government services to the breaking point. The same was true of the moral infrastructure. Like most midcentury Protestants, Eddy believed the bedrock of the social order rested on the twin pillars of home and church. Both were in short supply. The population of the prairie metropolis consisted primarily of unattached young men. Only a handful had church ties for reasons obvious to any careful observer. The city's few churches sold their seating by the pew at inflated prices, leaving newcomers with the equally humiliating options of standing in the back or being paraded to unused seats as a freeloader. No surprise that the sons of many a Protestant home made their community in neighborhood saloons, gambling halls, even brothels. Urban religion was in danger, Eddy feared, and without its civilizing influence, complete social breakdown loomed on the horizon.

But despite the gravity of the crisis, Eddy was in a celebratory mood. This September evening, his talk was to mark the beginning of a bold new experiment: the Chicago Young Men's Christian Association (YMCA). Even more than the organization itself, Eddy's address celebrated the broader impulse behind it, something he called *"religion in a work day dress."* Traditionally, Protestants understood the market primarily in reference to its intrinsic temptations to self-interest, greed, and dishonesty—a social space that functioned properly only by the steady infusion of Christian virtue. Of course, this influence was still needed, but Eddy saw the YMCA as the product of a new countercirculation in which business ideas and practices were imported into religion. Seeing that young men needed opportunities to develop Christian community, it was businessmen, not clergy, that took the initiative in promoting this new solution. If businessmen and professionals—lawyers, doctors, merchants, and even mechanics—were to apply their perceptive acuity and "rare mental discipline" to the cause of religion, Eddy preached, who knew what victories were in store? Where "pedlar of divinity" was once a term of derision, Eddy invited his audience to proudly apply their workaday skills to the cause of religion.[1]

We do not know for sure that a young Dwight L. Moody heard Eddy's talk, but it is certain that no one contributed more to the realization of his dream. Indeed, Moody took the idea much farther than Eddy probably intended. Raised outside traditional Protestantism and without formal religious education, Moody used business ideas and techniques not only to spread the message of God's love for individuals but also to transform that message. By the time Moody began his revival ministry in the 1870s, he had developed a set of interlocking assumptions about the nature of an authentic faith, a believer's relationship to God, and a modern approach to interpreting the Bible. And within a decade, Moody's modern evangelicalism, shaped profoundly by ideas imported from the world of business, had been grafted into the belief and practice of many middle-class Protestants.

DWIGHT L. MOODY WAS born in 1837, the sixth child of Betsey and Edwin Moody in Northfield, Massachusetts. It was a year remembered for a financial panic and depression so severe that it shook the nation's basic economic assumptions at their core. The Moody family could not avoid its impact. Though Edwin was a hardworking and frugal brick mason, his debtors' defaults swept him into financial ruin along with the libertines and real estate speculators. The resulting stress no doubt contributed to the heart attack that took Edwin's life when young Dwight was four. The Moody family's estate consisted of debts and a new set of twins, leaving Edwin's destitute widow with eight children to feed.

Betsey staved off poverty through connections to kin and her Unitarian church, a denomination most Protestants deemed unorthodox. Dwight was baptized in the church at six, and their minister faithfully paid the family home visits. The Moody home was loving, but never secure. Betsey was a proud woman, and this meant skipped meals and winter mornings without firewood. Moody would later recall his trauma as an eight-year-old briefly lent out to an ill-tempered elderly couple who lived a day's walk from his home.[2] Surely this uncertainty contributed to his being a poor and disruptive student. He was impulsive, hotheaded, and stubborn—characteristics that portended a future of failure by the metrics of mid-nineteenth-century business philosophy. A dozen terms of schooling reaped only a rudimentary literacy.[3]

Moody's less-admirable qualities were on full display in his impulsive move to Boston, against his mother's wishes, at seventeen. Confident in the strength of his bootstraps, he then impudently rejected his uncle's offer of employment, only to crawl back when he found that his narrow attainments made such self-making impossible. Unsteady start notwithstanding, Moody made good as a clerk in his uncle's shoe and boot shop. He yoked a winsome, confident personality to a ruthlessly pragmatic business philosophy born of poverty. He ignored existing agreements between clerks to equally divide sales opportunities, souring his relationship to his coworkers. But he did not care; business was not a communal activity.

Moody was more disturbed by his difficulties navigating the communal world of respectable middle-class Protestantism. He attended the Mount Vernon Congregational Church with his uncle as a stipulation of employment, but the weekly chore only further depressed his scant interest in religious things. It was the high-water mark of churchly Protestantism, a religious orientation marked by three key characteristics. First was a conviction that theological traditions mattered. Creeds, rituals like baptism and communion, and church organization and governance were all important markers between denominations. These topics were preached on Sundays, often in technical terms that were mind-numbing to the uneducated. A second characteristic of churchly Protestantism was its affirmation that religious authority resided in the institution of the church. God met and engaged his people in church, through a Bible carefully interpreted by ordained ministers and guided by tradition. Finally, churchly Protestantism meant that the evidences of an authentic faith were found inside the church—both in the vitality of the institution itself and in the functioning of the community it fostered. Christianity was primarily a matter of *being*—in church, in community—rather than doing or choosing. Children were saved under this same communal canopy of God's grace, unless they decided as adults to leave it. All this made church a comforting haven to established members, but a difficult community for outsiders to join. At this time especially, urban congregations were turned decidedly inward, focused on middle-class reproduction and foiling the "confidence men" angling for the benefits of church membership.[4] For a young illiterate Unitarian, it made for a cold and baffling initiation to orthodox Protestantism. And the brash and uncouth Moody had little that would appeal to the well-mannered and educated congregation.

Although a churchly orientation prevailed among respectable Protestants, a handful leaned toward an evangelical orientation. Among these was Edward Kimball, the Sunday school teacher who converted Moody to evangelical Protestantism. Unlike their churchly counterparts, evangelicals emphasized a personal relationship to God over church and tradition. They also tended to vest religious authority in the individual; that is to say, birthing an authentic faith was a matter of individual choosing, and maintaining that faith was a matter of following one's individual conscience and feeding one's soul through personal Bible reading, prayer, and authentic engagement in worship. But in the 1850s, among respectable evangelicals at least, this dimension was significantly muted. As a matter of course, they admitted that church and tradition were necessary evils to corral extremism, though they also believed these instruments might suffocate a sincere faith. Finally, these evangelicals believed that their faith, if truly authentic, would bring about some tangible good. For Kimball, this meant that he was on the lookout for outsiders like Moody. It was fitting, given Moody's future, that his conversion took place at work. Kimball felt led to call on Moody and offered him a simple explanation of "Christ's love for him and the love Christ wanted in return." He later judged this presentation as "very weak," but it deeply touched the lonely boy. It had demonstrated Kimball's personal concern and God's love. So Moody made a simple choice: he accepted the invitation to convert.[5]

The decision to accept Jesus settled the matter for Moody, but church leadership was not convinced. His first application for church membership was flatly rejected when he failed a rudimentary theological exam. For his examiners, conversion involved the mind as well as the will. Committed to joining the church, Moody spent ten months preparing for his next examination, but it did little more than solidify a lifelong dislike of theology. In the end, his examiners were swayed less by his theological proficiency than his sincere, if defiant, insistence that he would "never give up his hope, or love Christ less, whether admitted to the church or not."[6] Better to get such a boy within a church, where he could be guided properly. The experience made Moody suspicious of religious institutions and the barriers that theological traditions posed to uneducated believers.

Having learned the basics of the shoe business, a restless Moody tried his prospects in Chicago in 1856. His timing was impeccable. The prairie metropolis was booming thanks to its status as the terminus of most major rail lines in the eastern United States. Its many shoe manufacturers had no established distribution networks, and Moody easily found a position as a drummer, supplying stock to rural stores. These positions were important avenues to respectability and thus typically available only to white, native-born Protestant men like Moody.[7] As in Boston, he made unorthodox innovations to established business practice. At a time when rural retailers typically traveled to Chicago to purchase inventory, Moody shrewdly cherry-picked the most promising customers from hotel registries and train manifests, promising to visit them the next time. This became standard practice twenty years later, but it earned him bitter complaints in the 1850s.[8] Moody was rewarded handsomely by his employer, however. His base salary of $30 per week was well above the wage of an average industrial worker and nearly four times his Boston earnings.[9] Including commissions, he was earning $5,000 annually, which even by wage levels thirty years later placed him among the "well-to-do."[10] And with his returns on subsequent real estate investments and personal loans, his dream of accumulating $100,000 seemed within reach.

Despite Moody's economic success, he struggled to find a spiritual home within churchly Protestantism. He transferred his membership to the respectable Plymouth Congregationalist Church, but he found navigating its middle-class norms difficult. He was deeply wounded when, after speaking up at a prayer meeting, his minister advised him that he "could serve the Lord better by keeping still."[11] He also attended Methodist and Baptist churches but met similar resistance. He persisted, however, and eventually earned the respect of a small coterie of businessmen with evangelical sympathies. His first and closest friend was John V. Farwell, a devout Methodist soon known as the city's largest dry-goods wholesaler. Among the Baptists, he met the prominent attorney Cyrus Bentley, who later orchestrated the creation of International Harvester with its future president, Cyrus McCormick, another important Moody supporter.

Moody's devout business friends had the most important influence on his early faith. This was especially true during a period of evangelical-oriented renewal that spread across America's business districts amid a sharp, but brief, financial panic in 1857. In Chicago, Farwell and Bentley helped organize daily noon-hour prayer meetings that attracted an interdenominational following. To preserve the peace, they avoided theological and political issues and focused instead on heartfelt prayer, singing, and Bible reading, which all Protestants embraced. This was conventional piety in one sense, but it fostered revolutionary undercurrents. In an age of feminine and domestic-oriented religion, participants depicted the movement as explicitly male, literally erasing women from published illustrations and relegating their bodies to balconies and other peripheral spaces. They conducted meetings in business-district theatres, symbolically centering the movement in public economic life, removed from home and church. Devoid of ministerial oversight, the meetings thus became open space in which these men could reimagine faith in terms of their workaday lives. They brushed aside thorny philosophical conundrums. Rather than trying to square an all-powerful and all-knowing God with human freedom at the moment of conversion, for example, they made conversion another routine decision. It was a choice offered by God that anyone could accept or reject.[12]

The so-called businessman's revival positioned Moody as a religious insider for the first time in his life, and when Bentley and Farwell institutionalized the movement in the Chicago YMCA, he knew he had found a spiritual home. The YMCA straddled the space between church and the public square. It was blessed by the city's respectable denominations but was operated by pious businessmen independent of denominational control. While the noontime prayer meetings continued, members were also encouraged to invite acquaintances to the association rooms for wholesome evening recreation and Christian camaraderie.[13]

The "religion in a workday dress" that suffused the YMCA also spurred Moody to action, but, given his scant education, he was not initially sure what to do. Even reading the Bible aloud meant he faced "a great many of the words he could not make out and had to skip."[14] He decided to focus on tasks that leveraged his sales ability. Attuned to recognizing untapped markets, he focused on reaching working-class souls through tract distribution and filling the several pews he rented. The parade of unattached young men he brought each Sunday, including hungover saloon haunters, did not improve his reputation among the respectable set.[15]

Moody's primary vehicle for outreach was a Sunday school located in a notorious Near North Side neighborhood known as "The Sands." Ostensibly under the superintendence of Farwell, Moody had free rein to experiment with business-inspired outreach. He left the actual teaching to others, whom he selected without reference to their theological background,

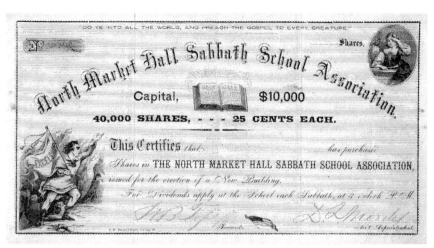

One of the "shares" Dwight L. Moody used to raise funds for his Sunday school.
Holders were told "For Dividends apply at the School each Sabbath, at 3 o'clock P.M."
in order to see the changed lives they were helping to bring about.
(Courtesy of the Moody Bible Institute Archives)

"Methodists, Calvinists, Liberals, rich and poor, high and low, learned and unlearned."[16] Whether the teacher continued was determined solely by the students, who were free to switch between classes at will. It was a market-based policy that one biographer claimed "would have made Mr. Darwin's heart glad."[17] Moody's primary focus was gathering students—by pony rides, pockets of candy, and occasional promises of new suits for Christmas. He later targeted parents and other neighborhood adults with food, clothing, and a 700-volume library.[18] Soon the operation was bursting with upwards of 1,500 students, making it one of the largest Sunday schools in the country. When this growth required a bigger building, he raised funds by issuing 40,000 "capital shares" at twenty-five cents each. The "dividends" were of a spiritual sort, available "at the School each Sabbath, at 3 o'clock."[19]

By 1860 Moody made the unconventional decision to "work for Jesus Christ" full-time. His announcement to do so without ordination initially "shocked" one business associate, though he later concluded it accurately reflected "the facts" since Moody's "work for the Lord was just as real and as vigorous at it had always been for his other employers."[20] "Vigorous" was an understatement. Early biographies recount Moody pouring out whiskey, barely avoiding beatings, and occasionally disbursing corporal punishment of his own in saloons, tenements, and slums. This religion of the working-class streets aroused suspicion among the city's ministers.[21] Few doubted Moody's sincerity, but many ministers questioned his propriety and, as the moniker "crazy Moody" suggests, his sanity.

Over the next decade, the mocking dismissal of Moody's work gave way to grudging respect. Initial legitimacy came by his business supporters, as when John Farwell brought Abraham Lincoln to visit Moody's Sunday school in November 1860. The onset of the Civil War solidified this support. Moody immediately joined the United States Christian Commission, an organization birthed by evangelical businessmen, including Farwell, to organize the spiritual and benevolent support of the Union army.[22] His tireless work ethic and prodigious organizational ability shone.[23] Personal transformations during this time also contributed to his growing respectability. In 1862 Moody married Emma Revell, daughter of a respectable shipbuilder, who helped school the future evangelist in the mores of the middle classes and polished his often rough edges. Though Moody would never be a gentleman, he now embodied the rough-hewn but "respectable" man of business that became his public persona.[24] The war transformed Moody personally. Walking through battlefields filled with the unburied dead and medical tents filled with hundreds on death's door sobered him. It led to his engaging in spiritual triage, first pleading for conversions from mortally wounded soldiers and later organizing religious services before battles, even leading them if no minister was available. It was a spiritual emergency that rendered propriety irrelevant. The pragmatism of Moody's end-of-life calculus was off-putting to some, but a greater number of once-skeptical ministers were won over by Moody's hard work and selflessness. He had proven himself in wartime.[25]

Perhaps the most striking confirmation of Moody's new respectability was the nearly unprecedented dispensation he received from the city's ministers in 1864 to establish a nondenominational house of worship, the Illinois Street Church. Moody's success at converting working-class adults through his Sunday school led to the same tensions with middle-class churches he had experienced as a new convert. A new independent church seemed the best solution.[26] Like other respectable churches, it was led by properly educated and ordained ministers. But as its colloquial name suggests, "Moody's church" also bore the unmistakable stamp of its founder.

WHEN THE CIVIL WAR ended, northern evangelicals mobilized to support the Union forces saw no rest in their future. Some continued their relationship with the Union army, supporting Reconstruction efforts in the South. But others, including Moody and most of his business allies, resumed "reconstructing" the urban North. Indeed, Chicago's growth was hardly dampened by the war. Its population tripled in the 1860s to nearly 300,000, roaring past Boston and Baltimore to become the nation's fifth-largest city. Concerns over vice, poverty, nascent labor unrest, and underequipped religious institutions were even greater now than before the war.

The new evangelical network that formed to address the "urban crisis" in Chicago and elsewhere used a new term for their efforts: "Christian work." Before the Civil War, the phrase rarely appeared in print and referred incidentally to ministerial tasks or the "work" of sanctification—that moral improvement God demanded of all believers. During the war, evangelicals began using "Christian work" to reference a particular type of lay-oriented religious activity. This did not include preaching or the defense of the faith "in formal debate," as one writer clarified. Instead, it was "to work for Christ . . . in everyday life," whether in teaching Sunday school, distributing tracts and reading scripture in "the homes of the poor," or other activities.[27] Moody understood his wartime activity as falling under this rubric, and in 1865 he helped organize the first in a series of annual "Christian Conventions" designed to limn the proper boundaries of this new Christian work in an urban context. The prominent attorney Henry F. Durant gave a keynote address titled "Christian Work the Duty of the Christian Church." Subsequent conventions attracted an impressive array of forward-looking pastors, seminary professors, politicians, and professionals. Together, they hammered out a fuller definition of Christian work. As the liberal Brooklyn minister Theodore Cuyler explained, appropriate "lay labor" included uncontroversial tasks like teaching in Sunday schools and operating benevolent societies. But he also included work traditionally reserved for ministers, like public prayer and singing, "proclaim[ing] the Gospel," and visitation. He still considered expository preaching (that is, interpreting the Bible), church discipline, and officiating baptisms and communion out of bounds. But this list of "distinctive ministerial duties" was notably shorter than churchly conservatives would compose.[28]

Moody was never content with mere discussion, however, and his new position as president of the Chicago YMCA after the Civil War provided a platform to develop Christian work by practice. He devoted most of his time to practical benevolence, which was also the least controversial part of the work. An employment bureau was finding work for 5,000 men by 1869.[29]

Bimonthly "Association sociables" (open to "everybody, irrespective of age, race, color, condition or anything else") taught proper middle-class etiquette and provided a wholesome atmosphere for unattached youth to meet future spouses.[30] At one point, he proposed building boardinghouses that would offer "the cheerful influences of a home,"[31] and he teamed up with the Chicago Library Association to open the first public library (without complaint of its Sunday operations). When his temperance stance was rendered implausible since visitors could not find something to drink outside a tavern, he spearheaded the installation of Chicago's first public drinking fountains.[32] But whether he was providing life's necessities or wholesome entertainments, Moody saw benevolence as the honey that trapped the unbelieving soul, a means of getting "hold of the hearts of the people."[33] This was reflected in Moody's ambitious plan to leverage the labor of YMCA members. He divided the city into districts, assigning a member to each and instructing him to meet every resident "with a tract in one hand and a loaf of bread in the other."[34] At this point, Christian work meant spiritual and physical ministry working in tandem.

Convinced that the work required a top-notch headquarters, Moody engaged in an ambitious building campaign and tackled the necessary fund-raising with his trademarked unconventionality. On one occasion, he created a fund-raising "committee" of sixty business leaders—when his primary targets were the committee members themselves. When donations lagged, he sold stock in the proposed building, this time promising real dividends from potential rental revenues from its well-appointed auditorium and retail shops.[35]

Moody dedicated the new YMCA headquarters in September 1867. Christened Farwell Hall to honor its main benefactor, it was a symbol in brick and mortar of a new hard-won reputation. Supporters now included a who's who of the Chicago business elite, including Cyrus and Nettie McCormick, lumber magnate Turlington W. Harvey, banker Elbridge G. Keith, foundry owner Nathaniel S. Bouton, A. T. Hemingway (grandfather of the famous novelist), mortgage lender James Houghteling, and department-store pioneer Robert Scott.[36] They appreciated Moody's pragmatic approach to ministry and his straight talk, tireless work, and Spartan lifestyle. In appreciation, they provided his family with a middle-class existence. His rent-free home was filled with donated bourgeois trappings. The Western Elastic Sponge Company furnished an astounding $157 worth of mattresses, and prominent artists donated family portraits.[37] Not all of high society embraced

Moody. The stuffy *Chicago Tribune* still complained that his interactions with clergy lacked due deference, though it now designated him a "peculiar and local institution" and a notable "lay exponent of Chicago Christianity" who brought the YMCA "to a high state of efficiency."[38] Meanwhile, his reputation as an expert in urban missions spread nationally through his Christian Conventions and internationally by YMCA networks.[39]

Moody's newfound respectability made him no more amenable to churchly Protestantism. Instead, he became increasingly convinced that the system designed to protect the faith was choking the life out of it. Why must God only speak and act in the world through traditional religious institutions? Did biblical interpretation really need to be constrained by a dense theological framework? Was conversion really so complex that it should be "the work of the elders" except in times of emergency?[40] Moody chafed at these assumptions. They created barriers between ordinary people and their God, made church feel claustrophobic, and made faith irrelevant to everyday life. He wanted something more.

MOODY'S RELIGIOUS RESTLESSNESS WAS but one manifestation of a broader backlash against Protestant middle-class cultural norms in the 1870s. The mass death and destruction of the Civil War, new scientific findings, the gritty realities of urban living—all of this challenged midcentury Protestant romanticism and spurred adoption of a new set of "realist" assumptions. In the literary world, this orientation was manifested in the desire of authors to gaze unflinchingly at "reality." It gave rise to writings filled with clear, empirically rooted descriptions and "natural," plainspoken dialogue. In philosophy, it contributed to the rise of a new pragmatism and scientific positivism. It was reinforced in new patterns of statistical thinking and "fact gathering" that fed later reform efforts. Natural selection presumed a realist framework, and social Darwinism purported to represent the fearless acceptance of underlying biological "realities," whatever the implications to traditional fairness or Christian ethics. The realist disposition was spread through the novels and magazines of elites but also by penny newspapers, dime novels, and urban-dwellers' own experiences with the realities of industrial life.[41]

Many self-described Christian workers in Moody's network combined realist assumptions and criticisms of churchly norms into an "evangelical realist" orientation. At its core were attitudes similar to its literary equivalent. Evangelical realists embodied a desire to face the "reality" of spiritual things regardless of the possible dangers of disorder, the offense to respectable sensibilities, or the complications to long-established theological tenants. They dispensed with sentimental views of God, the baroque symbolism of the sacraments, and the intricate theological systems undergirding denominational "orthodoxies." Positively, they wanted their faith and practice to reflect realist values. This meant reading the Bible in the same way that literary realists wrote their novels. The Bible, in other words, should be read plainly, as though it were a straightforward, empirically oriented description of reality. God was a person in an ordinary sense. And because the Bible was the "word of God," it should be interpreted as a straightforward communication. They believed that becoming a Christian, entering into a relationship with God, should provide both eternal life in the future and practical and measurable effects today.

For young Protestants who only knew churchly norms, evangelical realism was a strikingly fresh departure, uncharted territory in which to discover an authentic faith. But the assertion that the Bible was to be read "plainly" had appeared within American Protestantism before. And past attempts, by conservative churchly assessments, had not ended well. The reason was simple, conservatives asserted: God communicated truth through the natural world and the Bible in the same way. Both required properly trained "eyes to see" in order to discover accurate scientific or theological principles. Just as an uneducated observer might erroneously conclude that the sun revolved around the earth, so the amateur exegete might draw misguided conclusions from the surface meanings of scripture. Thus ministers were charged with the ultimate responsibility of superintending their parishioner's interpretations.[42]

In the 1870s, churchly conservatives had a stockpile of anecdotes to use against the "plain" interpretation of the Bible. It was a practice pioneered in America by "unorthodox" Unitarians and Universalists. It was used by numerous radical sectarians to justify all manner of social and moral deviations, including sexually promiscuous utopian societies. Even seemingly respectable, "scientific" projects could quickly ride off the rails.

The Adventist debacle thirty years before loomed large in the minds of churchly conservatives. Since the French Revolution, a small group of so-called premillennialists had begun applying a "plain" interpretation to biblical prophecy. Their core conviction that Jesus would physically return to earth and establish a literal 1,000-year earthly reign quickly spiraled into off-putting speculations. They searched prophetic texts for evidence of current events, proclaiming Napoleon to be the Antichrist and current wars to be Armageddon. Premillennialism also countered the prevailing idea that churches were responsible for bringing in God's kingdom through reform and mission work. Conservatives feared it bred an anarchistic disposition: civilization did not matter. In the 1840s, these fears came to a head. The leading premillennial advocate in the United States, William Miller, claimed that his esoteric numerical science had pinpointed the exact day of Christ's second coming to October 22, 1844. His followers quit their jobs, sold their belongings, and donned white ascension robes to wait for their savior on roofs and hilltops. After this, many Adventists drifted into heterodox waters, claiming Jesus had already returned "spiritually" or was incarnated in one or another sectarian leader. The moral of the story, respectable Protestants concluded, was that biblical interpretation without theological guardrails inevitably resulted in disordered belief and practice.[43]

Thus, a socially disruptive premillennialism prevented most respectable Protestants from embracing a "plain" interpretation of the Bible. But a small group, associated with an obscure British sect called the Plymouth Brethren, set about to cleanse premillennialism of its past excesses. According to the leading Brethren figure, John Nelson Darby, the problem stemmed from date setting. The Bible clearly taught that no one knew the day or hour of Jesus's return. And more, he asserted, this event coincided with the "rapture," an instantaneous gathering of all true believers to heaven. Only then would the other biblical prophecies be literally fulfilled. Darby's modifications seem arcane, but the rapture—an event no one could miss—served as a firewall to date-setting extremism.[44] Doctrinaire premillennialists, interested in prophecy as an end to itself, still speculated about current people and events. But these were harmless parlor games that always ended with the reminder that no one knew God's inscrutable plan. Pragmatic premillennialists, impatient with end-time chronologies, might dispense with such speculations altogether.

Darby's "futurist" premillennialism opened the way for a "plain" reading of the Bible, but his irascible personality and dogmatism limited his direct influence. Divisive and argumentative, he regularly separated from allies over minor points of theology. Even teachings on God's free gift of grace became legalistic nit-picking focused relentlessly on judgment and retribution. It soured other Brethren ideas that might have had wide and liberal appeal, such as the minimizing of denominational boundaries and a focus on God's love. For Darby, doctrine was an end unto itself; thus he complained that "the American line of things" was "work, not truth," and he disparaged the overly "active" Moody for his ignorance of basic theology.[45]

Darby's doctrinaire teachings held no appeal for Moody, but a trip to Great Britain in 1867 introduced him to a genteel Brethren network with connections to the YMCA. Leading this group was Darby's nephew, the broad and well-mannered William Pennefather. Hailing from an elite and politically connected Irish family, he was tutored by his uncle before becoming an Anglican priest and serving in the London borough of Islington. But he combined premillennialism with a warm spirituality that emphasized a personal, interactive relationship with God. George Mueller was another important member of the irenic Brethren network. A German immigrant to Bristol, Mueller embraced a simple biblical literalism focused on answered prayer. He boldly determined to operate an orphanage "on faith," without asking for donations of any kind. His publications offered thrilling anecdotes of God's last-minute provision to a worldwide following that, in turn, gave generously to his ministry. Both men modeled a practical faith producing measurable results that appealed to Moody. He was particularly taken by Mildmay, Pennefather's collection of ministries founded a few years earlier to serve the parish's poor residents. Its charitable pragmatism resonated with Moody's developing ideas of Christian work. Mueller, too, was a model of sorts. Although Moody was never shy about asking for donations, Mueller's taking the Bible at face value held great appeal.[46]

Moody returned to Chicago with new Brethren influences in tow and another that came of its own accord. A Brethren evangelist named Henry Moorehouse appeared one day at Moody's Illinois Street Church and asked to preach. Though initially ambivalent, Moody was transfixed by what he heard. Typically, ministers composed sermons to explain the meaning of a particular Bible passage and how it related to a larger theological and scriptural context. It required education and tended toward dry dissertations of Greek grammar or Hebrew culture. But Moorehouse modeled a new approach to the Bible. His weeklong series used a bricolage of scriptural texts to explain what the Bible had to say about a single topic: God's love. Each verse was taken at face value. He ignored immediate context and theological frameworks. Instead, he combined other isolated verses addressing the same topic into a cluster of ideas. Presuming the Bible could not contradict itself, he then shuffled and shaped these various ideas into a composite "biblical" answer. This created the powerful impression that the Bible contained a single unified message. Moreover, it was an all-sufficient text that could be used to interpret itself. Biblical interpretation did not require expertise in theology or history or the original languages. Anyone with good intentions and a Bible concordance (an exhaustive list of Bible references organized by topic) could compose a sermon.[47]

Irenic Brethren influences loomed large in Moody's blueprint for a modern evangelicalism. In the late 1860s, he engaged in a new activity, intense personal Bible study,[48] as well as experiments with short evangelistic talks. These were works in progress, to be sure. The pseudonymous theatre critic "Peregrine Pickle" compared listening to Moody with a trip "into the sewers" to "delve among the decayed dinners."[49] But any discouragement he felt from critics was compensated by a small but tight-knit group of allies. This included Moody's brother-in-law Fleming H. Revell, soon to become a dominant force in religious publishing, and Edward P. Goodwin, minister of Chicago's prestigious First Congregational Church. The second coming of Jesus held the "key to the Scriptures," they believed, and pointed the way forward to a new, relevant approach to the Bible. Small pockets of premillennialists also developed in St. Louis, Boston, New York, and other urban areas. They quietly corresponded, published magazines, and held small conferences in which they tried to make sense of the prophetic scriptures. Some were inspired directly by Darby and part of the Brethren movement; others remained in their respective denominations. Some had doctrinaire interest in the end times; others adopted premillennial conclusions as a consequence of their "plain" approach to Bible interpretation. But they all took great care to differentiate themselves from the disreputable practices and sects that had come before them.

Meanwhile, several setbacks in Moody's benevolent work made a focus on evangelism appealing. Problems started when a fire destroyed the YMCA building in 1868 only a mere four months after its dedication. Not properly insured, Moody suddenly faced a second building project. Many of his initial investors agreed to write off their losses, but they were less forthcoming with a second donation. The inferior structure replacing the first building compounded problems. The board of managers needed to rent the hall to cover their costs, but only less-respectable groups seemed interested in the space.[50] Moody grudgingly allowed Sunday political meetings and dramatic performances, but he finally balked at a fund-raising dance. The society pages gleefully reported Moody turning off the gaslights in the middle of the event and the dancers' determined continuance by candlelight.[51] The daily grind of benevolence work also wore Moody down. Employers complained about the caliber of workers sent their way,[52] while he complained about being "frequently and shamefully imposed upon" for railroad passes.[53] Perhaps lecturing himself as much as his audience, Moody warned that attempting too many projects simultaneously would lead to "a failure in all."[54]

Moody had long held that "a man without money in his pocket is not in a fit condition" for evangelism. But now he wondered whether it was more efficient to serve the body by first saving the soul.[55] By 1869, he was ready for work with fewer bureaucratic entanglements, and so he stepped down from the YMCA, though it was not yet clear what he would do next.

The 1869 Christian Convention that Moody hosted in Chicago evinced the growth of evangelical realist proclivities. Speakers rejected Bible commentaries as "cumbersome and mystifying" and called for "dry and dusty" dogma to be swapped for "practical Christianity" and simple teaching "more like the Saviors."[56] Others approvingly contrasted a personal relationship with God to "the machinery of the church." "The Holy Spirit was always near," one speaker explained, waiting for us "to let him into our hearts." This last appeal led a listener to shout that "the Spirit has come. . . . You have been calling for Him. . . . He's come, here he is," forcing organizers to quickly remove the man and offer a brief prayer for his "mental disorder." It was a sobering reminder that this new evangelical realism required vigilance, but it did not sway Moody from his growing interest in evangelism and a personal faith.[57]

The Christian Convention hinted at Moody's new direction, but the decisive shift came with the cataclysmic Chicago fire in October 1871. The flames that destroyed large swaths of the city's central core also decimated his lingering attraction to benevolence. What better inducement to focus exclusively on evangelism than watching a decade of benevolent work swept away? What stronger appeal to a more efficient ministry than walking through the ruins of his Sunday school, his church, and the seemingly cursed YMCA headquarters, now in ashes for a second time in five years? What better illustration of premillennialism—the transience of this world—than experiencing the literal flames of America's largest urban conflagration? The fire came in an instant; no one had predicted the day or the hour. If it was the responsibility of every Chicago citizen to raise the alarm of the impending fire, was it not also the responsibility of every believer, educated or not, to point nonbelievers toward spiritual salvation?

Despite deep exhaustion and growing restlessness, Moody could not abandon his Chicago ministries in their time of need and agreed to go east to raise funds for rebuilding. Fittingly, it was in New York City, walking down Wall Street, that Moody had a profound religious experience that confirmed his new direction. Away from his family and on the verge of a breakdown, he was "blessed . . . with the conscious incoming to his Soul of a presence and power" of God.[58] Moody rarely spoke of this event, for he was not given to emotional experiences. But his new direction communicated his conviction of having been called by a personal God to evangelism.

In 1872 Moody inaugurated a new ministry that eventually made him into a household name. At Theodore Cuyler's mission chapel for working-class men and women in New York City, he gave a gospel talk, a sermon in the style that Henry Moorehouse had given years before. He then honed his craft in front of YMCA audiences across the United States.[59] The reaction to "Mr. Moody's New Method of Impressing Scriptural Truth" was striking. The *Chicago Tribune* noted that "the vividness with which its great truths stand out" were "very remarkable." In Washington, D.C., "the religious book-store sold out all the pocket Bibles it had on hand."[60] Music was an essential part of this developing ministry, a vehicle both to engage his audience and, when needed, to control its excesses.

Moody's big break came from his British mentor, William Pennefather, who invited him to conduct revival meetings in Great Britain. He recruited song leader Ira Sankey, a former bank worker and tax collector he knew though his YMCA connections. But upon their arrival, they found that both Pennefather and the main financial backer for their meetings had died while they were in route. This led to a slower start and smaller venues at first, but they had the support of allies in the British YMCA, which they used to good effect. Using the British press to raise excitement while carefully maintaining decorum, Moody became wildly popular among the British middle classes.[61]

British media coverage was picked up in the United States, and by the time of his return, Moody had become a full-fledged celebrity. His American tour, starting in October 1875, built off his British momentum. He focused exclusively on large urban centers in the North, conducting weeks-long campaigns in Brooklyn, Philadelphia, New York City, Chicago, and Boston. Cavernous auditoriums, some built especially for Moody, were filled nightly, often with as many people sent away for lack of space. Remarkably, this nearly illiterate child of poverty had become an international phenomenon.

WHAT ACCOUNTS FOR MOODY's unprecedented success? Something of a cottage industry has tried to answer this question—one that surely has no single answer. At the time, the commercial press was suffering under a two-year-old economic depression. Many newspapers concluded that breathless reports and stenographic reproductions of Moody's talks were inexpensive ways to increase circulation. The media-generated spectacle took on a life of its own.[62] Moody's meticulous meeting preparations, made with a business eye, also contributed to his success. Local organizing committees composed of prominent businessmen handled the logistics—renting space for meetings, fund-raising, advertising, and coordinating hundreds of volunteers. Ministers were recruited to train hundreds more volunteers in the art of "personal work," evangelistic conversations conducted in the inquiry room after the service. These were the men and women who did the real work after Moody's mass sales pitch. "God's business is not to be done wholesale," he liked to say.[63]

Moody's maintenance of his reputation by aligning himself with a city's leading citizens was also instrumental to his success. He only accepted invitations from cities that had the unanimous support of its "evangelical" churches. This typically came by allowing his strongest constituency, business supporters, to exert their influence on their ministers. Moody then seated both groups, along with prominent politicians, on the platform behind him as he preached. This was an unprecedented practice for a religious service and provided a striking visual reminder to the audience that his message had the blessing of elites. On the platform, Moody embodied the figure of a no-nonsense man of business. He dressed in a business suit, ran the meetings with brisk efficiency, and tolerated absolutely no behavior that might transgress the norms of middle-class propriety.[64] His was a "commercial conception of Christianity," by one account, and he was "a salesman trying to sell a bill of goods."[65]

All these factors were so essential to Moody's success that one might forget the contents of his preaching. Contemporaneous commentary repeatedly emphasized the novelty of his message. Moody's ministry was "startling and quickening," one commenter noted. "It sweeps like a prairie-fire, it convulses like an earthquake, it scathes like the lightening, and deluges like a tidal-wave."[66] Unitarians described the revivalist as having "his pockets full of stones to stir up the slumbering churches and awaken the sleepy deacons." He was transforming religion with "the same dash and spirit by which business men and bonanza kings had revolutionized the business

This sketch of Moody preaching at his great Philadelphia crusade in 1875–76 shows the evangelist wearing a business suit with leading figures from the city sitting behind him. Their presence was a visual reminder of Moody's respectability. (Courtesy of the Moody Bible Institute Archives)

of the country."[67] Liberal Brooklyn minister Newell Dwight Hillis classed Moody with Phillips Brooks and Henry Ward Beecher as the three great prophets "of a new social and religious order."[68]

Capturing what it was that made Moody's gospel seem so novel is complicated. His was not a liberal theology, if for no other reason than he never embraced theology, period. Like any good salesman, the content of Moody's preaching was instrumental, designed primarily to compel an audience to the moment of decision. Thus part of the novelty lies in the fact that he eschewed doctrine of any kind, liberal or conservative. But it also came from the organizing principle that replaced traditional theological constructs: Moody's evangelical realist orientation. Observers noted how Moody lifted the romantic fog from spiritual things, how he saw "the invisible" and depicted "God and heaven and eternity" as "grand certainties."[69] His descriptions of biblical characters seemed so real that listeners could see them "walking the streets of New York."[70] Moody was reorienting listeners away from theology altogether. He regularly dismissed what he mockingly called the "little red light of Methodism, or your little blue light of Presbyterianism," in contrast to the unvarnished "light of Calvary."[71] For those who accepted this premise, Moody's "plain" explanations brought "new light" to a subject "so clear that one wonders how it was ever possible to have any other opinion."[72] The Bible became "a new book" under his tutelage.[73]

At the core of Moody's evangelical orientation, communicated in countless sermons, was the conviction that authentic Christian faith consisted in an ongoing personal relationship with God. God wanted a relationship with each and every person and acted like a human being would to achieve it. Conversion was a simple decision, like asking Jesus to telegraph ahead for a reservation in heaven.[74] In contrast to the Calvinist God who foreordained humanity's fall from moral innocence as part of a divine plan, Moody's God heard the news and then "came straight down to seek out the lost one." He vividly put his audience in the garden of Eden: "you can hear Him [God] calling 'Adam! Adam! *Where art thou?*'"[75] Moody's aim was to get both professing Christians and unbelievers "in love with God, in a personal knowledge of Jesus Christ, to know Him personally as their Lord and Savior, and as their Redeemer."[76]

An equally important part of Moody's evangelical realist orientation was his three-pronged approach to the Bible. First, building off his relational view of authentic faith, Moody insisted that the Bible be read personally—that is, as if it were a letter written directly to the reader. By Moody's estimation,

Bible truth came by a different process than either the "scientific" method of traditional Protestant exegesis or the "poetic" method popular among some liberals. The "word of God" took on a new literal edge. Read the Bible "as if it were written for yourself," Moody counseled, recommending a series of questions that focused on direct, personal applicability: any "duty for me to observe . . . example to follow . . . promise to lay hold of."[77]

Moody also assumed that the Bible should be read plainly, like one would read a newspaper. This logically followed from his personal reading. Surely God, like Moody himself, was capable of communicating his thoughts without philosophical acrobatics. Why not assume that God simply meant what he said in his word? And so, quite seamlessly, Moody displaced technical theological definitions developed over centuries with a word's colloquial use. What was the nature of true "faith" needed for salvation? It was "the same kind of faith that men have in one another" when engaged in business.[78] It was simply a choice, an act of the will, like reaching up and picking an orange off a tree or his son jumping off a table into his arms. Theological nit-picking about the "right kind of faith," Moody claimed, was like interrogating a beggar about which hand he used to accept a $10,000 gift.[79] Moody's sermons interwove Bible passages with modern anecdotes and clipped newspaper stories to illustrate their "truths." And these helps inevitably shaped the meaning of the passages.

Moody also took a practical approach to the Bible. Holy writ was not a theology book but a spiritual success manual capable of providing personalized instructions to the reader.[80] Moody saw the value of the text primarily in its ability to answer specific questions. "All scripture" was not only "God-breathed," according to one of Moody's favorite Bible verses, but also "useful." "When you read the Bible," he thus advised, "be sure you hunt for something."[81] "There is not a verse in Scripture where I am told to 'read' the Bible," he argued, "but again and again I am exhorted to 'search.'"[82] Moody was so wedded to the Bible-as-reference metaphor that he eventually stopped reading it in any conventional sense: "I would as soon read a dictionary that way now."[83]

In Moody's hands, the Bible became an all-sufficient replacement to church and tradition. Read personally, plainly, and practically as a personal letter, a newspaper, and a reference manual for life, it was a God-breathed, self-interpreting text. These convictions transformed the Bible into a sure basis of religious authority, rooted in an individual believer's reading without superintendence by ordained clergy.

Moody's evangelical realism also had a last component: the conviction that authentic faith would transform society in empirically measurable ways. Moody's was an active faith. It was not enough to simply believe or to be; the true believer also worked. And so Moody understood his revivals to be the beginning of a long-term project, a boot camp for Christian work. Initial preparations trained businessmen in logistical planning and engaged ministers in directing lay volunteers and mobilizing converted souls into a cadre of Christian workers, both lifelong believers and new converts. Moody's revivals primed the pump even as they illustrated what that city's believers, united across denominational lines, could accomplish. A "wonderful work could be done," he promised a New York audience, if only they "would wake up to the fact that they have a work to do" beyond merely "coming to these meetings, folding up their arms and enjoying themselves."[84] Moody ended each campaign with a "Christian Convention" like those he organized in the 1860s, focused on the practical mechanics of continuing the work.[85]

Thus Moody's revival campaigns helped spread a new evangelical realist orientation among Protestants across the United States. His talks encouraged listeners to understand the essence of authentic faith as an ongoing relationship to God, who interacted with individuals as a person. He offered a new source of religious authority: a Bible interpreted in a personal, plain, and practical manner. He encouraged his listeners to live an active faith and to judge the authenticity of their faith on its results instead of its doctrinal content or faithfulness to their denominational tradition.

Moody's evangelical realism complimented the premillennialism he had discovered among his genteel Brethren friends in Great Britain years before. This fact was not lost on the revivalist, who began privately claiming that Jesus's imminent second coming was the "key to the scriptures." Meanwhile, his close allies were making Chicago a leading urban stronghold for the doctrine. Long-standing advocates like Goodwin were joined by newcomers like William J. Erdman, the newly installed pastor at Moody's church. Meanwhile, Moody's brother-in-law Fleming H. Revell helped resurrect an interdenominational gathering devoted to premillennial Bible study. It quickly developed into the Niagara Bible Conferences, an important gathering of the country's leading premillennial advocates.[86]

Given Moody's connections to premillennial networks, it is all the more striking that he studiously avoided discussing the topic publicly before 1877. Clearly, his premillennialism was not a doctrinaire interest in end-times speculation; it was the inevitable result of interpreting the Bible plainly.

This pragmatism was clearly demonstrated in a miscalculation during his inaugural Brooklyn campaign. The city was home to Henry Ward Beecher, the best-known preacher of the Gilded Age, whom Moody had met at a Christian Convention in 1868.[87] After Beecher attended a meeting and gave Moody an interview, the revivalist privately revealed his premillennial convictions.[88] Whether Beecher was truly alarmed or simply saw it as an opportune distraction to his own personal scandals, he immediately told reporters that Moody was "a believer in the Second Advent of Christ and says it is no use attempting to work for this world." This revelation threatened the future of the campaign, so Moody adroitly refused any public comment on his views. When the *Chicago Tribune* concluded that Beecher must have been "mistaken,"[89] Moody said nothing to correct the error. For now, at least, accuracy was secondary to respectability.

THE APEX OF MOODY'S first American tour was his triumphant return to Chicago in October 1876. Newspapers that once mocked "Crazy Moody" now clamored for interviews. John Farwell and Turlington Harvey headed up the organizing work; retailer Marshall Field and meatpacking magnate George Armour donated generously. As elsewhere, nearly all of the city's newspapers and churches pledged their support. Volunteers reached every home in Chicago with a "personal" letter from the revivalist inviting them to attend the meetings. The city's Unitarians grumbled (Moody had alienated them during his early ministry), and a few staid denominational papers warned against Moody's methods. Moody seated the liberal minister David Swing on the platform, suggesting he cared little about the recent heresy trial prosecuted by conservative Presbyterians. The "Tabernacle" built for Moody was the largest structure of any kind in the city; it seated 8,000, with additional space for offices and "inquiry rooms" where personal conversations about conversion could be held. But even this was insufficient for the crush of people nearly three times larger clogging entrances on the first evening. Harvey, observing the inquiry rooms, declared he had "never seen people converted so easily."[90] By the end of the campaign, attendance estimates exceeded 1 million. Even the Democratic-leaning *Chicago Times*, which refused to promote the campaign, grudgingly admitted its success.[91]

In fact, the meetings had gone so well, and his respectability seemed so assured, that Moody decided finally to address the subject of premillennialism. The immediate cause was the tragic death of his friend Phillip Bliss, the song leader and hymn-writing celebrity. Bliss had agreed to continue the meetings after Moody and Sankey moved on to Boston. But en route to Chicago, a bridge collapsed under his train. Moody presided over a solemn memorial service for his solidly premillennial friend and then announced he would address the topic the following day, creating "no small stir." His talk emphasized premillennialism's practical implications. God promised that all scripture was useful, he told a packed auditorium, and the Second Advent fit that bill. It gave comfort, spurred people to work, and loosened the worldly temptations of fame and fortune. "My friends, it is perfectly safe to take the Word of God just as we [see] it," Moody explained. "If He tells us to watch, then watch! If he tells us to pray, then pray! If He tells us He will come again, wait for Him!" Not everyone left convinced. The *Chicago Tribune* sourly noted that Moody's previous forbearance in addressing the subject had shown "Christian wisdom." Yet many more were persuaded, and his careful defense of premillennialism was a turning point in its wider acceptance during the next decade.[92]

Moody triumphantly concluded his first tour in Boston, home to his conversion twenty years before, with his respectability intact. Whatever complaints lodged by hard-shelled churchly conservatives or the most forward-looking churchly liberals, he had swung the mass of respectable middle-class Protestants toward a modern evangelical orientation. Many Protestants from all denominations now understood conversion as a choice that inaugurated a personal relationship with God rather than a process whereby they entered a church community. Following Moody's example, they envisioned the Bible to be God's plain and direct revelation to individual believers rather than a text understood only in light of tradition and technical theology. They embraced the acceptability and desirability of a new sort of Christian work that was open to laypeople. It was work that would confirm one's faith and bring tangible results; it saved souls and changed lives. If enough people engaged in this Christian work, it might transform the world, even before Jesus came again to set the world aright once and for all.

TWO

The Problem of the Masses

The massive Tabernacle from Moody's Chicago campaign sat vacant for most of 1877 awaiting transformation into a new warehouse for John Farwell. But on the afternoon of July 25, it once again teemed with activity, raised from its slumber by fears of "an earthly kind." Railroad labor strikes that started in West Virginia had marched westward toward Chicago. The same middle-class newspapers that had puffed Moody's meetings now bellowed fears of class conflict into open flame. The police drew first blood on July 24, dispersing a largely peaceful gathering of workers with clubs and guns. Now, the city's "leading men" and their allies gathered at the Tabernacle to contemplate their next move.

It was the time "for practice" rather than preaching, the Reverend Robert Collyer declared, and the business classes attending received his benediction. John Farwell armed his employees and offered use of his delivery wagons to police, while about 5,000 former Civil War soldiers volunteered to patrol the city. Unfortunately, these undisciplined forces for order spurred their own wave of violence. In the days that followed, about thirty people died, mostly workers, and scores more were injured. Human costs notwithstanding, the *Chicago Tribune* worried most about property losses, flatly concluding that police should have opened fire on workers two days earlier.[1]

The repurposing of Moody's Tabernacle to the service of "law and order" signaled a shift in middle-class thinking about the "problem of the masses" over the decade. In the 1860s, YMCA founders had feared that fashionable elitism was excluding the city's young men and that folly and vice were ensnaring their souls. But now the danger lay in the working-class neighborhoods that simmered with resentment like overpressurized boilers ready to explode. Concerns of urban atomization shifted to fears of social combustion; a concern *for* the masses had metastasized into a fear *of* the masses.

But amid these worries, Moody's ministry fostered hope. Many middle-class Protestants had become convinced that his evangelical message was a powerful preservative of the social order. A personal relationship with God, they believed, facilitated self-governance by a transformed conscience. The Bible, plainly understood, provided a clear moral road map. This new faith, once rooted, sparked an impulse to spread the message further. Moody's ideas of evangelical social reform differed from a traditional faith in institutional carrots and sticks to maintain order. By Moody's calculus, religious institutions served only to coordinate the efforts of individual believers, increasing the circulation of a gospel that transformed society soul by soul.

Moody's experiments in efficiently spreading his evangelical message culminated in his founding of a training institute for Christian workers. Operating outside denominational control, Moody's Bible Institute represented its own danger to the established religious order. But the emergencies of the turbulent decade after the railroad strike eventually convinced many business elites that it was a risk worth taking.

THE LABOR UNREST CULMINATING in the 1877 railroad strikes was one social by-product of industrial production. Before the Civil War, only a handful of industries benefited from large-scale manufacturing. This changed thanks in part to newly reliable transportation and communication systems, new production processes, and increasingly inexpensive steam power to drive it all.[2] Industrialization produced new winners and losers—and with them, new resentments. Financiers and those manufacturers with access to capital became wealthy and powerful. An upwardly mobile middle class maintained positions of privilege by acquiring new education and skills. Others, including artisans and small proprietors, suffered a spiraling downward mobility as their once-necessary skills were displaced by machinery.

One of the core dilemmas raised by industrialization related to the long-standing tradition of autonomous work. According to traditional political economy, independent work was the birthright of free and virtuous white men, regardless of education or social status. In fact, it was economic freedom that guaranteed political freedom. But an industrial economy required employees—whether workers on the shop floor or the army of engineers, managers, and bookkeepers that designed the products and kept operations running smoothly. For both the successful and the struggling, autonomous work was an increasing rarity in a growing number of sectors.[3]

Were industrial work relations a threat to freedom or a more innocuous development? A moral framework called producerism shaped thinking on both sides of the debate. Producerism was a long-standing tradition in American political economy that linked virtue to work. It lionized "workers" as virtuous guardians of society and demonized nonproducers as threats to liberty and social stability. Traditionally, the catalog of nonproducers consisted of elites who siphoned off the rewards of productive work: capitalists, rentiers, speculators, effete intellectuals, and large southern slaveholders.[4]

For discontented wage laborers, it was a simple matter to include industrialists among those threatening their economic enslavement. But the business classes who self-identified as virtuous producers, despite their alignment with elites, needed a wholesale revision of traditional producerism. They still believed that most American workers—skilled workers affiliated with traditional craft unions, for example—were virtuous and shared the same basic values as themselves. Against mounting evidence, they asserted that anyone could work their way up the "labor ladder" to autonomous work. Thus the problem, by their alternate account, was the modern "non-producers" hailing primarily from the lower orders. These were the lazy "tramps,"[5] the dependent saloon sitters, and the political radicals or labor agitators looking for a shortcut. The immigrant "machine" politician embodied the problem, distributing unearned patronage from the neighborhood working-class saloon.

Recent unrest could be traced to the influence of these bad actors, business producerists claimed, rather than to the decline of traditional work autonomy. Thus, the future of the social order hung on "the masses" that fell between the hopeless nonproducers and the "respectable" middle classes. If they cooperated with the business classes, all would be well; but the social order would collapse if they succumbed to the temptations of drunkenness, resentment, self-interested voting, and rioting.

In fast-growing urban locales like Chicago, rising class tensions in the 1870s also had a particular religious inflection. The city's business classes were dominated by native Protestants, while many workers were new immigrants from Catholic, or even irreligious, backgrounds. In Chicago, tensions began in the mid-1860s when business elites thwarted enforcement of an eight-hour workday. This intensified after the fire when the business-led Chicago Relief and Aid Society provided disproportionate aid to the largely Protestant professional classes. But the final straw was differing views of alcohol consumption and Sunday Sabbath observance. When business leaders persuaded Mayor Joseph Medill to enforce Sunday saloon closings, the working classes united across ideological and ethnic lines to elect a leftist "People's party" for city government in 1873. The revolution was short-lived; working-class political groups splintered into warring factions, while business leaders consolidated around a deeply political but ostensibly nonpartisan "Citizens Association."[6] But the net effect was to link class interests with religious identities.

The links between religion and class led many business elites to seek religious solutions. Those who knew their history recalled an earlier religious crisis that arose in the early nineteenth century, when the threat of disorder loomed large on the frontier. Their forebears temporarily set aside their denominational differences and engaged a two-pronged campaign to convert the irreligious and then found churches, schools, and other institutions necessary to preserve the moral order.[7] The present crisis required a new campaign to convert the masses and create new religious institutions.

By the mid-1870s, the Protestant business classes had put their hope in the rising urban evangelist Dwight L. Moody to meet the challenge. Both the British and American press regularly depicted Moody as having special capacity to reach the working classes.[8] Hailing from a working-class background and with the verbal infelicities to prove it, he could speak to these men in their own dialect. Yet he hobnobbed with successful businessmen without any apparent resentment. He parroted their economic views in glib declarations, proclaiming that he could not "see how a man can follow Christ and not be successful" and that he believed hard work inevitably brought self-sufficiency.[9] It convinced top-tier business elites—the Dodges, the Goulds, the Rockefellers—to throw their support behind Moody's first U.S. revival tour regardless of their personal opinions of its content. Thus, many in the business classes were drawn by his message of God's love restoring social harmony. The "problem of the masses" was a matter simply solved by supporting Moody's attempts to spiritually reproduce himself en masse. Once converted, the working classes could be brought under the sway of churches and other traditional "civilizing" institutions.

But even before the 1877 railroad strikes, there were clear indications that Moody's meetings were not the one-stop solution his supporters anticipated. Moody's popularity among the middle classes was one culprit. As in most cases of limited supply, it meant that the silk-wearing churchgoers among his audiences crowded out the cotton-wearing workers.[10] His New York City revival meetings were typical: supporting papers noted the "intelligence and respectability" of the audience and listed the many "lawyers, physicians, scientists, and even editors" that embraced his message. Opponents complained that too many attendees were "of comfortable circumstances" and that the meetings did not touch "the densely populated poor."[11] For workingmen, hardened by want, the revivalist's neatly pressed business suit and platform filled with the captains of industry held no appeal. Thus, during Moody's Chicago meetings, German workers got no closer to conversion than mounting a beer-fueled procession featuring Moody and Sankey caricatures, mock sermons, and singing "in measure that would have startled that vocal evangelist."[12] The avenues by which Moody created and maintained his middle-class respectability undercut his effectiveness with the poor.

Moody understood the purpose of his revival meetings differently than his business allies. Most conservative Protestants maintained clear boundaries between religion and business; Moody's Christian work was essentially producerism applied to religion. He linked spiritual productivity to virtue, claiming those with "true faith in Christ . . . cannot help working for Christ."[13] He harbored ambivalence toward elite church leadership who sat on their laurels. Those ministers who supported him were inevitably engaged in active Christian work. It was spiritual productivity that signaled spiritual health, not proper dogma. Moody's business supporters understood the "revival" he was conducting as a simple matter of reaching the unconverted masses, but for Moody, the goal was engaging believers in Christian work. Both "the masses" and the believing church needed reviving.

What would a revived church look like? For Moody, the church, like a business, had no intrinsic value absent results. Thus its primary purpose was to coordinate, support, and encourage its members' Christian work. And the epitome of this ideal Christian community was his British mentor William Pennefather's Mildmay ministry. A key feature of the parish was a "Missionary Training Home for Young Women." It was originally inspired by German Protestant deaconess homes and exuded a pragmatic orientation. Initially, most women hailed from the educated middle classes, but it was open to women of any class or theological background who exhibited a "consistent Christian character, earnest love for souls, and a fair amount of intelligence and education." Students spent mornings in Bible study and practical training and afternoons applying these lessons in practical outreach. Over time, Pennefather hoped that new working-class converts would join the effort, creating a virtuous cycle that would transform the neighborhood. United by love and centered on Christian work, the Missionary Training Home embodied for Moody the essence of church life.[14]

Mildmay held such attraction to Moody that he had convinced a fellow Christian worker, Emma Dryer, to develop a similar center of Christian work at his Chicago church before leaving on his first revival tour. Dryer was a formidable force. Born in 1835, the college-educated Massachusetts native had taught at the Illinois State Normal University since 1864. Mutual friends introduced her to Moody in 1870, and after the Chicago fire, she demonstrated a prodigious capacity for systematic benevolence and a passion for evangelism. A pious Methodist, she embraced premillennialism after a near-fatal bout of typhoid fever. The ordeal opened her eyes to "the needs of this dying world," she later recalled, "especially for the fallen, wretched condition of the masses around me." At Moody's urging, Dryer started the "Chicago Bible Work" in 1873. Most features were borrowed from Pennefather. It had nearly identical entrance requirements, training, and outreach directed at working-class families. But the Bible Work also took a page from Moody's earlier YMCA work. Dryer divided up the city's most needy districts and assigned a "Bible Reader" to the area. The reader's primary responsibility was quite literally to inculcate needy families in the habit of daily Bible reading, but charitable services were given to create the proper home environment in which that reading would bear fruit. The Chicago Bible Work was a distinct legal entity, but Moody made it clear to Dryer that it should operate as an auxiliary of his church. It was his and Dryer's vision of an ideal Christian community. For all practical purposes, it was a religious settlement house, predating Jane Addams's Hull House by fifteen years.[15]

Moody's decision to make the Chicago Bible Work a woman's ministry was a practical solution to its potential controversy. As with women's seminaries of earlier generations, its "female" designation allowed the Bible Work to develop with relative autonomy. Moody understood this. Not only could women "most easily gain access to families," he pragmatically reasoned, but they also avoided the suggestion that he was challenging denominational authority over religious education, especially seminaries. "We'd find ourselves in hot water quick, if we undertook to educate young men," he told Dryer. Her educational credentials amply justified her directing a woman's ministry of this sort. But both Dryer and Moody saw the Bible Work as a model for a new type of religious institution, even a new church, organized around Christian work. Once it had proven itself effective and

*A young Emma Dryer, first superintendent of the Chicago Bible Work,
a ministry that would eventually morph into the Moody Bible Institute.
Highly educated and tough minded, she was a force to be reckoned with
in "Christian work." (Courtesy of the Moody Bible Institute Archives)*

respectable with women, they could quietly add men. At Dryer's insistence, Moody promised to assist in the work after what he thought would be a brief revival tour in England.[16]

Dryer's work embodied Moody's evangelical realism and his religious producerism. Her approach to the Bible reflected Moody's plain, personal, and practical assumptions about the text, and she encouraged both her workers and working-class charges to eschew denominational interpretations for their own Bible study. But Dryer herself was a particularly skilled Bible interpreter. Proficient in biblical Greek, she began publishing a set of monthly Bible lessons titled "Notes for Bible Study," which were embraced by women and men alike in premillennial circles across North America. Dryer's business-friendly assumption that Protestantizing working-class home life would ameliorate social unrest elicited support from Chicago's elite. Her wide circle of supporters included railroad tycoon John Crerar and the philanthropist and businesswomen Nettie McCormick, who became

Dryer's most important ally. Moody's close friend, lumberman Turlington W. Harvey, served as the Bible Work's legal guardian.

Although Dryer was never an ideological advocate for women's rights, her work nevertheless encouraged a radical democratization of church life in which members, regardless of sex or education, were empowered to interpret God's message and serve each other. Her female Bible readers pushed the boundaries of appropriate ministry for laypeople, let alone women. Her premillennial conviction that the world was in the midst of an end-time emergency justified her setting aside traditional gender roles for the sake of practical considerations.[17]

Moody's ongoing interest in the Chicago Bible Work casts a new light on his hopes for his revival tours. He had every intention of converting anyone who attended his meetings, but his real hope was to spur Mildmay-like ministries in each city he visited. This was why he organized Christian Conventions at the end of each revival campaign. Having initially rallied the city's Protestant leadership around his meetings, he hoped to then spur them and newly awakened Christian workers into permanent work after he left.

But like the hope that Moody would convert "the masses" single-handedly, the plan to start coordinated citywide movements of Christian workers fell short. His meetings revitalized the personal faith and devotional life of many middle-class Protestants, but the events rarely rose above sanctified entertainment. Even the Philadelphia revival organizer John Wannamaker ignored Moody's entreaties to engage Christian service full-time. Instead, the pioneering retailer transformed the railroad depot turned revival hall into his legendary department store.[18] Moody's Chicago revivals also yielded disappointing results. Anticipating a dramatic expansion in the Chicago Bible Work, he had encouraged Dryer to begin scouting sites for a new headquarters. Instead, the campaign monopolized his supporters' financial resources amid an economic depression and left an exhausted, rather than invigorated, laity. However one defined "revival," whether as mass conversions by a single celebrity revivalist or a mobilized movement of Christian workers, the railroad strikes underlined the fact that it had not yet come.

THE RAILROAD STRIKES INTENSIFIED a series of coercive projects inaugurated by the self-designated "better classes" against the lower orders. After the 1876 presidential election, southern elites wrestled control of state governments from majority rule and preserved it through voting restrictions, draconian Jim Crow laws, and terrorist violence against African Americans and their political allies. Northern business interests engaged suppression of the poor, of working-class radicals, and of ethnic political representation, often in the name of "civic reform." Fear of labor unrest spawned armories, "citizens groups," and "national guards" to protect business interests.[19]

Many of Moody's business supporters, now disabused of their faith in an easy solution, shifted their investment away from evangelism. Coercion, while not the ultimate solution, was the need of the hour. Doubts to its morality were placated by the justifications of many leaders within institutional Protestantism. Violence was a necessary evil for the sake of the social order, they claimed.[20] The true believers among Moody's business supporters still provided funding, but on a more limited budget.

The social unrest of 1877 also shaped the development of doctrinaire premillennialism. Moody's premillennial allies who quietly gathered at their summer conference the year after the strikes sensed opportunity in the pessimism that suffused respectable Protestantism amid the looming threat of social disorder. By their accounting, the great strength of their belief in the literal second coming of Jesus was that it gave hope in such times of discouragement. In addition, Moody's recent public advocacy of a literal Second Advent had encouraged middle-class Protestants to associate the doctrine with his now-popular plain interpretation of the Bible. The time had come to publicly advocate for their still-marginal beliefs.

Premillennial advocates could mark 1878 as a banner year. Their prophecy conference in New York City attracted urbane advocates. Overflowing crowds, including Moody's business supporters Turlington Harvey and John Wannamaker, witnessed their heady deliberations. That same year also witnessed the publication of *Jesus Is Coming*, the single most important defense of a literal Second Advent. It was written, initially pseudonymously, by William Blackstone, a successful real estate developer in the Chicago suburb of Oak Park and a friend of Emma Dryer. He had decided the year before to devote his efforts full-time to spreading the doctrine; this book was his first, and most important, contribution.[21] Both projects carefully addressed long-standing fears that premillennialism produced sectarianism and otherworldly extremism. The conference proceedings highlighted adherents' denominational diversity, the doctrine's practical benefits as a motivator for ministry, and their irenic feelings toward fellow Protestants not convinced by premillennial arguments. This was not Miller's Adventist extremism, which they rejected as deviating from "the faith once delivered to the saints."[22] Just as the Chicago fire had solidified Moody's premillennial convictions, the recent labor unrest now persuaded a wider audience. Blackstone's book and the published conference proceedings spread these ideas among an even wider circle and helped launch Fleming Revell's successful publishing career.

Yet just under the surface, this resurgent premillennialism harbored an undeniable pessimism and interest in esoteric minutia that were off-putting to many respectable Protestants. Their sunny claim that premillennialism increased evangelism was accompanied by the darker prediction that "the world will never be completely converted to Christianity." Instead, social disorder like the recent strikes would become more common. Some conference speakers also dove into weedy speculations about "the development of Antichrist" and the "ingathering of Israel" as "a separate nation, restored to their own land."[23] Blackstone, too, could not resist augmenting his practical justification for premillennialism with diagrams outlining the precise ordering of the "last days" and chapters distinguishing minute differences between "the Rapture and the Revelation." He would soon devote much of his energy to advocating for a modern state of Israel in order that biblical prophecy might be literally fulfilled. For many doctrinaire premillennialists, it was easier to busy themselves with esoteric calculations while they waited for their savior to come and make things right.

Moody's thoroughgoing pragmatism insulated him from the entanglements of doctrinaire premillennialism. He did not attend the New York prophecy conference, despite having taken a hiatus from revival work at the time. Apparently, he considered personal, rather than premillennial, Bible study to be more important.[24] Surely, he sounded more pessimistic after the strike. He, too, mourned that "this world is getting darker and darker," warned of God's judgment by fire, and proclaimed that "Christ will save His Church" only "by taking them [true believers] out of the world." But the ebb and flow of this rhetoric was dictated by circumstances. He compared the world to a "wrecked vessel" when his message needed urgency, but he could also lay out a utopian vision of a society where the fruits of the Spirit created a world of unemployed policemen and courts without "business."[25] Though helpful for motivating evangelism and holy living or for explaining failures in his ministry, his theological commitment was minimal.

The greater impact of the social unrest of 1877 was in eroding Moody's faith in human institutions and bolstering his religious individualism. Now commanding fewer resources from business supporters, Moody engaged a revival tour of second-tier industrial cities. The meetings, stretching from

Maine to California and from Texas to Minnesota, regularly exhibited Moody's frustration with the middle-class church that had proved immune to reform during his first tour. He used Jesus's parable of the Good Samaritan to bludgeon ministers who failed to help outcasts because it was not their "profession" and church leaders too distracted by archaic theological controversies to offer practical help.[26] He still insisted that "churches are the places to do effective work,"[27] but he warned that unless they "become inns for the fallen" rather than "aristocratic clubs for the few rich and respectable," God would simply replace them with "some other agency."[28]

Moody's imagining the church as an "inn for the fallen" was telling. Traditionally, "civilization" was embodied in and controlled by institutions with the right of coercive force—the state over the body, the school over the mind, and the church over the soul. Moody envisioned society consisting of autonomous religious individuals following the internalized voice of God. Thus institutions were only as beneficial as the individuals who controlled them. This was why Scribner's editor Josiah G. Holland described Moody and Sankey as "eminent radicals"; to them, politics, denominations, and "organizations are nothing, or entirely subordinate," while "individual reform is everything."[29] It was why an open letter, spearheaded by Moody and signed by representatives of the nation's leading denominations, asserted that praying for revival was the solution to "financial and political corruptions" and other threats to "our institutions and for the social fabric itself."[30] It explains Moody's growing impatience for "talk about reform": the real solution was individual "regeneration." Social reform was repainting the pesthouse; conversion was "the disease rooted right out."[31]

Moody's critique of respectable institutions at a time of growing social disorder could have easily brought his respectability into question; he allayed such suspicions by identifying himself with the social mores of business elites. In addition to their prejudice against various working-class activists, he embraced their regressive post-Reconstruction racial views. Moody exchanged his modest efforts at racial justice from his early ministry for a new role as the reconciler of whites in the North and the South. During forays into southern cities, he enforced segregated meetings, made deeply troubling alliances with racist promoters of the mythical "lost cause," and used insulting racial imagery in his anecdotes. "We once had the pleasure of speaking in Mr. Moody's church in Chicago," wrote one frustrated African American minister. In the North, he "does not allow any discrimination against his black brother," but in the South, he "has not the courage of his convictions."[32] Moody also opposed women's rights in a similar attempt to avoid controversy. Despite embracing the usefulness of women Christian workers, he strongly protested a modest discussion of women's suffrage because "he disliked to see such divisions." The women, in contrast, "thought their discussions had been conducted in the most amicable manner."[33] Francis Willard reported that Moody broke ties with her in 1878, both because of her criticizing women's meetings as part of "an outworn *régime*" and her suffrage work.[34]

In a sad irony, Moody's desire to protect his personal reputation came at the expense of others. In one sense, the pragmatic basis for his social views made it possible for women and people of color to occasionally make their own way in Moody's ministries; later, it led him to reverse his southern segregation policy in the mid-1890s. But in the aggregate, his social stands were weak. His fear of elite opinion limited the circulation of his gospel among the oppressed. And by treating racial justice and gender equality as controversial issues best ignored, he set a troubling precedent that many white evangelicals continue to follow.[35] The lion's share of benefits generated by his religious revolution accrued primarily to white men.

Moody continued conducting meetings in the 1880s, but after a decade of near-constant travel, he now sought new avenues of ministry closer to home. He had since moved his family to East Northfield, his childhood home. As a father of three children, including a ten-year-old son, Will, and an infant, Paul, he spent increasing amounts of time in a comfortably refurbished farmhouse, a world away from urban social problems. He focused his efforts on developing a seminary for young women (1879) and a preparatory school for boys (1880) located nearby and designed to provide poor children the middle-class education he had never achieved.[36] New efforts to promote and support Christian work reflected his bucolic surroundings. He started the Northfield conference in 1880 as a haven of "rest and spiritual refreshment" for "many tired Christian workers," conducted on grounds "well-fitted by nature" for "quiet communing."[37] The following year, he started a magazine with Fleming Revell. The sixteen-page monthly, titled the *Evangelistic Record*, was designed to support "Christian Workers and Bible Students" through columns on Bible study and occasional features on evangelistic techniques.[38]

All the while, Dryer continued to develop the Chicago Bible Work. Her immaculately kept statistics interspersed clothing distribution and other "errands to the poor" with "school prayer meetings" and "Number of Scripture conversations and readings." "Industrial schools" for children gave marketable skills while "inculcating neatness, order . . . and whatever will tend to their moral elevation." But she wanted the expansion that she and Moody had originally discussed and regularly reminded the revivalist of his promise to help. Moody appreciated Dryer's work, but he could not yet bring himself to engage in another project.[39]

IF MOODY'S COUNTRY LIVING allowed him to ignore the rising tensions between business elites and labor in the early 1880s, his urban allies had no such luxury. The stakes now were even higher than in the 1870s. For most city dwellers, wage labor had been the norm for the better part of a decade. During this time, economists had developed a new set of ideas about the nature of work and value. Traditional political economy made labor the basis of value. It was the work a person put into a product—the work that was an inseparable, often creative extension of a person—that gave things their value. Therefore a fair economic arrangement entailed workers to get their fair share of the labor value they had contributed. Even under the wage system, payment was a moral transaction. It was the just desserts of hard work and must at least equal the cost of living. But since technology was now increasing productivity by orders of magnitude, the task of disentangling the "fruits of one's labor" from the "fruits of capital investment" had become hopelessly complex. Instead, a new economic theory tied value to pragmatic use and therefore whatever price the market would determine. Value was not constant; it would ebb and flow with supply and demand. The radical implication of this theory was to make labor itself a commodity like any other. Wages were an expense that manufacturers should control as dispassionately as steel or coal.[40]

During a recession in the early 1880s, many business elites put the theory of labor-as-commodity into practice, cutting wages and hours without considering their human impact. Not surprisingly, many more workers now concluded that the industrial economy was a zero-sum game between themselves and owners. Their survival would come by collective action. Successful strikes in 1883 under the auspices of the Knights of Labor led to unprecedented increases in union membership. Meanwhile, labor unionists who would eventually form the American Federation of Labor began to rally in 1884 for an eight-hour workday for the same day's pay. What once seemed like a temporary disruption between business elites and labor now looked increasingly like a permanent divide.[41]

Chicago harbored one of the major fault lines between labor and capital in the early 1880s. Since the fall of the Paris Commune in 1871, the city had become a new leading center of radical politics worldwide. Meanwhile, Cyrus McCormick Jr., the newly installed managing partner of International Harvester, seemed intent on singlehandedly starting the class war many feared. Educated at Princeton in mathematics and the new science of economics, he implemented wage cutting with a ruthless efficiency that few before him had dared. Cost savings were poured into massive investments in technology that further simplified the work, expanded the pool of possible workers, and therefore further lowered wages. He dramatically increased productivity and profits, but on the backs of disgruntled workers.[42] And when it seemed that McCormick's practices would be adopted by other business elites in the city, frustrated labor leaders decided to take a stand. In October 1884 they threatened to begin a general strike on May 1, 1886, if an eight-hour day were not granted. Chicago's anarchists joined the movement, organizing a "poor people's march" for Thanksgiving Day. Its advertising circular sardonically listed reasons for expressing "thanks to our 'Christian brothers on Michigan Avenue.'" They provided unemployment, homelessness, hunger, and threats of being shot "by the police or militia if you refuse to die in your hovels, in due observation of Law and Order."[43] For evangelical elites, the sight of 3,000 marchers wending through their Gold Coast neighborhood, black and red flags unfurled, was difficult to ignore. Business elites feared that radicals, employing powerful religious rhetoric for radical ends, might sway the masses to their side.

Perhaps feeling pressured by his allies, Moody finally reengaged the "problem of the masses." The looming threat of unrest was even greater than that of the 1870s, despite the additional half decade he had spent recruiting Christian workers across the country. This led Moody to reconsider the source of the problem and its potential solution. Perhaps it was not enough for a Christian worker to be willing to work hard for Christ; reaching the working classes increasingly seemed like a special problem that required special training. Moody had successfully evangelized Chicago's working-class neighborhoods in the 1850s and 1860s. Might he not have special insight into reaching the masses today?

In the fall of 1884, Moody began holding Christian Conventions on the East Coast devoted to techniques for "evangelizing the masses."[44] Then, weeks after the anarchists' Thanksgiving march, Moody finally announced plans to expand Dryer's Chicago Bible Work. He proposed a new building to house and train 150 to 200 "city lay missionaries," both men and women. It would also feature specialized training in the Bible and other subjects to "fit them for mission work and for house-to-house visitation." Most important, Moody would serve as "one of its regular teachers" and would recruit other experts as instructors.[45] To push the project ahead, he conducted a month-long "Bible Institute" in Chicago and with Revell rebranded their magazine to the *Record of Christian Work*, filling its pages with effective techniques.[46]

Churchly conservatives were horrified at Moody's announcement of a new training school. It was one thing for a layperson like Moody to evangelize but quite another for him to teach others. At best, he was the exception that proved the rule. As one correspondent noted, while Moody's methods might bring results worthy of commendation, they "are not therefore of necessity the best for *imitation*."[47] Lay preachers were prophets, occasionally used by God to shake up the status quo; but religious education remained the responsibility of seminaries and ordained ministers.

Moody's business allies were less concerned by the departures from tradition than by the $250,000 price tag of his proposed training institute. In the fall of 1885, Moody redoubled his efforts at raising funds for the project, using a twofold strategy that emphasized threats to the social order and the relative economy of his solution compared to other options. The October 1885 issue of the *Record*, intended to stoke "interest red hot," contained no less than three appeals for funds.[48] One case noted the hundreds of millions of dollars spent on prisons in contrast to his paltry request to train evangelists. Another appeal, under the ominous heading "Dynamite or Gospel," warned how agitators had advocated violence to a menacing group of 5,000 socialists. "It is a loud call to the better class to carry the gospel without delay to these people," it explained, since "one riot would destroy more property in a day . . . than it will cost to carry the gospel to every soul in Chicago, and to erect and endow a training school for Christian workers."[49]

But churchly Protestants insisted that converting the masses was best accomplished by starting churches in working-class neighborhoods. In fact, the same month that Moody began his new plea for funds, New York City Protestants opened a "People's Church" in what they called the "Godless mile" on the city's East Side. Despite lingering doubts, Moody had agreed to conduct a month-long revival campaign at the new building to help the effort. His hesitation proved prescient. Upon taking the platform on the first evening, he faced a mere smattering of attendees.[50] "Where are the people?" he reportedly asked organizers, who sheepishly replied that they were "out on the streets." Fed up with believers who expected their Christian work to be done for them, the revivalist demanded that they "go out and get them." But at this point in class relations, that was all but impossible. When one intrepid organizer invited a saloon "crowded with working men" to the meetings, the only response was, "Who the hell is Moody?"[51] In the end, the seats were filled by churchgoers, and the inquiry meeting, designed for the unsaved, was filled with believers requesting prayer for relatives and friends.[52] Attendance never improved, and Moody unceremoniously abandoned the campaign after less than a week.[53] In a postmortem analysis, the *New York Tribune* feared that Moody's ministry had simply "lost its novelty,"[54] though that week he had also received an unsolicited invitation to Harvard University signed by 500 students. More accurately, the failure of the East Side revival was a continuation of the same difficulty in reaching the working classes that Moody had faced since becoming a celebrity revivalist.

The entire fiasco in New York left Moody more disillusioned about the effectiveness of traditional religious institutions, even his own revivals, but more committed to his new project. Before departing the city, he spoke to students at Union Theological Seminary. They should end the "patronizing air of building so-called missions" (like the People's Church?) and instead "work with your people individually, man by man." "Dig them out of sin if you have to use a pickaxe," he advised, and then, once they were saved, "set them at work." Rather than organizing mass meetings, they should conduct personal evangelism on a mass scale. The need of the hour was a school "to teach men how to lead" these efforts.[55]

But in the following months, Moody grabbed hold of another, even more radical, idea to solve the problem of the masses: perhaps what was really needed were Christian workers from a particular class. Acquiescing to the new state of class relations and taking a strikingly literal turn, he concluded that he needed to train Christian workers from the working classes. Reversing the traditional assumptions of respectable Protestants, he argued that the most effective urban missionaries would come from the same uneducated, working-class backgrounds as those they were seeking to convert.

Moody's first announcement of this new direction was made with a dramatic flourish in January 1886. During a visit to Chicago, he widely publicized a meeting to announce the latest developments for his proposed training institute. But he then strategically distributed tickets for the event "principally among the poorer classes . . . particularly to the non-church-going persons."

That he succeeded in attracting these classes, unlike in New York City, was a testament to the ongoing work of Dryer and other Chicago allies. It resulted in a striking inversion of the typical religious meeting. Reporters gawked as the ticketed poor sat comfortably while "Mr. and Mrs. East-of-Clark-Street" from the wealthy Gold Coast stood in back and in the aisles. Moody's talk made it no more comfortable for those churchly conservatives in attendance. He lambasted those who urged caution whenever "aggressive work for the Lord" was suggested. The Christian workers he would recruit were "workers" in a very literal sense—those who knew the struggles and concerns of the poor and could speak as equals.[56]

Moody's meeting sent ripples through the Protestant community, but class tensions had grown so significantly during the past year that many were open to such a radical departure. Once again, Moody's ally Cyrus McCormick Jr. stood at the eye of the storm. In early 1885 he pushed further cost-cutting measures, despite record profits. When workers went on strike in protest, his response was so belligerent that other leading businessmen, fearing a violent general strike, pressured him to back down. But that summer he was back on the warpath, firing top union leaders and replacing former strikers with pneumatic molding machines and unskilled workers. Rumors that workers were planning a coordinated response to McCormick's intransigence set the middle classes on the edge of panic; class war, they feared, was imminent.[57] So when Moody announced another meeting to discuss "city evangelization" designed to elicit financial and moral support from the respectable classes, he easily packed the auditorium.

The excitement was palpable when Moody rose to speak. Seated behind the revivalist were prominent ministers, Christian workers, philanthropists, and "many men of wealth" from "business and professional circles," including McCormick. Today he would discuss "what should be done with and for the workingmen," Moody explained, "the greatest subject before the people of today." How was it that an entire class of people—wage earners in "factories and shops"—still remained largely outside the church? It was a question Moody could claim some expertise in answering, for it was reaching this class, "not the tramps and not the rich," that had been his "one aim in life." It was a subtle but important distinction. Moody's aim was not to reach anarchists but the same "ordinary" workers that might be swayed by anarchistic arguments. It was evangelizing these men, "the bone and sinew of society," that was the key to social stability. Unfortunately, existing efforts were failing. Paternalistic "missions" made working-class people feel "that we look upon them as a sort of poor beggars that can not help themselves." Untrained Christian workers were unable to counter the arguments of "hard-hearted infidels and sceptics [sic]," who led workers astray. Ministers, in contrast, were overeducated and out of touch. They produced sermons that "soar into metaphysics away above their hearers."[58] Desperate times called for dramatic new measures.

If the city's Protestant establishment felt ambushed, the thunderous applause and laughter that punctuated Moody's remarks suggested that the respectable laity were on board. Using this momentum, he then announced his solution: he would recruit "workers from out of the ranks" of the masses "to reach the class of the people we are after." It was a new order of religious worker, modeled largely on himself, that he called "gap-men." This was not a "stop-gap" solution because ministers were in short supply; rather, it was a gap that educated elites were unable to fill. By using men that "know these poor people—how they live and what they need," these new Christian workers could succeed where their predecessors had failed.

But new recruits needed training, both in the use of the Bible and in effective evangelistic techniques, as well as coordination in their subsequent efforts. Chicago needed a new training and evangelistic organization that would cost $250,000. Now directing the pressure on his business supporters, Moody promised their financial support would allow him to dispense his years of evangelistic experience and create thousands of truly effective Christian workers. "Christianity has been on the defensive long enough," he concluded. "The time has come for a war of aggression."

Moody's announcement spurred a heated debate in the religious press. Liberal evangelicals like Lyman Abbott, editor of the *Christian Union*, echoed Moody's sentiments. The conversion of "the great class of dollar-a-day wage-earners" would come only by "men who have come up from the people without having come away from them," he asserted. These "shirt-sleeved preachers" could leverage their shared experiences and speak "in their own language." Trained ministers, in contrast, even those who had "a profound personal sympathy for the poor," could not do this work. "Their training, modes of thought, and even their vocabulary" were "ill-suited" to reaching this "congregation of the street."[59] Churchly Protestants would have none of this. One conservative Presbyterian recalled the "swarm of lay-evangelists" that followed Moody's Chicago 1876 revival, wrecking "irremediable mischief" in churches before returning "to soliciting life insurance and peddling subscription books." If lay evangelists were needed to address the present crisis, their work must be "done under the authority" of respectable denominations, "each supplying and controlling its own men." But a training school operating independently, as Moody proposed, would inevitably produce "a new form of sectarianism, if not a new sect."[60]

Whether concerned by denominational opposition or simply averse to the large price tag, Moody's business allies were slow to organize Moody's proposed training institute. Instead, as a consolation, they proposed that Moody hold a May revival campaign on the city's roiling Southside, cynically timed to coincide with the threatened general strike for an eight-hour workday. Moody reluctantly agreed, but as in New York, his hesitation was well-founded. The first evening, Moody addressed swathes of empty seats, exhorting the sprinkling of "wives [and] mothers" present "to bring to the meetings the men who [were] on strike."[61] The following day, May 3, a massive crowd of 40,000 protesters gathered at the gates of the McCormick factory. Police killed four strikers and injured hundreds more. German anarchists called for a protest at Haymarket Square the next evening and distributed pamphlets with a call to arms.[62] Moody's frustration was evident, warning listeners that "God is not mocked" and that "whatsoever a man soweth that shall he also reap."[63]

No one remembers May 4, 1886, for Moody's blistering sermon, which used Noah's flood to remind listeners that God will not allow sin "to go unpunished."[64] Rather, the day is noted for a bomb of unknown origin exploding in Haymarket Square, killing seven policemen and injuring many onlookers. The incident spurred hysterics in the "respectable" classes that exceeded even the railroad strike of the last decade. The mayor forbade all public assemblies the following day, an order Moody used to justify canceling the campaign he had not wanted to hold. When word reached the mayor, he quickly clarified that he had not meant to shut down the revival but hoped that "all those fellows . . . the dynamiters and Nihilists, I mean," would attend.[65] But the revivalist had already hopped the first train back to Northfield.

The mayor's clarification was too late, but Moody did not let the failure go to waste. "I am not speaking disparagingly of the different churches and missions now attempting to reach this class," he later told reporters, "but anyone with their eyes open can't fail to see that the masses are not reached. One of two things is absolutely certain: either these people are to be evangelized, or the leaven of communism and infidelity will assume such enormous proportions that it will break out in a reign of terror such as this country has never known. It don't take a prophet or the son of a prophet to see these things. You can hear the muttering of the coming convulsion even now, if you only open your ears and eyes."[66] Moody had made nearly identical comments in March, but it was only Haymarket that opened eyes, ears, and wallets. He secured $250,000 and a board of trustees consisting entirely of prominent Chicago businessmen. The McCormick family alone delivered $100,000, and Cyrus agreed to serve as a trustee. He was joined by old Moody supporters like John Farwell, Nathaniel Bouton, and Turlington Harvey, the department store magnate Robert Scott, and the Metropolitan Bank president Elbridge G. Keith. Moody made new friends as well; the department store magnate Levi Z. Leiter reportedly donated $10,000.[67] One newspaper cheered these donations as "the best possible arguments against the craze of socialism and anarchism."[68]

THE MONTHS FOLLOWING HAYMARKET only deepened the gap between the working classes and business elites. Police following the bidding of the business classes began a campaign of violence against political radicals. A sham of a trial eventually found eight anarchists guilty despite clear evidence to the contrary. Seven of the defendants were executed. Voting guilty alongside the other jurors was Moody's close friend, the railroad man turned evangelist James H. "Major" Cole. In this case, class interests trumped religion.[69]

Tempers flared the summer after Haymarket in a debate between John Farwell and several working-class Protestants in Chicago's leading labor paper, *Knights of Labor*. The paper had published a letter from Farwell calling labor demands unreasonable and lecturing readers to study the Gospels and "become a true follower of Christ." The working-class responses that followed mustered an impressive familiarity with, and commitment to, the scriptures. One anonymous "Wheelbarrow" noted Jesus's clear statement that it was easier for a camel to get through the eye of a needle than for a rich man to enter the kingdom of God. Perhaps it was Farwell, he suggested, who did "not believe the New Testament." Farwell was furious and unmoved. He could not understand how any authentic believer could critique the capitalist order on Christian principles.[70]

The same hardened attitude was exhibited by the doctrinaire premillennialists who gathered in Farwell Hall for a second prophecy conference the November after Haymarket. Designed to further consolidate the gains of the 1878 prophecy conference, the proceedings were notable for a new, less-than-conciliatory posture. Reverend Edward Goodwin gave the opening address with the same take-no-prisoners mentality that he had exhibited during a recent streetcar strike, when he called on police to "clear the streets if they leave a corpse at every step."[71] In his talk, he claimed, against all historical evidence, that premillennialism had "never been lost nor modified" by orthodox Christianity and that prominent postmillennialists like Lyman Abbott and Horace Bushnell had "abandoned the faith of the fathers." The concluding remarks of George Needham, conference organizer and former pastor of Moody's church, followed suit. He sourly insisted that premillennialism embodied the only "true principles" for a consistent approach to biblical interpretation. It was "a bulwark against the skepticism of modern theology," especially the "smoky and sulphurous match-light of mongrel Ayrian-German rationalism," and a "breakwater" protecting "the clean beach of a God-given theology" from "the jelly-fish theories evolved out of man's erratic consciousness, pride, and self-will." Moody once again skipped this prophecy conference, sending only a brief letter of regret that was printed in the official proceedings.[72]

In the context of yet another outburst of social unrest, doctrinaire premillennialists saw Moody's training institute as something more than a project to convert the working classes. Still an embattled minority in denominationally controlled seminaries, Moody's new organization could be the headquarters for a final evangelistic push before the rapture. In fact, several premillennialists, including William Blackstone, had gathered weekly with Emma Dryer to pray that Moody would organize such an institution. His success in mustering business supporters after Haymarket, they believed, was God's direct answer to their prayers.[73] This may be why the project has been mistakenly characterized "as a hedge against the New Theology and higher criticism" or as a means to inculcate premillennialism as protection against "apostate scholars."[74] But in fact, both Moody and his business board were pragmatists and too concerned with sectarian associations that would come with such a project. The new institute was "no theological scheme," Ira Sankey reiterated to reporters, but an attempt "to reach the lowest class of people," those that "ordinary agencies" of benevolence could not, with workers trained "especially for this class of work."[75]

Still, Moody exhibited his own tone deafness to working-class concerns after Haymarket. Now having lived with his celebrity for a decade, he was completely out of touch. McCormick's fateful decision to cut wages despite record profits in 1885 was flatly immoral according to older theories of labor and traditional Christian ethics. Though Cyrus drew the condemnation of his own mother, Moody remained silent.[76] In fact, he joined in such cut-rate practices. Showing exceedingly poor taste mere months after Haymarket, Moody joked with reporters about his own trouble with "labor agitators." He had offered to pay students at Mount Herman twenty-five cents per head to clear the campus of woodchucks, but their unexpected success led him to reduce his bounty to ten cents. The students ceased their pursuit of the pests in protest; Moody refused to budge.[77] Clearly, if Moody's Chicago project was to succeed, it would require gap-men—perhaps even more than Moody realized.

MOODY AND HIS BUSINESS allies incorporated the new ministry as the Chicago Evangelization Society (CES) in February 1887 and began hammering out plans. Theoretically at least, the CES constitution charted a blueprint for an institution that would have looked much like Moody's original inspiration at Mildmay. It specified no educational or theological requirements for entry—only "good Christian character," "ability," and membership in an "Evangelical" church. But to minimize controversy, it made the educational dimension of the work secondary. CES participants were designated as "workers," not students, and to "educate" them was but one facet of a broader agenda to "direct" and "maintain" their coordinated evangelism.[78] By the middle of 1887, the trustees had developed a plan of operation that they hoped would effectively reach the masses. It split Chicago into three districts, assigning a head evangelist to each.

Competing interests nearly sank the CES before it began. Denominational conservatives continued to strenuously object to Moody's plans, fearing a half-educated rabble of self-important Christian workers doing more harm than good. Under increasing pressure, Moody proposed a flurry of contradictory ideas, including his old standby of limiting the work of reaching working-class families to trained women. After all, he reasoned, "their sons will rule the city twenty years hence," and reaching families will "lay a foundation for this work . . . so deep and strong that it will last forever."[79] But Moody's business allies had no intentions of returning to indirect methods. The whole point of the Bible Institute was converting working-class *men*—a task that propriety dictated could only be done by other men. How else could Harvey promise in his fund-raising letter that they would "convert this dangerous element into peaceful, helpful citizens"?[80] The trustees codified these intentions in the new constitution, relegating the formation of a "women's department" to the bylaws. Meanwhile, Dryer soon became frustrated with the trustees' micromanagement. She was not about cede control of what she had spent almost fifteen years building, and she regularly ignored their directives. Nettie McCormick agreed, and since she controlled half of the family's $100,000 endowment, this ensured Dryer would not be cowed into submission.[81]

The conflict came to a head in July 1887, when Nettie sent Moody a set of proposed changes to the CES constitution. Caught in the cross fire and having extended significant social capital for a project that now seemed to be more trouble than it was worth, Moody resigned. Nettie followed suit, and the project appeared all but scuttled. Only the intervention of Moody's wife, Emma, who was close friends with both McCormick and Dryer, kept the CES afloat.[82] The resignations were formally retracted, but the core issues still festered.

In August 1887 the trustees hired Merton Smith as the first of Moody's promised army of working-class "gap men." Smith perfectly embodied Moody's new ideal Christian worker. A Scottish immigrant, he had drifted to Chicago as a drunk and a compulsive gambler. Unable to find work, he soon found himself living on the street and literally starving. He was contemplating a life of crime when he was befriended by members of Moody's church. Smith's conversion and reformation followed, after which he took charge of the Adelphi Mission, a ministry offering basic provisions and religious services to men on the street. His success was notable, guided by insights and sympathy for the "lapsed masses" that were born of his personal experience.[83]

Despite Smith's many appealing features, denominational conservatives stubbornly refused to cooperate unless they were given oversight of the work. Haymarket, it seems, only reinforced their belief that churchly institutions were required to impose order. Moody finally relented, agreeing that CES work would be done under the auspices of area churches and that new converts would be funneled into their congregations. Smith and two female assistants began their evangelistic work as a sort of trial run. For the next year and a half, they worked at an unrelenting pace. They conducted meetings on all sides of the city: in churches, theatres, missions, and tents. "There has been no place . . . too low to be visited and God's free invitation extended," Smith reported. "[S]ocial amenities, family ties, even reputation have been placed in God's hand and God's work has had precedence over everything." They established several new missions, visited "thousands upon thousands of souls," and distributed "hundreds of thousands of bills, dodgers, tickets and tracts." The fruits of this labor were 750 conversions,[84] a prodigious spiritual productivity. It was a heartening down payment on the potential of working-class gap-men, if multiplied a hundredfold as Moody had promised.

Whatever the promise, the various compromises forged to keep the peace left no one happy. Even after Dryer's work was formally merged with the CES in February 1888, she operated in relative autonomy, still ignoring trustee directives. Moody seemed most concerned with avoiding further confrontations with everyone involved. In October the trustees had enough. Blaming Dryer's intransigence for the lack of results, they forced her out and refunded Nettie McCormick's $50,000 donation.[85] But there were no indications that prospects were improving. Then, after hearing "from various quarters that the work of the C. E. S. has been a complete failure," Smith resigned in February 1889. From his perspective, the cause of that failure was the city's churches. Moody's policy to "do nothing to offend the denominations" was counterproductive, Smith complained, since "they were offended" from the start "and have been laughing in their sleeves at our cowardice ever since." He flatly declared that "the poor and the church are in a state of Divorce by mutual understanding," and "the church is indeed Dead" when it came to "any real consecrated effort to reach the masses." They did nothing to nurture the new believers in their congregation, and when they drifted back to old habits, the CES was blamed for insincere converts. In short, Moody's attempt to seek denominational approval had hamstrung the work. The city's churches would only cooperate after the fact, he concluded, when "constrained . . . by your manifested success."[86]

Smith's resignation was a wake-up call and spurred a new flurry of activity. The board approved construction of the institute building next to Moody's church, now located at the corner of Lasalle Street and Chicago Avenue. Moody also took new interest in supporting the work. Although he did not alter the policy of integrating new believers in cooperating churches,[87] he took Smith's other suggestions to heart. Most important, he moved forward with developing the educational wing of the ministry, forming the long-delayed Bible Institute to train Christian workers.[88]

To avoid suspicions of sectarianism, Moody knew he had to appoint leadership of the Bible Institute that would command the respect of the churches. His first choice was William G. Moorehead, a professor of theology at Xenia Theological Seminary. Moorehead embraced a moderate premillennialism and with it a plain interpretation of the Bible. He was a logical choice since he had led Moody's earlier month-long training institutes. But Moorehead was poised to take the presidency at his seminary and politely turned down Moody's offer.[89] Fortunately, Revell had another suggestion. He had made the acquaintance of an up-and-coming minister from Minneapolis named Reuben A. Torrey at a recent convention. Torrey held degrees from Yale University and Divinity School, embraced a similar "plain" approach to the Bible, and possessed a solid track record of successful interdenominational urban ministry. So it was no wonder that Moody reportedly claimed that "my mouth waters for him," sight unseen.[90] In Torrey, Moody saw a man he could put in charge of his entire Chicago operation. As Dryer later recalled, Moody believed the institute could be "a great evangelistic work," but it also "perplexed him." His heart was in Northfield, which "meant rest and home, and affectionate co-operation." Chicago, in contrast, was "an untried field."[91] Plus, Moody was now preoccupied with yet another project: rallying elite college-educated men for "the evangelization of the world in this generation." By 1887 this Student Volunteer Movement had over 2,000 student participants.[92] A man of Torrey's attainments could develop the Bible Institute on his own, with Moody's supplemental direction from afar.

A brief interview revealed another appealing trait of Torrey: his novel solution to the problem of reaching the masses. From his perspective, the social background of the Christian worker did not matter. Rather, he put his hope for effective ministry in a "power for service" given to rich or poor so long as they were rightly aligned with God. These ideas had appealed to Moody for some time, but he was untrained in theology and thus unable to clearly formulate them. But Torrey could, and his growing reputation for effective work seemed to back up his claims of spiritual power. As head of the Bible Institute of Chicago, he would prove the effectiveness of these ideas once and for all.

The meager returns on a decade devoted to evangelizing the masses left Moody all the more suspicious of human efforts and institutions. His lifelong struggle with churches, his failed attempts to organize centers of Christian work, and, most recently, the ongoing difficulties of starting the Bible Institute left him hungry for something new. He wanted a new spiritual technology, a supernatural "power for service" that would accomplish what both denominational conservatives and doctrinaire premillennialists claimed was impossible: the conversion of the masses and the restoration of social harmony.

THREE

Power for Service

It was April 18, 1889, and Reuben A. Torrey was ecstatic. For the last four months, the Minneapolis minister had conducted a test. He ceased taking a salary or even asking for donations, choosing instead to rely on God's provision through prayer alone. The experiment had produced "so many evidences of [God's] love & care," he wrote, "that it seems as though I ought to keep a record of His many kindnesses to me." The diary that followed recorded his "faith work." In the most thrilling of the anecdotes, prayers were answered when donors followed a divine impulse from the Holy Spirit to give, unaware of the need. Appropriately, Torrey kept this diary in an old ledger book, for it would be his accounting of God's miraculous provision.[1]

Torrey's attempt to rely on the power of prayer was one manifestation of a broader emphasis on spiritual power in the last two decades of the nineteenth century. The Holy Spirit was "the Spirit of the Age," according to historian Grant Wacker, the rallying cry of evangelicals.[2] Those reading the Bible plainly, personally, and practically saw passages on the Holy Spirit with new eyes. They rejected traditional Protestant assumptions that the Spirit worked through the church and noticed biblical references to a spiritual personality, a "he," who engaged the world directly. Those who interacted with this entity, they believed, experienced a dramatic influx of power for God's service.

What did Jesus mean when he promised that the Spirit would empower "even greater works" than he had performed? Some, like Moody, focused on conversions and dramatic transformation of individual lives. Liberal Protestants asserted that Holy Spirit power bubbled up from within Christian community, transforming society through ethical reforms. Radical evangelicals believed Jesus meant works of power—literal miracles—that hailed the coming kingdom and the disruption of the existing social order. These different answers would eventually divide former allies into distinct parties, but in the 1880s, this diverse coalition simply agreed that the power of the Holy Spirit guaranteed effective Christian work in demonstrable ways.

Torrey, more than most, incorporated all three answers into a powerful, if unstable, constellation of ideas that he brought to Moody's new Bible Institute. Borrowing across the theological spectrum, he ultimately formulated a radically individualistic spirituality that complemented the individualistic political economy of the Gilded Age. Experiences like "living on faith," he claimed, provided empirical evidence of a God who cared for him individually, communicated with him personally through the Bible, and empowered his work. It gave him unshakable confidence that God's power would set the world aright.

WELL BEFORE TORREY FORMULATED his understanding of the Holy Spirit, many other Protestants had wondered what a personal relationship with the Holy Spirit might entail. The question had troubled believers concerned with social order since the Puritans. All Protestants agreed that the Holy Spirit was the member of the Trinity that united believers to God. Churchly Protestantism followed their Catholic forebears in thinking this mediation came by particular corporate rituals. A believer encountered God by listening to the preaching of ordained ministers, through baptism, or in the sacramental bread and wine. To claim to hear God's voice directly was "enthusiasm," a form of religious disorder. History was replete with sad examples. During the Great Awakening, James Davenport believed God had ordered him to throw his possessions, including his trousers, into a bonfire of luxury items, all but ending the revival in New England. Innumerable sectarian leaders in the nineteenth century also used claims of God's personal revelation to challenge prevailing norms about human sexuality, family life, gender roles, and the political economy. However appealing individualistic religion might appear on paper (in the writings of Jonathan Edwards, for example), individual experience must always bow to the institutional authority of church, school, and government.[3]

Respectable Protestant aversion to individualistic religion began to diminish in the 1830s and 1840s. Leading the way were upwardly mobile Methodists who comported their once-disruptive theological tradition to upper-middle-class norms. Perhaps most important was Phoebe Palmer, a respectable New York Methodist who led a series of influential Tuesday evening meetings "for the Promotion of Holiness." She taught that personal holiness, even perfection, came by a second "conversion" experience, followed by an ongoing personal relationship to God. The potential for extremism was tamped down by the prevailing ideas of middle-class womanhood. Just as a wife's legal identity was absorbed by her husband in coverture, so a believer's will must be laid down and absorbed into the will of God. This "baptism of the Holy Spirit," Palmer explained, was an act of submission. It transformed the prophetic shout of the raucous revival campground into a private devotional experience—a quiet meeting in church, prayer in the parlor, or Bible reading at the table. The experience brought spiritual peace and offered no threat to the social order. Palmer's ideas resonated with the romantic impulses of the age and rapidly spread among respectable Protestants outside Methodist circles in the United States and Britain.[4]

Moody was initially unimpressed with Palmer's ideas, but over time he came to embrace a similar experience to different ends. Drawing again from ideas culled from his British allies at Mildmay, he shifted the relevant context from home to work, and the results from purity to power. Moody's unexplainable religious experience on Wall Street in the aftermath of the Great Fire, he concluded, was a direct encounter with God that empowered his Christian work. During his Chicago meetings in 1876, he began preaching about this "enduement of power." He carefully limited the effects of this experience to effective work rather than emotional experiences, prophetic revelations, or miraculous power. Nevertheless, these sermons, like Moody's premillennial revelations, "excited no little surprise" among respectable Protestants.[5]

By 1881 Moody was so taken by the idea that he published a book, *Secret Power*, designed to share "The Secret of Success in Christian Life and Christian Work." As the title suggests, the book drafted off the popularity of Gilded Age success manuals. But where secular manuals promised success for those who abided by traditional economic virtues of the preindustrial Protestant work ethic, Moody augured a strikingly modern vision for success, at least for Christian work.[6] "Power for service" came from outside the believer. It was a supernatural gift unrelated to a person's natural abilities, a spiritual technology available to anyone who sought it.

For Moody, this hope in Spirit power became all the more intense amid ongoing difficulties to organize centers of Christian work. God might well "take some tramp walking on the streets of Chicago and fill him with the Spirit of the Holy Ghost, and he would be worth a great deal more" than men of education, wealth, and influence, Moody explained during his initial Bible Institute announcement. "If a man is willing to be used of God—or a woman, either—God is willing to qualify you."[7] Although he might never persuade all professing Christians to engage in Christian work, he believed that a handful of supercharged, Spirit-infused workers, properly trained, could transform society.

Moody convinced many evangelicals of the reality of Holy Spirit power, less by the strength of his arguments than the story of his life. His teachings regularly conflated the person of the Holy Spirit with its power, at one point admonishing readers to "get more of the Holy Ghost" without explaining how one might "get more" of a person. Yet, how better to explain how a simple, uneducated salesman like Moody became an international religious celebrity? Thus many followed Moody in seeking this experience as the "secret of efficiency" in Christian work, believing it would allow them to "accomplish more in one day than they sometimes do in years."[8] But they would work out the particulars of the belief on their own.

MOODY HAD BEEN PREACHING Spirit power for only about two years when he began his 1878 revival meeting in New Haven, Connecticut. Among the crowds drawn to the famous revivalist was a young Yale seminarian, Reuben A. Torrey. An avowed liberal, Torrey had gone to the meeting with a group of students to "patronize" the "strange, uneducated man." But instead, he found himself transfixed. It was not Moody's arguments that swayed him, but a power he found difficult to place. "He may be uneducated," Torrey later recalled thinking, "but he knows some things we don't." The young man approached Moody afterward to ask his secret. The ever-practical revivalist simply explained that "the best way to learn is to go at it" and set Torrey and his fellow students to work in the inquiry room.[9] Torrey found the task of disputing for the faith with individual inquirers deeply satisfying and not unlike the legal career he had recently sacrificed for the ministry. It would be another decade before the two men crossed paths again, but Torrey would spend much of that time seeking the source of Moody's power.

Torrey's childhood could not have been more different from Moody's hardscrabble upbringing. Respectability was his birthright. He was born to a blue-blooded New England family in 1856; his father was a well-connected banker, a man who could lose his fortune in the panic of 1857 and gain it all back with lucrative government contracts to manufacture boxes for the Union army. Untouched by the war, Torrey spent an idyllic childhood on a palatial 200-acre estate in Geneva, New York. At ten, Torrey claimed, he traded both his father's Universalist faith and his mother's pious but decidedly nonevangelical Presbyterianism for a life of pleasure. He found

Reuben Torrey, the child of elites and Ivy League educated. His understanding of Christian work ironically inspired many evangelicals from the lower orders to take their faith in a radical direction.
(Courtesy of the Moody Bible Institute Archives)

his studies at an elite Episcopalian preparatory academy to be easy, and he matriculated at Yale when he was fifteen with plans to study law. There, he put his hedonism to work in a swirl of dancing, drinking, smoking, card playing, sports, and fighting.[10]

Torrey's faith journey began his junior year, when a series of fires in his father's factories and the crippling panic of 1873 again put the family in a precarious financial situation. Subsequently, upon learning he had not been accepted to one of Yale's prestigious secret societies, Torrey plunged into a deep depression, briefly contemplated suicide, and then promised God to become a minister "if He would take the awful burden off my heart." For a time, his behavior was even "more wild" than before, but he eventually joined the college church, adopted respectable Protestant norms, and fulfilled his vow to God by entering Yale Seminary.[11]

Torrey's faith, however sincere, did not last through his first year of study. After reading the eighteenth-century British historian Edward Gibbon, he fell into a profound agnosticism. Gibbon challenged the prevailing orthodoxies of his day, mustering substantial evidence that Christianity, like all human belief systems, developed and changed over time. He traced bedrock doctrines like the Trinity to pagan Greek sources, noting their absence from ancient Hebrew theology. The respectable orthodox belief that miracles ceased after the formation of the biblical canon was also of recent invention. These and other problems posed by historical consciousness haunted Gilded Age Protestantism. It left Torrey, who valued certitude above all else, "utterly at sea." "I made up my mind to find out to an absolute certainty the truth," he later wrote, vowing to "act accordingly" to what he discovered, even rejecting Christianity outright if it did not pass muster.[12]

Torrey's faith journey was oriented toward the guidance of the Spirit from the beginning. His pathway out of agnosticism wended through the Protestant liberal tradition, including key theologians from Britain and Germany. But he began with American Unitarians and transcendentalists, who emphasized an intuitive connection to God. He later reported being "a great admirer" of William Ellery Channing, Theodore Parker, and "others of the same or similar schools," including Ralph Waldo Emerson. The heart of the gospel for Parker was the love of God and others, sanctioned by "the voice of God in your heart" and the presence of "Christ and the Father abiding within us."[13] Emerson similarly argued that individuals should submit their wills to the God within, accessed by intuition rather than reason or willful self-making.[14]

After his encounter with Moody and his graduation from seminary, Torrey accepted a call to a Congregationalist church in Garrettsville, Ohio, where his liberal theology intermingled with his new interest in Christian work. His diary from the time recorded mundane parish work interspersed with interdenominational revival services, temperance meetings, and debates with local skeptics. Some of his sermons suggested a personal relationship with God, others a vague spirit-infused universalism that noted "some truth" could be found in every denomination and even non-Western religious traditions like "Buddhism, Judaism, Mohammedanism, [and] Confucianism."[15] He was drawn increasingly to a respectable evangelical Protestantism through the influence of his parishioners, especially Clara Smith, who he married shortly after his arrival.[16] But his reading was dominated by Charles Darwin and German liberal theologians.[17]

Torrey was still haunted by the doubts he had experienced in seminary, however. They became so acute in 1882 that he resigned his pastorate to "think himself clear" by studying in Germany.[18] Like other Gilded Age elites, Torrey struggled with the epistemological problem of attaining certain knowledge. But unlike most of his cohort, he never made peace with incertitude.[19] This was problematic, since the leading approaches to biblical scholarship spoke in terms of probabilities rather than certain truths. He found no satisfactory answers among the moderate Lutherans at the university in Leipzig. To keep "scientific questions of authorship" from disrupting the faith of laypeople, the biblical scholar Franz Delitzsch could only advise Torrey not to bring them up. "We tried to make him understand that in America men investigated these things & the preacher had to deal with them," Torrey complained to his diary, but these appeals went unanswered.[20]

Frustrated with biblical scholarship, Torrey moved to the university in Erlangen to study under F. H. R. Frank, a philosophically oriented theologian. Frank's lifework was a new theory of "Christian certitude" rooted in an individual's personal experience. A certainty of the existence of God, the transforming work of Jesus, and other core beliefs came by comparing one's life before and after conversion, he taught. Certainty, in other words, began in an existential leap of faith. Proof came afterward by examining the results of that faith.[21] By Torrey's thinking, this same principle could also be used to determine the Bible's reliability. Historical questions related to biblical higher criticism, questions that could not be answered with certainty, were ultimately irrelevant. What mattered was whether the teachings of the Bible could be productively applied to one's life. And these could be tested experientially. Surely, Torrey's own faith journey undergirded his later advice to "honest agnostics." Those searching for God should first read the Bible "a few verses at a time," he advised, with "a willingness to believe" and a promise "to act upon so much as you see to be true." If the Bible was true, he promised, their lives would be demonstrably better.[22]

Experience-based certainty opened the way for Torrey to read the Bible plainly, without the complications of biblical scholarship. In fact, he had already shown a preference for a rugged realist reading of the Bible at Yale. The approach was modeled in John Seeley's *Ecce Homo*, an ostensible biography of the historical Jesus. Seeley claimed to strip from Christianity the philosophical and dogmatic accretions of the last 1,800 years. He would accept only "those conclusions" about Jesus that "the facts themselves, critically weighed appear to warrant." "Facts" in this case constituted a plain reading of the gospel stories.[23] Seeley's realism was a lively alternative to stale churchly orthodoxy. It did not shy away from Jesus's impossible miracles or his radical condemnations of mammon. This plain gospel depicted faith as "a loyal and free confidence in Christ" rather than staid assent to theological dogma. Church was not a formal institution, but a group of believers united in their struggle to apply Jesus's teachings to society.[24]

As a follower of Seeley's Jesus, and free to find religious certainty in everyday life, Torrey cut his German studies short and returned to the United States. But where should he minister? Reflecting his growing realism, he believed that certainty would not be found in the safety of small-town Congregationalism or among effete urban elites, but in a working-class neighborhood in northeast Minneapolis.

MINNEAPOLIS WAS ALREADY AN up-and-coming urban center in the 1880s, the largest in the upper Midwest. When combined with St. Paul across the Mississippi River, its population numbered 300,000, putting it ninth in the country behind San Francisco. The surrounding fertile farmland and ample waterpower made it a dominant player in the world flour market, while railroads stretching west to Portland, Oregon, and south to New Orleans helped make it one of the major commercial and manufacturing centers between Chicago and the West Coast.[25]

Like other industrializing cities, Minneapolis faced rising class tensions, but the religious and ethnic composition of the city fostered a communal orientation that, for good or ill, shaped those relations. Members of Torrey's Congregationalist denomination dominated many of the city's business, political, and educational institutions.[26] Hailing from elite New England stock, they embraced a Pilgrim mythology. They were the bearers of "civilization" to the untamed western wilds and the teaming urban frontier. But numerical realities kept this tribalism in check. Congregationalists constituted just 3 percent of religious adherents in Minnesota, outpaced by Roman Catholicism and five other Protestant denominations. Indian peoples, whose religious traditions were not included in such censuses, were looming threats in the minds of many white residents, followed closely by political radicals and the irreligious "masses." Thus Congregationalists at least tolerated middle-class Roman Catholics and forged alliances with other American and European Protestants. An emphasis on the Spirit helped bridge these confessional divides. Outside explicitly religious domains, German and Scandinavian workers cultivated an industrial cooperative tradition. They promoted a model of collective workplace governance as an alternative to individualistic capitalism. It reaped moral benefits, advocates claimed, transforming one "drunken, disreputable guild" into "a responsible and respectable class of citizens" sympathetic to "law and order and public morality."[27] Cooperative endeavor benefited body and soul.

Torrey initially hobnobbed in elite circles but increasingly gravitated toward the lives of his working-class congregants. His Yale connections provided opportunities to lecture on German university life, to elicit donations from the governor, and to attend the city's elite functions. This was a world away from his Jefferson Street Church. Living in "a section of the city not supplied with church privileges," his parishioners, "largely dependent on wages," often struggled to put food on the table. Torrey offered a growing portfolio of social, educational, and religious services through his church, which functioned like a neighborhood center. He also incorporated smaller, but potent, symbolic changes, from renaming the congregation the "Open Door Church" to dispensing with the indignities of pew rents and choosing to labor alongside his congregants in the hot summer months, foregoing the traditional ministerial vacation.[28]

An article Torrey wrote in December 1885 reflected a new solidarity with this working-class congregation. Combining his growing communal convictions with appeals to a plainly interpreted Bible, he decried the overindulgence of the wealthy, especially when "earnest Christian men" struggled to support "families of six or seven or more upon $1.25 a day." It "must pierce the soul of the 'Son of Man' with keener anguish than ever the crucifying nails did his hands or feet on Calvary." More than tithing 10 percent, Torrey argued, rich Christians should "give eight-tenths more. Yea, 'sell all that thou hast, and distribute unto the poor, and thou shalt have treasures in heaven.'" This command is "binding upon all and a very literal interpretation would be desirable on the part of many." Torrey was no revolutionary; he focused on individual behavior over systematic critiques. He also stopped short of condemning all investments for profit. In an oddly literal rendering of a passage that condemned a servant "who *hid* his Lord's money in the *ground*," he argued that this forbade only "certain forms of real estate investment." But his conclusion that wealthy Christians had an obligation to invest most of their resources into "the intellectual, moral and spiritual elevation" of the masses was notable for a man of his background. He envisioned a kingdom of God on earth where wealthy believers gave freely and sacrificially, thereby ameliorating unjust disparities.[29]

Torrey understood Christians as constituting an organically united community, a body in which the Holy Spirit coordinated the actions of the whole. This reflected an increasingly popular understanding of society that would become the new basis for social science in the Progressive Era. Whether explicitly religious or more broadly secular, both understood conflict as unnatural, a sign of disease. The grossly unequal distribution of physical resources was like a clotted vein, and callousness to the suffering of fellow citizens was like a pinched nerve. This understanding of society as an organism produced a more sympathetic stance to the poor than social Darwinism's survival of the fittest. Yet it did not fundamentally challenge the power relations that created inequality. Instead, it depended, naïvely according to critics, on the goodwill of elites. "Reform" was limited to ameliorative measures.[30]

Yet the realist reading of the Bible inspired more radical efforts to Christianize society as well. There was general agreement among these reformers that the unconverted "masses" needed to be evangelized, and that middle-class church life should be reformed to accommodate working-class parishioners. But some went even farther. Taking the ethics of Jesus at face value, they suggested that social and economic systems needed to be Christianized. Washington Gladden, a pioneer of the social gospel, agreed that "no community can be saved without the salvation of the individuals," but he also considered industrial capitalism to be "diametrically opposed . . . to Christianity."[31] For these advocates, society must be "reorganized" on "the principles of Christ."[32]

Torrey did not criticize structural reformers, but he clearly understood conversion as the primary driver of reform. By reaching both "the masses" and elites, he believed he could further expand the social organism of the church and the coordinating power of the Holy Spirit. And by 1886, Torrey had demonstrated his ability to gather new converts. His church's original membership of eleven had grown eightfold over three years.[33] He expanded a Sunday school and opened a new mission in his neighborhood's commercial district. Increasingly, his attention was drawn to working-class evangelization over his traditional ministerial duties.

In June 1886 Torrey traveled to Chicago to participate in the inaugural meeting of the Christian Worker's Convention. The meetings were organized by John Collins, Torrey's seminary classmate and an urban missionary in New Haven, and George Clarke, a lawyer, real estate speculator, and Civil War colonel who founded Chicago's famous Pacific Garden Mission. They saw a need for an "intensely practical" gathering. Instead of "long philosophical essays or critical discourses," sessions would give space for discussions of effective methods and stubborn difficulties. They would act as a religious analog to a sales convention. Held a month after Haymarket, the first meeting attracted a wide audience, including coverage in the liberal-leaning *Christian Union*. On economic issues, the participants struck a conservative tone and focused almost exclusively on evangelization. Yet a thoroughgoing pragmatism provided space for progressive views on other social issues. Esther Frame, a Quaker evangelist, gave an impassioned defense of women in ministry using Paul's declaration that "there is neither male nor female." To the objection that "women can not preach like men," she retorted that she intended to "preach like a woman." Even John Farwell, so regressive on economic issues, dismissed the "forms and ceremonies" of traditional Protestantism as "ruts." "The ideal church," he thought, should be run on business principles. One final group emphasized themes that would become increasingly important to Torrey in the next year. They advocated for a "full Gospel" that offered both future salvation and a spiritual power capable of producing physical effects like miraculous healings. It was a power available to those who had a personal experience with God, a "Baptism of the Holy Spirit."[34]

The Christian Worker's Convention was a watershed for Torrey. He was elected chair of the convention and then president of the organization. His efficient oversight of the fluid proceedings attracted wide attention among many within the network, including Moody's Chicago allies Emma Dryer and Fleming Revell. Perhaps more important, he now saw himself not primarily as a pastor but as a Christian worker. This identity, taken with increasing literalness, would profoundly influence his future belief and practice.

OVER THE NEXT TWO years, Torrey began working out the implications of this new identity as a Christian worker. The most striking shift was a new emphasis on the personhood of God, especially the Holy Spirit, and the believer's relationship to him. He became convinced that the Bible taught that believers should experience a "Baptism of the Holy Spirit." Like Phoebe Palmer, he concluded it would inaugurate an ongoing relationship to God; and like Moody, he concluded it was accompanied by an influx of spiritual power. In fact, it became so important to Torrey that he ceased all work, shutting himself in his office and vowing not to preach again until he had gained it. Sitting in prayerful anticipation, he believed that God spoke directly to his heart, simply telling him that the gift was his and that he should "now go and preach." It occurred without emotional fireworks; rather, it was "the most quiet moment I ever knew."[35]

Torrey came to understand his experience of the Holy Spirit in the context of contract ideology. In the age of mass employment, the concept of contract became a catch-all solution to the ongoing problem of defining economic freedom. Traditionally, contracts were used to broker relationships and facilitate the transfer of goods. Legal precedents presumed the equality of both parties, freely submitting to the terms of the contract. But after the contract was executed, as in marriage, those relationships might become unequal. As part commodity and part relationship, modern labor straddled both arenas. In fact, marriage was an important influence on the legal interpretation of labor contracts. Much as the husband became the legal head of the family, the employer was legally granted exclusive control over both the work process and compensation. As the wife was subsumed into the husband's legal identity through coverture, the employee's labor was absorbed into the enterprise. In theory, at least, a worker had the freedom to refuse a contractual relationship or leave it at will, though vagrancy laws were often used to usurp that right. Thus for workers, economic freedom was limited to selling one's labor to the highest bidder. The work relations that followed were strictly hierarchical.[36] Torrey's Yale education was suffused with this contract ideology, and wage labor was an everyday reality for his current parishioners.

For Torrey, the Baptism of the Holy Spirit was the inauguration of a contractual relationship between God and a Christian worker. Like Palmer, he emphasized that the Baptism was "for me individually."[37] And like Moody, he insisted its purpose was to "make us effective" in "testimony and service."[38] But Torrey also emphasized *when* the Baptism of the Holy Spirit occurred. Since a valid contract required equal parties, it was important that the Baptism occur after God's free gift of salvation had transformed a sinner deserving damnation into a "child of God." As a "co-heir with Christ," he or she had the standing to freely choose to enter into this contractual relationship. It was a legal transaction primarily and thus need not be accompanied by strong emotions or demonstrations of spiritual power. It was like buying a piece of property, Torrey explained. "It is mine as soon as the deed is properly executed and recorded, though it may be some time before I enter into the experimental enjoyment of it."[39] But it was absolutely necessary to enter into God's employ—so vital that one should "stop his work right where he is" until it was achieved.[40] To do otherwise was to meddle on the factory floor without authorization, creating chaos.

The Bible served as the contract between the believer and God, specifying the terms for entering into the relationship. To help individuals achieve a true Baptism of the Holy Spirit, Torrey outlined seven steps that revolved around three primary activities. First, like a labor contract, the Baptism must be freely chosen with "an intense desire" and full awareness of the responsibilities that it entailed.[41] Second, entering the spiritual contract required a "total surrender to the will of God," including giving "myself and all I possess" to God's "control and use."[42] It involved "utterly renouncing every thought, every purpose, every desire, every affection of our own" and instead thinking Christ's "thoughts," forming "His purposes in us," and even feeling "His emotions and affections."[43] The final activity entailed a commitment to acting on God's direction, "prompt, exact obedience, without asking any questions" to every command in scripture regardless of how hard or impossible it might seem.[44] Christian workers, like their industrial counterparts, need not understand the entire process that was coordinated by management. Precisely following directions maintained order, whether following specifications for manufacturing or a seemingly arbitrary scriptural command.

As in other labor contracts, the Christian worker decided whether to remain or leave the contractual relationship. It was maintained by simple living "free from indulgence and surfeiting" and a willingness to "endure hardness, as a good soldier of Jesus Christ." It was voided by engaging in activities that impeded "the fullness of God's power," such as leading a "luxurious life" or "indulg[ing] extensively in dainties."[45] But Torrey believed God would always renew a revoked spiritual contract if the believer confessed and again abided by the contractual requirements.

The Bible also listed the requirements and rewards for Christian workers who lived under contract. In the broadest sense, the Baptism brought "power for service." Like Moody, Torrey understood this power as a sort of spiritual technology. It was "the Spirit of God coming upon the believer, taking possession of his faculties, imparting to him gifts not naturally his own, but which qualify him for the service to which God has called him."[46] And like all machinery, it required maintenance. Neglecting prayer and Bible reading would result in the loss of effectiveness. Spiritual power was like a battery. Electrical stores were depleted as the believer engaged in "service and blessing," Torrey explained, and "power would be maintained" only if it were "constantly renewed."[47]

But the Bible contained more than the general promise of power. Torrey believed that it was filled with specific promises to spirit-empowered believers. This was inspired in part by his German mentor, F. H. R. Frank. Frank understood the Bible to be God's covenant, or contract, with his chosen people—a record of God's promises and the requirements for their fulfillment. But Torrey emphasized an individual's relationship to God and his speaking to believers personally in the Bible, not to the community at large. "When you read a verse of scripture hear the voice of the living God speaking directly to you," he taught, the "living, present person, God, our Father, Himself talking directly to you in these words."[48] Torrey therefore individualized biblical promises and requirements. Search the Bible "for promises and appropriate them as fast as you find them," he advised.[49]

Torrey believed that God bound himself absolutely to every promise in the biblical contract. Once an individual discovered a "definite promise of God's Word" and fulfilled the accompanying requirements, he or she could have complete confidence that God would grant "the petition that I have asked of Him."[50] Torrey's God was personal, but the process was mechanical. The Bible was a Christian worker's toolbox, a catalog of specific, literal promises with guaranteed delivery. Believers made their requests through prayer, which Torrey flatly asserted was "God's appointed way for obtaining things."[51] Spirit-baptized believers were like faithful workers who could fearlessly stroll into their boss's office to demand resources for their job.

For Torrey, any biblical promise could be claimed "by meeting the conditions and risking all upon them."[52] Precision was important, since these requirements might "appear unreasonable or impossible." Yet once they were "definitely ascertained," they must be accepted without question.[53] This knowledge would come in part by careful Bible study. But ultimately, like other areas of one's faith, complete certainty came by experience, by "risking all." If God's promise seemed to fail, then the requirements were misunderstood.

Torrey's contractual understanding of the Bible overwhelmed all other interpretive concerns. Torrey could construe most any passage as a promise to him personally. For example, he wrote the phrase "Thou, God, seest me" on the flyleaf of his personal Bible. These were the words of Abraham's slave Hagar in the biblical text, but to Torrey, they were God's personal assurance that he saw his needs, desires, and struggles. The marginalia on the pages that followed contain the remnants of an intimate, intuitive, but contractually structured conversation between himself and God.[54] Torrey's Bible was not primarily a book of science, theology, ethics, or poetry but a living text, a medium through which God communicated to him directly. "I have come to the fork in the road more than fifty times," Torrey would say in terms incongruent to antebellum Protestants, "and in every instance where my reason and common sense differed from the Bible, the Bible had proved right and my reason wrong."[55] He dismissed the occasional inaccuracy in history and science as "a fly-speck in the corner" of "a great masterpiece of art." He never struggled with accepting the geological consensus that the Earth and life on it had existed for millions of years, and he insisted that evolution was not inconsistent with the Bible.[56] He later accepted premillennialism for the same personal and practical reasons as Moody. But he had no interest in end-times minutia. The exception to his otherwise densely marked Bible was the nearly pristine pages in the books of Daniel and Revelation, the hobbyhorses of doctrinaire premillennialists. Torrey's greatest concerns were always relational and experiential: "Is the Bible from God, and of absolute authority in faith and practice?"[57] Apologetics was simply a matter of living the faith.

TORREY WAS SOON TESTING the reliability of the divine contract through faith healing, a biblical promise that a growing network of radical evangelicals had claimed since the late 1870s. It was related in part to a broader "mind cure" movement that sprawled across many confessional divides. The rising popularity of faith healing, when current medical remedies were often worse than the disease, was not coincidental. But for evangelicals, it was simply taking God's clear biblical promises of healing at face value. Some dispensed with both doctors and medicine as a matter of principle, claiming that reliance on such "human means" demonstrated a sinful lack of faith. Torrey ceased giving his children medicine and for a time began praying for the healing of his parishioners and others who made requests.

But Torrey's public healing ministry was short-lived. In December 1886 he prayed for the healing of nineteen-year-old Cora Stickney, who suffered from leukemia—what doctors called "consumption of the blood"—and had been declared incurable. His faith cure initially appeared to be efficacious, but Cora died the following day. Unable to accept that God's word had failed, Torrey blamed the girl's faith, noting reports that she had expressed embarrassment over the faith cure. But the girl's mother, Anna, believed that God would raise her dead daughter and retrieved the body from the morgue. Anna was convinced that six days of prayer over the dead body had brought about a "partial resurrection" that was aborted, she tragically concluded, as "a judgment for my lack of faith." The medical examiner's conclusion was equally unsettings: Cora had been declared dead prematurely and had lain in the morgue half frozen in a coma. Newspapers across the country reported the grisly details. Though attempting resurrection had been too radical, even for the adventurous Torrey, he could not avoid the uncomfortable questions of reporters or escape the fact that Anna shared his absolutist logic.[58] After this incident, Torrey limited his practice of faith healing to the more-controlled setting of his immediate family, deciding that his public ministry was better devoted to evangelism.

Torrey fared much better in his other Christian work. In October 1886 he resigned his pastorate in order to operate the interdenominational Minneapolis City Mission. His monthly reports were filled with stories of transformed lives. Converts included typical "threats" to Christian civilization: a young drifter from Winnipeg in search of work; a "gray-haired" skeptic; a bartender who had not been to a religious service since his mother died; a "young Swede" who just dropped in but then "couldn't rest until [he] gave [his] heart to Christ"; a man just released from the workhouse, en route to commit burglary"; and an "actress . . . under the influence of liquor."[59]

To accommodate this steady stream of new converts who complained of being "frozen out" of respectable churches, Torrey started an independent "People's Church" under the mission's auspices. At one Christian Worker's Convention, he triumphantly reported on his congregation of "carpenters, stone cutters, masons, day laborers, small grocers, washerwomen and other people of very limited incomes and culture." Members included European immigrants and African Americans; numerous other nationalities, including "Chinese and Jews," attended regularly. It was "just as the multitude that was converted on the Day of Pentecost," Torrey explained. Independent of denominational control, their only creed was to "accept the Scriptures of the Old and New Testaments, which are the Word of God, as the only authoritative rule of faith and practice." They had few rules, since "where the Holy Ghost is, rules are not necessary, and where He is not, they are useless." Church work was conducted every day from dawn to dusk. Members often ate together, creating "a very loving kindly feeling," so much that "we are more a family than a church." When one member of Torrey's church lost his job, his grocery bill was paid by another congregant; he, in turn, paid it forward to help another family. Together, they set about to bring the Kingdom of God to their little corner of Minneapolis.[60]

The Christian Worker's Convention had grown during this time in both the number and diversity of its participants. The 1887 gathering in New York City attracted leading figures of the early social gospel movement, including Josiah Strong and Lyman Abbott. Reporters gave extensive laudatory coverage. They wrote of urban evangelism as the spiritual analog to big-game hunting and used martial metaphors such as "capturing souls" in contrast to their effeminate elite ministerial counterparts who were too concerned with theological minutia to be of any practical good.[61] Torrey's talks rejected formal doctrine. Street preaching "should be direct, earnest, [and] non-doctrinal," he argued, avoiding "all attacks upon Romanism." Focus instead on conversion, "and the doctrines will take care of themselves." Even questions "about the blessed Trinity" took a backseat to the concern "that you have a soul to be saved."[62] The Christian Convention's popularity continued the following year in Detroit, attracting notable participants like the wealthy philanthropist Grace Dodge, Toronto mayor W. H. Howland, and wealthy drug manufacturer turned mission founder Charles Crittenton. The Reverend J. H. Hector from California conducted a session titled the "Religious Needs and Possibilities of the Colored Race in America."[63]

Riding high on his growing success, Torrey decided to make his boldest and most literal test of the biblical contract to date. After reading George Mueller's famous autobiography and facing financial difficulties at the mission, he concluded that God had called him to live "literally by prayer." The biblical requirements "that it was wrong to run in debt to any man" (Romans 13:8) were clear, as was the promise of Philippians 4:19 that "if we trusted God and took our stand upon his plain word . . . He would see to it that our wants were met." Torrey paid down his personal debts and then began operating both the church and the mission as a "faith work" in January 1889. Living by faith was literally an all-consuming exercise, his complete dependence upon God's direct intervention for every need. "Every penny that came into my pocket, every mouthful of food that went into the mouths of my wife and children," Torrey recounted, "came in answer to prayer, sometimes in ways most direct and remarkable."[64]

Living by faith alone yielded irrefutable proof of God's faithfulness, Torrey later claimed, but his spiritual ledger, at least its first draft, recorded more ambiguity. Unlike Mueller's international reputation and massive donor base, Torrey's experiment was largely unknown outside the upper Midwest.

When press coverage ebbed, donations slowed to a trickle. Four months into the experiment, answers to prayer came by increasingly tenuous accounting tricks, like when he remembered funds "in our S. S. treasury to meet the deficiency." On another occasion, a coworker broke protocol to directly solicit funds. When Torrey found two silver dollars in his desk, was this evidence of miraculous provision or the need for better office organization? And when God provided dinner consisting of a two-day-old "bag of rolls & cakes some one had left," the "riches of God's grace" seemed to be running low.[65]

God's promise was supposed to be mechanically reliable; why, then, did these problems occur? Torrey's only possible conclusion was that he had inadvertently broken the debt proviso. But what God required was never settled with clarity. With his finances in a free fall, his policies oscillated erratically in search of God-pleasing practices. Initially, he thought having no savings whatsoever demonstrated his faith that "God can provide for the future." Later, he concluded the opposite: it "seems like running in debt to have your house a month & no provision for the rent," so he decided to "pay wholly in advance." But when financial troubles continued, he came to an even more radical conclusion. The only explanation, he decided, was that paying his landlord in advance was actually "putting him in debt to me."[66]

Torrey's final conclusion about debt was entirely logical given his communal perspective, but it would have had revolutionary implications for the morality of modern economic practices. If lending constituted an entanglement in debt as much as borrowing, then investments, banks, and commodity futures markets were immoral institutions. Rents and wages became insoluble dilemmas. Should payments be broken into hourly, even second-by-second rates—to be paid simultaneous with use? No wonder Torrey's last diary entry confessed deep confusion. And given its radical implications, it is also no surprise that this conclusion was silently eliminated from the version of the diary that the Moody Bible Institute published as a tract "to stimulate faith" after Torrey's death.[67] If the authentic Christian life was to be lived in an organic, interdependent community, the requirements of faith work became a philosophical cul-de-sac: one either was indebted to another person or placed that person in debt.

Ultimately, Torrey never followed through on his communal interpretation of debt. Rather, he went in the opposite direction, embracing a more thoroughgoing social individualism to complement his personal relationship with God. In another passage expunged from the published journal, Torrey explained that God's final provision in Minneapolis came through his wife, Clara, who apparently controlled funds independent of her husband and "gave a lot."[68] To consider his wife as an independent agent was a radical degree of economic individualism for the 1880s, but how else could he interpret this transaction to be answered prayer? And if even husband and wife constituted independent economic units, how much more were members of other social groups? Thus by Torrey's new accounting, both church and society were simply collections of independent individuals. Torrey was not accountable to his fellow man for his economic decisions, but only to God. He was not directly responsible for the physical well-being of the poor. In fact, God might be using those circumstances to guide that person just as he himself had been guided. Torrey's only responsibility was to sense the Spirit's direction and then obey it, giving to others when prompted but leaving their fate to God alone. Forced to choose, Torrey took religious certitude rooted in a contractual individualism over his earlier social Christianity rooted in an intensely interdependent community.

Torrey had narrowly evaded an empirical tsunami that would have swamped his certitude. But one final, permanent provision ensured that Torrey would never face that possibility again. Without any inquiries on Torrey's part (was it the movement of the Holy Spirit?), Dwight L. Moody extended an invitation to superintend the Bible Institute of Chicago. This meant God's future provision would come in the mundane form of a paycheck, and that his life of faith had been an "experiment" that both he and God had passed. God's faithfulness was concretized as an artifact of the past. It was this experience, Torrey later insisted, that made him "as certain that there is a God who answers prayer as I am that I exist."[69] God remained his faithful employer, the scriptures his ironclad contract, prayer his negotiation method, and Christian work his calling. These ideas would permeate his work at the Bible Institute as well.

WHEN TORREY BEGAN DEVELOPING Moody's Bible Institute into a center of spirit-empowered Christian work in the fall of 1889, he had no plans to replicate his college or seminary education. The institute was a thoroughly practical endeavor with an ethos inspired by his Minneapolis ministry and his work with the Christian Worker's Convention. Torrey's students would reach Chicago's masses and any other unbelievers they encountered under the direction and power of the Holy Spirit. Eschewing doctrine and traditional educational methods, they relied primarily on a spiritual technology, a "power for service" fueled by scripture, prayer, faith, and hard work.

As with Moody's and Torrey's other projects, the centrality of a personal relationship to God made doctrinal issues secondary at the institute. They actively sought wide denominational representation, attracting over forty by 1900.[70] Rather than composing a precise statement of faith sure to offend someone and introduce suspicions of sectarianism, they required that students be church members and that their pastors evaluate their fitness for Christian work according to their denominational standards. Unity centered not on doctrine but on a shared religious experience that began with the Baptism of the Holy Spirit—a nonnegotiable expectation for every student to achieve, along with a "thorough consecration" and an "intense love for souls." The institute's "creed," tellingly labeled the "*Act* of Faith," reflected Torrey's understanding of a Christian worker under contract. After a vague declaration of belief ("on the name of the Son of God," and "redemption through His Blood and life by His Spirit"), it moved to a submissive posture (belonging to God "by purchase, conquest and self-surrender") and finally to claiming biblical promises (provision "for all my hourly needs" and strength to overcome any "difficulty, inward or outward").[71] The institute was thus designed to produce trained workers for God while remaining compatible with any denomination.

Though Moody's simple gospel constituted the presumed theological center of the Bible Institute, this still allowed considerable leeway for more liberal influences. Though the Bible professor Wilbert W. White was not necessarily liberal, his Ph.D. from Yale under the liberal scholar William Rainey Harper suggests he did not fear modern criticism. Invited "special lecturers" were similarly diverse.[72] Biblical "difficulties," "the theories of the higher critics," and "typology and prophecy" were rare supplements to lectures devoted primarily to practical instruction.[73]

Whatever the doctrinal flexibility, the environment was not lax. Students were expected to expend every ounce of God's power for service. Torrey developed a rigorous two-year program designed to weed out all but the most committed. Admission was "only on trial," one brochure warned, and those "not adapted to Christian work . . . are frankly informed of the fact."[74] Success demanded "untiring energy" and a "willingness to endure hardness as good soldiers of Jesus Christ." This meant six-day weeks of morning classes, afternoon ministry assignments, plus additional manual labor for students unable to pay the four-dollar weekly room-and-board charge out of pocket. "We give no man anything," Torrey boasted; those "good for anything . . . will get through."[75] The Bible Institute was soon christened the

"West Point" of Christian service because, a former student explained, they learned only what they "need[ed] to know" and were expected to put that knowledge into practice lest it "become rusty from lack of use" or curdle into arrogance.[76]

Institute coursework taught students the English Bible inside and out as the Christian worker's primary tool. Over two years, students completed a summary of each chapter in the Bible, listing the "principal subject," the "leading lesson," its "best verse," and the "principal persons." Some books were engaged in even more detail; one exam on the Gospel of John required students to "give four leading incidents" of a key chapter and provide short summarizing phrases to arbitrarily chosen sections.[77] As salesmen and -women for Jesus, they were expected to know their product inside and out.

But even Bible study was not for its own sake; it was an "intensely practical" pursuit, especially focused on the task of evangelism.[78] Torrey's books, based on his classroom material, were designed for using over musing. His imposing 540-page textbook *What the Bible Teaches* was less a work of traditional theology than a legal index of the biblical contract. He discarded standard theological categories and instead organized the material in sections devoted to each person of the Trinity, to "Man," and more briefly to angels and the devil. These were the key actors in the contractual relationship—by Torrey's accounting, those that might either help or hinder Christian work. Mind-numbingly complex outlines, regularly extending four levels, organized hundreds of propositions and proof texts. "Beauty and impressiveness" were always trumped by "precision and clearness," he explained. Yet even seemingly esoteric subjects like God's omniscience always returned to relational themes and specific promises that students could claim, such as "He knows all man's sorrows" and "God's knowledge extends to the minutest particulars."[79]

Torrey's tellingly titled *How to Study the Bible for Greatest Profit* outlined those "methods" that brought "the largest results." It presented the benefits of Bible study in terms of quantifiable value in relation to the labor expended. The end was practical. To say the goal of Bible study was to "carefully and fully classif[y] its contents" was like saying "we are through with a meal when we have it arranged it in an orderly way upon the table." The Bible, like food, "is there to eat, digest and assimilate."[80] Like Moody, Torrey taught that the Bible should be approached with questions in hand. His "topical index" helped students sift through the mass of biblical content in search of the answer. Torrey spoke of his approach to the Bible as rigorously "inductive"—that is, it began with the mass of biblical data and allowed the general principles intrinsic in that material to emerge of their own accord. But of course Torrey's assumptions that undergirded the methods he taught, the headings in his outlines, and the topics in his indices influenced what his students saw (and failed to see) in the biblical text, thus significantly shaping their interpretation. The seeming objectivity of it all made these subtle influences all the more powerful.

A second facet of Torrey's curriculum focused on practical tools for evangelism. Training began in the classroom with technical instruction in music and giving "Bible Readings,"[81] as well as large amounts of rote memorization. Students were expected to study exhaustive lists of excuses people might give for not converting that were paired with effective scriptural responses.[82] One exam question asked for the twenty "principal difficulties that stand between men and Christ, and the Scripture to use in removing each."[83] But the real test came in their daily ministry assignments. Torrey almost always sent students to locales where the unchurched congregated—movable tents in working-class neighborhoods, a barge parked on the lake front, working-class saloons, or simply the bustling city streets. Preaching or music was used to attract listeners, followed by one-on-one interviews with potential converts. One of Torrey's favorite methods was simply to "go out and stand on the street and watch the people," praying to "the Lord to show you the right one" and then following the divine impulse to "step up . . . and lead him to Christ." "You do sometimes get arrested" or roughed up by detractors, Torrey admitted, but "God will take care of you."[84]

Torrey evaluated students' Christian work with elaborate bureaucratic instruments. Students listed the number of meetings they conducted and tallies of conversions on a "Weekly Report Card."[85] In addition, they kept a "Memorandum Book of Personal Work" in which they tracked demographic information of each evangelistic target, "time spent in conversation," "specific difficulty," and the "apparent result" of the encounter. New converts, in turn, filled out a card with their contact information, denominational preference, and comments on the evangelistic transaction. These were sent directly to Torrey as quality control.[86] The resulting statistics from these instruments were compiled as quantitative evidence for financial supporters. They also provided the fodder for weekly student evaluation meetings. Numbers did not lie: poor spiritual returns might signal a moral problem, a biblical misinterpretation, or simply that the student was not cut out for ministry.

Torrey was always clear that studies, techniques, and statistics were secondary to the Spirit. Once, when aggregate conversions dipped, Torrey canceled lectures and devoted the day to prayer. On another occasion, students called their own prayer meeting for spiritual power that continued past midnight.[87]

For all the bureaucracy, a family atmosphere prevailed. The entire institute, including Torrey and his family, ate together. Though Torrey was "earnest about . . . vital business," a student recalled, "he was always relaxed in private conversation, and was definitely not 'unapproachable.'" "[H]e would enter heartily into games," including a school-wide tennis competition,[88] "and was the 'life of the party.'"[89] The Bible Institute's magazine had a similarly familial feel; it printed correspondence addressed to Torrey personally and had a chatty manner.[90]

But the family atmosphere did not change the fact that each individual would be held accountable for his or her actions. The weekly "family meeting" where the practical work was evaluated was a case in point. By Torrey's description, given at a Christian Worker's Convention, he would "look over the blanks" and ask a student to stand. "I see there are eight inquirers talked with, two professing conversion. Won't you tell us about one of those who professed conversion?" Those without results had a more difficult interview in front of their fellow students. "I may seem rather savage here," Torrey admitted, "but we put the question right to them. They are there for business, to be taught how to save souls, how to do personal work."[91] Students were tested and evaluated as individuals. They were expected to have an individual experience of the Holy Spirit and a personal relationship with God. As much as possible, this information was tracked in a student's personnel file and summarized on an index card for administrators' handy reference. These assessments were unvarnished. Despite above-average grades, adequate financial provision, a "good tenor voice," and a reference letter from Moody's pastor in Northfield, "Phillip" was deemed "self-willed . . . [and] unwilling to listen to instruction" and thus was "dismissed for insubordination."[92] The key to both spiritual power and effective instruction was that the student maintain a posture of submission.

LEADING THE CHARGE AT Moody's innovative experiment in urban missions, Torrey believed he had found the secret to attaining sure religious knowledge and to success in one's life and ministry. It certainly seemed true in his life. Thanks to Torrey's growing reputation, he had become a hot commodity. He authored numerous books, including how-to manuals for Christian workers and spiritual reference works. They sold briskly over the next two decades and helped Torrey maintain an upper-middle-class lifestyle. Though less extravagant than his upbringing, his lifestyle was no less comfortable. Royalties purchased various urban residences and a beautiful summer home in Montrose, Pennsylvania. They paid for his children's college education, including Ivy League training for his only son. And having resolved the dilemma stemming from faith work in favor of economic individualism, Torrey was free to invest what funds remained to ensure the future well-being of his family. Torrey's wife, Clara, kept the family accounts. A thrifty woman, she tracked these investments in the unused pages of the same ledger containing Torrey's account of his "faith work." In a way, this literal accounting was an appropriate coda to the diary, since it too represented God's continuing material provision.

Although Torrey had ceased the active practice of "living on faith," his ostensibly successful experiment continued to produce personal dividends. With the often-tenuous realities of that experience safely in the past, its problematic details faded with time, Torrey gained from it an annuity of religious certitude. Torrey could comfortably forget that the empirical realities of everyday life might impede some plain readings—those times when, sincere faith notwithstanding, sickness went unhealed and rent unpaid. It was a conundrum that Torrey had narrowly avoided twice but, sadly, would soon face again.

FOUR

The Crisis of Evangelical Realism

It was a spectacle worthy of the Colombian Exposition that inspired it. In May 1893, D. L. Moody began a five-month evangelistic blitz of Chicago, coinciding with the World's Fair. It would be a fitting legacy for the revivalist and a telling indication of how his thinking about city evangelism had developed. Dispensing with a central auditorium and single revivalist, he lured nearly every prominent Christian worker he knew to join in the campaign. Some were seasoned veterans—quite literally in the case of Civil War major general Oliver O. Howard. Others were up-and-coming Bible teachers, the household names for fundamentalists of the next generation. The fiery southern Baptist transplant Amzi C. Dixon and the lawyer turned Bible teacher Cyrus I. Scofield both participated. The foot soldiers of the campaign were Bible Institute students. Moody did his part, conducting meetings in the symbolically poignant Haymarket Theatre, but the real impact would come by spreading evangelists across the city, working in tandem as a primitive form of spirit-empowered broadcasting. On a single Sunday, Moody's crew conducted sixty-five simultaneous meetings in forty-six locations in several different languages to over 62,000 people. The campaign, Moody hoped, would both evangelize the city and highlight the capacities of his Chicago Bible Institute to a national audience. And initially, at least, it seemed to succeed.[1]

Close to the entrance of the exposition's midway, another evangelical was hard at work. Anticipating the massive crowds that the fair would attract, the Australian minister John Alexander Dowie had built a small wooden tabernacle to conduct services. He, too, was interested in saving souls, but unlike Moody, he proclaimed a "full gospel" that taught Jesus had died to save both the soul from sin and the body from sickness. Every bit the promoter as Moody, Dowie created a visually stunning memorial to his "victories" above the platform consisting of discarded braces, crutches, and other medical devices abandoned as the sick sought healing through faith alone.[2]

Meanwhile, Reuben Torrey's Christian Worker's Convention had gained national prominence. Participants included settlement house pioneer Graham Taylor, the muckraking journalist Jacob Riis, "purity" reformer Anthony Comstock, and Senator Joseph Hawley.[3] The platform of the 1892 Boston convention was filled with leading citizens not only in religious circles but in "social and commercial and political" arenas as well.[4] The following year, Booker T. Washington traveled 1,100 miles to the Atlanta convention in order to give a five-minute talk. "I knew that the audience would be largely composed of the most influential class of white men and women," Washington wrote, "and that it would be a rare opportunity for me to let them know what we were trying to do at Tuskegee as well as speak to them about the relations of the races."[5]

This was the variegated face of "Christian work" ascendant in the early 1890s. Use of the term in published materials peaked in 1894, when it was used with greater frequency in American publications than "social gospel," "Christian service," or even "evangelism."[6] Some claiming the title "Christian worker" were trained ministers like Torrey and celebrity evangelists like Moody. But many more were former real estate agents and lawyers, farmers and shopkeepers, reformed drunks and gamblers. They followed God's call to transform the world through city missions, storefront churches, evangelistic tours, Bible schools, and healing homes.

But with the diversity of Christian workers came a diversity of how that work was expressed. New, sometimes disruptive ideas emerged regarding what the "plainly" interpreted Bible taught, what a personal relationship to God required, and what fruits an active faith might produce. On the surface, the movement of Christian workers seemed unstoppable in 1894; it would fall into crisis by the turn of the century.

MOODY'S PRAGMATIC ORIENTATION FACILITATED a theologically diverse network of Christian workers in the 1890s. His associates spanned the Protestant spectrum. Many of his premillennial and holiness supporters had grown worried about higher criticism and other innovations. But his work with college-educated students in the Student Volunteer Movement led to his recruiting moderate and liberal coworkers, including the future president of the University of Chicago William Rainey Harper and the Scottish evangelist Henry Drummond. Likewise, many of these students took their work in moderate or liberal directions—men like Robert Speer, John Mott, and Sherwood Eddy.[7] Moody was happy to cooperate with whomever embraced a personal relationship to God, some sort of plain interpretation of the Bible, and a desire to have a practical impact, especially through evangelism.

A similar diversity developed at the Bible Institute of Chicago under Torrey's direction. Most students were some sort of evangelical but held various denominational affiliations and theological orientations. Diversity also extended beyond religious categories. Women, who were completely shut out of most theological education at the time, constituted the most diverse group of students and many pushed beyond the limits of traditional gender norms. A former student turned reporter Margaret Robinson described how female students debated suffrage and "the question of the Biblical supremacy of man" but gave universal assent to "the heart of the question: 'Is woman not as good as man.'" She knew at least one self-defined "new woman" in attendance who unapologetically insisted that some women "might teach members of the stronger sex occasionally." Learning from one's husband "nowadays is good doctrine too," Robinson coyly observed, "if she has one and if he knows more about the Word than she does." But in any case, both men and women were encouraged to "see it for yourself, and think independently of every one but God."[8] Both sexes were also expected to share what they learned with others. Women took classes covering the "Exposition of the Scriptures" and "Plans for Preparing Bible Readings and Bible Lessons."[9] If the word 'minister' did not appear in connection with women, reports that an alumna "has charge of a Congregational church" were uncontroversial.[10]

The Bible Institute also attracted Christian workers from all socioeconomic backgrounds. According to an institute directory, students who did not enter full-time ministry after graduation engaged in diverse secular employments: in the professions (lawyer, engineer, doctor, and manager), working-class occupations (lumberman, teamster, janitor, laundryman, mechanic, and assembler), and everything in between (candy maker, auctioneer, journalist, cartoonist, and actor).[11] Some students attended the institute to supplement their college or seminary education with practical training; for others, it was a stepping-stone to further education. The famed social gospel minister Charles Stelzle chose to attend the institute only after Princeton and McCormick Seminaries rejected him. Students entering their studies with limited educational attainments typically struggled. Records indicate that few students were dismissed for a lack of scholastic ability, but many "became discouraged" and left on their own accord. One "slow, but faithful" middle-aged student had wanted to become a missionary to China but returned to farming in Ontario. Yet a "rather dull, but faithful, earnest, and conscientious" man plodded through the entire course of study and became a Methodist Episcopal minister.[12]

Though the student body was primarily white, there were a few students of color. Torrey did not make a concerted effort to facilitate a racially integrated community, but he followed his Minneapolis practice of not discriminating by race, either at the institute or at Moody's church when he became its pastor in 1894.[13] The institute's most famous African American graduate, the educator and civil rights advocate Mary McLeod Bethune, attended in 1894 with plans to become a missionary to Africa. At a time when interracial education was rare and even illegal in some states, the presence of African American students was notable. But Bethune's recollection of being "not unduly non-plussed" because of her race was hardly a ringing endorsement. She remained "the only Negro student" during her studies and, despite plenty of "cheerful greetings" and "blithesome chatter," reported only "one or two instances [of] close companionship."[14] One should not confuse the institute for an interracial utopia, a classless community, or a hotbed of evangelical feminism. Rather, these progressive characteristics were by-products of the institute's pragmatic focus on increasing the circulation of its gospel message. Whatever opportunities these students gained by their attendance were products of their own making.

The major avenue for uniting the student body was a shared religious experience intrinsic to Torrey's ideas about the relationship of Christian workers to their God. Bethune's interaction with other students was surely improved by her deep, near-mystical religious orientation, "a quickening and an awakening that I had not words to express from that day to the present."[15] Robinson insisted that the "new women" at the institute were fully accepted and "lovable, true, noble women, obedient to God and His teaching," even as they sought "the truth with the free unfettered minds that the Holy Spirit imparts."[16]

But the same experiential bonds that united the student body could also alienate others. Stelzle credited the institute for its Bible training and for breaking him of his conservative methods. But an all-night prayer vigil designed to help students attain the Baptism of the Holy Spirit baffled him. "Student after student joyously arose and shouted that he 'claimed the promise,'" he recalled, "[but] I couldn't see it. I remained on my knees until about four o'clock in the morning" while the meeting's unnamed leader "berated me for my lack of faith." Stelzle stayed true to his conscience, despite being "made the subject of special prayer" and other manipulative techniques, believing "honesty was better than having the approval of the Faculty."[17]

Yet it was the effectiveness of one's work in the shared project of evangelizing Chicago that trumped any other hindrance to unity. In fact, despite Stelzle's differing opinions about spirit baptism, Torrey considered him among the "most valuable" institute alumni.[18] Some instructors occasionally warned against higher criticism, but their primary purpose was to train competent Christian workers acceptable for any denomination. Thus the lumberman and the professional, the barely literate and the seminary educated, the conservative Plymouth Brethren and the liberal "new" women— all worked and studied together at the institute. They were united, not by doctrine, but by a passion to transform society one soul at a time.

AN ENTERPRISE UNITED BY pragmatic considerations required results, but by 1893 the sufficiency of these returns was an open question. Torrey's statistics tallied only about seventy-five conversions per month during the first year. Though better than any Chicago church could claim, it was dwarfed by the population growth of the urban metropolis.[19]

Moody believed the Bible Institute's full potential had not yet been tapped and planned his multipronged Columbian Exposition campaign to demonstrate that capacity. The campaign was headquartered on campus, and though each speaker and song leader ministered in his or her own way, the primary goal of each was to gather people so that "personal work" could commence. The foot soldiers in this effort were students at the Bible Institute. All told, nearly 2 million people attended at least one of these meetings. By historian James Gilbert's estimates, this was about 7.5 percent of fair attendees, outdrawing all but the exposition's top attractions.[20] How many converted to evangelical Protestantism was more difficult to quantify.

The glory of the World's Fair campaign lasted barely a month, thanks to the investigations of British reporter William Stead. Arriving the final day of the Columbian Exposition, he set about systematically investigating the conditions of the city. He spoke to rich socialites and prostitutes, upstanding citizens and criminals, businessmen and workers. His findings were a litany of poverty, vice, and class tensions. Maps charted blocks with dozens of brothels and saloons. Interviews told of poverty-stricken families and starvation wages. And by Stead's estimates, only 5 percent of workingmen attended church.[21]

Anyone following Moody's ministry for the last two decades knew exactly what Stead's numbers indicated. A detailed census of two of Moody's exposition meetings found that over 90 percent of attendees lived outside the city. Once again, Moody had reached the comfortable classes, people with the financial resources for travel or suburban living. Whatever "thousands of converted sinners and revived Christians" the meetings produced bled out of the city after the fair. Chicago was largely untouched and left footing the $60,000 bill.[22]

Stead was the bearer of bad news, but his intentions were to rally reform. Though some historians suggest his efforts mark the birth of a new social reform movement, it was the last gasp of an older coalition of evangelical realists. Stead's central theme, "If Christ Came to Chicago," was a well-worn trope. His critique that Christians acted like "members of a select club" that met only "for their spiritual edification" and "aesthetic indulgence" instead of "saving others" was often on Moody's lips. Unsurprisingly, Torrey sat alongside David Swing, Rabbi Emil G. Hirsch from the University of Chicago, and Unitarian minister Jenkin Lloyd Jones on Stead's "Federation of Ministers," while Moody's friend Turlington Harvey served on the newly formed Chicago Civic Commission.[23]

For reasons never specified but probably not coincidental, three of Moody's longtime business supporters, Cyrus McCormick, Turlington Harvey, and John Farwell, resigned en masse from the institute board around this time. Attempts to recruit other business leaders like Thomas Templeton, a longtime associate of Marshall Field, failed, and so the board tapped Torrey and Moody's son-in-law Arthur P. Fitt.[24] In Harvey's case, signs of disillusionment had first appeared in 1891, when he invested the lion's share of his money and time into a planned industrial community outside Chicago. His town, immodestly named Harvey, used restrictive covenants on land sales to prohibit alcohol sales and gambling. If he could not convert the city, better to start from scratch. Unfortunately for Harvey's bottom line, he could not find enough investors to buy into his utopian dream. The project left him teetering on bankruptcy.[25]

IF EVER THERE WAS a need for Christ to come to Chicago it was in 1894. The worst economic depression to date had brought staggering industrial unemployment rates of 20 percent nationwide. The exposition had delayed its onset in Chicago, but it quickly gained par that winter. One hundred thousand industrial jobs evaporated, with many more people struggling with wage and hour cuts. The city's ad hoc social services were overwhelmed.

Illustrating the social tensions of the day was a crisis at another utopian experiment, the company town of Pullman, just outside the city. Founded a decade before by luxury-railcar manufacturer George Pullman, it was hailed a "western utopia," representing "the identity of interest which subsists between capital and labor."[26] But Pullman's kinder capitalism, questionable even in good times, evaporated during the depression. He mercilessly cut wages by a quarter, and then, without adjusting his rates, he began subtracting Pullman rents directly from paychecks. This ensured profitability, but only by literally paying starvation wages. Workers struck, and by June 1894, the conflict had spiraled into a national railroad strike. President Grover Cleveland sent federal troops to crush it—over the protests of both the Illinois governor and the Chicago mayor. Violence ensued; thirty-four died.[27]

A similarly violent strike in 1886 had rallied clerks and skilled workers alike to the cause of law and order. Not so in 1894. This economic downturn, more than any preceding it, revealed a resentment against elites like Pullman that extended into the middle classes.[28] This was caused in part by the severity of the depression, which extended even into the comfortable classes.[29] But there also were deeper issues at play.

The financial crisis had been preceded by a twenty-year slump in the agricultural sector. Commodity prices had steadily fallen, eroding earnings despite record yields. What caused this unnatural state of affairs? Many farmers blamed elites. A complex system of graded agricultural commodities had imposed new middlemen between the farmer and the market. Grain-elevator operators and railroads took fees from farmers, quasigovernmental commodities markets set prices, and futures speculators made fortunes through dishonest maneuvers.[30] To survive amid falling prices, farmers needed to increase efficiency. But this came by expensive planting and harvesting equipment. It required more land, purchased from railroad operators or real estate speculators. These capital outlays in turn required loans from bankers. Unfortunately for farmers, Gilded Age monetary policy caused the value of the dollar to appreciate, further benefiting creditors and making the repayment of their debts more difficult.[31] Difficulties on the farm ate into the livelihoods of shopkeepers and other small proprietors. Thus by the 1890s, many in the hinterlands concluded the new system was rigged in favor of urban elites.

The economic difficulties of the 1890s shook the foundations of middle-class economic individualism. It revealed a complex interconnected economy with profound paradoxes that defied traditional economic logic. As farmers suffered under excessively low commodity prices, the urban poor starved. Virtue and hard work were disconnected from success. Newspapers reported bacchanalian feasting of elites, grotesque hundred-dollar-a-plate dinner parties designed only to shame competing hosts, while frugal families lost their life savings, homes, and farms.[32] The contract ideology and business producerism spouted by these plutocrats was a cruel joke, masking a conspiracy of epic proportions.

By the early 1890s, the moral backbone of Protestant America, farmers and small producers, had had enough. Critics were especially strong in the West and the South, and by the early 1890s they had formed the Populist or "People's Party." In the 1892 elections, Populists claimed nine members of Congress, three governorships, over 1,500 local offices, and over 1 million votes for their presidential candidate, James Weaver.[33] Though the Populist critique was rooted in the old producerist ideology, their solutions were unprecedented in redistributive reach. They proposed a graduated income tax, currency inflation by monetizing silver, and other government intervention, including ownership of railroads and utilities and facilitation of cooperative schemes.

But others within the middle classes still supported the economic status quo. They came primarily from the educated classes and were aligned with elite interests. These were the engineers, social and otherwise: lawyers, managers, accountants, and other knowledge experts. The changes in economic organization during the 1880s and 1890s that harmed the Populist base had been to their benefit. It was these professionals, implementing the draconian cuts on workers and calculating the railroad rate fees, that made farmers fume.

Professionals responded to the Pullman Strike as they had in 1886: with outrage and fear. There were exceptions to this rule, of course, like the crusading reformer Jane Addams, famous for her Chicago-based Hull House, an experiment in communal living, education, and social research. Yet even her mild critique of Pullman during the strike was deemed too radical by mainstream media outlets for publication.[34] The class divide spurred by the depression went straight through the middle classes.

The conflict between Populists and professionals had economic roots, but there were also wider ideological disagreements. As historian Robert Johnston argues, "middle class" was a powerful "imagined constituency," and both groups were battling over what it meant and who had the right to claim that identity. Substantial social and cultural benefits went to the victors.[35]

Each group had competing visions of the good society. The Populist, or "radical," middle classes valued democracy in all its messiness. The professional middle classes envisioned an efficient, orderly society controlled by educated elites. Radicals fought for the right of self-determination, including the right to make bad decisions. Professionals wanted to enforce order, even if that meant protecting individuals from themselves. The radical middle classes embraced a communal identity and conceptualized society as a hearty, self-correcting organism. Professionals, especially those engaged with business or law, saw society as a complex machine requiring constant adjustments from experts. The radical middle classes demanded economic fairness and a moral economy, even at the expense of a completely "free market." The professional classes continued to believe private property and contracts were inviolable.

Distinctions between the radical and professional middle classes were real, but they should not be overstated. These were differences of degree rather than opposing ideologies. All things being equal, both groups valued the democratic process, personal freedom, economic fairness, private property, and social order. But the core issues were real enough. When forced to choose, which value took precedence: democracy or order, economic fairness or private property, individual rights or communal responsibilities?

White participants in both groups shared a troubling racial ideology that manifested itself in different ways. Some Populists let critiques of the financial system wander into anti-Semitism. Prejudice against African Americans troubled other parts of the coalition. Meanwhile, the eugenics movement was the bailiwick of the professional classes.[36] Of course, many Populists were admirably tolerant,[37] and some professionals resisted the racial implications of eugenics. But for many people from both groups, racial ideology was a seemingly simple explanation for all that was right or wrong with the world, justifying the nation's imperialist expansion.[38]

If anything, the commonalities shared by Populists and professionals exacerbated the tensions. Professionals vehemently disagreed with the Populist critiques and solutions, but they fully understood its appeal, and this terrified them. If a large enough proportion of the middle classes were swayed, it might mean revolution.

The fears of elites only increased when Populists found their prophetic voice. Populists freely mixed the rhetoric of class warfare with religion.[39] Professionals winced as Populists painted Jesus as "a radical agrarian reformer and his circle of disciples a Galilean suballiance." North Carolina Populists unabashedly printed "Look to Jesus!" atop their printed list of approved candidates.[40] Observers of Kansas Populists described it as a "Pentecost of politics" and a "religious revival."[41] When the Christian socialist George Herron echoed Moody's institute-founding statement that "Revolution is not far off" without a "revival of love," it sounded like a threat.[42] Similar Christian rhetoric was deployed by Chicago labor activists.[43] The law-and-order crowd knew the power of religious rhetoric, and they trembled.

In March 1894, two months before the Pullman Strike, elites thought they saw the beginning of a religiously fueled class war. On Easter morning, businessman Jacob Coxey led about 100 unemployed men on a march from Massillon, Ohio, to protest government inaction and lobby for Populist policies in Washington, D.C. This "Army of the Commonweal of Christ" combined religious and militaristic imagery so appealing that it grew five-fold and spawned over forty imitation armies from as far away as California. These western "armies" violently took over trains to catch up with their eastern comrades. Many groups received food and other assistance from sympathizers along the way. Fearing a literal assault on the nation's capital, government officials stationed 1,500 soldiers in Washington and intercepted other groups before arriving. Although the protesters peacefully dispersed after their arrival, the violent railroad strikes that came shortly afterward suggested more trouble in the future.[44]

The use of religion by Populists was a devastating blow to Moody's project. To his failure of reaching the working classes, he could add the failure simply to keep order among the converted. The plain reading of Jesus's ethical teachings and early church life sounded radical. Evangelical realism seemed like a weapon that favored Populist reforms. After all, Jesus's sole act of violence was his clearing the temple of its moneychangers, the ultimate collusion of religion and capital. Moody's insistence that the Bible be put into practice now sounded ominous. The revivalist had inadvertently helped create radical evangelicalism—a movement that used the assumptions of evangelical realism for revolutionary ends.

RADICAL EVANGELICALS WERE LIMITED neither to members of the Populist Party nor to issues of political economy. In fact, while Coxey whipped up fears in Washington, another figure was raising eyebrows in Chicago. John Alexander Dowie was born in Scotland in 1847 and raised in Australia. He was college educated, ordained, and served a respectable Congregationalist church in Sydney. In 1878 he launched an independent evangelistic ministry to "the masses." Soon after, he became a professional faith healer and in 1888 immigrated to the United States, making his way to Chicago in the early 1890s. Dowie's claims of miraculous healing sat at the center of his work. He preached the doctrine and operated "healing homes" where the ill sat in rented rooms waiting for God's healing touch. He became increasingly popular, especially after 1894. While other ministries struggled to stay afloat amid the depression, Dowie's expanded; he opened more homes and started a weekly newspaper, *Leaves of Healing*, to spread his message and influence across the country. Dowie attracted followers across the economic spectrum, and these benefactors, large and small, increased the ministry's coffers. Eventually, he gained control of a full city block in a desirable South Side neighborhood.[45]

Dowie was no theological visionary; his views on faith healing were largely identical to what other respectable faith healers had believed since the late 1870s. Rejecting cessationism (that biblical miracles ceased after the apostles) and questioning the Enlightenment's stark division of the natural and spiritual worlds, a phalanx of modern faith-healing advocates emerged in the 1870s and 1880s.[46] Nearly all came from established denominations and upper-middle-class churches, including Presbyterians Albert B. Simpson and William E. Boardman, Episcopalians Charles Cullis and Carrie Judd Montgomery, and Baptist Adorniram J. Gordon. Some simply claimed faith healing was the "plain meaning" of scripture, while others, like Yale Divinity School seminarian R. L. Marsh, defended faith healing with Horace Bushnell and transcendentalists.[47] But nearly everyone initially agreed that faith healing should replace, rather than augment, doctors and medicine. And since this was a time when medical cures were often worse than the disease, many practitioners saw improvement in their health.

Dowie's innovation came less from the specificities of his belief and practice than from the ends to which he put them. His initial beliefs simply stated that God's miracle-working power was still available and that Jesus died not only to conquer sin but also sickness. Faith healing was thus an essential part of the "full gospel."[48] But riding Populist discontent after 1894, Dowie pushed the idea that seeking health through any other means was a heretical lack of faith. From there, it logically followed that doctors were agents of Satan, attempting to injure the faithful in both soul and body.

Whatever discontent professional medicine was causing in 1894, it was not because of its godlessness. The process of middle-class professionalization relied on religion as much as the rhetoric of their Populist opponents.

The professional respectability of doctors had been decimated by Jacksonian Era "democratized" medicine, when practically anyone could become a doctor by claiming the title.[49] But weeding out practitioners they deemed undesirable (often women, the poor, and people of color) required the right to exert social, political, and economic coercion. And one of the few justifications for such coercion was an appeal to morality. Elite Protestants of the previous century had skillfully used ostensibly "secular" moral appeals for explicitly religious ends. They passed blasphemy statutes, imposed Sunday Sabbath regulations, and mandated Bible reading in public schools despite the nation's secular Constitution.[50] Doctors used similar tactics to align the medical profession with the interests of the Protestant establishment, legitimating themselves as defenders of public morality. They even imitated religious language.[51] As practitioners of "orthodox" medicine, they argued, they had the same right to superintend the social body as "respectable" Protestant ministers had to oversee the nation's soul.[52]

The radical middle classes, especially in urban areas most affected by this new regulatory apparatus, resisted medical professionalization. It was yet another example of elite professionals restricting their right to participate in the health-care market with expensive licenses and educational requirements. If there were quacks and imposters, let market forces weed them out. Given this resistance to their professionalizing project and because they needed religious support, doctors largely ignored respectable faith healing in the 1870s and 1880s. Their occasional critiques were offered with the lightest touch.

But Dowie's critiques in the 1890s could not be ignored. His status as an ordained minister gave force to his moral condemnations of medical professionals and, consequently, the basis of their social authority. And Dowie's attacks had come at a particularly sensitive time. Several recent scandals had bolstered the Populist critique that economic self-interest, rather than altruism, was motivating medical regulators. Even the new science of bacteriology did not immediately diminish these suspicions; respectable newspapers like the *Chicago Tribune* printed hundreds of articles challenging the science for two years after 1894.

Thus medical professionals decided to pursue legal remedies against Dowie in 1895, presuming that the simple act of legal prosecution would sufficiently tarnish his reputation and neutralize his moral critiques. But their plan backfired. Dowie proved to be a formidable opponent in the courtroom. Harnessing the still-potent Populist discontent, he argued that a city hospital ordinance gave too much power to medical bureaucrats over the right of individual conscience on religious matters. Dowie was "simply practice[ing] his profession of minister of the Gospel," he argued, using only "prayer and the scriptural method of laying on of hands." On appeal, the court agreed, an embarrassing defeat for medical regulators.[53]

Dowie was exonerated, but the practice of faith healing suffered a precipitous decline among respectable Protestants soon after. There were numerous causes for this. As faith healing became more popular, failed healings inevitably increased, bringing the underlying assumption of God's guarantee of health into question. And notwithstanding initial controversy, advances in bacteriology were reaping statistically verified benefits. Finally, the use of faith healing by Dowie and other radicals now gave the religious practice a political taint. As a result, even faith healers like R. Kelso Carter began backtracking from their earlier prohibitions of medical means.[54]

Moody's hypervigilance for respectability pushed him ahead of the curve in rejecting faith healing. In fact, he always had been uncomfortable with absolute statements about the efficacy of prayer. After James Garfield was shot in 1881, Moody denounced those who claimed assurance equal to "their own salvation" that God would answer the nation's prayers for the president's recovery. "We cannot dictate to God," he argued. "The prayer of faith is not to make myself believe that just the very thing I ask will be done" but to engender "a trust in His love" regardless of what God decides.[55] Though Moody sometimes worked with respectable faith-healing ministers like Gordon and Simpson, he accepted faith healing provisionally, accompanied by "common sense." His was a complementary faith in both God and "a skilful [sic] physician or surgeon."[56] The belief that doctors had the right of first refusal to cure and the expertise to define both disease and health became the new orthodox view. Moody's view was identical to Lyman Abbott's assertion that although miraculous healings were possible, "the rejection of all means . . . is consistent neither with faith nor with common sense."[57] In 1895 Moody began making explicit public statements against the exclusive use of faith healing—to the great relief of the medical community.

But Torrey's views on faith healing went in the opposite direction. He spoke of faith healing at institute lectures, and by one account, he tried healing a student's optic nerve by anointing him with oil.[58] No longer living on faith, and with administrative duties crowding out heroic personal soul winning, Torrey retained faith healing as the last vestige of his direct reliance upon God.[59] His faith still required a personal experience of God's direct provision. As he wrote in a postscript to his faith work diary after moving to Chicago, "If I did not believe all the promises of the Word, I could never believe nothing [sic]."[60] Consistency and certitude trumped all other considerations, at least for now.

MOODY'S EVOLVING VIEWS ON faith healing, however necessary for the sake of respectability, created tensions within his realist interpretation of the Bible. Why were miracles less likely in the present if Jesus was in fact "the same yesterday, today, and tomorrow," as the Bible clearly claimed? What was the logic that determined modern miracles to be out of line with "common sense," but accepted Jesus's feeding 5,000 people with five loaves and two fish as a reasonable belief?

Liberals had a ready answer. The "plain" interpretation of scripture must be checked by science. The authenticity of the texts must be investigated with the latest critical methods, and its contents must align with new insights from anthropology, sociology, psychology, history, and comparative religions. The most liberal of these "modernists" rejected all miraculous events, past or present, as mythical, fraudulent, or otherwise explainable by natural processes. Moderate higher critics sidestepped the issue: debates about literal miracles were a distraction from the example of Jesus's life, his ethics, and his message of love that would revolutionize the world. The real miracle was that Jesus had inspired an intrinsically selfish crowd of 5,000 to share what they had with each other, so much that twelve baskets of leftovers remained. Theological modernism thus created a clear system to selectively read the example and ethics of Jesus plainly. But the cost was that this God could not be apprehended personally or directly. It was a God that acted through impersonal social forces and perhaps was an impersonal force itself.[61]

Those wedded to the idea of personal relationship to God turned to dispensationalism to address the problem of modern miracles. Dispensationalism was an esoteric interpretive system often associated with John Nelson Darby, the same British sectarian whose "rapture" doctrine addressed date-setting extremism among premillennialists. Dispensationalism addressed problems of historical development. Any careful reader of the Bible noticed that "essential" beliefs and practices changed over the course of human history and especially after the founding of Christianity. The basic mechanism of Darby's solution could be traced back to the writings of the apostle Paul. He argued that there was an old "dispensation" before Jesus, when the legal prescriptions of Moses were enforced, and a new dispensation after Jesus's death, when a "new covenant" was inaugurated. But unlike Paul, Darby argued there were seven dispensations, not two, and that during each, God had different ways of engaging humanity and different moral standards for believers to follow. This provided considerably more flexibility to address a variety of issues that arose from attempting to read the Bible plainly. Potential problems ranged from ancient practices like polygamy and the many prophecies about Israel that had not been literally fulfilled to modern miracles. . The present age was the sixth dispensation, he argued, during which miracles were rare. During a future seventh dispensation, all outstanding biblical prophecies would be literally fulfilled.[62]

American dispensationalists, some inspired by Darby, created an airtight science of scriptural interpretation distinct from both traditional hermeneutics and higher criticism. Leading dispensationalists often came from legal and engineering backgrounds and their systems reflected the same valuation for precise, absolutely consistent answers intrinsic to those professions.[63] Some Bible teachers pushed the dispensational idea to its breaking point, creating mind-bogglingly complex systems. But whatever variety they promoted, the same basic framework prevailed: scripture must be read and interpreted according to the dispensation for which it was intended.

Moody had several ardent dispensationalists in his circle of allies. The most important of these was Cyrus I. Scofield. Born in Michigan in 1843, Scofield's early adulthood was filled with embarrassing baggage. He fought with the Confederacy during the Civil War, married a Roman Catholic woman in Kansas, struggled with alcoholism, and was repeatedly accused of fraud, bribery, and abandoning debts. In 1880 he experienced an evangelical conversion. Soon afterward he met D. L. Moody and, with the scantest training under the venerable premillennial minister James Brookes, began preaching. He then divorced his wife and abandoned his two children in 1883 and remarried a year later. Though he never reckoned with his past sins, his forty-year ministerial career was largely scandal free. Trained as a lawyer, Scofield adopted an unabashedly legal approach to Bible interpretation that attracted a wide following, including Moody, it seems. In 1895, at Moody's urging, Scofield became pastor of the Congregationalist church the revivalist attended in Northfield.[64]

The key purveyor of dispensationalism in Chicago was William Newell. A graduate of the College of Wooster in 1891, he then attended Princeton Seminary but reported "escaping" before graduating. Newell was converted under the faith healer Albert B. Simpson and shared with Torrey a similar understanding of the relationship between the believer and the Holy Spirit. But he was increasingly taken by a doctrinaire premillennialism and dispensationalism. He also became a brash opponent of higher criticism. While William Rainey Harper was still allies with Torrey, Newell hotheadedly charged Harper of "doing more harm than Ingersoll and making more infidels than any man in America."[65] Despite this, Newell taught at the Bible Institute and later served as the assistant superintendent under Torrey for two years. Around the turn of the century, he began conducting large Bible classes. They became so popular that he made a weekly circuit of Chicago, Detroit, Toronto, and St. Louis.[66]

Scofield's first contribution to American dispensationalism was *Rightly Dividing the Word of Truth*, published in 1888. It would later be incorporated into his popular Bible correspondence course and then in the notes of his famous reference Bible, published in 1909. Newell communicated his dispensational framework through his classes, sermons, and Bible studies and eventually published a commentary on Romans that encapsulated his views.

Both Scofield and Newell followed Darby's teaching that there were seven dispensations from the creation of Adam to the last days, and that the present was in the sixth, or "church age." All scripture was inerrant and literally true, making every biblical miracle a real event. But they also emphasized that although "all the Bible is *for* us . . . it is not all *about* us."[67] They limited the parts of the Bible *about* the present dispensation to "Paul's letters."[68] Incredibly, they argued that the gospels and Acts were not intended for present-day believers. Jesus is "the Great Teacher . . . in a sense," Newell grudgingly acknowledged, but he was trumped by "those statements of Christian doctrine uttered by the apostle Paul."[69] Scofield similarly argued that the Sermon on the Mount was "the law of the *kingdom*," the final, future dispensation, "not of the *church*."[70] Neither Jesus's teachings nor his miraculous power were directly applicable to the present age.

Dispensationalism thus provided an alternative solution to a realist reading of the Bible. Though Pauline writings allowed for the possibility of miraculous healing, they were just as likely to advise taking "a little wine," which teetotaler dispensationalists read as "medicine." It carefully preserved "old-fashioned truths about sin, judgment, and hell"[71] and the historicity of miracles while imposing restraints on miraculous expectations. But the system's discarding of Jesus's ethical teachings and other modifications were breathtaking departures from traditional Protestantism.

Moody pragmatically determined that dispensationalism, though not ideal, inflicted less collateral damage to his realist convictions. Most important, it preserved a personal and interactive relationship with God. His final assessment on theological modernism remains something of a disputed point, exacerbated by his proclivity to say what others wanted to hear. But by the mid-1890s, he was expressing grave concerns about "the 'Modern Criticism' of the Bible," especially that, in denying "the old stories about Moses writing the Pentateuch and the sun and moon standing still," they might be "driving out the blessed gospel of Jesus Christ."[72] Moody's only recourse to imposing limits on his plain reading of the Bible would come by a dispensational framework.

IN 1896 THERE WAS no greater symbol of the looming Populist threat than the presidential campaign of William Jennings Bryan. Today, it is easy to look back at the Populist Party as a momentary flash in the pan, to take their opponents' caricatures at face value and dismiss the movement as a temporary aberration of Republican and Democratic dominance. But in 1896, the Republican Party was barely forty years old; Whigs were a living memory. If rural Populists allied themselves with urban labor, it could create a new permanent majority anchored in economic issues. And when Bryan was chosen to head a fusion ticket of Democrats and Populists, a new class-based politics seemed entirely possible.

A devout lifelong Presbyterian, Bryan melded the Populist critique with biblical language. Elites trembled at reports of Bryan's monumental convention speech, with its unforgettable metaphor of a "Cross of Gold." Perhaps they even heard the thunderous response from outside the Chicago Coliseum—extending fully twice as long as the speech itself. His accompanying admonition to not "press down upon the brow of labor this crown of thorns" and his subsequent campaign speeches filled with scripture suggested his ability to unite farm and factory with religious rhetoric. Terrified business elites and their allies spoke with their wallets; John D. Rockefeller alone contributed $250,000 to Republicans.[73]

William McKinley won the electoral vote comfortably but the popular vote by only a couple of percentage points. Bryan lost because of soft support among urban labor, perhaps in part because so few had been converted to his evangelical Protestantism. Elites breathed a sigh of relief, but the election was a wake-up call. Religion was not the easy answer to social disorder; in the wrong hands, it might also be the cause.

Moody was no less terrified than his business supporters. He warned a British friend that if Bryan won, he should "take his Boys Home" before chaos ensued.[74] These attitudes insulated him from personal criticism, but he never had a good answer to the growing concerns over the "misuse" of the Bible by radicals. And he seemed unaware of how close the superintendent of his Bible Institute aligned with their approach to the Bible.

Dispensationalism was too complicated for Moody to use himself, but in early 1897, he began giving new prominence to dispensationalists in his network. In March the *Record of Christian Work* featured a picture of Scofield on the cover and an article inside expressing surprise that "intelligent Christians accepted the views of Simpson, Dowie and others, that disease is in all cases the result of sin," or that any sickness "can be removed by the prayer of faith."[75] The following month, Scofield addressed readers' inquiries about biblical texts in a new column. A regular Bible lesson by Newell started the following January. Month by month, both men modeled a dispensational framework in all its complexity. Every answer was definite, free of mystery and ambiguity—perfect law from a perfect law giver.

Meanwhile, in Chicago, Dowie's legal victory did him no favors, as overconfidence reaped sectarianism. In 1896 he declared himself the autocratic "General Overseer" of a new "Christian Catholic Church" and imposed curious dietary restrictions based on his "plain reading" of the Old Testament. His growing collection of institutions, now including a bank and other secular institutions, was christened "Zion," an allusion to the postapocalyptic kingdom of God on earth. Ministers who disagreed were "the enemies of God," and he suggested he might become a modern "apostle" if his "humility" reached adequate levels.[76] Lest anyone miss his political implications, Dowie lashed out against democratic institutions, gleefully quoting a detractor who worried that his theology "would make a complete Revolution." He agreed: "If there is anything that I despise, it is that principle: government of the people, by the people, and for the people."[77]

Medical regulators fared little better in 1897, suffering under a reputation of being self-interested, power-hungry, tax-wasting elites. Their attempt to expand and modernize the state's Medical Practice Act that year, once a decennial ritual, suffered an embarrassing defeat.[78] A diluted revision passed two years later, but only with a remarkable exemption for those using "mental or spiritual means without the use of any drugs or material remedy."[79]

But it was the Torrey family that suffered most. In March 1898 their eight-year-old daughter, Elizabeth, became ill with diphtheria. Torrey's options were clear: he could pray, or he could allow the use of the well-proven antitoxin. He chose faith healing, and then, confident his prayer had been heard, spent the evening drafting a four-page letter of elaborate landscaping plans for the family's summer home.[80] But later that evening, he heard Elizabeth struggling to breathe. The panicked father called a doctor who administered the antitoxin, but it was too late to save Elizabeth's life. Distraught, Torrey berated himself for his daughter's death, though not for his reliance on prayer. Rather, he concluded that her death was God's judgment for his calling the doctor; all would have ended well if he had only believed. The following week, the grief-stricken Torrey had an emotional breakdown, then a restorative religious experience.[81]

A less-committed practitioner might have reconsidered the efficacy of faith healing when his fourteen-year-old daughter, Blanche, showed signs of diphtheria weeks later; astoundingly, Torrey took the "way of faith" once again. But, still shaken by his earlier loss, he drafted a note to none other than John Alexander Dowie, explaining his long-standing rejection of medicine and his recent failure of faith. "I asked guidance before" calling the physician for Elizabeth, he explained, "but now believe . . . I went my own way, not God's; the way of unbelief, not the way of faith." He asked Dowie to "pray, and to examine us to see if you can find any sin in the way," and he gave him permission to "read this letter publicly," confessing he had "dishonored the Lord and would be glad to have people know the failure was not in him, but in me." Dowie was out of town when the letter was delivered, but he kept it, along with a second note from Torrey rejoicing that his prayers had been answered and Blanche had recovered.[82]

Moody was heartbroken for Torrey but was initially unaware, it seems, of either the faith healing or Torrey's letter to Dowie. His awareness grew slowly. After hearing rumors of connections between the Bible Institute and Dowie in May 1898, the typically amiable revivalist responded swiftly. "I am greatly troubled about the divine healing," he wrote business manager Aymer Gaylord, and he forbade "any of Dowies [sic] papers in the Institute" or any "teacher about the Institute that has any thing to do with Dowie. If he is a man of God," he bluntly concluded, "then I am a fraid [sic] I do not know God." Students refusing medical attention were to be expelled.[83] Tellingly, Moody did not write Torrey of his concerns, and that summer, he sent Torrey to minister to troops mobilizing at Chickamauga, Tennessee, for the Spanish-American War.[84] In Torrey's absence, he invited a dispensationalist Bible teacher, James M. Gray, to set "forth what the Bible teaches on the subject" of faith healing.[85]

Upon Torrey's return in October, the Chicago YMCA summarily dismissed him from teaching a weekly Bible class, diplomatically explaining they wanted to emphasize "those truths accepted by all evangelical churches."[86] Moody asked Torrey whether this referred to "the Second Coming or Divine Healing." Torrey insisted, against all evidence, that it was a matter of hurt feelings;[87] meanwhile, YMCA managers continued to dance around their reasons for dismissal.

In the spring of 1899, Moody spoke publicly against radical forms of faith healing, blasting those who called doctors "devils." "Do not be carried away by the ravings of fanaticism," he warned his audience. "What would I do if I fell sick? Get the best doctor in Chicago, trust to him and trust to the Lord to work through him!"[88] As one newspaper headline stated, Moody's "REFERENCE TO DOWIE IS PLAIN," and the faith healer responded in kind. Taking Torrey's letters out of storage, Dowie read them publicly to his congregation and published them in his newspaper, *Leaves of Healing*. Torrey "did not call upon you to pray the prayer of faith that saves the sick," he goaded Moody, "for he knew that you were utterly impotent to do so." Instead, "he came to 'that crank Dowie.'"[89]

Dowie's public revelations forced Torrey to finally come clean with Moody, who frantically reversed course. Torrey should "say nothing," and rather "push the old truths to the front," he warned. Since it took "two to get up a quarrel . . . we should keep quiet and do our own business."[90] But reminders repeatedly surfaced of the damage. When a frustrated Chicago YMCA administrator wrote Moody of their ongoing dispute, he complained that Torrey "well understood" their reasons for dismissal, "reasons which, perhaps, he did not care to have brought to your attention."[91]

MEANWHILE, MEDICAL REGULATORS WERE furious about the new faith-healing exemption in the 1899 Medical Practice Act. But they realized that simply arguing for their own efficacy or against faith healing as quackery would not work. They needed to restore their reputation as moral guardians of the social order. So they began a new campaign that emphasized the danger of faith healing to children by ignoring effective treatments and spreading infectious disease throughout the city. Dowie's recent sectarian turn had made him a perfect target.

In July 1899 medical officials announced an investigation of the death of a girl whose father, a Dowie follower, had refused to provide "medical aid." The *Chicago Tribune* wrote supporting editorials critical of parents who deny "what most people call 'necessary' medical assistance" to their children.[92] In mid-August, the State Board of Health announced that it would track the number of children who died under faith healing "with a view to securing a special statute from the next Legislature forbidding so-called faith healers to practice upon children." The subsequent death of a child under Dowie's direct care seemed to provide the "positive proof of criminal malpractice" that regulators promised would "drive Dowie's institutions out of Chicago."[93] It became a topic in the mainstream and medical press from New York to Los Angeles, with every article focusing on the safety of children.[94]

As medical officials focused increasingly on child endangerment, Dowie saw another use for Torrey's letters. How could Dowie be a dangerous sectarian when the respectable Torrey had done the same thing? Dowie ordered his followers to distribute pamphlets with lithographic reproductions of Torrey's letters, Bible Institute letterhead prominently displayed.

An awkward silence followed, until an exasperated young Presbyterian minister, Frank DeWitt Talmage, son of a renowned Brooklyn divine, had enough. In an October 1 sermon, Talmage read Torrey's letters to his congregation, accused him of "criminal negligence" for allowing "his baby [to] die without a doctor," and demanded that he "right himself before the world or leave Moody Institute and take his position in Zion's tabernacle, where he belongs."[95]

The next day, most of Chicago's major papers covered the scandalous revelations, some on the front page, and many reprinted Torrey's letters in full. National newspapers already following the Dowie story now dragged Torrey into their coverage as well. The timing could not have been worse for the struggling Bible Institute: it was the first day of its tenth anniversary celebrations, designed by Moody to rally the waning support of the city's elites.[96] Instead of the triumphant beginning to the week of festivities, Moody and Torrey held an emergency closed-door meeting, leaving a church full of celebrants shifting uncomfortably in their pews. Moody emerged from the conference "frowning" and "unaccompanied," refusing any comment to the gaggle of reporters. Torrey did not deny writing the letters, but he insisted that his "Christian science has scriptural limitations" and stubbornly reiterated his belief "in the efficacy of prayer."[97]

Later in the week, with the scandal still festering, Moody flatly denounced faith healing in the strongest terms to date. A supportive editorial in the *Tribune* recounted that although Moody believed prayer can "heal sick souls and moral ailments," the revivalist "has no patience with the assertion that prayer can heal smallpox and diphtheria and set broken bones." For these "man-made diseases," a person "should send for a physician instead of 'battering the gates of heaven with ineffectual prayer.'"[98]

Torrey was stunned by this renunciation of faith healing; perhaps referring to Moody, he wrote to his wife of "persecution . . . from a most unexpected quarter."[99] Emma Dryer, a lifelong believer in faith healing, later was forced to admit that Moody's "views of this subject changed somewhat, before he died."[100] But Moody's declaration was effective. It tamped down the controversy before it spiraled out of control.

Despite their campaign to protect child victims of faith healing, Chicago's medical professionals politely diverted their eyes from the controversy, delaying an already planned initiative against Dowie by two weeks. They apparently found Torrey's explanations sufficient; after all, he had called a doctor for one of his daughters and had spoken out against Dowie's equation of "drugs, doctors and devils."[101] The inquests of child endangerment directed at Zion for identical sins never reached Torrey.[102] As one of the elite, he was granted his right to a private family tragedy. And by showing restraint, medical officials only reinforced their association with the Protestant establishment. In exchange, there was no doubt that forbidding medical intervention contravened respectable orthodoxy.

THE WORST TRAGEDY FOR the Bible Institute of Chicago came just weeks after Torrey's disastrous revelations, when Moody's chronic heart condition caused him to collapse at a revival meeting in Kansas City. Though he lingered for a time, he died in December, leaving the institute in disarray. Torrey, hired as the solid foundation for the institute's respectability, had become its loose footing. On his deathbed, Moody passed over the heir apparent and appointed his son-in-law and personal secretary, Arthur P. Fitt, to serve as president instead.[103]

Moody's death became a propitiation for Torrey's sin, overshadowing the scandal. It produced an outpouring of goodwill for the Bible Institute and front-page retrospectives of Moody's work. Even Dowie, who prophesied Moody's imminent demise, seemed a little taken back at the swiftness of its fulfillment. "O my God, you know I did right," he piously declared. "I publicly, openly, warned him that he would die" unless he recanted "the things which he had said against Thy servant and against Zion." Yet Moody was "with God," Dowie concluded, since "he erred" largely from ignorance.[104]

Torrey took a leading role at Moody's memorial service. Preaching on the text "Moses my servant is dead; now therefore arise," he urged his listeners to begin working for a great revival to honor their fallen leader.[105]

However confident Torrey's public face remained, his religious certitude had lost its vital core. His final word on faith healing, written twenty years after the scandal, was an unsystematic hodgepodge attempting to salvage his earlier views in light of modern medicine. Torrey believed that faith healing might supersede medicine, but he was also careful to give doctors the final word in determining the authenticity of a miraculous healing. To salve his conscience over his daughter's death, he asserted that it was "sometimes" sinful to use medical means after starting with faith healing, since "the doctor gets all the glory and God none." But he also obliquely warned that "many excellent Christian people" have gone "beyond what is written in the Book of God," choosing to let "themselves or their children die rather than" using "rational means." "There have been many sad tragedies along this line," he noted, without direct reference to himself, and these brought "the Bible truth of Divine Healing into great disrepute."[106] Elsewhere, he warned readers that the devil might suggest "all manner of difficult or even ridiculous things as the will of God, thus getting him into perplexity and . . . spiritual agony." But his only advice was to "wait for God to make the way perfectly clear,"[107] without explaining how that clarity might come.

MOODY'S DEATH MARKED THE end of respectable evangelicalism's hermeneutical innocence, when a "plain" meaning of the Bible could be embraced, at least ostensibly, without concern of negative externalities. Only radical evangelicals persisted in that practice. They put their health and safety on the line and, in so doing, put the social order in jeopardy. The irony was that radical evangelicals came primarily from the downwardly mobile "masses," the population whose evangelization Moody promised would stabilize the social order. In short, not only had Moody reached far too few working-class souls, but those that he did reach were no less "disordered" by the standards of the professional middle classes. The entire premise of evangelical realism seemed terribly naïve at best, and in some cases, outright dangerous.

Some "respectable" Protestants were better positioned than others to address the fallout from radical evangelicalism. Churchly conservatives could sit back and calmly shake their heads; Dowie, after all, represented the very thing they had been warning against. Princeton professor Benjamin B. Warfield and Methodist editor J. M. Buckley had been long-standing critics of modern miracles. Both saw their respective denominational traditions as the solution to the radicalism of a plain interpretation.[108] Theological modernists warned against the dangers of unscientific biblical interpretation, while dispensationalists, with some hermeneutical acrobatics, could also navigate around the problem of miracles.

With the common ground of evangelical realism lost, the once-diverse coalition fragmented. During the Dowie scandal, William R. Harper, Torrey's former ally and now president of the University of Chicago, warned against the "incalculable injury" that the Bible Institute "and similar institutions" were inflicting on Christianity.[109] By this, he later clarified, he meant "particularly the narrow and unscientific conceptions" of the Bible "taught by many of the instructors in Moody Institute." His observations and the witness from "a score of ministers" in Chicago confirmed the damage. Corresponding with Harper about his Bible Institute comments, the respected British minister G. Campbell Morgan, who was teaching a course at the institute, agreed that he would not "defend . . . the vagaries of some of those who have been most intimately associated with its work." Yet he insisted that "the amount of good done by the Institute far outweighs the harm" and suggested that Harper's higher criticism might be the real danger.[110] These differences would only become more pronounced with time.

Thus, nearly all "respectable" Protestants, of whatever stripe, agreed that Moody's assumption of a "plain" interpretation of the Bible was now untenable. The handful of respectable evangelicals who rejected the alternatives to churchly conservatism—radical evangelicalism, dispensationalism, and liberal theology—became increasingly isolated. For the Bible Institute to survive the twentieth century would require a different basis.

PART TWO

Christian Consumers

FIVE

Religion on a "Business Basis"

When Henry Parsons Crowell first entered the oatmeal business in 1882, few took him seriously. He knew nothing about the milling process, and his newly purchased mill in north-central Ohio was in laughable condition. Other millers considered Crowell a fool, and by the business logic of an antebellum economy, he was. But he could have cared less. Crowell was part of a phalanx of forward-looking businessmen that considered physical equipment secondary to a business's intangible assets. It was a calculus that transformed the face of business over the next thirty years.

The oatmeal market suffered under the weight of too many competitors, with prices often falling below production costs. Crowell saw the solution in the mill's overlooked Quaker trademark. And so, at a time when most consumers shoveled their oatmeal from open barrels, Crowell's product appeared on shelves in sealed, two-pound boxes. Richly illustrated advertisements saturated local, then national, print media. Both package and ad featured the iconic Quaker, always smiling jovially and holding a scroll on which was written the single word "Pure."

By 1891 Crowell had absorbed most of his competitors, but even his unparalleled success did not convince some of his more reluctant partners. By their older, more-traditional producer orientation, his promotional techniques were a half step away from outright chicanery. But as long as he sat atop the company's rigid corporate structure, these opinions could not stop the sprawling nationwide operation from marching in tandem with his designs. In 1901 the permanency of his plan was marked by a newly organized corporation, the Quaker Oats Company. Crowell not only had dragged his own industry into the modern era, but he also was among the early pioneers that demonstrated these techniques could be applied to practically any consumer good. Through the trifecta of trademark, package, and promotion, a consumer society was born.

Crowell's second major life project began before the ink was dry on Quaker Oats's incorporation papers. And like his initial business investment, Crowell saw potential where others did not. The Moody Bible Institute was in crisis, hemorrhaging both money and goodwill. But it, too, had a key intangible asset: it was founded by Dwight L. Moody. Crowell became president and quickly incorporated his business ideas into this religious work without a second thought; Moody already had made borrowing such concepts unremarkable. But the business strategies themselves were new and thus would transform the purpose of Moody's institution even as Crowell stayed true to the founder's business spirit.

HENRY PARSONS CROWELL WAS born in Cleveland, Ohio, in 1855. His father, Henry Luther, a successful shoe merchant and devout Presbyterian, died of consumption when his son was only nine. The Crowell family was well-to-do. Unlike most dying fathers, the elder Crowell was greatly concerned that Henry and his two brothers "might be ruined by his prosperity" without his guidance. Henry attended the Greylock Institute, an elite boarding school in Massachusetts that prepared young men for business careers or an Ivy League education. He had plans to attend Yale and would have been classmates with Reuben Torrey, but at seventeen, he showed signs of his father's consumptive lungs and returned to Cleveland to work the family business. Crowell now took a new interest in religion, especially after hearing Moody, who was not yet famous, give a Bible reading in a Cleveland church. He was taken by Moody's approach to the Bible and never forgot the revivalist's encouragement "to dream great things for God." Moody's unparalleled success confirmed that "God didn't need his men educated, or brilliant, or anything else," only "a man," and Crowell determined to be one of them. He could not preach, but already he was confident he "could make money and help support the labors of men like Moody." "If you will allow me to make money to be used in Your service," he prayed to God, "you will have the glory."[1]

After encountering Moody, Crowell's reading of the Bible became radically personal and individualized. A passage from Job, "He shall deliver thee in six troubles: yea, in seven there shall no evil touch thee," became God's personal promise to heal his lungs in seven years and then bring him success. Crowell had a simple confidence in the absolute reliability of this promise, but unlike Torrey, he did not care how God worked. His healing might well come by medical professionals and wealth by business acumen. Thus, when his doctor gave orders to spend the next seven years in the open air, it was like the voice of God. Crowell followed this medical advice to the letter, traveling extensively and continuing a life outdoors even though he felt fully healed a year early.[2] Upon returning home, he married his true love, Lillie Wick, in 1882. But when she died in 1885 before their first child was yet two, God's promise that "no evil will touch thee" must have seemed exceedingly narrow.[3] His experience of a second tragic death inoculated him from any theology that equated sickness with sinfulness or promised absolute health to the faithful.

Crowell's seven-year sojourn, which spanned the continent, provided him with a sense of the national market and shaped his approach to business. After four years of leisurely travel on both coasts, he turned to work. He made handsome profits on a farm in Fargo and horse breeding in South Dakota. In both cases, he narrowly averted natural disasters and realized his profits only by the resale of the businesses. It foreshadowed a career in which he profited more by extracting wealth from farmers than his own agricultural productivity. As he saw it, "I would rather get into a business where if I made a mistake, I could correct it." Weather and crops could not be tamed.[4] Crowell's demand for control was reflected in every enterprise that followed. Though his demeanor was quiet, prepossessing, and deliberate, he refused to compromise as long as he was convinced it was the "best" course of action. But he could just as stubbornly insist on abandoning projects or approaches when he concluded they had failed. He was, according to his biographer, a "Breakfast Table Autocrat"—a title Crowell seemed rather fond of. [5] And it was clearly displayed when he entered a new line of work with the proceeds from his second farm sale: the Quaker oat mill in Ravenna, Ohio.

Oat milling was a young industry in the 1880s. Though oats were used widely in farm-animal troughs, they were largely absent the breakfast table. The influx of German immigrants, who did eat oatmeal, led to the country's first oat mill midcentury and a niche market that grew with the population. One among them, a former grocer named Ferdinand Schumacher, largely created the industry. He was the largest producer when Crowell purchased the Ravenna mill. Schumacher embodied an older business ideology, focused on productive capacity, efficiency, thrift, and bulk sales. It had made him a wealthy man.[6]

Crowell turned traditional business logic on its head. He bought the oat mill primarily for its two intellectual assets. The more conventional asset was an innovative processing patent to cut oats with blades, which was shared only by Schumacher. It produced a higher quality product with less waste, giving Crowell an advantage over most of his competitors. His business partner, the engineering and milling savant James H. Andrews, relentlessly improved designs. Following pioneers like Andrew Carnegie though still against conventional wisdom, Crowell also discarded existing equipment, regardless of condition, whenever doing so sufficiently increased efficiency. His second asset, the Quaker trademark, was the primary draw and the foundation of his unconventional strategy. Only a handful of other companies were selling branded products, packaged for retail sales and supported by aggressive marketing campaigns.

The validation of Crowell's methods came with astounding rapidity. Within five years, his mill was the third-largest producer in the country, and within the decade, his $25,000 investment was worth half a million dollars, a twentyfold increase.[7] But Crowell suffered with everyone else under the crippling crisis of overproduction. He spearheaded an early attempt to control supply through a type of cooperative corporation. Leading producers, still independent, bought shares in a shell company designed to coordinate production levels, share profits, and buy up competitors. But by the late 1880s, it was falling apart as members fudged on their obligations and enterprising capitalists built new mills merely to extract money from the association. It was already unviable when the Sherman Antitrust Act outlawed such combinations in 1890.

Success required control, Crowell concluded, and his next effort to tame the market in 1891 operated under that premise. A new corporation, the American Cereal Company, was formed by Crowell and five competitors. Its plan of operation, authored by Crowell, focused first on exerting autocratic control over all member mills through a single management structure. It forbade any entangling agreements with other competitors that might impede its complete corporate autonomy. Crowell's plan also specified creating a reputation of unsurpassed quality. A diversification policy was designed to create stability against fluctuations in supply and demand for particular cereals and economic conditions in particular geographic locations, and to find uses for by-products or other unmet secondary businesses. Finally, it proposed aggressive marketing designed to "create a demand for cereals where none existed" using a "single trade name" under which all of its business would be done.[8] Crowell became the managing shareholder of the largest oatmeal producer in the country. Whatever his other competitors thought of him, he could no longer be ignored.

Crowell's ideas were so counterintuitive to a producer orientation focused on minimizing costs that even profitability could not justify it.

By the traditional logic, the company would be even more profitable if it stopped "wasting" money on expensive new machinery and frivolous advertising. Schumacher was Crowell's most reluctant partner, joining the company only under duress, when he lost his new, uninsured mill to a catastrophic fire. A traditional proprietor, he reportedly "found it almost impossible to delegate authority and responsibility to subordinate hands," even choosing to handwrite his business correspondence rather than use a secretary.[9] To the insult of losing control of his business were added what he thought were injurious promotional budgets that topped $500,000 by 1896.[10]

Unswayed by Schumacher's protests, Crowell and a group of young executives pushed ahead, moving the company headquarters to Chicago, the agricultural commodity capital of the world, in 1898. But shortly after the move, Schumacher fomented a shareholder revolt with other conservatives and ousted Crowell from management. Crowell remained a major shareholder and thus able to comfortably support his daughter and new wife, Susan Coleman, a Vassar-educated teacher. But it was a stinging professional setback that left him literally with nothing to do.

As in earlier times of trial, Crowell focused on his faith. Living in the wealthy Gold Coast neighborhood adjacent to the Bible Institute, he met William Newell, the school's associate superintendent and a leading dispensational advocate. At Henry and Susan's invitation, Newell conducted a weekly Bible study on the Epistle to the Romans with a small group of their friends. Crowell was thoroughly taken by his dispensational system and abandoned his naïve plain reading. Under Newell's influence, he also came to believe that he now had a responsibility to judge proper belief and practice using the tools of dispensationalism. Thus, while he once had been "friendly toward anything which affirmed itself 'Christian,'" now he would refuse to blindly follow a minister's views. Newell also introduced him to a new theological standard related especially to how the Bible was interpreted and a personal relationship to God. After this, Crowell became what his biographer called a "business-priest," seeing business as more than "his way of making a living." It had become "his altar where he serves the King."[11]

Crowell's newly invigorated faith changed neither his hardball business tactics, which he used to regain control of the American Cereal Company a year later, nor his novel business practices, which he immediately reinstituted once he returned to the helm. Schumacher ultimately admitted defeat, selling his shares and retiring. After this, Crowell's policies were enshrined as the unfaltering rule at the newly reorganized Quaker Oats Company. His charitable giving was generous, as he had promised God, often equaling about 65 percent of his income. But his faith was congenial to fully enjoying what remained. He owned multiple palatial estates, shuttled a corps of servants across the country with the family, and hosted elegant dinners. He was still the president of Quaker Oats, but as it now required less of his time, he was ready to tithe not only his finances but also his business acumen.

IN 1900, AFTER MOODY's death, the Bible Institute trustees had put on a brave face. They legally renamed the organization the Moody Bible Institute (MBI) in honor of its founder and vowed to continue his work. But behind the scenes, MBI was suffering a crisis of leadership. Arthur Fitt found his ascension to the presidency both unexpected and unwanted; despite being an excellent administrator, he almost immediately began looking for a replacement. Meanwhile, other trustees tried removing Torrey from the board due to "serious differences of opinion . . . ab[ou]t faith healing, etc.," which they found "very hampering."[12] However, this proved all but impossible, and the board limped along with Torrey in tow. Whether from frustration or old age, two more long-standing and prominent trustees resigned in January 1901.[13]

Finances at MBI fared no better. With Moody's Northfield ministries, the institute's leaders organized a "Moody Memorial Endowment" that fell far short of their $3 million goal.[14] Fund-raising for day-to-day operations also suffered. When Turlington W. Harvey declared bankruptcy in 1900, MBI lost his $10,000 promissory note from the original endowment.[15] The McCormick family's giving had plummeted precipitously as the new century approached, ceasing altogether in 1904.[16] Although substantial contributions would occasionally surface, the noncommittal $150 donation from pioneering bicarbonate manufacturer John Dwight—or worse, the $25 token from former mayor George Swift—was increasingly the norm.[17]

Torrey's actions did little to help matters. His bumbling attempts to differentiate his views on faith healing from John Alexander Dowie's only made things worse. In a final defense, sent to the *Chicago Tribune*, he took considerable pains to pinpoint the precise moment his notorious letter was delivered to prove that his daughter Blanche was healed without Dowie's help.[18] This, of course, missed the larger concern that he endangered his daughter's life by ignoring proven medical therapies. After this, he mercifully turned his attention to starting a worldwide revival. He reconvened the Christian Worker's Convention in September 1900, but none of its former prominent participants answered his call "to wait on God for Power."[19] And after a fruitless year of revival work, it seemed God also was a no-show. A frustrated Torrey began lashing out in all directions, until he dejectedly admitted "that conditions never were less hopeful."[20] His tantrums left "everybody east" in Northfield "down on Mr. Torrey," and Fitt complained that "his letters . . . have been in such poor spirit and tone that I have nothing to say."[21] Certainly, Torrey's crushing personal losses and professional reversals made his sour mood understandable, but it left the institute, in the words of one chronicler, "a Syrian ready to perish."[22]

No wonder, then, that Fitt hopefully asked Crowell to become a trustee in May 1901, or that Crowell initially declined, blaming his other "responsibilities and obligations already assumed." But Crowell had a change of heart in December and began attending board meetings.[23] As in business, however, Crowell wanted control. Where the earlier business elite had given Torrey free reign over day-to-day operations, Crowell began quietly consolidating his influence. He was elected to the MBI Executive Committee in February 1903 and a year later was elected president.[24] He held the reigns for the next forty years. At eighty-nine, he still walked to the institute every Tuesday to preside over its two-hour board meetings.[25]

Crowell's rise to power at MBI was facilitated by Torrey's leave of absence, granted so that he could conduct revival meetings in Melbourne, Australia. In fact, the timing of the request with Crowell's change of heart in December 1901 hardly seems coincidental. Torrey had prayed specifically that God "would send me around the world preaching the Gospel," he later recalled, and claimed to have been given a divine revelation of its fulfillment. His God still interacted with him in a deeply personal and miraculous way. Given the circumstances, the trustees were happy to send him across the Pacific for what would become a worldwide evangelistic tour.[26]

CROWELL'S FIRST TASK AS head of MBI was to recruit new leadership. He immediately began courting James M. Gray as a replacement dean in Torrey's absence. Gray was a Reformed Episcopal minister from Boston with broad civic and ecclesiastical ties. He taught at his denomination's seminary for two years but was best known as an independent Bible teacher. Gray already had occasional connections to Moody's Chicago work that Crowell wanted to make permanent. He was planning to overhaul the institute into something "much wider and more effective in its scope than the old," he explained, and wanted Gray's help. "MBI would be a magnificent base from which to do a great work," he promised.[27] Gray initially hesitated, wanting the old leadership cleared out, but this was not Crowell's style. Fitt had promised to cooperate, leaving only Torrey as a wildcard. And asking him to resign was unwise, Crowell counseled, since "we want his hearty co operation when he returns to this country." Ever the expert in managerial politics, he begged Gray for a personal interview since the issue required the most "careful handling" being "so broad and far reaching in their effect."[28] Gray was convinced. At the September 1904 trustee meeting, he was simultaneously elected to the faculty and the board of trustees and appointed dean with "the powers and duties of the superintendent . . . until the further order of the board."[29]

If Torrey would eventually become Crowell's Schumacher-like nemesis, Gray was his trusted theological engineer. Gray's so-called Synthetic Method of Bible interpretation was a hit among upper-middle-class Boston audiences in the 1890s. It was rooted in dispensationalist ideas, asserting that God acted according to different rules at different times. But it avoided the overly technical and absolutist stances that plagued some dispensational systems, including Newell's. For all Newell's early influence on Crowell, his unstable personality and harsh outbursts over minor points of theological difference disqualified him from consideration. Later revelations of an opium addiction and a controversy over a sexual indiscretion, first confessed then retracted, confirmed Crowell's decision.[30] Gray, in contrast, was solid. With genteel manners born of his privileged background, he knew how to make dispensationalism palatable to the professional classes. Rather than highlighting obtuse points of doctrine, he positioned his views as simple "Bible Christianity."

Important to Crowell was Gray's treatment of the touchy issue of modern miracles. Generally speaking, "the era of public miracles" ceased around 70 C.E., Gray explained, and a new era of miracles would begin after Jesus's second coming. But because of his Reformed background, he jealously guarded the divine prerogative, allowing that God "reserves the sovereign right" to allow modern miracles "when it promotes His glory." In other words, though God typically worked through "ordinary" means, miraculous claims that did not appear fanatical to middle-class society might in fact be evidence of God's hand. Still, most miraculous claims were counterfeits, either figments of a misguided imagination, "natural causes" mistaken for miracles, "mind-cures," or perhaps even demonic manifestations. The primary "miracles . . . transpiring in our own time" were "the conversion of men and women from all nations and tongues."[31] It was this sort of clear, modest reasoning that Crowell sought from his primary theological technician.

With the theological controls safely under Gray's direction, Crowell set about bolstering the business and civic representation on the Board of Trustees. Crowell had political and business connections spanning Chicago's elite networks and extending even to golf games with Warren G. Harding in the 1920s.[32] But tellingly, new board members were much more homogeneous in their religious views than under Moody. Crowell's recruits included the prominent Chicago produce wholesaler Thomas S. Smith and executive Robert L. Scott Jr. from the department store Carson, Pirie, Scott & Co. High-profile legal figures included municipal court judge McKenzie Cleland, who ultimately was forced to resign over an extralegal probation scheme, and prominent attorney H. S. Osborne, who stirred passions at his Presbyterian church by proposing it operate "on the radical evangelical plan of the Moody church." Crowell's flashiest recruit was William Whiting Borden, the multimillionaire son of a Chicago real estate baron. In 1912 the Ivy League–educated Borden made headlines by becoming a missionary overseas. He was ordained at the Moody Church. When he became ill and died overseas less than a year later, he left a sizable financial donation to the institute while his selfless sacrifice generated goodwill for the religious institution to which he was most closely associated.[33]

A well-operated bureaucracy also required competent managers. Crowell built up MBI's administrative capacity, offering annual salaries of between $1,800 and $2,250 for middle managers and between $3,000 and over $5,000 for top management and marquee teaching positions. These rates kept pace with averages for railroad executives. By 1909 the institute's business manager had fifty employees and an annual budget of $150,000.[34]

As at Quaker Oats, Crowell drafted a "Plan of Operation" that outlined his proposed reforms for MBI. His designs included consolidating institutional power in a corporatized structure and then experimenting with innovative organizational structures to facilitate effective ministry. Moody originally had based the institute's governing structure on the Chicago YMCA. The male trustees controlled the property and addressed financial issues, while a fifteen-member "Board of Managers" was legally vested with authority over its operations. Harkening back to original negotiations with Nettie McCormick and Emma Dryer, the constitution specified that between six and nine of these management positions, approaching a two-thirds majority, must be filled by women.[35] This had been ignored

This photograph of the MBI "Printing Bureau" is one of several staged scenes of the institute's offices used for promotional purposes. The professionalism portrayed was an important part of MBI's self-understanding and shaped both the faith and religious practice of its workers in important ways. (Courtesy of the Moody Bible Institute Archives)

in practice after Dryer's departure; instead, Torrey, in consultation with Moody, oversaw day-to-day activities. Crowell considered such ad hoc arrangements dangerous. To further consolidate power and ensure a "professional" (that is, male-dominated) operation, Crowell formally dissolved the Board of Managers and transferred all its responsibilities to an enlarged board of trustees. He then further consolidated power in a three-member executive committee—composed of himself, Gray, and Fitt—and reduced the quorum for the fifteen-member trustee board to four. This smaller committee's responsibilities included formally investigating potential trustees according to new, stricter religious standards. No longer requiring church membership, the committee made sure that potential trustees held "views of the truth" that were "commonly held by the evangelical churches" and provided "evidence of conversion and consecration to Jesus Christ."[36] The unwritten standards behind these vague specifications were firmly in the hands of the executive committee.

A well-organized bureaucracy, however important, would not solve MBI's lingering existential crisis. Concern over disorder, especially after MBI's faith-healing scandal, made its initial purpose to convert the "masses" undesirable. But without this focus, there was no obvious reason for the institute's existence. Practical training was all well and good, but denominational seminaries had begun offering similar instruction by this time. MBI needed a new purpose, and Crowell was intent on discovering it. He initiated multiple strategies, sometimes simultaneously. As in business, he cultivated his successes and abandoned any old "machinery" that proved to be inefficient.

TO FACILITATE NEW MINISTRY experiments, Crowell's plan of operation split MBI into four departments that reported independently to the Executive Committee. He consolidated all financial decisions and professional fund-raising under the "Business Department." The Bible Institute work continued under the "Educational Department." This had a secondary benefit of limiting Torrey's influence to one department, which Crowell had diluted further by appointing Gray as a second "co-ordinate dean."[37] Crowell deemed MBI's school-by-mail program worthy of its own "Correspondence Department." Started in 1901, it was probably inspired by William Rainey Harper's pioneering correspondence courses of a decade before.[38] But Crowell's primary interest and hope lay in the "Extension Department," an "evangelistic work" that used "the Institute as a 'base.'" Ultimately, he thought it would become more important than the Bible Institute itself.[39]

Crowell was sure that the Extension Department could fill an important need in the religious landscape for organizing citywide revivals. He envisioned MBI as a one-stop revival shop, replacing local committees that typically had varying levels of competency. The Extension Department would bring in an evangelist and organize the revival's logistics, whether the physical needs of fund-raising, auditorium rental, and advertising or the spiritual needs of coordinating prayer, training volunteers, and ensuring that converts were funneled into cooperating churches. The sole responsibility of a local committee was to cover any financial shortfall not met by freewill offerings. Over time, MBI's growing expertise would lower the cost of conducting revivals.

The idea of coordinating revivalism was not unique to Crowell; a few denominations had started similar evangelistic bureaus. But he saw MBI as having some distinct advantages. Most important, it could broker cooperation across confessional lines and thus tap a larger pool of financial and spiritual resources.[40] In addition, Crowell planned to employ a corps of extension workers, professional evangelists on salary. This eliminated the ever-present suspicion of financial motives when freewill offerings were taken to cover campaign costs. Salaries also meant control. The Extension Department could impose standards on the content of the revivalists' preaching and dictate their schedules, even at a moment's notice. In return, MBI revivalists gained the institute's seal of approval, and with it, the potential to broaden their sphere of influence outside their particular denomination or geographic locale. It was professional revivalism.[41]

Thus to Crowell's mind, the Extension Department would increase the quantity and quality of revivals in the United States, solve MBI's existential crisis, and provide a constant revenue stream.[42] As the institute developed a national reputation for consistent, efficient, and professional revival work, it would develop its own gravitational pull. Why should a local committee take on the logistical hassles of a revival when they could delegate it to MBI? Why trust an unverified revivalist when MBI had a stable of engaging and trustworthy evangelists at the ready? Why would a talented evangelist set off on his own, facing deprivation, suspicion of motives, and the hassle of endless bureaucratic details, when MBI offered financial security and the luxury of focusing exclusively on their calling to preach? Using the logic of the market, MBI would become a self-perpetuating center for revivalism, creating a clear raison d'être and a fitting memorial to Moody's evangelistic ministry.

Crowell began courting potential extension workers to fill the roster before he finalized the plans for the Extension Department. Some of his choices suggested a broader definition of "evangelistic" work than Moody would have held. One of Crowell's more-interesting recruits was the former president of Princeton Seminary, Francis L. Patton. That Patton agreed to give a series of lectures under the auspices of the Bible Institute was a gratifying boost to its respectability. A decade before, he was complaining to fellow Presbyterians about the "arbitrary and unhistorical system of interpretation" common in Moody's circles, while grudgingly admitting that "few, I fear, know the English Bible as they do."[43] Patton's subject, "The Fundamentals of Christianity," foreshadowed Crowell's and Gray's growing concerns.[44]

The Extension Department plans explain why Crowell wanted Torrey's "hearty cooperation"; for as Crowell developed his plans, Torrey's worldwide revival tour, which included New Zealand, India, and Europe, had made him a celebrity revivalist in his own right. Upon Torrey's return to the

United States in 1903, the *Chicago Tribune* mused that "Moody's Successor" may have been "Found at Last," though it was not yet confident enough to put him on the front page.[45] Like Moody, Torrey and his evangelistic song leader, a charismatic former MBI student named Charlie Alexander, toured Great Britain to similar effect.[46] Over the next two years, the religious press breathlessly tracked their work, recounting the pair's role in various awakenings. Torrey's past scandals forgotten, these accounts kindled hopes that a "coming revival" would spread to the United States. Crowell saw Torrey's celebrity as the means to establish MBI's reputation in the revival business. They could use his upcoming American tour as both a trial run for logistical matters and, once the kinks were worked out, an advertisement for their services.

Torrey had hitherto operated his revival work independently, but in 1904 Crowell began gingerly steering him back under MBI's auspices. Torrey initially responded positively to Crowell's plans. He was happy to let the institute to handle mundane organizational details and to eliminate monetary suspicions with a salary. But when he realized that Crowell planned to require local committees to guarantee a specific amount of fund-raising at Torrey's future stops, the evangelist balked. It went against his principle of relying on God alone to provide. "I do not criticize Dr. Gray for doing it," he explained to Fitt, who now had become his strongest ally at MBI, but he flatly refused to agree to the policy for "fear it would injure my work."[47]

This minor quibble aside, the Extension Department seemed poised for success in July 1905. The most exciting development was finding a director to build up the department to its full potential. Joseph Calhoun was a Presbyterian minister of a substantial 900-member congregation and an increasingly popular evangelist. He had some administrative experience with the Presbyterian Evangelistic Committee, a nearly identical operation, and close connections to well-known revivalists like J. Wilbur Chapman.[48] Gray had first approached Calhoun to become an occasional extension worker, but Calhoun was so taken by Crowell's plans that he offered to become its director. They quickly agreed, and Gray began arranging an exhaustive speaking schedule for Calhoun at major Bible conferences and revival meetings in midsized cities. Even better, Torrey had sent word that he was planning to tackle the United States that winter. Calhoun suggested keeping Torrey occupied in major metropolitan centers with a nationwide blitz of extension workers in secondary markets.[49] The timing seemed providential.

But despite its seeming promise, the plans for professional revivalism did not last the summer. Calhoun's tenure ended before it began when the Associated Press leaked reports of the agreement. Whether because of denominational pressure or his own second thoughts, he backed out of the arrangement. His reasons, first "nervous & heat trouble" and then his congregation's refusal to accept his resignation, seemed especially flimsy when he took up the identical position under his Presbyterian denomination a year later.[50] A fuming Gray was left on the hook for his already-scheduled speaking engagements, and the abrupt change did little to suggest the reliability of the new Extension Department.

Torrey added to the Extension Department's woes after receiving his proposed itinerary from the Executive Committee. His response expressed gratitude for Crowell's "active interest" and willingness "to put his business sagacity at the disposal of the Institute," but he tartly insisted that any attempt "to dictate how we shall conduct our meetings . . . goes too far" and claimed his God-given "liberty" to abandon the scheme altogether.[51] Crowell scrambled Daniel B. Towner, a longtime music instructor at MBI, to patch things up with Torrey in London. He negotiated a truce that preserved Torrey's relative autonomy.[52] But soon, Torrey's intransigence would become the least of Crowell's problems.

NEWSPAPER HEADLINES OF TORREY's British revival meetings had focused on his gospel message. They noted the many prominent elites who lent support. For the pious Cadbury family of chocolatiering fame, this bond was made permanent when Torrey's bachelor song leader Charlie Alexander married into the family. Papers more interested in conflict than romance reported Torrey's increasingly testy exchanges with Unitarians and higher critics.[53] But largely unreported was Torrey's role as an inadvertent "John the Baptist" of global Pentecostalism.[54]

Pentecostals typically described their faith as a "four-fold gospel" that was, at its core, largely indistinguishable from Torrey's belief and practice. They, too, saw the essence of their faith lying in a personal relationship to God, independent of church and tradition. They embraced the imminent, any-moment return of Jesus that encouraged Holy living and hard work but had no interest in obtuse chronologies. They held to a belief in Holy Spirit Baptism that would empower a person for Christian work that included miraculous power. They also embraced faith healing along the lines of Torrey's early views and Dowie's lifelong convictions.[55] All things equal, Torrey fit nicely within the Pentecostal tradition, but there was one important difference: the movement consisted primarily of radical evangelicals, often from working-class or Populist backgrounds, whose active faith was unadulterated by professional middle-class conventions. Religion was a means of social critique and revolution rather than an anodyne for the masses.

It is difficult to pinpoint a single source of the Pentecostal movement, but Dowie figured prominently. His Zion community, now a full-fledged utopian community outside of Chicago, was an important node in a nationwide network of radical evangelicals. And most Pentecostals followed his unflinching absolutism in putting faith before physical safety or middle-class convention. Other communities also emerged around the country, some with direct connections to Torrey and the Bible Institute under his tenure. This included Frank Sandford's "Holy Ghost and Us Bible School" near Lewiston, Maine. Sandford visited the institute in 1895, and Torrey was so impressed that he sent Bible Institute students to work at his ministry that summer and gave a ringing endorsement. His Bible school, modeled in some respects on MBI, was founded in 1897 as a "faith work." It quickly took a dark turn when the community fell into malnourishment and Sandford began claiming that he could cast out demons. He eventually proclaimed himself to be God's special representative on earth before Jesus's physical second coming, taking the title "Elijah." [56] Radical evangelicals flocked to the school, often for short periods of informal study before returning to spread the good news in their hometowns.

The man usually credited with formally codifying Pentecostalism's most distinctive practices was Charles Fox Parham. He was born a sickly child in 1873 to struggling Iowa farmers. The family's move to a farm outside Cheney, Kansas, brought no substantial improvement to their situation. After a basic education, including time at the Methodist Southwestern College, he was licensed a Methodist minister in 1892. But within two years, he had rejected theological education and denominationalism as a hindrance to the Holy Spirit. This did not stop him from reading widely, including works by Torrey. He visited Dowie's Zion and Sandford's school and then started his own "faith work" in Topeka. It featured a healing home and a Bible school with students devoted to Bible study, prayer, and practical work among the city's working classes. [57]

As the new century approached, Parham became convinced that they were on the cusp of a final worldwide revival. Then on the symbolically poignant morning of January 1, 1900, a miraculous sign of the new era appeared: students began to speak in foreign tongues, like the apostles of old. This, they believed, would allow them to fan out across the world in an end-times mission blitz, for "the fields were white unto harvest."[58] As the practice of tongues spread to other independent ministries through informal networks, it created a powerful impression that God was at work independently of human efforts. There were also self-defined "apostles" of Parham's message. Perhaps the most important of these was a Louisiana-born African American minister named William Seymour. In 1906 he brought the message of the "latter rain" and the practice of tongues to a Los Angeles Mission on Azusa Street. Here, the movement took on a multiethnic and multiracial character and, with this change, new symbolic potency for both promoters and opponents.[59] From Los Angeles, it spread up the West Coast, into the South, and into most major urban centers of the East and Midwest.

The practice of speaking in tongues was Pentecostalism's most emblematic and controversial feature, but even this, at least in its original form, was simply Torrey's underlying belief in Spirit Baptism taken to its logical end. Pentecostals held to an ongoing and interactive relationship with God that was no different from what Torrey advocated. Like Torrey, they used the biblical terminology of a "Baptism of the Holy Spirit" to describe the beginning of that relationship. Tongues was not simply a sign of power; it was itself a useful "power for service." These were literal foreign languages, Pentecostals believed, useful for missions. Later, when a growing body of evidence from the mission fields and elsewhere made this assertion untenable, a new claim of "glossolalia" was put forward. It was a heavenly language with no earthly equivalent and thus served less practical ends.[60] Torrey, for his part, did not publicly criticize the movement until 1913. His attacks used stereotypes common among respectable middle-class critics that depicted Pentecostals as immoral enthusiasts. But in theory, he made no objection to the "gift of tongues" occurring in modern times, for "if God sees fit to do it, He can . . . and will do it."[61] This same stand was held by some self-identified Pentecostals.[62] As with Torrey's views of faith healing, there was no consistent criterion by which to differentiate his views from these radical insurgents.

Thus Pentecostalism was difficult to distinguish from the variegated holiness networks that also included MBI. They, too, advocated for a turn-of-the-century revival and even used a type of dispensational logic. The main difference was that while MBI personnel argued that recent revival movements constituted *a* revival, Pentecostals asserted that it was *the* revival that would mark a dispensational transition just before the second coming of Jesus. This meant they were now in the seventh and final dispensation—a time when even the stodgiest dispensationalist would agree that miraculous signs again became commonplace. And by the same logic, a new dispensation meant that all bets were off—everything was malleable as new rules and a new order was established. Doctrinaire dispensationalists like Cyrus Scofield vehemently disagreed, insisting that the rapture of the church was the definitive sign, and thus Pentecostalism was illegitimate. But to outsiders, this seemed like theological nit-picking. The primary difference was that Pentecostals used dispensational ideas to justify revolution rather than to prevent it.

What would this new dispensation look like? The most radical Pentecostals combined a plain rendering of the book of Acts with Populist, occasionally outright leftist, political convictions. Pentecostals typically referenced the Old Testament prophet Joel, quoted by the apostle Peter at Pentecost, promising a "latter rain" in which God would "pour out My Spirit on all mankind" such that "your sons and daughters will prophesy, Your old men will dream dreams, Your young men will see visions." Miracles would be commonplace, and the Sermon on the Mount was in force. There was no distinction between "Jew or Greek" or "male or female," leading to significant challenges to the reigning racial and gendered social order. In fact, nearly every miraculous sign that Pentecostals claimed could be paired with an encroaching dimension of professionalization: speaking in tongues was a protest against educational requirements on the mission field; God's direct prophetic word countered seminary and complex hermeneutics; faith healing protested professional medicine; and faith work was a protest against modern accounting. Pentecostals insisted that God was on the side of the downtrodden and was making his preference known through miraculous signs. God was calling the respectable classes to repent through them. True believers must choose either worldly success among the professional middle classes or faithful adherence to the pure gospel.

Most early Pentecostals were drawn from the working classes, southern "plainfolk" evangelicals, and urban communities of color that typically operated outside of MBI's purview. But there were enough intersections and a shared vocabulary to raise concerns among some of the respectable classes. Many important Pentecostal leaders, including Frank Bartleman, Francisco Olazabal, and Marie Burgess, were students at MBI during Torrey's tenure, and many more were inspired by Torrey's writings.[63] These connections were even more direct overseas. "I can only say of myself," recalled one German Pentecostal who dated the movement's beginnings to one of Torrey's revival meetings, "that a marvelous gentle stream of fire came down over me from above."[64]

Torrey was largely oblivious to most Pentecostals being anything other than Holy Spirit–filled believers, perhaps with a questionable interest in tongues. Crowell and Gray were also slow to notice the movement's growth, being preoccupied with the continuing difficulties in the Extension Department and, in 1906, what seemed like the beginnings of an open rebellion by Torrey and Fitt to Crowell's plan of operation.[65] Gray's heavy speaking schedule on the Extension Department circuit left little opportunity for him to see the growing Pentecostal excitement spreading at MBI. Even Fitt seemed to think they were entering into a unique period of revival and began using the same "latter rain" terminology as Pentecostals. As editor of MBI's magazine, the *Institute Tie*, which was resurrected shortly after Moody's death in 1900, he began promoting these ideas. At one point, he suggested that the present revival had been prophesied by the late Hudson Taylor, the venerated founder of the China Inland Mission, and that "immediately following . . . the Lord Himself will come." Even when the authenticity of the prophecy was challenged, Fitt refused to back down, instead printing a signed affidavit from a missionary who claimed to have heard the utterance firsthand. "The Institute Tie is not a yellow journal," his last editorial word on the subject stated, "but it knows a good thing when it sees it."[66]

Pentecostal networks were fully developed in Chicago by late 1906. Not surprisingly, some of the first converts lived in Dowie's Zion community. Pentecostalism was a welcome renewal amid financial mismanagement and a crisis of leadership that led to Dowie's ousting. Pentecostalism also made beachheads in the city limits. William Durham, a Baptist Christian worker from Kentucky, had noted what he believed to be "gifts of the spirit" on display at his North Avenue Mission. In March he made a brief trip to Los Angeles to visit Seymour and the Azusa mission. He spoke in tongues and brought the practice back to Chicago. His mission quickly became a midwestern center of Pentecostalism, responsible for many prominent future leaders, including Aimee Semple McPherson, and sending many missionaries from its multicultural congregation across the globe. William H. Piper was another important Chicago Pentecostal. Initially an elder at Zion, he became disillusioned in late 1906 and founded the Stone Church on Chicago's South Side. He initially resisted the Pentecostal message but embraced it in the summer of 1907. His magazine, the *Latter Rain Evangel*, edited by Anna Reiff, became influential in the movement and spread the message widely.[67]

Torrey had spurred revival excitement at MBI during revival meetings held in the fall of 1906. Like other times he believed himself to be on the cusp of momentous events, he began a diary, recording for posterity the mundane facts of his revival schedule and successes.[68] After Torrey's departure, according to Fitt, "a special outpouring of the Holy Spirit" was experienced by the student body. It was a time of "confession and reconciliation," he explained, and with "little or no false fire or extravagance."[69] Torrey was ecstatic. "I trust the Holy Spirit is still with you in power," he wrote, "and that you are being used to win others to Christ."[70] Gray was also pleased, expressing confidence that "you will have wisdom to guide the situation."[71] But at reports of "another outpouring," Gray became concerned and wrote to Fitt, hoping that "the same Lord keep the pestilence from us in these days"—by which he meant the "dread" disease of Pentecostalism "raging in the city."[72]

When speaking in tongues occurred at MBI in May 1907, administrators were horrified. Fitt immediately moved to quash it, instructing the men's superintendent "to fire instantly any student who has the gift of tongues."[73] This was followed by a scathing critique of the tongues movement in the August 1907 issue of *Institute Tie*. Though the magazine had largely avoided religious controversies before, it now unreservedly condemned tongues as a "delusion . . . foisted by the devil upon an underfed church." Its aberrant behavior "would be very absurd if it was not so humiliating to the name of Christ."[74] These measures did not stop a second wave of Pentecostal activity from hitting MBI in the fall.[75]

Torrey, in contrast, was not overly concerned by recent developments. "Of course, there is always danger of excesses," he wrote to Fitt when learning the news. "Just trust God and things will come all right."[76] It was a similar reaction to the news the year before that Dowie had been ousted from Zion. "Dowie I thought was a humbug, but I thought there were a good many honest people in it," he told Fitt, and "the idea of a model city is not a bad one." The new director Frank Voliva, who helped bring Zion into the Pentecostal movement, Torrey thought "to be thoroughly honest," and he suggested if Fitt was willing to "help them out any by giving them any of our printing, I should be glad to see it done."[77] When Zion was swept into the

Pentecostal movement, it was no impediment to Torrey making a visit, nor to their inviting him to preach.[78]

THE WAVES OF PENTECOSTAL revivals sweeping across the country drove home an important lesson to Crowell: like the oatmeal market, the cost of entering revivalism was simply too low to corner. Though coordinated citywide revivals required planning, "wild-cat" evangelists could preach at will. And if one of these Pentecostal meetings achieved critical mass, as happened repeatedly, it could become citywide, even nationwide, without sophisticated planning.

Torrey's continuing intransigence illustrated another important lesson: the best trademarks cannot talk back. Torrey had his own ideas and a will to resist instructions, and since he was a celebrity in his own right, Crowell had no leverage over him. Torrey could create excitement, but he was impossible to govern and thus had little value to Crowell's Extension Department scheme.

Seeing the writing on the wall, Crowell dissolved the Extension Department altogether in 1908. It was just as well. A scathing article by the venerable editor Arthur T. Pierson protested the very sort of "revival machinery" that Crowell planned to use: "extensive organization, elaborate preparation, expensive outlay, studied notoriety, display of statistics, newspaper advertising and systematic puffing." Though Crowell undoubtedly would have avoided "spectacular sensationalism, dramatic novelties, and sometimes doubtful complication with secular and political issues," this was too fine a distinction. Moody's son Will had been especially critical of how many present revivalists focused on fund-raising, which he called "the very antithesis of everything that . . . my father stood for all through his ministry." Only "Mr. Torrey and one or two others" were exceptions to the rule, and Torrey's fund-raising policies were at odds with Crowell. Apart from these, Will concluded, "the whole evangelistic work seems to be thoroughly commercialized."[79]

Evangelism was the bread and butter of MBI, and various efforts continued. Crowell served on the board of the Laymen's Evangelistic Council of Chicago, a self-styled "Business Men's Movement" focused primarily on the professional classes. During a 1910 summer open-air campaign in Chicago, the institute left the street work in working-class districts to the rescue missions while its students focused on the noon meetings "in the very heart of the business district" that attracted between 300 and 1,000 professionals daily.[80] But in any case, these efforts were local events, a far cry from the sweeping plans Crowell had envisioned.

Even with the setbacks, Crowell's modifications to MBI paved the way for other ministry experiments that might prove its usefulness to professional middle-class Protestants. And just as Quaker Oats helped naturalize the techniques of modern consumer capitalism in the promotion of other consumer goods, so MBI naturalized these corporate strategies in the religious world. As former employees went to other organizations or started their own ministries, these techniques followed. The more commonplace these practices became among evangelicals, the more convinced evangelicals became that they had nothing to fear, and perhaps everything to gain, from leveraging the techniques of modern capitalism.

The rise of Pentecostalism convinced Crowell and his allies that there was more work to be done to make modern evangelicalism safe for middle-class consumption. It was not enough to believe in revival. Without proper controls, even that holy desire might easily veer in "dangerous" directions and challenge the social, economic, and cultural status quo. But here, too, he would find that the ideas of modern consumer capitalism could help. Crowell had jumped the gun with his Extension Department plan; only after he and his religious team had safeguarded evangelicalism from radicalism could they then return to addressing MBI's existential crisis and begin developing avenues for it to influence the wider religious world.

SIX

A Consuming Faith

Stephen Woodruff completed his studies at Moody's Bible Institute in 1898, believing he was called to the ministry. But with no ready opportunities, he took a job in the printing office of the Chicago-based *Farm Implement News*. By 1905 it seemed that God had called him to a secular career, but he worried his hard work had gone unnoticed by his superiors. Fearing a life without advancement, he began studying Walter Dill Scott's famous textbook *Psychology of Advertising* to better his prospects in the publishing world. One evening, Woodruff returned to MBI to attend a lecture by James Gray on homiletics, the science of constructing effective sermons. As the talk proceeded, Woodruff realized that the principles Gray outlined could "be applied to advertising." Ambitious fellow that he was, Woodruff sprang at the opportunity now before him. The writer of the weekly advertising column had forgotten to submit his copy before leaving on vacation, and so, Woodruff later wrote Gray, "I took your subject [and] prepared an advertising article from it." The editor liked the piece so much that he printed it and asked Woodruff to write the following week as well. "Needless to say," Woodruff concluded, "I was at your next week's lecture."[1]

Although Woodruff's brief writing career ended when the regular columnist returned, his work was now noticed. He was soon hired as an assistant editor and then into a management position. Then, in a final twist, a new opportunity arose for Woodruff to combine his long-standing desire to serve God with his newly acquired business acumen. He applied to be the publishing agent for MBI's newly revamped magazine. He was hired because of the experience he gained through the application of spiritual principles to secular advertising.

Woodruff's experiences capture a fluidity between sacred and secular that is missing from most accounts of the rise of consumer culture. Many evangelical professionals considered business practices of all kinds to be uncontroversial reservoirs of spiritual insights. Their experience at work provided metaphors for understanding their faith and techniques for effectively practicing it. Evangelicals like Woodruff felt at home in the pages of Scott's book. Its advice on using emotional and sympathetic appeals, its five stages of human choosing, its taxonomies of decision makers, and its warnings that "individuals are different" and make their choices by "divers [sic] methods" confirmed their experiences in personal evangelism.[2] But the exchange went both ways. Secular advertisers were happy to borrow insights into human psychology from religious professionals who spent years cajoling sinners to choose salvation. Both advertisers and evangelists were tackling the same problem of individual human choice, and both groups welcomed any art or science that gave them an advantage.

In the ideological overlap between modern consumer capitalism and religion, evangelicals at MBI forged a consuming faith. By the first decade of the twentieth century, a new set of ideas and practices, nascent in the industrial capitalism of the Gilded Age, had matured. It provided solutions to sticky ideological issues caused by the decline of autonomy at work and a new set of corresponding opportunities to create identities through the consumption of goods and services—now more plentiful to an ever wider proportion of the population. These same ideas were useful to evangelicals of the professional classes. The dangers in evangelical realist assumptions, they believed, had been vividly demonstrated in the "excesses" of Pentecostal revivalism. It had made Christian work without close superintendence appear dangerous. In the same consumer-oriented ideas, they found the means to create a faith that was both appealing and safe for middle-class consumption. They helped transition evangelicals from Moody's conviction that an authentic faith produced Christian workers to a new ideal embodied by the savvy consumer—a believer who rightly judged and appropriated correct belief and practice from the options in the religious marketplace.

ANY DOUBTS THAT CORPORATE capitalism was the new normal were laid to rest during the first decade of the new century. The same depression in 1893 that galvanized Populist discontent also spurred a wave of unprecedented corporate consolidation. When the merger mania subsided in 1904, over half of these new corporations now controlled over 40 percent of their respective industries, while almost a third controlled 70 percent or more.[3] Traditionally, enterprises of any size were temporary, dying with the entrepreneurs who created and controlled them. But twenty years of developments in business law and organizational strategies had granted the gift of eternal life to any enterprise that remained profitable. Corporations became legal persons by the mid-1880s, able to own property and engage in contracts, thanks to the Supreme Court's inventive interpretation of the Fourteenth Amendment. Loosened state regulations made the act of incorporation, complete with the benefits of legal immunity, routine where they had once required a special act of a legislative body.[4]

The large corporation had become a "natural" part of the business landscape with important repercussions for the patterns and meaning of modern work. It meant, lingering myths of the "labor ladder" notwithstanding, that a majority of the population would spend their working lives as employees, not independent proprietors. And with increasing regimentation of managerial organization, it also meant a decreasing amount of individual creativity in that work.[5] This was even true for many entrepreneurs and workers in small shops. If they serviced large corporations, they were beholden to their massive gravitational pull and thus were hardly different from other corporate employees. Neither was the corporate form limited to the manufacturing, transportation, and communication sectors. Thanks to massive mail-order companies, wholesalers, and new chain stores, the world of corporate work encroached increasingly on the retail heart of traditional middle-class proprietorship.

By the turn of the century, labor activists had already begun shifting strategies to accommodate the new realities of corporate capitalism. They exchanged demands for work autonomy for moral claims to a "living wage," safer working conditions, and job security. This new stasis would develop in fits and starts, but the end result was less-meaningful work for many people and the bare exchange of labor for cash—corporate servitude traded for more disposable income and free time.[6] The demise of autonomous work did not end the desire of Americans to exercise their economic freedom, but the arena in which that freedom was exercised shifted from the shop floor to the retail store.

Consumers developed a variety of scripts to follow when transforming the act of consuming into part of a modern identity. Some followed the road of hedonistic excess and conspicuous consumption.[7] But for most consumers, it was a more discriminating process. Consumption could also be the means to self-betterment by education, for example.[8] And for nearly everyone, the pattern was created, then as now, by *avoiding* the consumption of some things. Choices were shaped both by the desire for pleasure and by purity—not simply lust, but also fear, and even duty.[9] Consumers made their decisions within a wider matrix of beliefs and practices. The consumer revolution was less a matter of morals than mechanics, specifically the displacement of work as the primary means by which one's economic identity was constructed.[10]

Consumer culture thus encouraged a definition of what it meant to be authentically human that placed a particular emphasis on choice. For those embracing the new neoclassical school of economics, for marketing professionals, and for business elites, among others, society consisted primarily as a collection of rational-acting individuals. It was the freedom to choose, whether by voting, marrying, or shopping, that differentiated civilized humanity from the beasts.

The centrality of choice resonated most strongly with an evangelical disposition. Authentic faith was an individually chosen, personal relationship with God. And it was the act of choosing specifically that made one's faith authentic. Thus children who had reached an age in which choice was theoretically possible needed to authenticate their faith by making their own decision for God. It was not enough to be baptized and raised in the church; God has no grandchildren, conservative evangelicals liked to say.

Though it was perhaps impossible to escape the influence of a modern consumer identity, not everyone was influenced equally, especially in their religious belief and practice. Churchly conservatives, as before, thought about their faith in communal terms, drawing primarily from metaphors of the family. Liberals, increasingly inspired by modern scientific ideas, also had powerful counterweights to a consumer identity. Social science had taken a Darwinian turn. This meant first and foremost that the population, rather than the individual, became the basic unit of analysis.[11] Social gospelers, eager to align with social science and sometimes key participants in its creation, shaped their religious convictions accordingly. The future of religion was in the group—in society—and God's working through it. Higher criticism reinforced this idea with evidence that even the holy books of scripture were not the product of a single author writing under God's inspiration, but the product of communities that evolved over time. God worked in and through societies rather than interacting with individuals. Liberals incorporated consumptive practices into their religious identities, especially after World War I.[12] But it was always in tension with scientific conceptions of humanity that exerted equal, if not greater, influence. Conservative evangelicals' individualistic ideology had little communal ballast and few external cultural references apart from consumption.

Of course, business interests could also be of a divided mind in their embrace of rational individualism, but advertising, the language of consumer culture, consistently spoke in an individualistic key. Corporate structures and the collaborative nature of modern production mitigated a purely individualistic understanding. Advertising professionals might use insights from group-oriented psychology to manipulate customers. But as historian Roland Marchand has noted, ad creators discovered early on that consumers wanted their products "introduced to them in ways that gave the appearance and feel of a personal relationship." They sold "the American dream," offering "new and satisfying forms of individualism, equality, personal interaction, and cost-free progress within the emerging mass society." What made advertisers "modern" was the "extent to which they . . . achieved subjective qualities and a 'personal' tone."[13] The individualistic appeals of the conservative evangelical message might have been at odds with modern science, but it had much in common with consumer culture.

Consumers wanted a personal touch in their mass consumption, but how does one have a personal relationship with a faceless corporation? Unlike older companies that had a limited group of owners with full responsibility for corporate actions, the modern corporation had virtually unlimited owners with limited liability. Managers, the ostensible decision makers, were mere employees, answerable to stockholders, who could be fired at will. So who was this corporation? This relational conundrum mattered especially for corporate food processors, whose product required that consumers to entrust their bodies and health to an amorphous entity whose only end was profit. It fell to the advertisers to humanize the conglomerate.

Henry Crowell addressed the problem of corporate personification with the trademarked Quaker. Advertising, he realized, was the medium through which the company initiated a relationship with customers. It began with establishing familiarity. From the 1890s onward, readers of most major urban newspapers and nationally distributed middle-class magazines were bombarded with graphic-intensive ads designed to make the trademarked Quaker figure synonymous with oatmeal. Product packaging was another medium for advertising. Each trip to the store was another exposure to the brand, which was especially striking early on, when Quaker Oats was one of the few stand-outs in an otherwise drab, crowded general store. Crowell's Quaker became the face of oatmeal.

Advertisements created a rapport between the company and consumer. The Quaker Oats advertisements were clever, entertaining, and pleasant to look at. Sometimes, the Quaker was depicted self-consciously in incongruous settings, with a knowing wink to the reader. Crowell took advantage of his sealed packages to pioneer the use of "premiums," small gifts from toys to china that were free with purchase. This was not simply to spur demand through greed; it also forged a relationship with the consumer, engendering loyalty to the brand through gift giving. For consumers still unsure of the product's quality, the company distributed free, sample-sized packages of Quaker Oats to entire midsized cities. It built elaborate displays at World's Fairs and other exhibitions, where attractive personnel, often dressed in Quaker garb, served free samples of Quaker products to hungry attendees. In each case, the promotion was designed to create a human face for the corporation. The Quaker Oats man was your favorite grandfather who lavished you with gifts, joked around, and did not take himself too seriously. But he also loved his customers and was watching out for their well-being. They knew that behind the horseplay, Quaker Oats was deadly serious about the purity of its product; the scroll with the single word "pure" was never far from the Quaker's hand. It was the associations of Quakers to the characteristics of trustworthy people that first convinced Crowell of the value of his trademark, "values like goodness, purity, honesty, plainness, and robust heath."[14]

The problem solved by corporate advertisers like Crowell was almost identical to the problem conservative middle-class evangelicals faced in personifying and personalizing the ineffable God. For evangelicals, the personhood of God was paramount, but respectability demanded that this God interact indirectly and through mediation rather than through the direct and disruptive ways of the Pentecostal spirit. Yet these very constraints on the Godhead, common in a churchly orientation, were what first frustrated Gilded Age evangelical realists, including Moody and Torrey. Allowing God to communicate personally and intervene directly in the world made him seem like a real person. Placing strictures on God's actions made personhood a formality, a legal fiction like the corporation.

Was there another way to realize God's personhood without social disruptions? Crowell saw the answer in the same methods that he used to personify his corporation. It meant respectable Protestants did not need to return to a churchly orientation to counter disorder. He could create a new "respectable" middle-class evangelicalism as long as its theology imitated the conventions of advertising and its believers acted like modern consumers.

A typical advertisement by the marketing-savvy company Quaker Oats, whose president, Henry P. Crowell, led the Moody Bible Institute after 1904. Note the sentimental pitch of the ad, including the protective stance of the friendly Quaker figure and the appeal to both "scientific opinion" and "experience." Also note the scroll, on which was written the single word "PURE." This appeared in nearly every Quaker advertisement of the era. Similar types of appeals were made in a religious context as well. (Personal collection of author)

JAMES GRAY AND OTHER dispensationalists took the lead in conceptualizing an interactive relationship with God that was safe for professional, middle-class consumption. Their efforts are typically associated with the Keswick Holiness Movement, named after a series of conferences in the Lake District of England that started in 1875. The movement was self-consciously interdenominational, and most participants hailed from respectable backgrounds. There were numerous intersections with Moody's evangelical networks at Mildmay, and in the 1880s and 1890s, many of the same speakers also shuttled throughout Moody's American networks. In Great Britain especially, the movement's focus was constructive and experiential, devoted to promoting a heightened spiritual existence and devotional fulfillment that they called the "higher life." But especially after the emergence of Pentecostalism, those labeled "Keswick" in the United States took a more defensive turn and a doctrinal orientation toward dispensationalism. Charles Trumbull was one of the leading figures in the American movement. A close confidant of Cyrus Scofield, he was also the editor of the widely circulating *Sunday School Times*. It was once a theologically broad publication embodying the full range of evangelicalism, but it narrowed considerably under his guidance, becoming the leading voice of the Keswick movement. Other leaders included Gray, William Newell, and Scofield. Nearly every teacher hired at MBI under Crowell and Gray's tenure also fell in this category. If dispensationalism was the science of the fundamentalist movement, Keswick would be its heart.[15]

Keswick advocates remained allied with Torrey and other respectable holiness advocates and had plenty in common. They, too, taught that a believer's relationship to the Holy Spirit was contractual, that it required complete submission by exchanging one's will for God's, that the special relationship could end at any time, and that it produced spiritual power. It was as much a departure from traditional Protestant teaching as were Torrey's beliefs.

But Keswick advocates also made key modifications to earlier holiness teachings that they believed had led to social disruption. They marked the difference by substituting the phrase "filling with the Holy Spirit" for the phrase "Baptism of the Holy Spirit" that Torrey and most Pentecostals favored. They also understood the believers' relationship to God as closest to a relationship between a consumer and a corporation rather than a worker and an employer. Thus they conceptualized the act of submitting to God as part of a consumer transaction that provided freedom from sin rather than part of a relational state of divine employment. It was also markedly different from traditional Calvinist theology, which taught that the process of ridding one's life of sin, called "sanctification," was a lifelong project and came through hard moral exercise, or "working out your salvation." Keswick, in contrast, understood sanctification as a service done *for* you by God in exchange for oneself, fully submitted. To "put sin away" was something impossible for anyone to do, Scofield taught, "but the Holy Spirit can."[16]

It followed that the "power for service" Keswick advocates anticipated differed from the power that Torrey and other evangelical realists had expected. For Torrey, "power for service" was open-ended; it was alien and supernatural, ungovernable and unreasonable, manifested in whatever way God thought necessary. God worked directly and sometimes miraculously though a person, whether to save and guide or to heal. Keswick, in contrast, limited this "power" to internal revitalization that flowed in an orderly manner to increased ministerial effectiveness. Where Torrey claimed that Moody's ministry was successful because he was "definitely endued with power from on high," Keswick advocates insisted it "was his sincerity and goodness. He was good through and through. He was the same in the dark that he was in the light."[17] Keswick advocates held that effective ministry was a function of holiness. Power "comes down from God, enters into my life, revolutionizes it, uplifts it, energizes it, and enables me to go out in His name and win others for the Saviour [sic]."[18] Although this too was an alien and divine power, it was limited to internal transformation.

The choice of metaphors used by Keswick advocates to describe God's power emphasized governability over God-inspired spontaneity. Radical evangelicals used metaphors of fire and wind;[19] Keswick metaphors preferred electricity. This choice tellingly required knowledge and experience with technology common only among the urban middle classes. Gray's analogy that the Holy Spirit illuminated a mind "in the knowledge of the truth" in the same way that Gray waited for the dynamo to send light to his darkened classroom would have meant little to a tenant farmer.[20] But even more notably, electricity was a source of power that neither destroyed nor intrinsically controlled direction. "This thing is a trolley system," Newell said of the spirit-filled life, and the believer is a streetcar. It has "no ability to run" on its own. Electricity powers the car, and then the "car does the work and carries the passengers." In the same way, God "says I will put my divine electricity in you. Oh how easily we go ahead when He is working it in us."[21] The power of the Holy Spirit caused the believer to move, and direction was dictated by the track—that is, by a dispensational interpretation of the Bible. To leave that track was to leave the power wires that follow them. The believer was not a ship pushed as the Spirit of God directed; rather, all believers ran along the same track, mechanically picking up passengers.

Keswick advocates also muted God's guiding voice. Torrey insisted that one might "walk with God," by which he meant living "in communion with Him . . . to be every now and then speaking to Him or listening while He speaks to us . . . .liv[ing] in the real, conscious companionship of God."[22] In contrast, Keswick understood a believer's "fellowship with God" primarily as a list of spiritual disciplines: self-examination and confessing sin, keeping God's commandments, "loving the brethren," being "separated from the world," and avoiding "false teachers."[23] The one exception that otherwise proved the rule was God's direct prompting to evangelism. Following the divine impulse to share one's faith was mandatory; other promptings were highly suspect and always tentative.

Believers accrued evidence of a relationship to God by internal feelings of comfort and peace, not by demonstrations of miraculous power. The Christian life was like laying on a feather bed, Newell explained; it required only our "letting go" and allowing Jesus "to give us His rest and his peace and his joy." Gray also regularly thought about his message in connection to rest, peace, and comfort. "I believe God is making me a real blessing here," he wrote from Eagle's Mere, Pennsylvania, after describing its idyllic beauty, noting how his message and "work have fitted into the situation peculiarly."[24] God beckoned his followers to peace and rest, just as the Quaker promised security to those who purchased his product.

Keswick holiness, when combined with dispensationalism, was a modern evangelicalism that was safe for middle-class consumption. Dispensationalism provided a way to hold to an ostensibly "literal" interpretation of the Bible within the norms of the respectable middle classes. These were Christians who also visited doctors, took medicine, borrowed money, lived in nuclear family units, and placed their lives under the guidance and direction of professional experts who worked according to a scientific expertise they need not understand. Indeed, the dispensational system itself was an example of modern professionalization. The plain meaning of the Bible was an engineering problem; dispensationalism was a system to address it. Like other products of engineering, it could be used by nonexperts, especially after 1909, when the dispensational scaffolding was literally imprinted on the pages of scripture in the *Scofield Reference Bible*. Its copious notes "explained" troubling passages, and carefully culled cross-references made connections between otherwise unrelated texts. Scofield's Bible quietly inculcated millions of readers into the complicated dispensational system as if it was intrinsic to the scriptures themselves and simply "discovered" by their careful reading.

The Keswick religious experience mirrored the contours of therapeutic religion in ways functionally indistinguishable from its liberal analog. God was intoned as "the Great Physician" in one popular tract by MBI administrator John Riebe, but unlike Torrey, the only healing imparted was "spiritual surgery upon a broken heart." "Spiritual joy is independent of congenial environment, circumstances or occasions," Riebe explained. Thus "[w]ealth never yet made a happy home. Poverty never yet made a miserable home. . . . No set of conditions can produce misery apart from the condition of the character itself."[25] This diminished the need for social reform; one needed only to let God transform his or her inner disposition, accepting divine comfort despite physical circumstances. Keswick dispensationalists had a different pathway to enlightenment than liberal therapeutic religion, but the destination was virtually identical. For both, God's day-to-day interactions with believers mirrored a corporation interacting with their customers. God and Quaker Oats alike were assuring from afar, satisfying, and empowering. This was the faith Crowell and Gray would promote through MBI.

AFTER THE FAILURE TO corral revivalism through the Extension Department, Crowell turned to the other ongoing experiments he hoped would build MBI's constituency, promote its Keswick-infused dispensationalism, and ultimately to justify its existence. One important avenue was publishing. "Middlebrow" print culture, both books and magazines, was rapidly becoming one of the most important arenas in which a middle-class identity was being constructed. If MBI was to play a role in shaping that identity, it, too, must produce the printed word.[26]

Before 1907, MBI had two narrowly delimited publishing projects. The *Institute Tie* had been resurrected shortly after Moody's death.[27] It was intended to serve as the house organ for MBI, designed to "keep donors and friends of the Moody Bible Institute informed of the work" and to act as a "'tie' to unite our students, past and present." Initially, the magazine was something of a touchy subject because Moody's magazine, the *Record of Christian Work*, had been the official organ of his various ministries. Arthur

P. Fitt, who served as the *Tie*'s editor, assured both readers and Moody's son Will, present editor of the *Record*, that they had no intention of creating "a general magazine" that would in any way compete. True to Fitt's word, the *Tie* was basically a printed re-creation of daily life at MBI. It published a smattering of lectures from institute teachers, lesson outlines, Bible study helps, evangelistic strategies, alumni news, and even meal hours and department schedules. For supporters, the *Tie*'s lists of donations, "extracts of donor letters," and annual reports "tied" them into the institute network as well.[28]

The second publishing avenue available to Crowell was the Bible Institute Colportage Association (BICA), but financial troubles and murky connections to MBI made it a less-than-ideal vehicle. Moody started the BICA in the mid-1890s, but it was only incorporated shortly after his death. Though its board consisted entirely of current MBI personnel, it was legally independent. Fitt was its president; institute business manager Aymer F. Gaylord served on the board; and another MBI administrator, William Norton, controlled its day-to-day operations. Moody's widow, Emma, had also served on the board. Torrey took her place after her death in 1904, though he rarely attended meetings. The original purpose of the BICA was to sell inexpensive paperback editions of gospel literature. By 1900 it had produced over 100 different publications, employed 600 independent booksellers across the country, and distributed over 3 million volumes. But a year later, it lost the second-class postage rate that had made the enterprise financially feasible. So in 1903, the BICA looked to expand into higher-margin publishing to support its charitable work. But this proved difficult. All BICA printing was done by Fleming H. Revell, now an MBI board member. He owned the plates and legal rights to put out higher-priced cloth editions of the same books designed for middle-class audiences. He rebuffed BICA inquiries, claiming exclusive copyright to all the works in the BICA catalog. There were significant revenues at stake. The books at issue included the *Cruden's Concordance* that Moody had helped popularize as a "must-have" Bible reference. The dispute became heated, and MBI trustee meetings no doubt became awkward affairs. Though a tense détente was negotiated through arbitration, it left the BICA teetering on insolvency.[29]

In November 1905, Fitt proposed starting a weekly religious newspaper in order to solve the BICA's financial crisis, expand its profile, and promote the turn-of-the-century revival of which Torrey was now a major part. But tellingly, Fitt thought it wise to run the idea by the Executive Committee of MBI before raising the idea to his own board. Crowell and Gray thought it would be an excellent auxiliary to the Extension Department (still operating at the time) and promised "the Institute would add its cooperation as far as possible." But the following March, the BICA board disagreed and tabled the proposal.[30]

Then in January 1907, when it was clear that the Extension Department was faltering, Crowell borrowed Fitt's ideas to revamp the *Institute Tie*.[31] In its new form, the *Tie* would be a general-interest religious magazine, "the arm by which the Institute may reach out over the world month by month." Torrey and Gray were appointed as coeditors in chief, and photographs of both men were placed on opposing pages of the full-spread announcement—a visual reinforcement of their watchful eyes over the project. They would be more than "mere ornaments," the announcement promised, giving "active and personal interest in the paper."[32] James Gray would compose a running commentary on the whole Bible, directed at the "average layman." Torrey's scholarly reputation was put to use in a column answering "Puzzling and Practical Questions." This column precipitated another first: the magazine's use of a copyright to maintain exclusive rights over Torrey's words. He also contributed Bible study notes, though all indications suggest this was an afterthought borne of his protest. Initially, despite the announcement's promises, Fitt did most of the work. But Gray quickly saw the value of the "editorial department," the first feature of each issue addressing current events, and he soon became its lead author and thus the collective voice of the institute. Torrey remained largely uninvolved except for his directly authored contributions.[33]

Promotional efforts for the new magazine took a page from Crowell's work at Quaker Oats. They targeted a middle-class readership and initially, Gray criticized some of Fitt's features that suggested "the cheap little papers." The price of an annual subscription was doubled to $1.00, signaling the intended audience, even as an "introductory rate" kept the price at its old level.[34] Current subscribers were asked to submit names of friends, who were sent a "sample" three-month subscription. A special expanded issue was published in July 1907, coinciding with the major Bible conferences around the country, where representatives distributed free copies. A new name for the magazine would provide a clear break from the old format, but this proved a source of contention between the new editors. Gray dismissed the proposed titles "Christian Progress" and "Study & Service." He hoped Torrey would either accept his idea, "The Christian Tie," or suggest something else with "a little poetry & sentiment . . . [s]omething that appeals to the imagination just a little." When deadlock ensued, they were forced to launch with the old title in place.[35]

The *Tie*'s new content sparkled despite the old banner head. Its soothing editorial voice was calibrated to middle-class readers perplexed by the contemporary religious landscape. An initial editorial titled "Some Things We Believe" assured readers that the magazine was nonsectarian. Another editorial used current theories of "crowd psychology" to explain undesired election results and the spread of "unbelief" in traditional Christian doctrines, and to reiterate readers' "obligation of witnessing for Jesus Christ." Gray was generally pleased with the first effort, but he advised that future editorials be "thoughtful, terse, instructive, critical or playful as the situation calls, but chary of quotation."[36] Still, the initial reception was strong. Influential individuals were reading "the editorials with interest & profit," and Gray had heard there were evangelists in Philadelphia distributing their promotional materials and "urging subscriptions."[37]

Torrey and Gray displayed clear differences in their first contributions to the *Institute Tie*. Despite Torrey's reputation for combativeness, his column was a moderating influence. To the inquiry asking whether "the institutional church" was not "detrimental to the real work of the church as set forth in the New Testament" (a common dispensational attack on socially oriented church work), he insisted that physical and intellectual services "may be a valuable auxiliary" as long as they "are kept in thorough subordination to the spiritual." To skeptical questions about the YMCA, Torrey insisted, despite his earlier troubles with the Chicago branch, that "as a rule they are doing an immense amount of good." His monthly commentary began with the Gospel of John, the place he recommended all new believers begin their Bible study. The interpretations he offered were merely a starting point that "the student should carry . . . further for himself." Gray, in contrast, began with the book of Genesis, as he typically recommended, to highlight the orderly progression of God's grace through dispensational history. And though he, too, claimed the study was "not an exhaustive exegesis," it did explain "the real nature of the revelation of God as it unfolds itself from age to age."[38]

In the end, Torrey's and Gray's editorial differences were more complementary than contradictory. But Torrey would soon conclude that Crowell's changes in other departments were a more serious matter.

AFTER THE LAUNCH OF the new *Institute Tie*, Crowell turned his reforming eye to MBI's Education Department. These reforms would be among the trickiest to negotiate. To limit instruction to evangelistic techniques was problematic since they might be used to spread a radical message. But expanding into formal theological study was to raise suspicions that it had ambitions to become a seminary, or worse, that it was promoting sectarian beliefs. There was also internal resistance: a proposed set of minor curriculum changes the year before was strongly opposed by Torrey. Thus, in deference, Crowell's early reforms nibbled around the edges. He recruited new respectable faculty, including Howard W. Pope, a graduate of Yale University and Seminary, to be the superintendent of men. MBI also explored cooperative relationships with Wheaton College and the YMCA for supplemental educational offerings.[39]

But after the collapse of the Extension Department plan and amid new concerns over Pentecostalism, Crowell shifted his stance toward Torrey to something still civil but uncompromising. A revision to his "Plan of Operation" now included a sweeping set of educational reforms. Torrey's older nonlinear class schedule was replaced by a "graded" system that split coursework into introductory and advanced sections. Graduation now required a new capstone thesis. More professional, the system also better accommodated the sequential dispensational approach to biblical interpretation. Crowell also proposed to dilute Torrey's influence further by adding a third dean. Scofield's name was floated, but this was never implemented. Torrey protested these changes but continued to cooperate thanks largely to Fitt's diplomatic acrobatics.[40]

The keystone of Crowell's new educational reforms was a massive building project to facilitate MBI's professionalization. A new administrative building would provide proper office space, new classrooms, a gymnasium, hospital rooms (further distancing it from faith healing), and a 10,000-volume library. The old building would be converted entirely into a men's dormitory, and a second new building would replace the "seven old-fashioned dwelling houses" used by women students. New consolidated housing would improve efficiency while meeting the middle-class needs for "parlors or reception rooms," an auxiliary library, "chapel for devotional meetings," and "storage for trunks, accommodations for laundry work, adequate pantries, etc." These new facilities, Gray insisted, would improve "the development of the social and inspirational life of the students."[41]

Physical spaces shape the organizations they house. Crowell's new buildings signaled the end of the older MBI ethos under Torrey as part family-run business and part enlarged parsonage. The old building had combined the domestic, educational, and bureaucratic functions under one roof. Torrey's role as pastor of Moody's church next door meant the institute borrowed freely from its sacred space as well. The new plans imposed strict segregation between domestic, educational, and corporate space and carefully circumscribed sacred space. In fact, during the planning, both the Moody Church and Crowell's architect independently proposed a joint-use building. Since the church's primary space needs occurred on the one day that the institute did not hold classes, this was by far the most efficient and cost-effective solution. Still, Crowell rejected the idea and any direct connection to the church beyond occasional short-term ventures. Anything more suggested favoritism, even sectarianism, should the Moody Church go off the rails. And since Crowell had no authority over the church, he had no guarantees. But more to the point, he wanted MBI above the fray of local churches. He was positioning the institute as a new type of religious organization: a supplier without any ecclesial ties of its own.

Crowell's promotional expertise would be required to raise the $350,000 necessary for the building project, which was almost a third more than the original endowment. Crowell targeted wealthy philanthropists, as was typical. He contributed $50,000 himself and offered naming rights to anyone donating the full cost of a building. But he understood that contributors, like investors, exerted influence. Thus his plans outlined "principles to govern the raising of money" that included enumerating donors "who must not be appealed to."[42] He offered various "premiums" for donations that had specific theological content. By offering Gray's "How to Master the English Bible" or *Institute Tie* subscriptions, they induced ideological allies to give; perhaps convinced the open-minded to adopt MBI's theological position; or, as last resort, repulsed those diametrically opposed to their mission. Crowell also worked to diffuse donor influence by encouraging a broad support base of many middle-class donors of moderate means.

Crowell's fund-raising appeals took various tacks. He highlighted the potential to professionalize Christian work, for example, suggesting that MBI was creating "splendid workers with the right training." But a project of this magnitude also needed an overarching story to sell it. They settled on presenting MBI as the living representation of its late founding namesake and the building project as his Chicago memorial. To widely disseminate their message, they used press releases and other standard practices, along with the unusual strategy of planting "puff pieces" as legitimate news stories in the religious press. At one point, they contemplated hiring Hugh C. Weir, a reporter known for writing adventure and "real crime" stories and later a Hollywood screenwriter. The campaign would culminate with an elaborate anniversary-week celebration featuring "distinguished Bible teachers and preachers the world over" and, as a promotional coup, a building dedication on Moody's birthday in February marking the twenty-fifth anniversary of the institute's founding.[43]

There was only one problem. Crowell's timeline for fund-raising and construction required the Bible Institute to have been founded in 1886 so that the twenty-fifth anniversary would be in 1911. Yet every piece of letterhead of the last decade had proudly declared that MBI was founded three years later, in 1889. This was only a minor issue to Crowell; sacrificing historical accuracy to elicit an emotional response is a hallmark of modern advertising and the cornerstone of his Quaker-themed promotions. (In fact, they had briefly contemplated using 1885 before the building timeline was firm.) But such date changing was flatly dishonest to Torrey, who had the disastrous ten-year anniversary celebration in October 1899 indelibly burned into his memory. He wrote a heated protest.[44]

To Crowell's mind, Torrey's objection was just another problem to be solved, so he sent Fitt on a mission to find evidence that, articles of incorporation notwithstanding, MBI had been founded in 1886. Like a dispensationalist handling the Bible, Fitt "discovered" that the founding date was January 22, 1886. This was the day of Moody's iconic meeting where he publicly appealed to Chicago's business classes for funds. It was as close to February as possible and also positioned MBI on the side of law and order, with Moody prophetically warning of the social disorder that came to pass that May at Haymarket. But of course, this had been only one in a long line of such "announcements" stretching back to 1884 and forward to 1889. Torrey was unimpressed with Fitt's research. "It would be very nice if we could make the date of the Bible Institute coincide with Mr. Moody's birthday," he scoffed, "but in order to do that we would have to change history and that is a somewhat difficult thing to do."[45] Torrey's objections were lost on Crowell, who without further consultation with Torrey, proceeded to use the 1886 founding date on institute documents and promotional literature. Torrey protested the "deception," snidely asking "to know who the students were in 1886, [18]87, [18]88."[46]

By this point in mid-1908, Crowell was ready to make an uncompromising stand for control of MBI, regardless of who it alienated. Torrey fell first. In addition to the date controversy, his protest against going into debt for the new construction was ignored. Torrey then was notified that the Executive Committee had chosen Charlotte Cary to be the new superintendent of women. Torrey had hotly protested her nomination because she disagreed with him about the Baptism of the Holy Spirit, holding to a Keswick stance. His concerns dismissed yet again, Torrey suggested, as a last-ditch effort, that he return to his old role of superintendent—a position eliminated long ago. Even Fitt recognized the futility of his request. "The work has enlarged so much since those days," he diplomatically explained, "that I don't think one man could do what you [once] did." Days later, Torrey resigned, noting he "could not conscientiously continue when things were done of which I so heartily disapproved." Crowell asked Torrey to reconsider his resignation but without offering any concessions; he would remain only on Crowell's terms.[47] Torrey could cope with different opinions, but he could not bear to be ignored. His only remaining connection to MBI was his ostensible editorship of the magazine. This was precisely what Crowell wanted: Torrey's association without his input.

Five months later, Fitt also resigned, citing that MBI was "suffering from criticisms which point to me personally—my manner, my words, my letters, my acts," by persons "prominent in Christian work." He refused to name his accusers, but he also refused to "continue as a Christian worker while such criticisms remain unchallenged." Many were shocked at the resignation, including Will Moody. Torrey claimed he would not have resigned had he known Fitt's plans and feared it was giving unnamed administrators "a free hand to enjoy what others with great labor have built up." Given the state of MBI when Crowell first came, this was not entirely fair, but since Crowell had accepted Fitt's resignation without protest, it also was not entirely inaccurate. Rather than immediately filling Fitt's position on the Executive Committee, they gave his duties as executive secretary to Gray "until further action." In the meantime, Crowell and Gray served as an Executive Committee of two. Unencumbered, they set about developing MBI's corporate culture, revising its curriculum, and reorienting its theology.[48]

Crowell's hard line against Torrey was simply the final step in his transformation of MBI into a fully corporatized entity. As early as 1907, Crowell had implemented changes in what it meant to be an employee of MBI. When the director of the evening school, John Hunter, was called to serve as the part-time assistant pastor of Moody Church, Crowell denied the request. Despite ample precedents for this sort of personnel sharing, he explained that the work of "a tired man" with "divided interests and diversified thought" would not be done well.[49] New policies were implemented to control the outside engagements of institute employees; since "the highest welfare of the Institute" came first, even a person's Christian work had to be cleared by the Executive Committee. Vacation policy specified one month per year, during which "no work should be done, such as preaching, singing, writing, &c." Like other middle-class professionals, leisure was necessary; in fact, it was a "sacred" duty. There was no summer moonlighting. Since vacation time was time paid by the institute, any event "for which compensation is received" must "be paid into the Institute treasury as at other times."[50]

The last showdown with intransigent employees came right after Torrey's and Fitt's resignations. Daniel B. Towner was the long-standing head of MBI's Music Department. He had a decade-long career in secular music before becoming associated with Moody in the 1880s. A well-known performer, he was also a prolific gospel song and hymn writer and had compiled several best-selling hymnbooks. When an audit revealed that Towner was pocketing royalties on a new book, a four-month battle ensued. Towner claimed to be operating under a policy first set up by Moody himself and tried to leverage his reputation, threatening to resign if he could not maintain his royalties. The Executive Committee would have nothing of it; they made it crystal clear that his high salary came with the expectation of their having full rights to his work product, with no exceptions. His bluff called, Towner quickly backpedaled.[51]

With the last of the old guard, now corralled, Crowell wrote a note of uncharacteristic sentimentality to Gray. He was "deeply touched by several of your recent letters," he explained, and was convinced that God "has bound us together in the Institute for some great work. . . . He has cleared away everything that does not make for harmony that our course may be plain and straight." New "friends and supporters" are on the horizon, he assured Gray, and "we are about to enter upon a new era of prosperity and efficiency."[52] But not everyone was so sanguine about the changes. MBI was "paying higher salaries, spending more on advertising, doing more of an up-to-date business character than in the old days," Fitt wrote to the institute's business manager Aymer F. Gaylord, but it remained an open question to him "whether the present is as well-pleasing to God as the old."[53]

CROWELL UNVEILED YET ANOTHER project in October 1908, shortly after Torrey's resignation. A new foreign-mission department was designed "to make the Institute the greatest missionary educational center in America." In light of the "growing interest in foreign missions throughout the country, especially among young people," they saw a niche that MBI could exploit: educational opportunities for both currently active missionaries and new recruits. The center would include classroom and office space, as well as housing for missionaries on furlough. But the honeypot was a "comprehensive Missionary Library" of at least 5,000 volumes "kept thoroughly up-to-date, giving the need and condition of every country in the world, and the work of every missionary society." This alone, they estimated, would draw the estimated "600 to 800 young people" currently participating in various "Missionary Study Classes" into MBI's student body. In addition, the plan proposed a mission museum, holding "curios, photographs, etc.," that might "help to make foreign peoples and customs more real to students." A new mission course would include the standard Bible curriculum but also specialized mission "research work."[54]

The idea for the mission department paralleled many of the strategies Crowell first proposed for the Extension Department. It would increase institute enrollment and expand its influence with denominational bureaucracies.[55] Crowell and his people saw a twofold opportunity. On the one hand, they planned to service missionaries associated with denominational mission organizations. In fact, they made special provisions in the curriculum "to specialize" along whatever lines were determined "by his own denominational Board." But of course, MBI training would not be additive free. Denomination-specific training was offered alongside classes teaching a dispensational approach to the Bible. The other opportunity was to service missionaries not affiliated with a particular denomination. Many denominational missionaries complained that Pentecostals were wreaking havoc on the foreign field, arriving ill-prepared and unsupported and spreading controversial beliefs.[56] This, in turn, raised suspicion of all unaffiliated missionaries, even from "respectable" independent mission boards like the China Inland Mission. Thus MBI could serve as a validating agency for respectable independents, even as it forged connections to and exerted influence on denominational agencies.

The proposed mission department was capital intensive and reputation sensitive. To help with both areas, the Executive Committee sent an extensive prospectus to Mrs. Mary Borden, wife of the Chicago real estate baron and a close friend of Crowell's wife, Susan.[57] Much of the May 1909 issue of the *Institute Tie* was devoted to an introduction of the the mission department by its director, the respected missionary and missiologist Edward A. Marshall. The issue also included a page displaying the photographic portraits of its business and civic-oriented trustees.[58]

Appealing to denominational conservatives was a tricky business that required MBI to adhere strictly to respectable middle-class culture. A shift was detectable as early as 1905 in revisions to the school catalogs and bulletins sent to prospective students and donors. These promotional materials included a cursory note of MBI's proximity to "a teeming population of the middle and lower classes" to the west of campus, but then shifted focus eastward toward "one of the finest residential quarters in the city." Potential students were wooed with descriptions of the various libraries, museums, and parks of the city and noted its location a mere six blocks from Lake Shore Drive, "one of the most attractive promenades to be found in any large city of the country."[59]

Gray maintained a crisp corporate demeanor with students. He apparently never called anyone "by their first names even though he knew them well" and, unlike Torrey, "did not mingle in their social gatherings or outdoor recreations."[60] In 1908 he issued a stern memo on dress code laxity after having "observed members of the faculty during this warm weather sitting in their offices without coats or vests."[61]

Other changes were more substantial. In the catalog following Torrey's resignation, all references to the "Baptism" of the Holy Spirit were summarily replaced by "filling," and the year after that, "filling" was exchanged for a generic reference to "the developing and deepening of the spiritual life."[62] One annual report noted a lack of "outbursts of what might be called revival feeling" but suggested that "the growth of spiritual life and character has been more uniform and steady," and in one administrator's opinion, "more satisfactory."[63]

By the early 1910s, administrators had developed an elaborate "Policy Manual" dictating numerous aspects of institutional life and conduct. Many policies were written to maintain MBI's respectability and the corporate control of its image. The manual specified everything from schedules for cleaning restrooms to policies for married students who became pregnant. In the latter case, "due regard . . . to the proprieties in such cases" required that the woman "be cared for away from the Institute at the time of confinement." It dictated that employees should give no letters of endorsement for publications, specified how much detail to record about students dismissed from the institute, and delimited the narrow conditions under which male students might transgress the habits of "good breeding" and eat in the dining hall without coats (only so long as "they wear shirt waist and belt"). Students suspected of insanity should be brought to the house physician and, if their condition was confirmed, should be quietly admitted to the "Psychopathic Hospital" using "blanks for the purpose" that "are kept by the Superintendent." When contacting the afflicted person's relatives, care should be "taken not to use the word 'insane' in any telegram." "Women practicing on the pipe organs in the auditorium" should be "accompanied by a settled woman student." A "skilled dietitian" was employed to address complaints about food quality. Double rooms for men should have two beds. Vaccinations were required for employees. In some cases, specific sectarian organizations were outlawed, deemed "inimical . . . to the interests of the Institute."[64]

As the specificity of the policy manual suggests, the students and faculty were themselves a form of promotion for the institute. MBI served as a sort of test kitchen demonstrating the effectiveness and purity of its message. No longer conceptualized primarily as workers learning on the job, students were treated as products of the Bible Institute. Their work was important, but they must also model what it meant to be the thoughtful consumers of pure religion they wanted all believers to become. For this reason, it became increasingly important to screen applicants to the Bible Institute. Administrators increased education and age requirements, with mandatory remedial English courses when needed. It was also for this reason that Gray thought it important to counter the assumption that MBI attracted "only men or women of very limited educational attainments." In fact, one-third of recent or present students "were college-trained," he proudly declared.[65] By highlighting the college and seminary men, the attorneys, the businessmen, and the medical doctors enrolled at the Bible Institute, they were advertising that MBI's evangelicalism was appropriate for professionals.

In an increasingly racialized society at the turn of the twentieth century, the desire for respectability led to new racial restrictions for the student body. Although African American students could matriculate, a new policy implemented in October 1909 specified that they "be accepted on the condition that they board and room outside our buildings." A deeply offensive letter was sent to current students of color at this time, explaining that these requirements were needed to prevent "embarrassment . . . should white and colored students room and board together." It disingenuously assured them it was "motived [sic] quite as much by consideration for you as for any white brother" and insisted that the "comparatively few colored students" they enrolled (no doubt fewer after this policy) would be "heartily welcome." Racial logic of the lowest common denominator prevailed since "the relations between the races are different in different sections."[66]

Racial exclusion opened the way for MBI to reach a new constituency of "respectable" white southerners. It also allowed the school to benefit from the rampant racial coding of the time. In fact, the *Institute Tie* was already using those tactics to deal with the ongoing challenge of Pentecostalism. One article noted, "from recent personal observation of the Pacific Coast," that the tongues movement "has largely died out there" since those "affected with it chiefly are the colored people," and only a "few white people associate with them."[67] Racism was incorporated into calls for foreign missionaries. One graphic depicted highly racialized figures, representing different countries, whose height was made proportionate to the "size of the parish of each white missionary." A massive Sudanese man in a loincloth took up the entire foreground.[68]

As promotional objects, women students at MBI had their options increasingly circumscribed to the expectations of middle-class consumers. Preaching classes were exchanged for a series of "Special Courses for Women" covering "sewing, handiwork, cookery, home management and home nursing." By 1916 all women were required to take these classes, raising protests from some. This policy was modified in 1922, but only to exempt from the course those women demonstrating proficiency in domestic skills. No provision was made for women wishing to take preaching-oriented coursework.[69]

The *Institute Tie* reflected the new domestic orientation for women. One woman writer chided male preachers for exhorting women "to be true to their homes," but only because "they are going to be anyhow." Instead, the writer proclaimed, pastors should encourage women to reach "the higher planes of fellowship with Christ." She encouraged women likewise to study "the higher Christian life," and, defining her audience with subtle racial coding, she reminded them that the "blue eyes" of their children "are nothing as compared with white souls."[70] For women especially, a consuming faith, oriented toward domestic life, had drowned out calls to Christian work.

FOR THE COMFORTABLE BOURGEOISIE, MBI's new formulation of conservative evangelicalism was a viable alternative to the liberal theology produced increasingly by divinity schools and seminaries. A Keswick-warmed dispensationalism maintained the belief and practice of a personal relationship to God without Pentecostal excess. When a critic complained of the "mechanical" and "materialistic" nature of dispensationalism, MBI Extension worker L. W. Gosnell needed only to glance at "the corner of his library containing books on the Holy Spirit," which set "forth the highest spiritual privileges of the Christian life."[71] Keswick-infused dispensationalism offered a semblance of continuity to Moody's earlier evangelicalism. True, there were sacrifices to be made, most obviously a social component to their ministry. But on the whole, the safety offered by this new system, and its compatibility with contemporaneous modes of thinking, made it worthwhile. Those finding dispensationalism too complex need only accept its conclusions. Just as one need not understand the science of electricity to flip a switch, so ordinary churchgoers could trust the experts and devote themselves instead to the devotional piety that Keswick offered.

Thus Keswick dispensationalism addressed the needs of middle-class Protestants already committed to an evangelical orientation. But for Protestants outside these narrower networks, there was a larger chicken-and-egg problem that remained unresolved. Keswick dispensationalism was a historical novelty and as such seemed to many denominational conservatives like another form of sectarianism. It needed a history—a claim to orthodoxy. In the same way, Crowell and Gray wanted the Bible Institute to represent a respectable alternative to liberal Protestantism and churchly conservatism, but as a nondenominational institution, it had no established theological resources from which to draw. In fact, the past two decades of radical evangelicalism had only highlighted that the closest thing MBI had to a tradition, evangelical realism, was shifting sand. They were grasping for a nondenominational "orthodoxy"—a modern "old-time religion" that did not yet exist.

SEVEN

Pure Religion

Frank Hagerty was a dealer in grain, animal feed, and flour in Arch Spring—a now-defunct speck of a town in west-central Pennsylvania. He was a world away from Chicago, but he could not escape its products. The grain he sold, raised in the surrounding farmlands, was no doubt touched by McCormick farm equipment. He had probably also leafed through his share of Montgomery Ward or Sears and Roebuck catalogs. But on this spring day, the Chicago institution on Hagerty's mind was the Moody Bible Institute, to which he was writing a letter of thanks for a complimentary copy of the *Institute Tie*. It was a publication he "shall be glad to receive in the future," he explained, since he had "the greatest interest in the success of the work founded by Mr. Moody." Given this affection for the revivalist, it was a little surprising that his letter was not going to D. L. Moody's son Will in praise of the *Record of Christian Work*. But Hagerty had heard rumors "that there is danger of the Unitarian influence at Northfield." In contrast, he had "never heard such intimations about the 'Moody Bible Institute'" or that anyone associated with it had deviated from their promotion of "the whole Bible, the Atonement, and the Divinity of our Lord Jesus Christ." He enclosed a modest donation of eight dollars with a promise, if finances allowed, to "give more substantial aid" in the future.[1]

Moody's Northfield ministries were not the only worrisome institutions to conservatives in the first decade of the twentieth century. As fear of radicalism turned many respectable evangelicals in a churchly direction, they were surprised by what they found. Rather than a quiet haven to harbor the long-standing traditions of their denomination, they met new voices intent on aligning that tradition with a particular form of modernity. Perhaps it was an article in their denominational paper questioning the virgin birth of Jesus; or their church's young pastor discounting the Old Testament miracles; or their son, back from the denominational college, spouting Charles

Darwin. In each case, the institutions that were supposed to ensure religious purity seemed themselves to be infected with a new contagion. And it seemed to be spreading to nearly every respectable middle-class denomination across the country. Some, like Frank Hagerty, had already begun rallying around MBI or other institutions that they believed embraced the "Whole Bible." But many others felt isolated, perhaps totally alone, in their concerns.

What could be done to address the modernist threat? Lyman Stewart, an oilman from Los Angeles, believed he knew the answer. God had blessed him financially, and he was now ready to give back. He would sponsor a hard-hitting exposé of the "new theology," a sort of spiritual "muckraking," and then send it free of charge to every minister and Christian worker in the United States. It would spur a movement to purify the denominations of modernity's errors.

Stewart enlisted the help of Henry Crowell, but like many others who had done this, he would find that he had recruited a partner intent on controlling the project. Crowell had a very different idea about how to address the problem of modernism: not by religious journalism, but by developing a new theological product. It would be a modern orthodoxy compatible across denominations and rooted in an evangelical orientation. It was a project that was both combative and constructive, producing a nationwide coalition of conservatives who no longer completely trusted the theological judgment of their denominations. Once constituted, that group would require servicing. And so it would also be a permanent solution to the still-nagging question of why an institution like MBI was needed. The project, eventually known as *The Fundamentals*, would change the face of Protestantism in the United States.

Other projects to formulate a nondenominational "orthodoxy" had always failed in the past. But Crowell had new tools at his disposal that his predecessors did not, born of modern business. The project would succeed not by creating another traditional creedal orthodoxy but by replacing doctrine with the performance of orthodoxy facilitated by modern promotional techniques.

LYMAN STEWART WAS BORN in 1840 in Cherrytree, Pennsylvania, and raised by devout Scotch Presbyterian parents common on the west side of the state. He received a fifth-grade education before entering the family tanning business, but at nineteen he was inspired by Edwin Drake's success in the new business of petroleum. After several failures, an inauspicious military service for the Union army, and a few courses in finance and accounting at Eastman's Business College in Poughkeepsie, Stewart began his oil career in earnest. With his brother and lifelong partner, Milton, he made his first big claim in 1867 and soon was earning $1,000 per week. He married and seemed poised to enter a life of plenty. But some ill-advised investments left him bankrupt in the early 1870s, and he was forced into the ultimate humiliation of working on salary.

Stewart continued to struggle financially until he moved to the largely untapped oil fields of Los Angeles in 1882. Initially, this project also seemed destined to fail. Unreliable partners exacerbated the difficulties of unexpected geological formations. But by the early 1890s, his newly formed Union Oil Company finally took root and began generating healthy profits.[2]

Stewart shared a common stock of ideas with other modern business leaders, including Crowell. Both men were involved in combinations that tried unsuccessfully to limit production of their respective commodities. Both were stifled by middlemen that impeded their access to the end consumer. Both fought internal battles with more-conservative partners who resisted vertical integration and other modern organizational methods. Stewart even experimented with new uses for crude, from ink to lubricants, eyeing consumer products as a way to escape the tyranny of the open commodities market.[3]

But Stewart also held ideas, born of the boom-bust cycle of the oil business, that were markedly different from Crowell's. The nature of oil was capital intensive. It operated on high-stakes gambles that yielded high returns, not on incremental business that slowly accrued rewards. He was thus regularly forced to push Union Oil to the edge of bankruptcy and faced challenges to his financial liquidity even amid substantial wealth. In addition, both the price of his product and the shares of his company were subject to the fickle whims of the open market. He controlled Union Oil on the narrowest margin through a complex set of holding companies. Maintaining basic corporate governance often consumed significant portions of Stewart's attention. Though he apparently enjoyed the work, it came with generous portions of stress, fear, and exhaustion. Thus Stewart understood business as intrinsically unstable, in perpetual crisis, and as a Darwinian battle for survival.

The existential threat of Stewart's business operations was Standard Oil. He loathed John Rockefeller. It was perhaps born of a reasonable fear, but eventually it metastasized into an unfortunate sort of conspiratorial thinking. Stewart indiscriminately applied this reasoning to Roman Catholics and secret societies. And as Stewart divined Rockefeller's liberal religious proclivities from his rival's significant financial contributions, he drew similar conclusions about the dangers of theological modernism.

Stewart's conspiratorial tendencies were not helped by the timing of his new interest in religious things. Stewart had held a semblance of Moody's plain, practical, and personal Bible interpretation in the 1870s and in California had joined the local Presbyterian church and YMCA branch. But only when his business achieved some stability in the 1890s did he begin devoting himself seriously to religious causes. It was amid the concerns over social unrest in 1894 that Stewart first attended the Niagara Bible Conference, still operated by Moody's premillennial friends. He adopted an ardent doctrinaire premillennialism and embraced their warnings of "the great apostasy." James Brookes's journal, *Truth*, stood out to Stewart, especially its "note of warning" against those teaching the "error" of theological modernism. It was here that the idea first struck him to "[send] this magazine to all the ministers in America," though nothing became of it. He attended Moody's Northfield conference and embraced the many teachers there who combined dispensational Bible interpretation and Keswick holiness teachings. He returned to California with his personal faith reinvigorated and a new concern for "error" in tow.[4]

In the first decade of the twentieth century, Stewart began the process of methodically dismantling his substantial fortune and carefully distributing it to various religious causes. Like Crowell, he had felt called by God personally to earn money for religious ends. "Luke 12:33 was impressed very strongly upon my mind," Stewart recalled, especially its command to "Sell that ye have, and give alms." At the time, "I did not have anything, apparently, that I could sell, and the obligation was upon me for making provision for my family." But now he took the call seriously. After placing a "comfortable" amount in his wife's name, he began giving strategic donations that be believed would lay "deep, strong, spiritual foundations" on the West Coast. In 1906 his philanthropy included sponsoring a Los Angeles revival campaign led by Thomas Horton, an evangelist and Bible teacher most recently associated with John Wannamaker's Bethany Church in Philadelphia. But Stewart found he was unable to recruit any Christian lay workers to assist with the meetings. There was clearly a need for training in personal work, and the popularity of several Bible classes conducted by Horton convinced Stewart he had found his man.[5]

By 1908 Horton's work in California had evolved into a Bible institute that used MBI as its template. The Bible Institute of Los Angeles, known almost immediately as "Biola," was designed as a "city evangelization and Bible Training work." Horton gathered doctrinaire premillennialists to direct its operations. William E. Blackstone was hired as its ostensible superintendent, though he was often away on other engagements. His assistant, Robert A. Hadden, was thus more involved in day-to-day operations. Hadden was a popular dispensational Bible teacher and an early graduate of MBI. Stewart provided Biola with 1,000 shares of Union Oil stock as an endowment.[6] As he explained to Arthur P. Fitt, they were "endeavoring, in a small way, to copy it [MBI] in our own city." Through Hadden's connections to MBI, they collected all the bureaucratic instruments "used in the work" and requested "everything & anything that will be suggestive." But they attempted to borrow more than ideas from Chicago: Reuben Torrey, who was already contemplating leaving MBI by this time, agreed to consult for Stewart, while Hadden unsuccessfully recruited James Gray to teach.[7]

Stewart also began donating money to the Bible department of Occidental College in 1906, a relationship through which he experienced the "dangers" of theological modernism firsthand. Stewart had definite expectations that his $3,000 annual donation granted him the right to influence both hiring decisions and course content. The department director, John Baer, sought to appease Stewart, especially early on, but he was unwilling to compromise on his right to hire moderate- and liberal-leaning faculty, ignore dispensationalism, and preserve academic freedom. Stewart repeatedly butted heads with Baer and ultimately concluded that it was "a sin for a Christian to contribute to the support of Occidental" and warned others against it. Though Stewart's intransigence on such matters was no more ingrained than Crowell's, he had less patience and far less savvy. Direct confrontation and threats were his instruments of choice.[8]

Stewart's increasing frustrations with modernism were shared by a growing collection of conservatives across denominations. One of the leading voices was Amzi C. Dixon. The son of a North Carolina Baptist preacher, Dixon was converted under his father's preaching, studied law at Wake Forest, but then felt called to the ministry. Though he never finished seminary, he had a notable preaching ability that propelled him after 1877 through a series of pastorates northward to Brooklyn. His brother, Thomas Dixon Jr., had authored the notoriously racist novel *The Clansman*, which became the basis for the film *The Birth of a Nation*. Unfortunately, Amzi was also a staunch opponent of racial equality, though he couched his views in the "respectable" terminology of northern racism.[9]

At Moody's recommendation, Dixon devoted himself to preaching evangelistically and training Christian workers in the 1880s. He became an active proponent of a Keswick-style understanding of the person and ministry of the Holy Spirit. Rather than praying that the Holy Spirit "be poured out upon us" as at Pentecost, Dixon noted, it was better "to realize that he is already with us."[10] During Moody's Colombian evangelistic campaign in 1893, Dixon became concerned with the tolerant liberalism on display at the interfaith World's Parliament of Religion.[11] After this, his tack became combative, and he stridently opposed the social gospel movement, scientific evolution, and higher criticism. As a Baptist, he was particularly concerned with his denomination's flagship school, the University of Chicago. It had become a fount of modernist theology, funded with Rockefeller money.[12] His concerns only grew when he accepted the pastorate at the Moody Church across town in 1906.

In August 1909 Dixon was invited by the Los Angeles YMCA to speak on the dangers of liberalism. Stewart, amid his struggle with Occidental, attended. Dixon's talk was an extended critique of *The Function of Religion* by University of Chicago professor George Burman Foster. In a series of smart rhetorical turns, Dixon argued that the book, more than being unorthodox, was actually un-Christian.[13] Although Dixon's anti-Catholic bias remained undiminished, he observed that even Catholics were theists who believed that the Bible was God's revelation to humanity and in Jesus's deity. Dixon spoke of theological modernism like an infectious disease that threatened to destroy Christianity. He noted that Foster had in fact been an orthodox preacher only a few years before, but now the professor was claiming that "there is not a single Bible believer today" among either theologians or the educated laity. Dixon repudiated Foster's characterization, arguing that "many of the strongest, manliest men in the business world" believed that the Bible was "the inspired word of God." But how corrupt higher education had to be for Foster to have come to such a dire conclusion.[14]

Stewart saw himself in Dixon's "manly" cohort of true believers. He had fretted that modernist theology was infecting his denomination and even Moody's work at Northfield. He had agonized at the thought that Moody's son Paul was suggesting "pernicious literature of the Chicago University" to readers of the *Record of Christian Work*; what "a great grief to the true friends of Northfield," he lamented.[15] But now, thanks to Dixon's talk, he saw that it was a problem that extended beyond his own denomination and personal networks. It was pervasive across traditions and geographic boundaries. As with Stewart's business efforts, the time had come to take a substantial risk, with the potential of a massive payout. He had conducted smaller experiments in literature distribution—Bibles to Spanish-speaking Catholics; several thousand copies of Blackstone's premillennial defense, *Jesus Is Coming*; and complementary copies of the hard-line dispensationalist journal *Our Hope* to spur future subscriptions.[16] But now, he was ready for something greater, and he believed Dixon was the perfect man to head the charge. He felt "very deeply the importance of asking him for a personal interview," Stewart recalled. When the two men met, Stewart explained his idea: he wanted to create a new monthly magazine, tentatively titled "Testimony," to "set forth in attractive form the fundamentals of Christianity and correct the false teachings of the 'Destructive Criticism.'" Then he wanted to spend $300,000 to send it "to all the (English speaking) preachers, missionaries, and Bible teachers in the world." To Dixon, it was "of the Lord." *The Fundamentals* project had begun.[17]

DIXON IMMEDIATELY ALERTED MBI's Executive Committee to Stewart's plans upon his return. Gray was excited; he and Cyrus Scofield had been "talking and praying along the same line," he explained. Crowell also had demonstrated similar interests. Several years before, MBI had paid for Princeton Seminary president Francis Patton to give talks on the "Fundamentals of Christianity." And a month before Dixon approached them, Crowell and Gray had discussed a "series of tracts for wide distribution bearing the imprint of the Institute & dealing with the fundamentals of the faith as a counter-irritant to the current assaults upon it."[18]

Neither Crowell nor Gray seemed all that impressed with Stewart personally. A couple of years earlier, Gray had sneeringly referred "some rich oil king" associated with Biola and joked about creating "a trust of all these Institutes & set[ting] ourselves up as Bible Barons."[19] But $300,000 was nothing to smirk at, and they agreed to cooperate. Dixon was thrilled. He saw in the project a long-coveted opportunity to cultivate closer ties with MBI; his pugnacious southern style had apparently not sat comfortably with his next-door neighbors, who had rebuffed his earlier entreaties. But fighters were needed against the forces of modernism, and by aligning with Dixon, they would have direct access to the operations of this new project.[20]

Stewart laid out his vision for the project most clearly in a letter inviting his brother Milton to join him in what he called "the real business of the true Christian life." Denominational education had been corrupted, he explained, and thus was becoming a channel "of evil rather than of blessing." Poison poured into the Baptist and Methodist denominations by their flagship universities in Chicago and Syracuse. Both were funded, he noted, with Standard Oil money. And now Presbyterians seemed next in line. The "remedy" was to mobilize the faithful to clean up the channels. And this was done, as with other reform efforts, by sounding the alarm through the religious equivalent of muckraking journalism. He would rally the "orthodox" to take back their denominations in the same way that civic reformers mobilized "citizens" against political machines. The publication he envisioned would feature punchy, 2,000- to 4,000-word articles by leading conservative voices that would explain the dangers of modernism and promote the conservative alternative. Milton thought this was a spiritual investment opportunity worth taking and agreed to cover a third of the cost.[21]

The line between muckraker and crank was a fine one, and Stewart started making plans to ensure the new publication would be respectable. Though writers should fearlessly call liberals out for their many errors, he forbade name calling, even though their opponents said and did "things which otherwise would seem idiotic."[22] The reputations of the author would be important; thus any potential contributor "who has 'queered' himself before the church by giving at any time expression to unsound views" was to be eliminated from consideration.[23] But he also suggested they form an advisory board of "prominent ministers and laymen" from "the leading denominations." Purely symbolic, the board would nevertheless "insure a hearing from 'hide bound' denominationalists" who might otherwise ignore the project.[24]

Stewart designed the project as a top-down operation. No conference of conservative scholars was called; no denominations were queried for input. Rather, Dixon formed an organizing committee consisting of four men. He, Gray, and Torrey (at Stewart's request) met together, and William J. Erdman, the premillennialist former pastor of Moody Church, was consulted by mail.[25] This coterie compiled a list of about forty possible contributors who were in their judgment "true to Christ and the Bible."[26] They also created a list of possible topics, ranging from "The Personality of God," "The Testimony of Real Science to Real Christianity," and "The Second Coming of Christ" to attacks on various "Modern Apostasies." Then Dixon drafted a letter to potential contributors, outlining the project and requesting they choose a topic from the enclosed list.[27]

Dixon also gave Stewart an opportunity to weigh in on the committee's choices, encouraging him to veto any topic or contributor that did not meet his approval.[28] Stewart was not shy about making suggestions. He had Dixon add "The Personality of the Devil" to the list of topics and also suggested he add a column devoted to alerting readers to "unsound teachers." There were other "plain truths," he obliquely noted, that should be addressed as well. But he knew this would be controversial and recommended they not be mentioned until after "attention and confidence have been secured." At one point, Dixon offered to communicate through Giles Kellogg, a trusted ally of Stewart in both religious and secular work who was administering the donated stock, "so as not to burden you" with the mundane details of the operation. But Stewart would have none of it; he wrote hundreds of letters with suggestions ranging from adding more British contributors to specifications for type selection, paper quality, and margin size.[29] "I trust that you will not feel hampered by such suggestions as I may feel led to make," he wrote to Dixon, since the work "has been on my heart for years" and his financing of the project "will perhaps be the greatest work of my life."[30] As the holder of the purse, Stewart could not be ignored.

Yet Stewart's control was far from dictatorial. He designed the project, incorporated as the Testimony Publishing Company in Chicago, to be formally independent of his direct control. Convinced that "a strong and efficient organization" was needed, he specified a seven-member Executive Committee, structured like a modern corporation, so "that the death or disability of any one will not seriously interfere with the work."[31] Stewart declined to serve but selected four of its members: Dixon; Torrey; Elmore Harris, the Baptist founder of the Toronto Bible Institute; and Louis Meyer, a Jewish convert, Presbyterian evangelist, and ardent premillennialist based in St. Louis. He also asked the prominent attorney Philip Mauro to join the board, but he declined.[32] This left three positions open for Dixon to fill. Seeking to curry favor from MBI, he chose Crowell; Thomas S. Smith, a fruit wholesaler and MBI trustee whom Torrey later noted "is very closely connected with Mr. Crowell";[33] and a businessman turned Methodist evangelist D. W. Potter. All board decisions were made by majority vote.

Given Dixon's location, it made sense to base operations in Chicago, a decision that would have far-reaching implications on the project. Dixon selected Thomas Stephens, editor of the *Moody Church Herald*, to oversee

A group photo of the three major power brokers at MBI who also played a leading role in The Fundamentals *project: Henry Crowell (left), James M. Gray (center), and Thomas S. Smith. Crowell and Gray, especially, were largely responsible for putting MBI on a modern "business basis." (Courtesy of the Moody Bible Institute Archives)*

business operations. Both the business and editorial offices were located at Moody Church immediately adjacent to MBI's campus. But even more important, it meant that Crowell and Smith formed half of what Dixon called the "resident committee," a four-person majority block of the board in Chicago that exercised disproportionate guidance over the project. The other members scattered across the country were consulted by mail but rarely participated in the actual deliberations. So significant was Crowell's and Smith's influence that outsiders regularly confused them with the anonymous "two laymen" funding the project.[34]

Beginning with the first meeting, it was clear that the Executive Committee had a different vision for the project than Stewart. The Chicago committee, especially, envisioned the project creating a new interdenominational orthodoxy. They made a series of executive decisions about the project's future that transformed Stewart's muckraking ideal to a reference work. As

Dixon later wrote to Stewart, they thought the project's primary purpose should "be a positive statement of the fundamentals of Christianity." Instead of a monthly magazine, it should take a "book form," published quarterly, to "make it permanent and not temporary" and thus "secure it a larger reading from preachers." Instead of snappy articles attacking modernism, they envisioned a collection of scholarly, closely argued essays by leading theologians. As such, they did not need Stewart's suggested advisory board; rather, "the names of the writers on the cover will give it greatest weight." Stewart's title, "Testimony," also had to change to reflect its new purpose. The title "which most strongly impressed all the Committee" was "Back to the Fundamentals: A Testimony," later simplified as *The Fundamentals*.[35] Stewart trusted Dixon's instincts, but it seems that he did not completely understand that their proposed changes were altering his designs. At one point, for example, he asked how a monthly magazine could be issued in "book form."[36] In any case, he made no initial complaints.

But Stewart was quick to complain when he saw a newspaper article noting rumors of the project, and worse, that a Los Angeles–based donor was backing the endeavor. He had insisted that Dixon maintain strict secrecy about his involvement. This was not simply a matter of modesty; since all of his wealth and the donation itself was in Union Oil stock, any word that Stewart was seeking liquidity might either drive down the stock price or encourage attempts at hostile takeovers. Stewart was livid, both at the committee for leaking details of the financial arrangements and at Dixon for giving them that information in the first place. Torrey admitted responsibility for the leak. Unaware of the need for secrecy, he had been trying to "stir up the curiosity of people." Dixon apologized and assured more discretion henceforth.[37] In the end, the story went nowhere and a disaster was narrowly avoided.

Meanwhile, Stephens, the business manager, set about the task of organizing the massive project. Collecting, organizing, and updating hundreds of thousands of names and addresses, tracking expenses, and determining methods to measure the project's effectiveness was a massive bureaucratic undertaking. Much of the physical mailing and address maintenance was farmed out to third-party professionals,[38] but even still, the project would have been impossible without persons well-versed in business methods.

The task of determining who should receive the publication was left to the Executive Committee, with input from Stewart. The clear preference was to extend circulation as widely as possible. But it was cost prohibitive, even with Stewart's substantial donation, to send a publication to every English-speaking Christian in the world. Cost per copy, including postage, hovered between eight and nine cents,[39] limiting the circulation to several hundred thousand copies. To maximize their reach, they targeted religious leadership in hopes of creating a global mesh of recipients. If they could not reach each professing individual, perhaps they could get the publication in the hands of someone they knew. That way, each copy had the potential to influence tens, even hundreds, of additional laypeople, especially if, as Stewart hoped, they "preach[ed] sermons from it" or passed it on to friends after they read it.[40] Thus the organizers set out to track down every possible minister, missionary, seminarian and seminary professor, YMCA and YWCA secretary, and Sunday school superintendent. In addition, they collected the addresses of organizations—libraries, college-level Bible and theology departments, various "reading rooms," and religious newspapers and periodicals. As an experiment, Stewart also requested that copies be sent to about 3,000 Roman Catholic priests.[41] Their first list totaled about 175,000 recipients compiled from directories, denominational yearbooks, and sympathetic contacts inside denominations and other religious organizations. The mailing list was regularly updated and grew to over 300,000 addresses;[42] printing a single volume consumed two freight cars of paper.[43] Amid the idealism of the project, there was a striking realism in their calculations. Stewart acknowledged that, like all advertising campaigns, "only a small percentage of the whole" would be convinced; it was the sheer scale that made him hopeful it would be "a large number."[44]

Yet it was clear that the differing visions for the project led to a different understanding of *how* the publication would promote "pure religion" to its audience. Stewart's journalistic understanding lent itself to an older direct-marketing model. Like a mid-nineteenth-century druggist, he was merely getting the word out regarding the spiritual disease and its cure. As Stewart later recalled, the project's genesis came secondhand, after he had noticed the American Tobacco Company's marketing and believed that "the children of the Kingdom certainly should be as wise in their generation as the children of this world."[45]

But promotion was Crowell's bread and butter. "What the artist is to the picture, or sun to growing plant," one corporate insider waxed, "advertising has been, is, and will be to Quaker Oats."[46] During Crowell's twenty years in the business of marketing, his vision of its potential exceeded simply broadcasting a message; it could be used to gain and maintain market power. If he could successfully translate these techniques for a religious context, he could upend the religious world.

CROWELL USED PROMOTION TO several ends simultaneously at Quaker Oats. Most directly, it alerted consumers to the existence of his product, increased demand for oatmeal in general, and generated goodwill for the company. It created the public face, and a personal touch, for a faceless multinational corporation, as discussed earlier. But when promotion was combined with trademark and package, it accomplished something magical: it created a new commodity over which Quaker Oats had monopolistic control.[47]

The problem of overproduction that Crowell and other producers faced in the early oatmeal market was, more accurately, a problem of market power. Initially, oatmeal was one of many consumer goods that were undifferentiated commodities. In general stores and other retail outlets, oatmeal, like nails or sugar, was typically shoveled out of large barrels without reference to the producer. In these types of markets, wholesalers who controlled large distribution networks held the power when production exceeded demand. They pitted one supplier against another in a death spiral to unprofitability. Traditionally small retailers were also at the mercy of the wholesaler, especially before reliable transportation networks made product distribution less difficult.

The triad of package, trademark, and promotion shifted the balance of power from the wholesaler to the manufacturer. By selling Quaker Oats exclusively in two-pound packages, Crowell literally removed his product from the commodity stream. The trademark on the package granted a de facto monopoly. All that remained was to increase demand for that exclusive product. Using the latest technology and discriminating standards, Crowell ensured that Quaker Oats was the highest quality oatmeal on the market. (But never one to waste, he sold lower-grade product under off-brands or as animal feed.) Relentless promotion cemented the reputation of the product. Advertisements proclaimed its purity, and samples allowed consumers to experience it firsthand. Oatmeal might be acquired anywhere, but Quaker Oats, the new standard for quality oatmeal, was only available from Crowell.

Thus insulated from the vagaries of the market, Quaker Oats's promotional team could turn to "warning" against the dangers of the open market. The sealed package, emblazoned with the Quaker image, was an implicit contract with the consumer for oatmeal that was guaranteed pure. The open barrel, in contrast, had no such assurances. Who manufactured the product? What care was taken to protect the fragile contents in transit? Even worse, the open barrel in a retail establishment offered many stomach-turning possibilities. Quaker Oats promoters engaged in its own investigative reporting, offering stories of a retailer sitting "on the nice, soft flakes," pocket knife in hand, fingernail "trimmings falling into Rolled Oats to be retailed at 4 cents a pound." At another retailer, an open barrel in a "nice, warm, sunny window" was a perfect bed for a "Tabby Cat. Ten pounds of oats with cat hairs for 35 cents. Who wants the first ten pounds?"[48] In an age where "pure food" was of increasing concern for consumers, a sealed package that showed evidence of any mishandling was a powerful inducement.[49] If consumers found anything wrong with their product, they could write Quaker Oats directly, and the company would make it right.

There was an irony in a promotional strategy challenging the safety of the wholesale chain. In the early days of mass production, a product's distributors generated consumer trust. Since confidence was created through personal relationships, buying from an unknown manufacturer seemed like a risky proposition. What if something was wrong with the product? How could the consumer get redress? Wholesalers solved this problem. They purchased the products from manufacturers they knew, moved the physical product through their network of trusted regional distributers to local retailers (providing credit as needed along the way), and guaranteed the product they distributed. The difference between a suspicion-generating peddler and the respectable retailer lay in this chain of provenance brokered by wholesalers. The retailer personally knew his wholesaler and on up the line to the importer or manufacturer. Although consumers could not hold the manufacturer directly responsible, they knew that there was someone that could. By controlling this chain of trust, wholesalers held the power and reaped immense profits as a result.[50]

Leveraging media outlets, some now with national audiences, producers like Quaker Oats sidestepped the wholesaler and appealed directly to consumers. Clever advertising and free samples primed the retail pump. Consumers demanded Quaker Oats of their retailer, who did likewise to the wholesale representative. Branded goods held no upside for wholesalers, and so, not surprisingly, they resisted stocking them. But the brilliance of this strategy was that their opinion no longer mattered. With increasing competition in the wholesale sector, it would be impossible to completely shut out branded goods. As a stop-gap measure, Quaker Oats could serve as its

the "best" on the topic, but "because his name is the mightiest single personal force in Great Britain, back of any truth." The assessments of the first volume reflected their different understandings of the project. For Dixon, it was "worthy of being adopted as a text book on the Fundamentals of Christianity." Stewart admitted to its technical quality but worried "that unless the book is lightened up somewhat by articles of a more interesting character to the average reader, the book will not be attractive to as large a number as we are desirous of reaching."[59]

The differing visions for the project shaped the perception of the intended audience. The Chicago contingency imagined an audience of college-educated ministers and seminarians; Stewart perceptively understood that it would be difficult to "[reach] the 'higher-ups,'" but there were "many thousands of ministers who are very poor" with limited education and available reading material "who will receive Testimony gladly."[60] He also rightly perceived that hard-hitting exposés would have more appeal than scholarly treatises. This fundamental disagreement continued for the duration of the project. Stewart repeatedly complained that "an undue portion of effort" was given to "articles intended specially for the more scholarly" readers, failing to make "sufficient allowance for the lack of education and spiritual instruction among a very large portion of the Christian ministry."[61]

Whatever Stewart's misgivings, the subsequent response to the publication portended great things for the project. Conservatives produced a consistent flow of appreciative correspondence to the business offices. Stephens reported receiving "thousands of letters of unqualified commendation" after the first volume "from all parts of the country." The greatest appreciation was expressed by "pastors, and especially from students in various theological seminaries, indicating the great need and timely appearance of this book." In June, he was still receiving a "large volume" of responses to the first volume, far beyond Stewart's expectations. In fact, responses remained strong throughout the span of the project. In late November, Stephens reported receiving between 300 and 500 letters daily. A year and a half later, he was still reporting between 200 and 400 letters daily. In the fall of 1911, he estimated he had received 50,000 letters to date, half containing requests of some sort and the other half simply offering "heartfelt appreciation." The strongest response came after the ninth volume in early 1913. Stephens sent packages with hundreds of these letters for Stewart to peruse.[62] All told, the project elicited nearly 300,000 letters and cards. Stephens estimated that the substantial correspondence—not including mundane communication with the postal service, changes of address, and the like—weighed 1,800 pounds.[63]

The project leadership was encouraged by friends and opponents alike. A favorite letter came from a liberal minister accusing them of setting back "the progress of the Kingdom" by making "it more difficult for the world to accept the general principles of Biblical criticism."[64] Someone associated with the project responded that "your letter of criticism gave me greater pleasure than almost any letter of appreciation" since it "clearly proved, first, the necessity of sending out the volumes" as well as "the fact that the Lord is using and blessing our feeble efforts." "To us of the Orthodox School," it explained, higher criticism "is nothing but shear infidelity"; inasmuch as they were "hindering the spread of it, we are profoundly thankful to God."[65]

The "resident committee's" strategy favoring scholarly reputation over an author's precise theological alignment proved prescient. "I am as a rule suspicious of publications which are sent free," one anonymous correspondent reported, since "they usually proceed from cranks." But "the names of the contributors" left the letter writer "immediately reassured," and upon reading the first volume, he or she felt "the book leaves nothing to be desired."[66] An admiring editorial in the *Christian* reported "preachers of various denominations have told us with what gratitude they have come into possession of copies of the book."[67] Some ministers began using the volumes for Bible studies.[68] Another correspondent reported that the wife of a former governor had organized reading groups for "high society" women.[69] At least two other magazines reprinted full articles from *The Fundamentals*, to Stephens's delight.[70]

Throughout the outpouring of correspondence ran a repeated refrain that suggested the most important outcome of *The Fundamentals*: the work created an imagined community of Protestants united in their opposition to theological modernism. Stewart mused after reading a bundle of letters that many recipients, "like Elijah," felt "that they alone were standing for the old truths." But upon "finding that there are many other loyal men gives them renewed courage."[71] A missionary in British Columbia wrote how "ordinary men," before *The Fundamentals*, were "fenced around with great learning and scholarship," such that they "shrunk from attempting any attack" on higher criticism.[72] But no longer; embattled conservatives had found their people.

DESPITE STEWART'S HOPES TO the contrary, the project followed the template of the first issue for three additional volumes. A parade of respectable conservative scholars wrote highly technical articles attacking higher criticism and defending a handful of subjects uniting churchly and evangelical conservatives: the deity of Jesus, the Virgin Birth, and the Incarnation. The only relief from weighty considerations "the tabernacle in the wilderness" or "the recent testimony of archeology to the scriptures" was the occasional personal testimonies and a snappy list of "tributes to Christ and the Bible by brainy men not known as active Christians."[73]

By the fourth volume, even sympathetic observers were noting a problem. The common ground between thoughtful conservatives and the corporate evangelicals organizing the project was so narrow that it had already been traversed several times over. A reviewer for the *New York Observer* insisted he marched "shoulder to shoulder" with *The Fundamentals* on "the Bible and of doctrine" but could not help suggesting that perhaps "only one paper, instead of five, on the inspiration of the Scriptures" would suffice. More articles should be devoted to "other fundamentals of Christianity" of "equal prominence." As it stood, by obsessing too much "upon one 'fundamental,'" they threatened to harm its reception among "thoughtful readers."[74]

But therein lay the rub: beyond the narrow confines already considered, there were few subjects that would unite every conservative Protestant. Missouri Synod Lutherans recommended that *The Fundamentals* address "Original Sin, Free Will, the Means of Grace, and the Origin of Faith"— topics sure to alienate Arminian conservatives.[75] Stewart's evangelical allies were similarly unwilling to compromise their obtuseness for the sake of a broader audience of churchly conservatives. "The subject you assign to me does not appeal to me," C. I. Scofield sniffed in response to one of Dixon's suggestions. Instead, he offered to write several articles setting "forth the distinctive messages of Paul, to show that which is revealed only through him," though such a series would have only appealed to the dispensational faithful.[76] To Stewart's carping for an article on prophecy, Dixon replied he had received but one submission, and it was so "meagre" that he discarded it.[77]

Financial difficulties added to Stewart's discontent. The depressed state of the oil-securities market and an ongoing price war with Standard Oil was creating liquidity problems. He began debating ways to cut costs, floating the idea that they continue sending the publication only to those requesting it. But Stephens warned against that course; the incoming correspondence suggested that many were now appreciative of the work who had once been suspicious.[78] The "resident members" of the committee agreed and strongly recommended against Stewart's suggestion. The design of the project was to create "a reference" that pastors would turn to "when they have questions." Forcing recipients to request future copies would cut down on its overall effectiveness. It was Stewart's money, but to make such a change, he would be forced to explicitly overturn the committee he appointed to oversee the project. Dixon followed up with an additional inducement. He assured Stewart that the committee would let up on the subject of "destructive higher critics" after the fourth volume and turn "to positive statements of the Truth." This, Dixon tantalizingly promised, would include "prophecy, the doctrines of Grace [dispensationalism], the Second Coming of Christ and answers to modern apostasies." Stewart relented and, in preparation, began appealing to Scofield for articles on prophecy and dispensationalism.[79] But Dixon would not be around to see through on his promise to Stewart. After the fifth volume was published, he accepted a call to the Metropolitan Tabernacle in London and resigned his editorship.

Stewart took the disruption as an opportunity to try to recapture the project's balance of power from the "resident committee" in Chicago.[80] Dixon's departure became a convenient excuse to expand the size of the Executive Committee to eleven, and to expand the committee's responsibilities to approving content. He handpicked the new members, including his Biola superintendent and close ally Thomas Horton.[81] He appointed Louis Meyer as the "executive secretary" and head editor. Meyer would send potential manuscripts to the entire committee, and "those approved by the largest number of the members would be published." This proved to be too unwieldy to be practical, and so they decided Meyer should send each potential article to four committee members of his choosing. If anyone raised an objection, it would automatically be sent to everyone for a vote.[82] Stewart also took the opportunity to create a subcommittee on finance, which consisted of Crowell and Thomas Smith. Whether he was trying to limit their influence to business matters is not entirely clear, but both still made recommendations on manuscripts.[83]

With Meyer taking the lead, it appeared that Stewart was back in the driver's seat. The reorganization broke the power of the Chicago committee, moving the editorial offices to St. Louis and placing Stewart on par with Crowell. Indeed, amid the transition, a puzzled Meyer wrote to Stewart about Dixon's repeated references to decisions of "the Committee." Whatever Dixon meant, Meyer flatly asserted, "I am sure that it is not the Committee of which I have been a member." Stewart took other steps to shore

Project organizers felt especially pressed to address two sects. First on the docket was the "Millenial [sic] Dawn," known as the Jehovah's Witnesses. This was especially troubling to conservative evangelicals for its claims to a simple biblicism and its focus on the end times. In fact, Biola was repeatedly mistaken as being part of the movement by FBI agents investigating the sect during and after World War I. A clear line needed to be drawn. Moody's old associate, seminary president and ardent premillennialist William G. Moorehead, cleverly highlighted the sect's resonances to liberal Protestantism. Both belief systems asserted that Jesus "was not Divine" and that "his atonement was exclusively human, a mere man's"—and thus his "resurrection" was merely spiritual since "His body was not raised from the dead."[93] A similar tack was taken with Christian Science, which they called "Eddyism" after its founder, Mary Baker Eddy. A common form of metaphysical healing among the middle-classes, the phrase "Christian Science" was sometimes used to refer to any sort of faith healing or belief in answered prayer. But these resonances were ignored. Instead, author Maurice Wilson made it too sound like a liberal analog. It was based in the desire "for a comfortable life here" rather than in the hereafter. It taught that God is a "principle" rather than a "person," that traditional prayer mistakenly treats God as human rather than divine, that sin is an illusion, and that the atonement is "the exemplification of man's unity with God." Jesus was not resurrected; rather, he hid away in the tomb.[94] To oppose these "dangerous" sects thus required that liberalism be rejected as well.

It might seem strange that a project attempting to formulate "old-time religion" would tackle economic subjects, but two articles were included to ensure that, whatever this "orthodoxy" was, it would be compatible with modern consumer capitalism. One article, written by the venerable editor of the *Missionary Review*, Arthur T. Pierson, aimed to explain Jesus's "ethical system on the subject of money." But more than anything, it was a demonstration that a dispensational approach to the Bible made its "plain" interpretation safe for the modern middle classes. Rather than looking for particular commands in the text, Pierson sought the general "principles" of Jesus's teachings. For the sake of convenience, he claimed, readers could simply refer to II Corinthians 8 and 9, where these ideas were "gathered up and methodically presented by Paul." By his rendering, Jesus's economic principles were in complete harmony with modern capitalist assumptions. God owns everything ("the principle of stewardship"), and therefore to challenge inequality was to challenge God's decisions. In fact, God gives much to those who have proven themselves faithful and trustworthy (the "law of recompense"). Moreover, poverty might be caused by spiritual deficiencies. The "principle of investment" reinforced the secular practice by spiritual analogue and, with it, the reliance on investment experts. Jesus's famous command to a wealthy man to give away all he owned was re-rendered. It was not because "having great possessions . . . was wrong"; rather, it was because the man's "'trust' was in riches." But the lion's share of the article sidestepped knotty ethical issues altogether. It focused instead on the proper principles of charity, like giving generously to missions.[95]

A second article, "wisely written" in Stewart's opinion, was titled "The Church and Socialism." In it, Charles Erdman tackled the social gospel movement directly. It was considered to be so important by both Torrey and Stewart that it found its way into a volume otherwise devoted to evangelism.[96] Erdman showed a certain level of sophistication in his treatment of socialism. He acknowledged that as an "economic theory," abolishing private capital was not necessarily incompatible with Christianity. Yet he eliminated from consideration a Christian socialism as an unholy amalgamation that violated both socialism and Christianity, and he dismissed the social gospel as "discard[ing] the fundamental doctrines of Christianity" for "a religion of good works." He also sidestepped the most salient socialist critiques of capitalism by claiming it belonged to a "social creed offered as a substitute for religion." His understanding of the Bible's economic message was deeply regressive. Jesus's teachings had no more to do with "questions of political economy . . . than with those of physical science." Thus the church had no right to dismiss economic laws on moral grounds, just as it had no right to dismiss natural laws. The socialism practiced by the early church was "designed to meet a special crisis"; it was not "an abiding principle of Church life." Moreover, the scriptural admonitions to masters and slaves should be applied to owners and employees. Economic morality was limited to individual choices. "The hope of the world is not in a new social order," he concluded, "but a kingdom established by Christ."[97]

WHATEVER STEWART'S SATISFACTION WITH the publication, by 1913 he was positively impatient that his long-standing requests had not been fulfilled. He was still waiting for an article by Scofield on "Law and Grace" and an article "on the subject of 'Prophecy, Fulfilled and Unfulfilled.'" Meanwhile, many dangers remained unaddressed, including "the great peril to the church from secret societies" and "the false teaching and political ambitions of Roman Catholicism." He was not shy in reminding Meyer that "these were the things that largely influenced me originally in the undertaking of what has resulted in The Fundamentals." To exclude them was to thwart the reason for Stewart's donation.[98] Meyer promised that subsequent volumes would have doctrinal teaching and exposés of spiritualism, Romanism, and secret societies and would include a list of recommended books. The final volume, he promised, "will be limited to articles on 'Prophecy,' or rather 'the Premillennial Return of the Lord.'"[99]

A month after this promise, in March 1913, the elderly Meyer fell ill. In June, his wife informed Stewart that Meyer had lost his mental capacities.[100] This meant that Stewart needed to find another editor to complete the series. Stephens thought that Stewart had the right to choose someone "more inclined and more able to carry out your wishes." Since Stewart was "the man to whom God has given the vision" and funds to pay for the project, it was only right that he help shape its "editorial character." He recommended Scofield, but Stewart worried that he was too busy to be reliable. Instead, he chose Torrey, who was close at hand and eager to please.[101] He also chose another Californian, Presbyterian minister and college president John Balcom Shaw, to replace Meyer on the Executive Committee. It was a choice that left a number of people in Chicago "aghast." Those opposing the choice never explained themselves at the time, but it was surely related to rumors that precipitated Shaw's trial for sodomy in 1917. Whatever the case, Shaw was another reliable vote for Stewart's interests.[102]

The contents of the final volumes under Torrey's direction confirm his amenability to Stewart's wishes. In fact, he reverse engineered the approval process by first learning what articles Stewart wanted published and then selecting four members of the Executive Committee he thought would approve them. Thus these final issues were aligned closest with Stewart's true intentions for the project. He finally got an article from Scofield on "Grace"—a piece practically indecipherable for those unaccustomed to dispensational teaching.

Torrey's greater success as editor came by his administration of the project rather than its contents, but at a significant cost: it irreparably damaged Stewart's relationship to his Chicago allies. Stewart had originally assumed that The Fundamentals, conceived as a muckraking exposé, would seamlessly transition to a traditional subscriber-based magazine. But when the project took on a more book-like character and a quarterly distribution schedule, he began making contingent plans to offer subscriptions to Biola's new magazine, the *King's Business*. Started in 1910, it was nearly identical to MBI's magazine, especially after Torrey became its chief editor in October 1912.

Stewart requested access to *The Fundamentals* mailing list in January 1913 to begin sending sample copies of the *King's Business*. Stephens expressed clear discomfort. Some addresses had been shared with the explicit understanding that they would be used for no other purpose. Stephens ran the idea by Crowell and Smith on the finance committee. Their ruling—no doubt related to the advantage it would give Stewart's competing magazine—was that it would smack of "commercialism." Meyer, seeking a compromise, thought Stewart could use the list as long as its scope remained west of Denver to avoid "encroaching upon the sphere of other Bible Institutes." But Crowell and Smith would not budge. If Biola wanted such a list, they must gather it themselves.[103]

Stewart backed down, expressing his pleasure that the committee was "so loyal to its rules," but he then immediately formed plans to get around these objections.[104] Claiming financial difficulties, he insisted that the last three volumes would be sent only to those who sent in a coupon that would be enclosed in the ninth volume. By his reasoning, he would have a right to the resulting list. He had technically gotten it of his own accord, with each recipient freely contacting him. Catching wind of Stewart's plans, Crowell and Smith strenuously objected. Crowell wrote to Stewart directly, using his best political charms. Stewart must have foreseen "just such crisis as the present one," he noted, "and realizing the weakness of human nature," he therefore invested authority in the committee. But Stewart ignored these charms. His proposal was neither a crisis nor "commercialism," but "a perpetuated testimony," pure and simple.[105]

To ensure that Stewart would get his mailing list, Torrey then orchestrated an Executive Committee coup. In August 1913 he convened a meeting of the committee at his summer home in Montrose, Pennsylvania, under the guise of mundane editorial business so that Crowell and Smith would not bother to come. Then, without Moody Bible Institute representation, he pushed through a raft of administrative decisions, first officially transferring control of the project materials, the remaining Union Oil stock, and the mailing list to Stewart and then forbidding use of the mailing list by anyone without unanimous consent, effectively denying MBI access.[106] Crowell was furious, but there was nothing he could do. After this, Torrey was so despairing of the committee's disunity that he was ready to continue the fight against modernism without it.[107]

But in the end, even Torrey would not deliver everything Stewart wanted. With time short, Stewart had insisted that "two subjects, which we had in mind from the very outset" and were "of the greatest importance," be included: a warning against secret societies and an article by Scofield addressing "The Jew in Prophecy." He was convinced that Scofield's contribution would not only make "the great truths of the Scripture very real" but also dramatically "increase interest in the Study of the Scriptures." He told Torrey to scuttle an already-agreed-upon issue devoted to personal evangelism in order to create room. But by the time Stewart had communicated his desires, it was too late to change without incurring significant additional expense and delay. And since Stewart was now funneling his sales of Union Oil stock to his brother so as not to lose control of the company, he admitted defeat.[108]

An article on secret societies, written by Charles Blanchard, suffered a similar fate. Problems began when Torrey accidently chose Thomas Smith to review the article. Perhaps still stinging from the mailing-list debacle, Smith objected to its contents, forcing a review by the entire committee. "I knew that he was opposed to secret societies," Torrey apologetically explained to Stewart, but he "is very much affected by Mr. Crowell's judgment of things."[109] To Stewart, it revealed that the MBI contingency did "not fully comprehend what the real purpose governing The Fundamentals has been," at least according to his own intentions.[110] And apparently, neither did Torrey: days before the final volume went to press, he nonchalantly wrote to Stewart to say that he was dropping Blanchard's article because, upon further review, he considered it to be "a weak presentation of the case . . . very wordy, very carelessly written."[111] Stewart pleaded with Torrey to revise it as he wished but to include it, but his letter arrived too late for Torrey to comply.[112] Stewart would later send out a supplemental pamphlet on secret societies to The Fundamentals mailing list after the final volume. But few took note then, and fewer remember it now.[113]

Crowell remained unappeased. He was rarely bested in political wrangling and seems never to have forgiven Stewart for beating him. Though collaboration on The Fundamentals project dramatically improved Torrey and Gray's relationship, Crowell's anger festered until Stewart's death in 1923. Even a year after The Fundamentals project was complete, Gray was forced to hastily wire Torrey, withdrawing an article he had sent to the King's Business. He was compelled to do so by the protest of "two of our trustees who were on the Fundamentals committee," he apologetically noted.[114]

WHAT WAS THE LONG-TERM impact of *The Fundamentals*? By traditional religious measures, one could argue that the project was a failure. Theologians, denominations, and even future fundamentalists largely ignored its contents. Its focus on higher criticism was too narrow, many of its particular concerns were too dated, and its writing was too technical for all but the most patient readers to plow through. As a fundamental declaration of faith, it somehow lacked both comprehensiveness and coherence. The formation of the Executive Committee created no new alliances and strained some that already existed. The project did nothing to unite the diverse contributors; they never sat in the same room nor had any contact with other authors. In some cases, "contributions" were simply articles repurposed from other sources with the authors' approval.

Yet *The Fundamentals* was not a failure. It left a substantial fourfold legacy. First, the project created a substantial mailing list of self-selected conservative ministers and religious workers. Stephens was still sending out a not-insignificant 85,000 copies of the eleventh volume and predicted a slight increase for the final volume.[115] These names were free for Stewart to use after the project was completed.

Second, the publication created a group identity for isolated conservatives and evangelicals. No longer alone, they now felt like they were part of a larger nationwide community. This gave them the courage to fight even if they were the only fundamentalist in their town. And they in turn influenced a broader circle of laypeople and ministers. If each of these newly minted fundamentalists articulated their "fundamentals" differently, they were united at least in the conclusion that theological modernism was not only wrong, but not even Christianity.

Third, *The Fundamentals* as an artifact provided a means of identity formation. It was a powerful totem, especially when, immediately after the final volume was published, Torrey set about editing a handsome four-volume edition that was organized by topic for easy reference. Whether or not they got any use, these books were a means to identify with the movement to "reclaim" the "fundamentals."[116]

A final contribution of *The Fundamentals*, a trial run for creating and recreating a modern "old-time-religion," was arguably its most important. By 1910, advertisers were already adept at creating "old-fashioned" reputations for new corporate entities. They used emotional association, sentimentality, and references to "good old days" that never actually existed. This was Quaker Oats's bread and butter, whether through its jolly Quaker character or in the racial key of the Aunt Jemima brand it purchased in 1926.[117] *The Fundamentals* worked the same way. It was not a substantive creedal formula for "old-time religion" but an enactment for modern times. Fundamentalism was not the inscription of particular doctrinal beliefs on the minds of its readers; it was an empty reference for an "orthodoxy" that followed the contours of a conservative evangelical orientation, a theological vessel that individuals could fill with their own doctrinal particulars. There were limits to its elasticity, but as anthropologist Susan Harding smartly observed, it functioned as a discursive form in which one talks about the faith.[118] *The Fundamentals* offered signposts and served as a center of gravity for an evangelical "orthodoxy" that was impossible to capture in creedal form. This means of creating, and seamlessly re-creating, "traditional" religion—always fresh and always relevant—came by business methods.

The fact that *The Fundamentals* project was not overwhelmed by hardline dispensationalism, doctrinaire premillennialism, or rambling conspiratorial speculations about secret societies was ultimately due to contingent factors: the busyness of potential authors, available funds, and healthy amounts of miscommunication, misplaced manuscripts, and dumb luck. Yet there was a method to the project's madness, one that was perfected and then regularly repeated over the next century.

Uniting a diverse coalition of evangelicals and churchly conservatives required a new orthodoxy that had a fabricated reputation, a patina of tradition, and the appearance that it could coexist with distinctive denominational beliefs and practices. In this way, *The Fundamentals* completely revolutionized the nature of "orthodoxy" across nearly every denomination using seemingly conservative materials. In so doing, it served as a scaffold for the movement, but once that movement took on a life of its own, no one noticed that the scaffolding had collapsed.

EIGHT

The Name You Can Trust

"A Cosmopolite" and "a National Layman"—so the Presbyterian newspaper *Continent* characterized Henry B. F. Macfarland in 1913. His varied and distinguished career gave ample reasons to agree with this claim. Macfarland certainly had a distinguished career. He started as a political journalist and became one of the founders of the famous Gridiron Club. In 1900 he was appointed by President William McKinley to be president of the commissioners (mayor) of the District of Columbia. He implemented many municipal reforms of the "city beautiful" movement. He then began a third career in law, which already reaped "a number of notable cases to his credit." All the while, he continued faithfully, but quietly, engaging in lay religious work as a Sunday school superintendent, a church member, and a member of the boards of organizations like the Red Cross. Though a "familiar of Presidents and statesmen," he was "first of all a Christian" whose "faith has been the dynamic of all his activity."[1]

Thus when Macfarland claimed to "know what many laymen are now thinking," a broad swath of America's elite thought him worth listening to. It certainly generated excitement when he made this pronouncement at a 1918 conference in Philadelphia. No ordinary gathering, this was the fourth and last of the great premillennial prophetic conventions that began in 1878. "The intelligent world" had once believed it was bringing "its own millennium," he explained, led by German-trained "men of science and philosophy." But the Great War that still raged had "shattered" this hope, revealing "the real character of Germany" and leaving the world to search "for a new theory." That theory, he argued, was premillennialism.

Even secular people hoped for "an appearing of God, as the only One who can help," Macfarland claimed. His friend John Mott had told him that although the pulpits in Europe were silent on the subject, the laity regularly expressed "their hope that the Lord Himself may return to set all things right."

Thus the second coming of Jesus had become as important as his first, "the most important subject before the American people and the world today."[2]

Given the context, it is hard to blame Moody Bible Institute's leadership for thinking that premillennialism would spur a revival of conservative evangelicalism and sweep away the modernism they opposed. *The Fundamentals* had introduced premillennialism to conservatives as a bulwark against encroaching higher criticism. And now, it seemed, the "intelligent" world understood that naturalistic philosophy and evolutionary science was too unstable to support civilization. The nation needed the certitude and stability of their dispensational approach to scripture, motivated by Christ's imminent coming, to tackle the threat of political radicalism at home and abroad. MBI was ready to help provide training, guidance, and organization for that work. But by the early 1920s, it was clear that they were mistaken. They had miscalculated the stability of their message, the nature of their audience, and their ability to control the fundamentalist coalition they helped muster. Soon they would be in full retreat and fighting even to maintain their claim to the name evangelicals trusted: Dwight L. Moody.

BIOLA BLOSSOMED INTO AN important center of West Coast fundamentalism—an ironic outcome given Lyman Stewart's earlier principled premillennial stance "that it was a serious mistake to put the Lord's money into brick and mortar." In 1910 he had contemplated facilitating "a chain" of independent but loosely "affiliated institutions" that would train "a large force of consecrated workers" without significant overhead.[3] But he was finally "forced into" building up Biola. Once committed, he did things right, so much that his buildings elicited accusations of "extravagance" by MBI trustees. Stewart thought Henry Crowell's decision to pave MBI's new administration building with marble gave him little ground for such critiques.[4]

Stewart also strove to develop Biola's presence in print by the *King's Business*, a project greatly assisted by his possessing a mailing list of almost 100,000 self-selected fundamentalists. Sample subscriptions instantaneously made the *King's Business* a leading voice of the movement. Stewart took the leading role in its design and contents. He demanded a "definite dispensational character to indicate just where the institute and the *King's Business* stand."[5] Whether its readers were dissatisfied with the contents or unable to afford the subscription, circulation dropped precipitously when the free distribution ended. By the summer of 1918, it had only 5,000 subscribers. Stewart's solution, as always, was more articles on prophecy.[6]

Biola's biggest hurdle to national prominence was geographic isolation. Although the opening of the Panama Canal in 1914 and constant improvement of rail lines helped considerably, it would be another decade before California became a significant cultural rival to points east. The clearest demonstration of this was the underwhelming "World's Bible Conference" organized by Stewart and Reuben Torrey. It was designed to coincide with printing the final volumes of *The Fundamentals* and the 1915 World's Fair in San Francisco, the Panama-Pacific International Exposition. But they could persuade few of their allies to make the trek. In the end, scheduling complications and construction delays at Biola resulted in a disappointing conference, largely forgotten to posterity.[7] Biola's national prominence would grow in the 1920s, but even then it was overshadowed by the likes of Aimee Semple McPherson, who embodied a West Coast style and the use of dramatic flair and celebrity culture for religious ends—a better portend of evangelicalism's future.[8]

Thus MBI became the dominant institution among fundamentalists in the 1910s. As *The Fundamentals* project had plodded on, MBI leaders had worked behind the scenes to capitalize on the new constituency the publication created. Preparations began in 1909, when Crowell maneuvered the Bible Institute Colportage Association (BICA) into a closer relationship, adding himself and Thomas Smith to its board "to 'bridge' the interests of both organizations" and "secure . . . the highest efficiency in co-operation and singleness of purpose."[9] With MBI's resources, the BICA increased its office space, enacted new business strategies, and added new books to its catalog by leading fundamentalists like Torrey, James Gray, and others. It produced new tracts—short essays designed for evangelistic purposes and sold in bulk for free distribution. The recently acquired tract series by faculty member Howard Pope had wide appeal in mainline churches; one denominational board acquired 96,600 items over a year.[10]

A rebranding of MBI's magazine, *Institute Tie*, was made easier after Torrey resigned his nominal editorship.[11] Its new title, the *Christian Workers Magazine*, was announced in October 1910 and reflected that its reach extended to "Christian workers generally" without other connections to MBI. But Moody's son Will saw a more devious reason for the title change. "Possibly I should not have written as I did," he half-apologetically explained to MBI business manager Will Norton, "but there was a very definite statement made to me" when the *Tie* was started that it would not "enter the general religious field." The new name, by his estimation, was an obvious attempt "to try to come as near to calling it the RECORD OF CHRISTIAN WORK as possible."[12] Intentional or not, MBI's magazine had everything to gain by the confusion. With Torrey gone, it was transitioning from a personality-driven publication to one where the corporate entity itself embodied a distinct and independent reputation. Associations to Moody's earlier work would only help with this. During *The Fundamentals*, the magazine aligned itself editorially with the project, though it was careful to avoid mentioning MBI's direct involvement. It also began attacking modernists directly. An extensive editorial critiquing the *Biblical World*, the magazine of the University of Chicago, noted that modernism might represent "A New Type of Christianity" but reminded readers that "the Founder of the old type of Christianity" had warned of "false prophets" in the last days.[13]

Even without *The Fundamentals* mailing list, the *Christian Workers Magazine* had greater success expanding its circulation than its West Coast rival. New promotional schemes included a "scholarship program" that encouraged students to sell subscriptions in their hometowns. They were given sample copies, promotional materials, and assurances that "200 or 300 subscriptions" would pay for a year of schooling.[14] It guaranteed that those unable to afford MBI's modest room-and-board expenses could at least sell. Nonstudents hawking the magazine were promised "Bibles, Books, Fountain Pens" and, for a mere 200 subscriptions, a new piano. All this helped create a "country-wide" audience from "all evangelical denominations."[15]

The Executive Committee also set about expanding MBI's influence. Prominent conservatives outside of Chicago were invited to become trustees, including Charles Trumbull, editor of the influential *Sunday School Times*, and Winnipeg-based grain magnate Sydney T. Smith.[16] They also retooled the Extension Department in 1910, hiring "a small corps of Bible Teachers" to serve as the face of the institute in particular regions. If "reviving" interest in things of God was part of their mission, they were equally focused on disseminating a correct interpretation of the Bible. Primarily acting as promotional agents for MBI, they also engaged in fund-raising whenever possible.[17]

Crowell's and Gray's choice of extension workers suggested a new focus on attracting "respectable" white southerners as students and donors. The best-known of these was Bob Jones. Ambitious and independent minded from the beginning, he chafed "under . . . [MBI's] control" and eventually left to begin an independent ministry. In 1926 he founded his self-named university, which became a citadel of southern fundamentalism. MBI also

This promotional photograph depicts the offices of the MBI Extension Department in 1925. Newly constituted in 1910, the department focused on sending out Bible teachers for promotional, evangelistic, and fund-raising purposes. Carefully posed, the photo depicts a professional, male-dominated—but woman-operated—office. (Courtesy of the Moody Bible Institute Archives)

tried to lure Louis Sperry Chafer to the department. Although he, too, went his own way, he had a good working relationship with Chicago. Strong ties between his independent dispensationalist Dallas Theological Seminary and MBI continue to the present day.[18] Given the new focus on southern whites, it was perhaps inevitable that "the status of colored students" would again become a topic of discussion among the trustees in 1913, but no recorded modifications were made to its already-restrictive policy.[19]

Much of the executive committee's institution and network building was done in preparation for what they hoped would be an influx of donors, students, and subscribers after *The Fundamentals*. But the grand gesture inaugurating the new phase in the movement was a Prophecy Conference held at MBI in February 1914. It was perhaps an extension of an early idea of Amzi Dixon's to hold "general testimony conferences" in major cities to reinforce the publication by bringing together "the great defenders of the faith." Planning at MBI began the year before, and it was described as one of several post-*Fundamentals* "Forward movements."[20] In fact, had not finance-induced delays pushed publication to the following year, the conference would have coincided with the release of the final volume. The choice of a Prophecy Conference to consolidate the influence of *The Fundamentals* speaks to the tenor of the times and the centrality of premillennialism to the project. This was not their fathers' premillennial convention. It would no longer argue for the *compatibility* of premillennialism with "respectable orthodoxy" and active Christianity. Now they would claim it was a *necessary* tenet of orthodoxy and a central means of mobilizing an aggressive coalition in a battle against modernism.[21]

Respectability remained as important for the forthcoming conference as with *The Fundamentals*. On the conference call, MBI organizers highlighted conservative denominational representatives, including the moderator of the Presbyterian Church (U.S.A.) (and Crowell's pastor) John Timothy Stone and several other seminary professors and presidents. These names appeared before the larger block of lesser-known American and Canadian evangelicals who were the real driving force of the conference. Among these were Cyrus Scofield; his close friend Arno Gaebelein, editor of the hard-line dispensationalist journal *Our Hope*; and the up-and-coming Baptist minister William B. Riley, a southern transplant in Minneapolis. As a premillennial conference, it was unable to attract most of the important conservative names who had agreed to participate in *The Fundamentals*. But organizers made up the deficit with an audacious, and occasionally ludicrous, appendix in the published proceedings listing "Some Exponents of Premillennialism" throughout history. The list included the early church fathers as well as those better known for their contributions to science, philosophy, and literature, including Isaac Newton, William Occam, and John Milton. Sprinkled among this illustrious body were Scofield, nearly the entire faculty of MBI, and other important fundamentalists. With premillennialism spread so widely, how could it possibly be sectarian?[22]

Few of the ostensible premillennialists from history would have felt at home amid Riley's attempts to divine the "signs of the [end] times" in the buildup to world war, or Gaebelein's railing at higher criticism as "the theological forerunner of the Antichrist," or the symposium on modern Zionism filled with all manner of end-time predictions that even the conference announcement had insisted would be avoided. Some speakers offered more balance. Denominational conservatives testified how they became premillennialists,

*An iconic photograph of the 1914 Prophecy Conference organized by MBI
administrators. The conference was an attempt to consolidate the coalition of
conservative Protestants rallied by* The Fundamentals *project. Note the respectably
dressed audience. (Courtesy of the Moody Bible Institute Archives)*

and Torrey emphasized the doctrine's personal and practical ramifications.
Gray conducted a concluding "consecration meeting," at which he explained
how to attain the fullness of the Holy Spirit in Keswick fashion.[23]

At the apex of the conference, on the final evening, Gray proposed a
"Testimony" for attendees to approve, enumerating what could now be
called the "fundamental truths of our holy faith." "The existing conditions
in the professing church" required this statement, it claimed, and it called
on "the people of God in all denominations . . . to contend earnestly for the
faith" that it encapsulated. Many of its brief ten points would have been
familiar to readers of *The Fundamentals*. It reinforced conservative evangelical assumptions, put the Bible forward as "our *only* authority," and included
premillennial belief with other "essential" doctrines. It omitted subjects of
churchly concern and defined "church" as a simple aggregate of individual
believers, akin to a "consuming public," rather than as an institution or
community. The "great mission of the church" did not include establishing
justice in the world, serving the poor, worshipping God, or following in the
steps of Jesus. Its sole purpose was "to evangelize the world."[24]

The composition of this statement of faith borrowed from the methods of *The Fundamentals*. It was written almost entirely by Torrey[25] and then approved by a committee of five that was selected by Gray. Yet it was publicized as a product of "The Conference" because those attending the evening session "unanimously adopted [it] by a rising vote." The entire conference proceedings were published by MBI. A prefatory note explained that if the publication produced funds in excess of the conference costs, they would be used to send gratuitous copies *Fundamentals*-style "to theological students" and others engaged in Christian service.[26]

The results of the conference were beyond what MBI officials had anticipated. About 2,000 people from thirty-four states had attended, and a "spirit of unity and love" had prevailed. It spawned other meetings across the country, and the proceedings went into a second printing.[27] Thomas Stephens reported the conference to Stewart as "a marvelous success," with "[t]he power of the Holy Spirit . . . upon every speaker" and the auditorium "literally packed at every service."[28]

The doctrinal statement approved by the conference helped solve a sticky problem at MBI. The institute adopted the statement as its creedal standard and made its acceptance a requirement for graduation. Yet they could continue to insist MBI was ecumenical and nonsectarian since it was approved by an interdenominational gathering and no MBI official had technically composed it. The trustees ordered that MBI "literature occasionally" include "the 'conference Testimony'" along "with a declaration that it represents our convictions & has our endorsement."[29]

Another victory for MBI during this time was its acquisition of the popular Scofield Correspondence Course. Conducted by Scofield personally beginning in 1890, it laid out the dispensational method now embodied in his popular reference Bible. By the early 1910s, Scofield was in ill health and worried about the financial solvency of his family. After lengthy negotiations, he finally agreed to sell the course, including the exclusive rights to his name, for $10,000. This was a coup, since Scofield had started a competing Bible school in Philadelphia. In fact, when the Philadelphia school's administrators learned of the exchange, they begged MBI administrators to let them purchase shared rights for $5,000. They were politely informed that the "proposition, to speak briefly, seems . . . unwise from a business and administrative point of view."[30]

MBI leaders were quite literally accumulating theological assets from around the country with the goal of creating a one-stop shop for a new orthodoxy. In the coming years, they regularly entertained offers to acquire other Bible schools and fundamentalist journals.[31] When necessary, they were not shy about defending their trademarked products.[32] As a result, MBI quickly became a central hub of the new fundamentalist movement.

FUNDAMENTALISTS WERE NOT THE only ones creating transdenominational networks in the early twentieth century. Theological modernists had been working informally across confessional lines for at least twenty years, typically in academic circles, and forging a new basis for a modern faith rooted in method rather than creedal content.[33]

Another project included some of D. L. Moody's moderate protégés and culminated in the formation of the Federal Council of Churches (FCC) in 1908. It maintained Moody's pragmatic orientation, focusing on developing a unified response to social issues and an organizational basis for denominational cooperation at home and abroad. Thus, in contrast to fundamentalists, FCC organizers believed that "the relation of labor to capital" and other social questions required "united and concerted action if the Church is to lead effectively in the conquest of the world for Christ." Moreover, they explicitly excluded creedal considerations from the purview of the FCC; members would agree to disagree on all but practical matters. It was organized as a deliberative and democratic body, not like the streamlined corporate organizations of fundamentalists. Thus the FCC, like the denominations it represented, promoted its agenda in a manner that was slow and incremental.[34]

Although the FCC was distinct from both modernism and the social gospel, these lines were muddied in 1912 when Shailer Mathews, a professor at the University of Chicago and a nemesis of fundamentalists, became its president. After this, the tentative support that fundamentalists gave to the FCC largely evaporated.

The Fundamentals had rallied conservatives, but it united liberals as well. The *Constructive Quarterly* was a telling imitation of sorts. Edited by Episcopal Silas McBee, it embodied an older, organic vision of ecumenism. Diverse religious groups each offered a summary of their distinctive beliefs and practices in the hopes that participants might discover common ground.[35] The *Quarterly*'s constructive character notwithstanding, its first issue also provided space to attack the competition. Mathews took the lead, using those who would soon be called "fundamentalists" as a foil against which he defined his project. The enemy, by his account, were those who "prefer a bald literalism" and were "frankly opposed to anything like critical thought" associated with "the various Bible Institutes . . . in Chicago, New York, Minneapolis, [and] Los Angeles." They were obstructing the progress of his project, in which "the real content of the Gospel is being rethought in the terms and under the influence of evolution and democracy." He compared his opponent's approach to scripture to sectarians like the "Millennial Dawn" and radical evangelicals like "Dr. Dowie" and "the 'Holy Rollers.'" Appealing to middle-class prejudices, he emphasized that the roots of premillennialism was in "the apocalyptic literature of Judaism." It was, at root, no different from other "sects" and thus not "truly representative [of] Protestantism of America."

Yet even as Mathews painted his opponents as outsiders, he tellingly complained that "our business men" fail "to see that they know less about theology than do properly trained ministers." He rejected the proposition that business leadership in church work brought "unqualified success," preferring "scientific management" instead. In fact, he claimed he would choose "the sovereign God of Calvinism," which he found anathema, over "a bureaucracy of business men."[36]

Gray was quick to respond to Mathews's article with a thoroughly uncon-structive response that the *Quarterly* refused to print.[37] But since his real audience was denominational conservatives, he was happy to use the pages of the conservative-leaning *Bibliotheca Sacra*. Mathews's criticisms of Bible institutes "can be reduced to one" factor, he flatly stated: "We still believe the Old and New Testaments to be the inspired Word of God, and take them at their face value." Gray drew parallels between their views and respectable conservative institutions like Princeton Seminary. And far from being logi-cally associated to sectarians like Dowie, it was "Bible Institutes of the right sort" like MBI that were "the antidote to these extremes." He traced the "real cause" of radical evangelicalism to Mathews's "awakening Protestant-ism." For by diminishing the reality of miracles in the Bible, its proper place, modernists were forcing spiritually hungry people to seek the miraculous in their everyday lives, producing extremism. Mathews's errors, Gray omi-nously warned, would culminate in the "man of sin"—in antichrist.[38]

Mathews continued the dispute the following year in the pages of the *Biblical World*, which he edited out of the University of Chicago. "We are . . . now in the midst of an extraordinary attempt to force Christianity against the current of modern culture," he wrote in clear reference to *The Fun-damentals*. "Men are spending enormous sums of money" to convince Christians that "scientific thought . . . [is] atheistic."[39] A leading voice of the social gospel, Washington Gladden, joined in critiquing this "Dangerous Crusade," which he described as "the business of biblical defense." It was "bibliolatry," he complained, making biblical infallibility "the test of popular orthodoxy." "A concerted and organized movement" of "popular evangelists" and "a number of wealthy men," fundamentalism sought to replace "the scholarly study of the Bible" with "propagandism." Putting forward a dangerous binary view of the Bible, the movement's efforts were causing the educated to leave the faith. This left ignorant fundamentalists filling pews, exerting even more pressure on "timid ministers who do not wish to expose themselves to the imputation of heresy." Liberals must fight back and reach the "plain man," but this would only happen if denominational leaders refused to acquiesce to the fundamentalist crusade.[40]

MBI officials saw no need to respond to Gladden, but a series of attacks emanating from a magazine for Methodist Sunday school teachers elicited a swift response. Three of the offending articles were written by Harris Franklin Rall, a professor at the Garrett Biblical Institute, which was associated with the Methodist-affiliated Northwestern University. Using MBI's published proceedings of the recent Prophecy Conference, Rall made a compelling case that premillennialism was incompatible with traditional Methodism. This, of course, struck at the heart of MBI's project and prompted an unprecedented full page "Special Announcement" in the May 1916 *Christian Workers Magazine*, promising a response from eminent conservatives Charles Erdman and William H. Griffith Thomas. The articles, published over several months, were accompanied by pictures of the stately stone buildings of the author's respective institutions at Princeton Seminary and Wycliffe College in Toronto to highlight their established credentials. Both men focused on accusations that premillennialism manipulated the biblical text, that it predicted the destruction of the institutional church, and that it was essentially pessimistic, thus discouraging evangelism and "social service" and encouraging social anarchy. Premillennialism, they insisted, was a long-held doctrine, the result of a "plainly" read Bible. Liberals rejected it because of their unscriptural bias, and the "excesses" these enemies accused the doctrine of generating were ad hominem attacks based on outliers. Erdman echoed his diluted definition from *The Fundamentals* and continued to insist that differences with postmillennialists were minor matters. Thomas's sprawling response was more polemical and included a defense of the Scofield correspondence course, which critics complained relied on definitions that were "mechanical and artificial in the extreme" and produced "unwholesome tendencies." The real question, by Thomas's estimation, was whether dispensationalism was true.[41]

Always on the lookout for promotional opportunities, MBI leaders used the controversy to promote its magazine. With funding from William Blackstone, they sent the August issue to about 30,000 Methodist ministers across the country.[42] Still, it was striking that they could not muster a sufficiently prominent Methodist defender. Perhaps this was part of the reason they considered the proposal of Methodist Arno Gaebelein to "promote the Institute thru his meetings and magazine" and extended an offer to Dr. Edward F. Cook, former missionary secretary of the Methodist Church, South, to head the Mission Department despite some reservations he apparently expressed with their doctrinal position.[43]

As the dispute dragged on, a pattern developed in MBI's selective responses to modernist critiques. Attacks mocking MBI as old-fashioned, overly "literal," or out of step with modern criticism were either ignored or trumpeted. Accusations of sectarianism or incompatibility with mainline denominations were repudiated in the strongest terms. Modernists depicted fundamentalism as a "theological obsession" that "especially appeals to the lay mind, and huge sums of money are being spent to further it."[44] "Propaganda" was a regular refrain, as were warnings of its "Jewishness," its antiscientific character, and, counterintuitively, its incompatibility with modern business.[45]

MBI's leadership in the early fundamentalist movement was solidified by liberal attacks. MBI benefited both from Crowell's institution building and the accident of geography that placed them in the same city as the major advocates of theological modernism. For liberals seeking something concrete to blame for a movement they did not understand, MBI was an obvious choice. This allowed Crowell and Gray to rally other conservatives to their defense; the resulting editorials and articles cemented the institution's reputation. When Shailer Mathews's premillennialism-attacking pamphlet *Will Christ Come Again?* was sent out *Fundamentals*-style to pastors across the country, a Baptist minister from Lewiston, Montana, saw it as a veiled attack on "the Moody Bible Institute." It would have greatly pleased Crowell that the man's "sympathy in the controversy was with the Institute" rather than his denomination's flagship university.[46]

AS THE WESTERN WORLD became engulfed in world war, MBI's stars seemed perfectly aligned. The rallying call of "the fundamentals" was pitch perfect for the times, a generous attempt to find common ground across confessional lines. Numerous liberals, late to the party, attempted their own project to determine "What Is Fundamental."[47] MBI used a masterful turn of phrase to promote itself as "The West Point of Christian Service." It captured both the growing militarism of the times and the keyword "service," which historian David Kennedy notes was a powerful "rhetorical vessel," that encompassed both "the autonomy of the individual will and the obligation of the individual to serve a sphere wider than his own."[48] MBI modernized its relationship to the military during this time. In addition to sending faculty members to minister to mobilizing troops, it focused on literature distribution. In 1918 it had raised about $7,000 to distribute about 150,000 pieces of literature, typically coordinated with the military hierarchy.[49]

MBI's promotional machine was in high gear. The institute sent trial subscriptions of the *Christian Workers Magazine* to over 50,000 recipients, with the ongoing religious controversy adding spice to their other offerings. The magazine was filled with advertisements ranging from Quaker Oats and typewriters to a full array or religious merchandise for Christian service—organs, magic lanterns, commentaries, and communion sets. Montgomery Ward advertised a "Missionary Bureau" service that sent the supplies and comforts of home overseas.[50] MBI did its own share of advertising. One ad for the Extension Department boasted a corps of twelve workers photographed in neatly tailored suits and, for the three women on staff, elegant, if unadorned, dresses. The idealized consumer of MBI's religious product was repeatedly depicted as an upper-middle-class white professional man and his family.[51]

The education departments were also flush. By 1917, MBI's student body numbered over 1,000 and included the likes of an unnamed Princeton University graduate and medical doctor, who considered the education worthy of delaying entry to the mission field.[52] Enrollment in MBI's correspondence courses had grown to over 3,000 by 1915 and increased steadily after that. The Scofield Bible Course was the crown jewel, supported by several other new courses in doctrine, Bible study, pastoral training, and New Testament Greek. The trustees briefly considered a full-fledged course equivalent to a B.A. for ministers destined for smaller rural parishes, conducted in cooperation with mainline denominations. Telling of MBI's success was the development by liberal Congregationalists of a competing "Chicago Christian Institute" in 1917, though its courses aligned more with a liberal arts degree than with MBI's biblical and practical focus.[53]

MBI administrators used both students and faculty for promotional purposes. They accrued teachers like the former president of Westminster College Robert Russell, who came aboard in 1915. His appeal to educated conservatives was apparently worth a generous $5,000 annual salary. "Those inclined to sneer at the orthodox and evangelical faith as no longer accepted by the scholarly must account for Dr. Russell," Gray crowed in an editorial."[54] As the primary "product" of MBI, the student body was heavily regulated before, during, and after their attendance. Those who did not pass muster for entrance were sloughed off to the correspondence course, with the promise that completed coursework would count toward a degree should they be accepted. Whatever the reality, ads for the course depicted businessmen or upper-middle-class families in well-apportioned home libraries completing coursework.[55]

The outlook of the defenders of old-time religion at MBI bore the markings of a particular sort of modernity amenable to business, engineering, and law. A talk given at MBI by the evangelist Herbert Booth, son of Salvation Army founder William Booth, was typical. Launching into an extended metaphor of the spiritual life as an automobile, he theorized a "spiritual law of adjustment" that would warm the heart of any mechanic. Elsewhere, Dixon argued that there was no inconsistency in resisting evolution, or "science, so-called," and their own claims of certain knowledge. The "modern thought" of the previous fifty years had run along two lines. One, aligned with engineering, "the finding of old laws" such as steam, electricity, and radio "and applying them to new uses," had been overwhelmingly successful. The other, aligned with modern science "discovering the origin of things," had failed.[56] This mirrored their view that the "applied science" of dispensationalism bested higher criticism's search for origins.

Fundamentalists' confidence was bolstered when the onset of World War I caught modernists by surprise. Premillennialism was on the ascent, they thought. They noted Wellesley professor Vida D. Scudder was sounding an awful lot like a pessimistic premillennialist in her 1917 essay on religion and civilization in light of the war.[57] And she was not alone. The atrocities of the war were taking their toll on the optimism that had driven the liberal project since the turn of the century. Had fundamentalists bothered to look, it was clearly a premillennialism of a different order, but no matter: geopolitical events seemed to be undeniable fulfillments of biblical prophecy, leading many a pragmatic premillennialist into its more esoteric branches and all manner of intemperate predictions. Advertisements for the *Christian*

Workers Magazine highlighted essays by Gray about "the Christian's relation to war in the light of prophecy" and about the Great War in "relation to the battle of Armageddon mentioned in the Book of Revelation" and "to the end of the age."[58] Even Torrey was lured into an unseemly pamphlet war with Shailer Mathews on premillennialism.[59]

By 1918, modernist attacks on premillennialism were filled with a hyperbole that suggested desperation more than domination. In January, University of Chicago theology professor Shirley Jackson Case accused premillennialist advocates of being part of a conspiracy against the war movement that was funded by German sources.[60] Liberal editorials warned that premillennialism "cuts the nerve of patriotism and prevents it followers from heartily supporting the government." Some suggested that its effects in "religious circles" were similar to the International Workers of the World in labor.[61] Case's full-blown argument in July reached hysterical heights. Premillennialism, he warned, was "a serious menace to our democracy," a "virus . . . injected into the spiritual veins" of churches. Its "distributing centers" in major cities spread dangerous literature. Ministers, often well-meaning, "advocate[e] this harmful delusion" without "realizing the insidious character of their message," while teachers of "innocent youths" are indoctrinated in its tenets by the *Sunday School Times*. The money spent in distribution was incalculable, and whether it came from "German gold" or "would-be loyal citizens" was unclear. But its "Teutonic" quality and tendency to bolster the anarchistic "I.W.W. propaganda" against "organized society" and the war was undeniable.[62]

Case's fear mongering was a bit much, even for the *Biblical World*, which, to its credit, published an article challenging some of his assertions.[63] But the main point that the doctrine constituted a virus weakening the American body politic was a charge fundamentalists took seriously. The United States had entered the war in 1917 to make the world "safe for democracy." This began shifting the national conversation from apocalypse to terms that favored modernist positions. Wartime mobilization undermined fundamentalism's modern individualism. The military draft, government oversight of the economy, and the resulting shift from consuming culture to collective sacrifice augured a communal orientation. Indeed, modern advertising techniques were now used by George Creel to whip up nationalist fervor, transforming "the war into a religious crusade."[64]

MBI's leadership had been faithful supporters of the war effort from the beginning, but other premillennialists had some explaining to do. Torrey especially had been burdened by greater nuance in his understanding of international politics, born of worldwide travel and ongoing friendships with German evangelicals. Thus, when the United States first entered the war, his support was half-hearted at best. He disparaged Woodrow Wilson's call to spread democracy and mocked elites who trumpeted their "sacrifices" for the war effort. Such "propaganda" coming from Biola created concern at MBI and no doubt among other respectable evangelicals.[65] In this context, it was more important than ever to depict fundamentalism as an integral part of the nation. Most evangelicals rallied around MBI as their best chance of doing this.

MBI continued to defend premillennialism, but now its message was accompanied by an overbearing patriotism. Its personnel helped canvass for Liberty Bonds, and they exceeded their commitments to the Red Cross when "some of the Chicago churches" failed to meet their obligations. The imminent return of Jesus meant they must always be ready to give account, and during the present crisis, this "path of duty" was to support their government "to the last dollar and the last man."[66] It reported on its work among soldiers, praising the "new religious spirit" in the armed forces.[67] Amid the enthusiasm, MBI took care to maintain propriety; respectability remained a front-and-center concern. This meant that when the former professional baseball player turned celebrity evangelist William "Billy" Sunday came to town, their support was muted. A write-up in the *Christian Workers Magazine* dutifully noted Sunday's message "rings true to the gospel" without "false note . . . with regard to the fundamental teachings of the Scriptures" and his support for the war effort. But it expressed concern that "his platform methods may not please all." Apart from lending members of the music department to the crusade, they thought it better to stand as well-bred observers rather than participants.[68]

As to whether a Christian might in good conscience participate in war, dispensationalists had a ready answer. Social gospelers and radical evangelicals were the ones that tried to apply Jesus's pacifist ethics to the present age. As dispensationalists, it was a small step to begin arguing that God operated differently in his distinct spheres of influence—the state and the church—in the same way that he chose to act differently in different historical periods.[69] Thus, violence was absolutely righteous as a "government truth" but forbidden as a "church truth," William Newell explained.[70] To speak against "the soldier business" was wrong. In essence, dispensationalists had reinstated the public/private distinction that Moody and Torrey had fought so hard to erase. But it mirrored the logic of professionalization, which allowed upstanding citizens to examine bodies as medical professionals, to defend the guilty as lawyers, and to engage in cutthroat tactics in business. That Newell called soldiering a "business" akin to "carpentry" was not coincidental; business was business. Especially in time of war, Christianizing the secular realm was not only foolhardy but also sinful.[71]

Patriotism combined with overweening confidence generated attacks in the pages of the *Christian Workers Magazine* that were unprecedented in their vindictiveness. The conspiratorial linking of fundamentalism to Germany led conservative evangelicals to an obvious retort. It was theological modernism that had direct ties to that "abomination of abominations . . . that ripe, rank, rampant, rotten new theology made in Germany." Even as they criticized liberal pacifism, they also argued that German barbarism, with all its alleged atrocities, was the logical end of an unholy alliance of evolutionary theory, radical politics, and liberal theology. Fundamentalists were the real defenders of democracy, of traditional Protestantism, and of the industrial order.[72]

The formal end to hostilities in November 1918 exacerbated the conflict between modernists and fundamentalists. Victory abroad led to peace negotiations based on Wilson's fourteen-point plan. The last of these points was the development of a "League of Nations," a democratic deliberative body that would broker international disputes, better coordinate international trade, and keep the peace if necessary. This had long been a dream of modernists, and, in fact, many leaders in the FCC had helped develop the League of Nations.[73] The project helped revive some of the prewar optimism, recasting the war as atonement rather than apocalypse. Western society underwent a crucifixion-type experience of supreme sacrifice only to experience resurrection and perfection.

Fundamentalists had their own explanation of recent political developments. They saw the League of Nations as an entirely expected imposition of a one-world government predicted in prophecy—though most were careful to specify that it was merely a precursor, while the actual organization would come after the rapture.[74] Neither were they surprised by the formation of an "Interchurch World Movement" designed to unite Christianity into a single organically unified institution. This, too, was fulfilling prophecies of a world church, they believed, portending the rise of antichrist.[75] Thus the same events that reinvigorated modernists only reinforced premillennialists' confidence. The stakes had never been higher for fundamentalists:

any cooperation with these liberal-tinged projects was assisting in Satan's end-time rebellion.[76]

Thus, with both fundamentalists and modernists supremely confident in their opposite conclusions, the already high-pitched battle was pushed to new heights. Like the influenza outbreak that claimed more lives than the war, fundamentalists saw a broad demonic conspiracy infiltrating society. It produced outbreaks across the country, like the series of strikes from Seattle to Pittsburgh and the anarchist bombings that in June 1919 hit eight cities within an hour. They did not accuse modernists of anarchism per se, but it certainly had contributed to the "present state of social, industrial, and political confusion."[77] Rooted in evolutionary science, it relieved individuals of personal responsibility for their actions, preached an ethic of "survival of the fittest," and limited religious endeavor to the physical world.

Modernism also had taken root in seminaries and college theology courses. Thus embedded in these institutions, it would, fundamentalists feared, continue to impart its corrupting influence on the next generation of ministers, like an infectious disease. *The Fundamentals* had raised awareness of the problem and rallied conservative Protestants to battle. But if pure religion was to survive, the scattered outposts of orthodoxy would need to unite.

THE IDEA OF UNITING fundamentalists into a formal organization first surfaced at a meeting at Torrey's summer home in Montrose, Pennsylvania, in late 1918. Torrey, William Bell Riley, and several others made plans to hold a conference on "the fundamentals of the faith" the following summer. This conference would mark the formal beginning of the World's Christian Fundamentals Association (WCFA). By Riley's account, he had been chosen to lead the association, but Torrey reported events differently. At the original planning meeting, William Evans, a former professor at MBI, had been "placed at the head of it," Torrey explained to Gray, but he "ran against so many snags that . . . he gave it up." Riley then swooped in to take charge. But he too had competition. Presbyterian minister Mark Mathews had put forward a competing idea to unite fundamentalists the year before that was focused on uniting distinct denominational families on separate creedal bases and ridding all of modernist impurities. He insisted this was the better basis of organizing the movement.[78]

Gray had his own project to unify fundamentalists using Bible institutes as a base. He had planned a conference at MBI, "World Evangelism and

Vital Christianity after the War," in February 1919, and he invited Torrey to help him organize the movement with others who would attend. But Torrey turned down the invitation, deeply skeptical that Bible institutes were the right basis for such an organization. He agreed "heartily" that such a movement was needed, but the basis should be broader, he explained, including "seminaries . . . the ministry, and . . . place[s] of other leadership." To work, the organization needed to be "a real representative company of those who are agreed on the fundamentals." This meant that they could not require "the acceptance of premillenarianism [as] a condition" since "there are other questions that are more fundamental." If Gray was interested in organizing a broader coalition of this sort, Torrey pledged his support.[79]

Since the conference was already planned, Gray pushed ahead without Torrey. "German militarism is dead," the conference announcement flatly declared, "but [the] German theology that made it possible still lives." This was a new rallying cry to the same imagined audience that they had rallied for the 1914 Prophecy Conference at the end of *The Fundamentals* project, but it exhibited stark binary thinking, hints of paranoia, and an ungainly confidence in dispensational premillennialism. Its results would not be limited to "words," they promised, but would "be followed by an aggressive forward movement." The announcement had in embryonic form what would become major features in a future WCFA. They invited evangelists, conservative "editors of denominational journals," and representatives from Bible institutes to discuss future cooperation. There were also the trademark features of MBI-led endeavors like sessions on "church efficiency." Typical of Crowell, the conference doubled as a promotion for MBI. It was scheduled to overlap with their weeklong celebration of Moody's birthday. It eventually evoled into a "Founder's week" conference that MBI still conducts each year.[80]

The conference promoted "the same fundamental truths" and embodied "the same tone of spiritual life . . . as in the days when Dwight L. Moody preached in the same auditorium," *Christian Workers Magazine* reported. Yet it seems unlikely that Moody would have declared that "we are now in a fight and we must hit hard." Likewise, the claim of one speaker that the purpose of Bible institutes was to disseminate "Christian truth" missing from seminaries and should serve as havens where true believers can send "their children . . . without any danger of their faith being weakened or totally destroyed" were the exact opposite of Moody's designs for MBI.[81] Speakers declared that just as Germany was not the enemy of one nation but "of mankind" and "civilization," so, too, modernism was "not the foe of Methodism" or other individual denominations but "of Christianity."[82]

The real business of the conference was conducted offstage. Participants in the Bible school discussions asked Gray to form two committees that would create educational and theological standards, respectively, for Bible institutes. Gray agreed and also offered to head the theological standards committees with Scofield and Torrey. (Theirs was a simple task, since they simply adopted the 1914 Prophecy Conference creed written by Torrey.) Most important, the discussants agreed to attend the upcoming WCFA conference, where they would report on their progress.[83]

A federation of Bible institutes would only work if MBI and Biola took the lead, but Gray, like Torrey, had cooled to the idea before it began. Responding to Gray's update of the conference developments, Torrey held firm to his earlier concerns and then piled on more. Scofield's school had "no thorough and well systematized course," he complained, and the classes at Riley's school in Minneapolis were "very inadequate," taught entirely "by one person, and that a woman." In fact, MBI was the only "Bible Institute in the country that I would be willing to be classed with." Apparently, spending a few days with his Bible School compatriots soured Gray to the idea as well. "The plan is not of my devising," he explained to Torrey, but he thought it "best to give them an opportunity to express themselves." In any case, he seriously doubted that "anything would come of it."[84]

The World Conference on Christian Fundamentals in Philadelphia in May 1919 did little to stoke either man's enthusiasm in the Bible institute idea and all but quashed Gray's interest in any sort of fundamentalist organization. Gray especially disliked Riley's leadership. Riley maintained a tempestuous southern plain-folk disposition despite his Minneapolis address. His opening declaration that future generations would see the conference as having greater import than Martin Luther's ninety-five theses was not only preposterous but seemed vaguely sectarian. Riley also took a hamfisted approach to controversy devoid of political finesse.[85]

Unlike MBI's careful attempts to obviate denominational authority, the WCFA defied it. The various committees formed at the conference looked a lot like the beginnings of a new denomination. They were responsible for coordinating "Colleges, Seminaries and Academies," periodicals, Bible conferences, and foreign missions. And in this context, the WCFA doctrinal statement seemed less like a set of lowest common denominators on which all "orthodox" denominations agreed than a new sectarian creed. Practical considerations also made the WCFA unappealing to those concerned with maintaining a professional middle-class identity. The committee on colleges, for example, "resolved" that it was "Christian duty" to avoid sending one's child to any educational institution that did not adhere to their "fundamental" doctrines. This certainly would boost the enrollment numbers of Wheaton College, whose current president headed the committee, but it would have made a professional career in many technical fields impossible. It was a stricture that neither Gray nor Crowell had followed when educating their own children. MBI's philosophy, embodied in a fund-raising appeal, was for "Christian parents . . . [to] send prospective college students for two years to Moody Bible Institute" to buttress "their faith" before continuing elsewhere.[86]

Even before the WCFA convention ended, it was clear that MBI would be an ambivalent partner at best. Other committees promised to propagandize for the movement (periodicals), forbid the teaching of human evolution (colleges), "perfectly systematize . . . [the] Bible study movement" (conferences), and withhold support from any mission board that "knowingly" sends out "unregenerate men" (missions). Gray's committee on Bible institutes, in contrast, asserted it was "obviously premature . . . to take any further action" and only offered to host another meeting. By November, both he and Torrey agreed that "hitch[ing] up" with the other Bible institutes was a bad idea and commiserated that "the movement . . . was being conducted on altogether too narrow a plan." Torrey still held out hope that he could reform the WCFA. But Gray skipped the next planning meeting, cryptically suggesting that Riley may have felt that "I have not shown an entirely cordial spirit of cooperation with him." He agreed to speak at the second WCFA convention in June 1920, hosted by the Moody Church (now removed a mile down the road from MBI). The *Christian Workers Magazine* printed a positive, but brief, synopsis.[87] Records at MBI suggest this was the end of their cooperation with the organization.

IF THEIR BRIEF PARTICIPATION in the WCFA had taught Crowell and Gray anything, it was that they needed to reestablish MBI as a leading voice of the fundamentalist movement on its own terms. This was demonstrated in yet another revision and rebranding of their magazine in the fall of 1920. It now sported the larger "standardized form" of middle-class periodicals like *Literary Digest* or *New Era*, as well as a new title: the *Moody Bible Institute Monthly*. An announcement noted that "by a strange turn of affairs," the

Christian Workers Magazine "has now become too narrow," and with the Red Scare, perhaps vaguely threatening. Better to suggest a consuming public rather than "workers," Christian or otherwise. The new title emphasized that MBI was "turned to by thousands of earnest and sincere Christians all over the world" who wanted "advice, instruction and comfort" amid "these dark days of apostasy." Because the magazine was the primary voice of the institute, it was only right that its name "should be formally attached to it, and its standard thus flung to the breeze."[88]

The Moody Bible Institute, a name over which they had full legal control, was thus positioned as shorthand for pure religion. The theme of purity was driven home with the cover illustration on the new magazine's first issue, penned by the "Christian Cartoonist" E. J. Pace, now also an MBI faculty member. It depicted two imposing cliffs positioned on either side of an immense chasm. One side, crowded with figures marching behind the standard of the cross, was labeled "The faith which was once delivered unto the saints." The other side, sparsely populated and crumbling, was labeled "Modernist theology." Below each was a series of descriptions contrasting their modern form of old-time religion with its corrupted alternative ("The Bible IS the Word of God" versus "the Bible CONTAINS the word of God"; "Man is the product of special CREATION" versus "the product of EVOLUTION" and "a SINNER" versus "the unfortunate VICTIM of environment"). Above this scene was the caption "NO MIDDLE GROUND—ONLY A CHASM."[89] The following month, an editorial approvingly quoted a "liberal" pastor from Chicago who declared there to be only "two camps, namely, the Moody Bible Institute Camp, and the Chicago University camp." All the better, in MBI's estimation, that liberals also associate "Moody" with "the faith once for all delivered unto the saints."[90] The meaning was clear: individuals, churches, even entire denominations must decide whether to align with the institute or go the way of modernist apostasy. There was no third option.

A binary model served MBI's interest by obscuring some of its novelties, rallying denominational conservatives to its defense, energizing its followers, and providing a clear choice to new converts. But it also had downsides that became all too evident. Thanks to the efforts of the WCFA, the fundamentalist movement swept up varieties of plain-folk and Populist believers that always created concern within MBI's walls. These were a far cry from the stodgy Philadelphia Presbyterian, the urbane Atlanta Southern Baptist, the ambitious Los Angeles Methodist, or the stolid Lutheran farmer in the upper Midwest that they envisioned as the backbone of the movement.

M**OO**DY BIBLE INSTITUTE M**O**NTHLY

Volume XXI	September, 1920	Number 1

NO MIDDLE GROUND-ONLY A CHASM

"The faith which was once delivered unto the saints."

Modernist theology

① The Bible *IS* the Word of God. — the book which contains the word.

② The Bible *CONTAINS* the word of God. — the word which contains the book.

③ Jesus Christ is *THE* Son of God in a sense in which no other is.

③ Jesus Christ is *A* son of God in the sense in which all men are.

③ The birth of Jesus Christ was SUPERNATURAL.

③ The birth of Jesus Christ was NATURAL.

④ The death of Jesus was EXPIATORY.

④ The death of Jesus was EXEMPLARY.

⑤ Man is the product of special CREATION.

⑤ Man is the product of EVOLUTION.

⑥ Man is a *SINNER* fallen from original righteousness, and apart from God's redeeming grace is hopelessly lost.

⑥ Man is the unfortunate *VICTIM* of environment but through self-culture can make good.

⑦ Man is justified by *FAITH* in the atoning blood of Christ, result: supernatural regeneration from ABOVE.

⑦ Man is justified by *WORKS* in following Christ's example, result: natural development from WITHIN.

| James M. Gray | J. H. Ralston |
| Editor | Associate Editor |

20 Cents a Copy. $2.00 a Year

The cover illustration from the inaugural issue of MBI's reworked magazine, now called the Moody Bible Institute Monthly. *It shows MBI's strategy to depict the fundamentalist/modernist debate as a binary choice between "orthodoxy" and "modernist theology," which the publishers would assert was not Christianity at all. The goal was to appeal to churchly denominational conservatives leery of the potential for evangelical disorder. (Courtesy of the Moody Bible Institute Archives)*

Showing little concern for middle-class respectability, these radicals would not abide direction from MBI any more than they would from their own denominations. Worse, they made it all too evident that fundamentalist "orthodoxy," like the evangelicalism that inspired it, could be used to disruptive ends. As more-strident and less-deliberate voices became the public face of fundamentalism, MBI retreated from the movement it helped create.

By 1921, MBI's relationship to the WCFA had become an outright liability. Both Riley and his key ally, New York pastor John Roach Straton, also of southern extraction, exuded a Populist, antidenominational rhetoric. Their heresy hunting in the Northern Baptist Convention became so extreme that they alienated denominational conservatives. This included Curtis Lee Laws, the editor of the conservative Baptist journal the *Watchman-Examiner*, who is typically credited with coining the term "fundamentalist."[91] A series of editorials in the *Moody Bible Institute Monthly* over the next three years chronicled MBI's disavowal of the "fundamentalist" label. In January 1921, Gray wrote a 1,000-word editorial to distance MBI from the WCFA. He admitted speaking at the recent Chicago conference but disclaimed any "leadership" in the movement and reaffirmed his belief in "the need and desirability of denominations in this age."[92] In March the *Monthly* condemned those who left their denominations for having "too much of the 'holier-than-thou' spirit" and shirking their duty to "bear testimony to the truth" where they were.[93] April editorials battled accusations that MBI had formulated a "creed which has been adopted by a chain of Bible Institutes" and suspicions that it now constituted "a new denomination." Instead, they posited a new "dividing line" in Protestantism: "modernism versus evangelicalism."[94] In 1922, Gray insisted that MBI was not part of the WCFA and that he had "no inside knowledge of its affairs."[95]

But MBI's efforts to distance itself from the movement that it helped create came too late to avoid collateral damage. While intemperate voices had divided Protestantism into "two camps" and called for "battle royale," moderate liberals quietly laid claim to the middle ground. No one was more masterful at this technique than the mild-mannered minister Harry Emerson Fosdick. In his widely reprinted sermon "Shall the Fundamentalists Win?," he expertly positioned himself between the "reckless [liberal] radicals gifted with intellectual ingenuity, but lacking spiritual depth" and those "who call themselves the Fundamentalists" intent to "drive out of the evangelical churches men and women of liberal opinions." These were not "conservatives" who "can often give lessons to liberals in true liberality of spirit," he clarified. Neither did he accuse those who simply held conservative opinions on various topics to be the problem; there was room for debate. The issue, he argued, was that self-described fundamentalists had transformed a random smattering of topics into nonnegotiable beliefs: "stakes" that "mark out the deadline of doctrine around the church." The virgin birth, he noted, had not been mentioned by either Paul or John. And since biblical inerrancy, premillennial belief, and opposition to evolution could not be found in the historic creeds, there was little warrant to claim they were "essential."[96]

Fosdick's argument put Gray in an impossible position. Either he could accept that these "fundamentals" were not essential parts of the historic tradition, and thus undermine his claims to represent long-standing "orthodoxy," or he could argue the point, which only served to confirm the hopeless irascibility of the movement. A frustrated Gray chose the latter.[97]

Despite Gray's subsequent vindictiveness, he had already quietly granted Fosdick's point on premillennialism and dispensationalism. In a striking departure from past opinion, Gray admitted in April 1921 "that orthodoxy as generally understood, does not of necessity include Premillennialism." Other views were wrong, he insisted, and he found it "difficult" to understand "how any Christian can thoroughly study the Bible and not discover that truth." Yet he would not call them a "heretic."[98] In August, Gray also modified his dispensational views on the Sermon on the Mount in response to a Mennonite inquirer, whose denomination quietly but consistently interpreted Jesus's teachings literally and directly. It had some "application . . . [for] the present time," Gray grudgingly admitted.[99]

MBI's theological "purity" was now looking rather muddied by their own standards, and with their respectability endangered again by radical voices within the fundamentalist movement, secular discussions of purity—at this time filled with racist implications—became all the more important. But it turns out that this "secular" idea had complicated implications for their theological views. To be a virulent racist—to engage in extralegal lynching or race riots, for example—went against respectable middle-class mores. MBI's leadership would vigorously condemn these actions. But "respectable" racism, the prejudice of the professional white middle-classes, was an important marker of their respectability. Thus they partook in the same deeply offensive concern about "the negro problem" that swept the white middle classes, especially as rural southern African Americans immigrated to northern cities during and after World War I.[100] They repeatedly defended the anti-Semitic *Protocols of the Elders of Zion* because it seemed to confirm some of the finer points of premillennial theory even as it mitigated accusations of its "Jewishness." There was no record of MBI challenging the justice of Jim Crow, and it considered the benefits of the Ku Klux Klan to be an open question in the early 1920s.[101] It condemned the Chicago race riots a year late and with equal approbation to the supposed black assailants. It showed little courage in the cause of racial harmony. When an African American alumna called MBI in a panic during the rioting, running low on food and having not slept for days, administrators only mustered a prayer meeting on her behalf.[102]

But for all MBI's deficiencies in matters of race, it avoided the full-throated racialized gospel that prevailed among the Ku Klux Klan and much of mainline Protestantism.[103] This had less to do with race than the fact that it contradicted an evangelical gospel grounded in individual choice. Because choosing was the central means to verify sincere, authentic belief, "orthodoxy" could not be limited by race. It was in their interest to position "unredeemed" nonwhite society in as menacing a fashion as possible so that they could then claim to be the *solution* to that problem. Thus editorials in the *Monthly* repeatedly insisted that the *Protocols* were not anti-Semitic because they only referenced secular Jews—those that ceased hoping for the messiah. Observant Jews were granted toleration, and those who converted to Christianity were held in the highest esteem. The same ambivalent dynamic was evident in Gray's attitude toward eugenics. "If spiritual 'eugenics' were given its proper place," he mentioned in passing, "the physical side of the same subject would not be giving the trouble that it is."[104] All physical problems, whether labor unrest or fears of racial purity, had spiritual solutions.

At the beginning of the Red Scare, MBI produced a poster-sized ad proudly displaying a "real American 'Melting Pot'": twenty-six neatly coifed MBI students of all races and ethnicities, labeled with numbers for easy reference. These, it claimed, were "the Answer to Labor Unrest." From Irish to "Porto [sic] Rican," Italian to "American Negro," Syrian to "Russian Jew," "German-Bohemian" to Japanese—all were "'agitators' for righteousness" and the antidote to the "paid agitators" of labor unions "busy among workers." It was "the gospel of Jesus Christ, which makes men of whatever class or nationality upright, industrious and peaceable."[105] It was entirely in their interest to diminish "inferior" religions and position Protestant Christianity as the protector of civilization, but this faith must be transferrable across racial lines. In the business of religion, as in the business of consumer goods, controlling who consumed your goods was neither practical nor desirable.

Representatives of Different Nationalities Among Men Students—Winter Term, 1920

(1) Porto Rican, (2) Irish, (3) American Bohemian, (4) Swedish, (5) English, (6) Czecho-Slovak Bohemian, (7) Scotch, (8) Assyrian, (9) South African (English descent), (10) Russian Jew, (11) Italian, (12 and 14) Canadian, (13) Dutch, (15) Russian, (16 and 17) Norwegian, (18) French, (19) American Negro, (20) Syrian, (21) Japanese, (22) Finnish, (23) Armenian, (24) German Bohemian, (25) German, (26) American.

This photo was used in several different contexts to represent MBI as a solution to urban disorder. In one case, it was used for a large poster (too large to be reproduced here) that was distributed to donors. Above the picture was a blaring headline: "The Answer to Labor Unrest." Text beneath it called the heterogeneous group "agitators for the gospel." In the larger format, each numbered figure had his name and a descriptive paragraph that personalized him beyond simply a racial or ethnic label. The photo illustrates MBI's complicated relationship with both labor and race. (Courtesy of the Moody Bible Institute Archives)

Products were sold with the promise that they could transform, regardless of skin color. But in the same way, it was important that both consuming religion and mass consumer products be advertised as a product designed for white middle-class consumption. In both modern capitalism and a religious system presuming its framework, interminable dilemmas to questions of race proliferate.[106]

AMBIGUITY OF CONSUMPTION NOTWITHSTANDING, there was no question about the need for MBI to control its virtual trademark, Dwight L. Moody. Despite his death over twenty years before, Moody remained a popular, even poignant, symbol of respectable evangelicalism unsullied by discord. He was, in other words, the epitome of a rallying point for white professional evangelicals.

MBI had continued to trade on its association to Moody throughout the controversies of the previous decade, but in 1922, liberals began grumbling. Many evangelicals during this time had begun asking what side Moody would have taken in current controversies. Given the revivalist's aversion to conflict, it was a fight bound to happen. Liberals could rightly note that fundamentalist heresy hunting and premillennial speculations were out of step with Moody's public persona. Fundamentalists could rightly note the importance he placed on premillennialism in private, his reservations about higher criticism, and the centrality of a personal, freely chosen relationship with God as the central fact of authentic religion.[107] The first liberal questions on the matter were met with a swift response from the *Monthly* in a multipage editorial and a reprint of Scofield's dispensationalist-tinted portrait of "Moody as I Knew Him."[108]

The following year, a second series of challenges to MBI's claim to the Moody name came from Northfield. The long-standing cordial relations between Moody's Chicago and Northfield ministries had steadily deteriorated after some financial disputes in the late 1910s. By 1920, they were no longer on speaking terms for theological reasons. To an inquiry into why the *Record of Christian Work* refused to carry MBI advertising, Will Moody wrote plainly that he could no longer "recommend any young person . . . attend the Institute" or take "its correspondence courses." In fact, he had heard of "an organization" that refused "to employ any further graduates of the Institute in their work" because they were schismatic and "pharisaical," making premillennialism "the touchstone of orthodoxy" and thus "a point of cleavage" rather than "of union between Christian people." MBI, Will concluded, simply had "departed from the spirit and attitude of my father."[109] The following year, he publicly expressed further frustration with premillennialists for causing divisions "at a time when Christian forces should be united as never before."[110] Then in 1922, soon after Fosdick's sermon, he requested that Gray cease using "Moody" in connection with the Bible Institute.[111]

The executive committee made a half-hearted attempt to follow up on Will's inquiry, but it ultimately concluded it was better to let the matter drop in hopes that it would go away. But the next year, Moody's younger son Paul, the president of Middlebury College and more liberal and impetuous than his brother, wrote a public letter to the *Christian Century*. He thanked the liberal magazine for a recent editorial on his father and worried "that he was becoming a veiled figure for this generation," especially his tolerance for higher critics like George Adam Smith. By present standards, his father was "a conservative," Paul admitted, yet "he was, *for those days*, a liberal." Moreover, he concluded, "were he living today," Moody would be "more in sympathy with" men "like Fosdick," who preached "the love of God and the power of Christ," than with those fundamentalists persecuting "them because they will not subscribe to certain shibboleths."[112]

This was too much for MBI's leadership. Gray asked Torrey to respond publicly "because of your long intimate acquaintance with D. L. Moody, and also because of what you know of the present spirit and attitude of the Institute." Torrey agreed, especially since the article also reflected poorly on him.[113] Torrey's article proceeded to argue that he, a man who knew Moody only for the last decade of the revivalist's life and largely through correspondence, was better informed about his views than his own family was. Calling Paul's letter a "Gross Calumny of his honored Father," he took him to task on every point. Moody "was a conservative of the conservatives" and had stated in private that Smith "was doing the Devil's work." "Mr. Paul Moody has a right to his own convictions," Torrey indignantly concluded, "but he has no right to misrepresent his father in order to justify his own apostasy from the faith."[114]

This forced Will to enter the fray. He insisted that, notwithstanding his own conservative theology, he was certain that his father would no longer be in sympathy with the Chicago institution that now claimed his name. Torrey served again as MBI's hatchet man, accusing the *Christian Century* of "trying to use Mr. Will R. Moody as a cat's paw to draw their own chestnuts out of the fire."[115] If the tone of both articles was much harsher than what was typically allowed in the pages of the *Monthly*, it was justified by the existential nature of this challenge to MBI's institutional identity. But these harsh rebuttals were always followed by positive assessments of Moody from their particular interpretation, explaining what he "believed and taught, and how he taught it." They also printed multiple letters of support from those who "knew" Moody in one way or another.[116]

Yet another liberal critic picked up the theme in 1924. Elmer W. Powell, a prominent Baptist minister, wrote an article containing a litany of accusations, suggesting that the present "management" of MBI had risen to power by way of a hostile takeover. Premillennialism was a required tenet of their creed, he argued, and "fundamentalism" had been developed under their auspices. All this had alienated the Moody family from MBI.[117]

These charges elicited a rare public response from Crowell. His parsing was at times so narrow as to flirt with outright dishonesty, but it reveals how seriously he took the accusations. He was on the most solid historical ground when noting that Gray's first association with MBI was at Moody's invitation, and that MBI had cordial relations with nonpremillennialists since both John Greshem Machen and William Jennings Bryan had spoken at the institute. But it was only true in the narrowest sense that Gray had no part in preparing a premillennial creed, since he had selected the committee that did and then approved their work. And though employees were not required to sign the creed, all students did in order to graduate. Even more egregious was Crowell's assertion that "Fundamentalism as a movement was neither developed nor propagated by the Institute" since Dixon, now known as the editor of *The Fundamentals*, "was never connected with the Institute." Of course, Crowell failed to mention that both he and Smith had served on the Executive Committee and that Gray had helped draft lists of contributors and subjects.

But there was one accusation that gave Crowell greatest pause: the idea that Moody's name was taken by "the Institute after his death as a 'trademark for commercial ends.'" Crowell's substantial donations to MBI would protect him from accusations of personally enriching himself by Moody's name. And he argued with all integrity that MBI's change of name occurred before his arrival. But there was no denying that Moody was indeed serving the exact function of a trademark, both for the promotion of their religious product and for fund-raising.[118]

The rift with the Moody family was all but permanent after these public battles. Torrey's assertion that Moody had said that George Adam Smith was "doing the devil's work" was particularly egregious to Will, who wrote to Gray protesting that his father "could never have said such a thing." "Well, he did," Torrey told Gray, and the fact that Will questioned this demonstrated that he "did not understand his Father." In fact, Torrey continued, Moody had expressed concerns for his son in one of their last conversations. "Of course, I do not feel at liberty to repeat that conversation unless I am compelled to," he said.[119]

A final series of letters from Will to the MBI trustees in 1925 capped the controversy. He asked pointed questions about MBI's fund-raising and its rumored movements toward becoming a seminary, and he challenged their continued use of his father's name. Crowell's response was unbending. "The name possesses much value for the Institute itself. It is its creed practically," he tellingly argued, designating "that for which the Institute stands doctrinally, and guarantees its fidelity to the truth." It also had "become a rallying cry for evangelical believers in all denominations and in all lands."[120] Will openly despised MBI's leadership after this, especially Gray. When MBI began printing an article originally appearing in the *Record of Christian Work* as a tract, Will demanded that all references to his magazine be removed. It must have been published many years ago, he mused, "certainly long before he was president of the so-called Moody Bible Institute."[121]

During the public controversy with the Moody family, MBI leadership was more careful than ever to distance itself from the fundamentalist movement. In 1924, after an auto accident incapacitated Riley, Torrey gingerly approached Gray about participating in the upcoming WCFA convention. "The time has come when we can make the Christian Fundamentals Association what it ought to be," he promised, freed of "the unfortunate things . . . that have sometimes happened." But that ship had already sailed. After consulting Smith and Crowell on the matter, Gray politely declined. "The Institute's supposed leadership in the Fundamentals Association has brought us much trouble and loss in the last two or three years," he noted. And though they would not "shrink from suffering for our faith," they had no intent of being "charged with leading an organized movement to disrupt the churches."[122]

Gray and Crowell were not alone in their aversion. A year prior, Louis Sperry Chafer expressed similar dismay. "The fundamentalist movement has been reduced to the influence of about four men: Dr. Riley, Dr. Munhall, Tom Horton, and J. Frank Norris," he complained. "Just what these four plunging men will do before they are checked remains to be seen. But it certainly is a great embarrassment to the rest of us."[123] By 1925 even Torrey had grown disillusioned; displeased with Riley's return to leadership, he refused to speak at the Memphis conference despite already being in the city for a series of evangelistic meetings.[124] With allies like these, it was no surprise that the convention would falter soon after.

THE *MOODY BIBLE INSTITUTE MONTHLY* would continue to report on the activities of self-described fundamentalists, positioning itself as an "outsider" to the movement, though differences rarely extended beyond the degree of argumentativeness and skill in political finesse. Like self-described fundamentalists, MBI also attacked evolution throughout the early 1920s, culminating with Gray's assertion that "a Christian Cannot Be an Evolutionist."

This illustration captures MBI's sense of identity as a "Power House of Practical Christianity." Diverse groups of students enter the school and are professionalized and purified for work in various fields and geographic regions. The illustration was printed in the institute's May 1916 bulletin. (Courtesy of the Moody Bible Institute Archives)

This, he claimed, because he defined "evolution" as "a theory which undertakes to account for, or to explain, the origin and course of the universe independently of God." But when the Scopes Trial commenced, this coverage dropped precipitously. At William Jennings Bryan's death, an editorial complained that "had our council been sought, the fight would not have occurred in the place and under the circumstances in which it did." And when fundamentalist activists forced through antievolution legislation, they prophetically opined that many of these laws would "recoil against the position they are enacted to promote or maintain," and that without a change in the debate strategy ("appeal[ing] to reason, to thoughtful argument, to calm logic and limit[ing] ourselves to statements of fact"), "the 'victors' may in the end be the losers." Torrey, ever the odd man out, continued to insist that Christians could be both evolutionists and thoroughly orthodox, to Gray's consternation.[125]

Whether institute leaders liked it or not, an important part of MBI's consumers were obtuse fundamentalists, plain-folk evangelicals, and a growing population of upwardly mobile Pentecostals. The institute awkwardly negotiated the interests of its various constituencies. It gave space for Gaebelein to fulminate about Pentecostalism's beginnings "among colored people" and conspiratorial claims that the same "enemy of God and His truth, Satan," was behind both it and modernism. Then MBI turned around and allowed faith healer Fred F. Bosworth and other "respectable" Pentecostals space to protest.[126] The only perceptible dividing line between sectarian and saint on many matters was how it played to middle-class sensibilities. MBI's caginess about the "fundamentalist" label did not adversely affect its reputation among self-defined fundamentalists. The rambunctious Fort Worth–based Baptist minister J. Frank Norris approached MBI about taking over his substantial bookstore operation in 1923, rent free and including complementary advertising in his weekly newspaper. It was Crowell who was "unfavorable" to the proposition.[127]

Thus, the demise of the WCFA and other culturally militant forms of fundamentalism was of substantial benefit to MBI. This was the state of affairs Crowell had desired all along. It allowed the institute to quietly, and thus all the more effectively, exert influence over churches, individuals, and organizations as a purveyor of religion, guaranteed pure.

Epilogue

Moody Bible Institute continued to exert immense influence over conservative evangelicalism after the fundamentalist-modernist controversies of the 1920s. Having proven itself an expert in organization, it served as a primary hub of an informal religious network that spread across America and the world.[1] It is difficult to think of an interwar fundamentalist that did not have or attempt to establish some connection to MBI. Interestingly, this included Reuben Torrey, who at the end of his career returned to teach at MBI and serve as an extension worker. After Lyman Stewart's death, tensions rose between Torrey and Biola trustees over undisclosed issues. Even a preacher of Torrey's considerable stature found it difficult to continue without any institutional affiliation, and since he would have no administrative authority, Henry Crowell was happy to have his scholarly and "orthodox" reputation under the auspices of MBI.

By all accounts, the relationship continued amicably until Torrey's death in 1928. But the same stubborn differences between his holiness theology and MBI's new Keswick orientation had not changed. It resulted in an awkward exchange between James Gray and Torrey's daughter Edith in 1931, when MBI wanted to rework a section in Torrey's correspondence course on the Baptism of the Holy Spirit. Since the Torrey family still held the copyright, Gray needed their permission. Torrey's teachings were too close to "Extreme Pentecostalists" like Aimee Semple McPherson, Gray explained, and they had been rejected by most major dispensational premillennialists. Edith was horrified by Gray's inquiry. She flatly rejected his request and demanded that he never mention "this matter to my mother as it would surely cause her even greater distress than it has caused me."[2]

In the 1930s and 1940s, MBI became a key relay between the older fundamentalist movement and the welter of new institutions that formed the organizational backbone for self-described "evangelicals" in post–World

War II America. The National Association of Evangelicals, the National Religious Broadcasters, and the Christian Booksellers Association (the leading force in evangelical publishing today) all came into being, at least in part, through MBI's direct efforts. Fuller Theological Seminary in Southern California, an important center of "neoevangelical" influence, had roots at MBI, including the trustee Thomas Smith's son Wilbur. Add to this the organizations of former employees and students, and the list would stretch for pages.[3]

MBI's various outreach departments flourished after 1930. Radio became its newest foray starting in 1926, headed by Henry Colman Crowell, the technologically savvy son of the president. When the institute's station, WMBI, sought to expand its broadcasting hours and signal strength in the 1930s, it needed to make the case to regulators that it was a nonsectarian, educational ministry. And unlike the raucous fundamentalist radio broadcasters on unregulated Mexican border stations, WMBI had to take care to be nonoffensive. An undated "Policy Statement" for guests, dating sometime after the 1960s, carefully explained the Federal Communications Commission requirements that they "refrain from making derogatory remarks about individuals, groups or other religions." This meant not mentioning those "with whom we disagree" by name.[4] Quantifying the reach of radio is difficult, but statistics from the 1940s and 1950s report between 40,000 and 60,000 letters being received from listeners annually.[5] The *Moody Bible Institute Monthly*'s circulation approached 30,000 before the Great Depression took its toll. But it rebounded quickly; it had nearly 75,000 subscribers by 1946 and had topped 110,000 by 1966. It would increase to 250,000 in the mid-1980s before going defunct, with many other magazines, in the Internet age.[6] Correspondence courses grew steadily to about 7,800 students annually in 1953 but then exploded to 40,000 active students in 1960.[7] Extension workers and faculty members conducted thousands of meetings in most states, reaching hundreds of thousands of people.

MBI continued to be troubled by the tension between an intrinsic individualism that negated racial categories and the tug of often-racist middle-class norms. Generally speaking, it has stayed abreast of broader cultural shifts, whether for good or ill. Its exclusionary racial policies were reversed in 1938, much earlier than other fundamentalist institutions, but the document outlining the change was labeled "not for . . . general circulation." A note in the policy manual suggested they emphasize that students of color were "under the supervision of the Superintendent."[8] Likewise, radio guests in the 1960s needed explicit reminders that if they found it "necessary to make a distinction," they should refer to African Americans "ONLY as 'Negro,' 'colored man,' 'colored brother,' or 'colored friend.'"[9] Today, MBI considers it a point of pride that it remained in the city while most evangelical colleges, like Biola, migrated to the suburbs. The neighborhood has now been gentrified significantly—increasing the value of its significant landholdings while also limiting its ability to expand. But it was, for most of its history, located at the seam between a poorer working-class West Side and the elite Gold Coast neighborhood to the east. Moody had been within walking distance of a large African American population in the nearby Cabrini Green public-housing complex until it was torn down in the early 2000s. Many students engaged in different types of "Christian work" there. MBI attracts far more students of color (and faculty) today than it did in the early twentieth century, but many issues related to race remain unresolved.[10]

Women students had their ministerial options hamstrung in ways and for reasons that Dwight L. Moody would have never approved. The theology of "purity through submission" intrinsic in Keswick holiness developed into a system that many women have found to be dysfunctional and oppressive. Shirley Nelson's thinly veiled, semifictional account of her years at MBI provided a poignant description of these dynamics during World War II.[11] In 1977 author Patricia Gundry wrote a conservative statement of feminism, *Woman Be Free!*, based, like any good evangelical work, on her personal study of the Bible. When she began lecturing on the subject, she was banned from MBI media. In the face of growing conservative complaints, her husband, Stan Gundry, a professor at MBI, was asked to resign two years later.[12] Based on early disciplinary records, it seems that MBI has always attracted small groups of gay and lesbian evangelicals, but that is a history still to be written.

Another somewhat ironic source of MBI's cultural influence came by way of its engagement with science. The Moody Institute of Science (MIS) was started by Irwin Moon, a lay evangelist who had a penchant for God's creation and a desire to evangelize those who might not attend a typical evangelistic service. Moon was a promising student and received a physics scholarship from Yale, but he turned it down to attend MBI instead. Thus his "science" was largely self-taught and often tended more toward subjects familiar to engineers, like electricity, rather than biology. In 1930 Moon began conducting evangelistic campaigns using simple scientific experiments to demonstrate theological ideas. In 1938 he caught the attention of Will Houghton, the new president of MBI. He incorporated Moon into

MBI's Extension Studies Department. When mobilization for World War II began, Moon conducted demonstrations for soldiers, promising to give his scientific apparatus worth about $20,000 to anyone who "can prove to me that any statement in the Bible is untrue." In 1944 he completed his first film, which became part the award-winning series *Sermons from Science*. These films were widely utilized by the U.S. Air Force during new recruit training in the 1940s. Over two years, they were shown almost 9,000 times and reportedly produced 2,500 conversions.[13]

Thanks to Moon's prodding, MBI also played a leading role in the formation of the American Scientific Affiliation, an organization of Christian scientists still in existence today. The professional values impressed on its early formation, requiring that members be educated scientists and not amateurs, made it a leading voice for integrating an "orthodox" Christian faith and "mainstream" science. Today, it defines "orthodoxy" by ancient creeds rather than a personal relationship to God and is a leading advocate for the compatibility of Christianity and biological evolution.[14]

MBI's wheelhouse remained technology and engineering rather than science per se. Its aviation division, first proposed in 1946, has been a top trainer of missionary pilots and certified aviation technicians around the world. It moved from the Chicago suburbs to Tennessee in the late 1960s. In 1986 one author estimated that a Moody graduate was taking off every four minutes on average from somewhere around the globe—often from treacherous, small patches of cleared land in remote forests and jungles. At that time, at least, over half of all active missionary pilots were trained at MBI.[15]

But dwarfing all of these other forms of outreach was the prodigious output of MBI's publishing arm. The Bible Institute Colportage Association was fully incorporated into MBI in 1941 and rechristened Moody Press. By 1959 it was producing 18 million pieces of literature per year.[16] Early on, this material reached well outside conservative evangelical circles. In 1943 Dale Carnegie, the ever-chipper father of modern self-help techniques, recounted how his childhood home was filled primarily with books "of the Moody Colportage Library." His mother apparently had designs that he become "a Methodist minister" and "would be thrilled to know that her son was privileged to have correspondence with the Moody Bible Institute."[17] Moody Press has always focused primarily on the evangelical market, but it never limited itself to self-identified fundamentalists. In the late 1960s, MBI trademarked what had been the long-standing understanding of its customers: Moody was "the name you can trust."

MBI FURTHER REFINED THE methods of creating and re-creating old-time religion through business methods while working tirelessly behind the scenes to create modern evangelicalism's institutional infrastructure. But as an organization, MBI has become far less prominent over time. Innumerable imitators borrowed its methods to create their own Bible schools, colleges, independent churches, radio ministries, magazines, and other "para-church" organizations. MBI eschews political activism, which may also diminish its present influence. But its long-standing alignment to Republican politics will doubtless continue. Meanwhile the Religious Right embraces the individualistic, business-friendly modernity that MBI pioneered. Whether promoting creation science or voicing skepticism of global warming, it resists any science incompatible with individualism or public policy presuming a social ill not caused by individual choices.

MBI has continued to wrestle throughout its history with the difficulties of maintaining a pristine reputation for "pure religion" amid the completely free market of religion. A corporation might dominate a *single* market, but only governments can regulate an economy. Crowell's strategy worked at Quaker Oats only because American capitalism is not an entirely free market; it has laws and courts to which a company can appeal for relief when someone appropriates a trademark without authorization. This legal apparatus also mediates separations when partnerships do not pan out, and it bars troublesome ex-employees from posing as company representatives. But no legal controls exist for religious movements in which "the market" is metaphorical and uninstitutionalized. Inasmuch as there is legal overlap between religious and business institutions—that is, as to the specific honest dealings of a corporate entity—MBI has maintained a pristine reputation for straight financials and no funny business. But it remains vulnerable to guilt by association whenever a self-described evangelical experiences a fall from grace.

To combat the challenges of the religious free market, conservative evangelicals at MBI and elsewhere find as much utility in the categories of "fundamentalism," "Holy Roller" Pentecostal, and other "radicals" as do their liberal opponents. Such groups served, and continue to serve, as spiritual junkyards that hold and dissipate the inevitable toxic by-products of the evangelical project. One believer's principled stand, or bold act of faith, or encounter with God, can also become another believer's "extremism," when disruptive outcomes result. In such cases, conservative evangelicals are happy to accede to secularists that "fundamentalism" represents a dangerous "other" as long as they can position themselves between it and the other "extreme"—projected as an all-encompassing "liberal" religion devoid of "real" Christian content or sincerity. Most Protestants, rank-and-file evangelicals included, want to be identified with this imaginary "center" that is always conveniently positioned over one's personal convictions.[18] It was a strategy destined for success.

For all of MBI's midcentury promise and influence, its prominence slowly eroded toward the end of the millennium for reasons, it seems, that were largely beyond its control. Born with the birth of a mass market in which a single brand appealed to the consuming masses, MBI failed to make the transition to the market segmentation that spread widely through the economy after World War II and came into its own in the 1960s.[19] Henry Crowell died in 1943, and no other marketer has served a major leadership role at MBI since, leaving the institute to plod forward utilizing policies their brilliant leader had established for an earlier era. Defending and developing a single trademark made it too slow and old-fashioned for a modern, agile market with virtual communities that dissipate as quickly as they form.

The new segmented religious marketplace is serviced by innumerable niche players, a stream of religious celebrities that includes ministers, Bible teachers, authors, singers, and healers. But the real power behind these individuals is the religious media conglomerates that work symbiotically with them. Their centralized bureaucracy, indeterminate (even secular) identities, and multiple brands allow them to service efficiently a diversity of religious consumers, both literally and symbolically.[20] Thus, after Billy Graham especially, the evangelical marketplace has irreparably fragmented in ways that mirror the secular economy. It is left to the charismatic authors, pastors, and syndicated radio and television hosts interwoven in this mass media machine to provide the personal touch for each respective segment. The corporate powers remain in the background.

The amorphous boundaries of evangelicalism since the 1980s to the present reflect this pliable, segmented evangelicalism. It is the old-fashioned Pentecostalism of Joyce Meyer; the historicist premillennialism of Jack Van Impe; the Old Fashioned Revival Hour of Jerry Falwell; the evangelical hipsters in the emergent church movement, who appropriate a full range of religious traditions to achieve a particular aesthetic vision; the quasi-Reformed, beer-drinking "New Calvinists"; and the mash-up of Jonathan Edwards and Ayn Rand in Minneapolis Baptist minister John Piper's neo-Puritanism. It is the mature Willow Creek megachurch in suburban

Chicagoland; the sandal-wearing megachurch of Rick Warren in suburban Orange County; the multiracial "health and wealth" megachurch of Joel Osteen in Houston—still slightly suspicious to some white evangelicals; and the slightly too-liberal "Love Wins" megachurch once led by Rob Bell in Grand Rapids, Michigan. It is the "fundamentalist Harvard" of Wheaton College; the media-savvy Liberty University, whose paradigm-shifting "business plan" and 90,000 online students have made it the world's largest Christian university;[21] the more-militant, homeschool-oriented Patrick Henry College; and the southern fundamentalist holdovers Bob Jones University and Dallas Theological Seminary, still openly dispensational after all these years. It is the "praise-and-worship" industrial complex churning innumerable variations of the same individualistic praise songs to God at every tempo for every denominational style. It is the Contemporary Christian Music scene, with analogs for every musical genre, from death metal and bluegrass to hip-hop. It is the innumerable magazines for every segment of the evangelical population—a *New York Review of Books*–inspired *Books and Culture*, a *Time*-inspired *Christianity Today*, and everything in between. Each publication is carefully designed for segmented markets of pastors, men, women, and more, and most are owned by the same company. All of these things and more are the logical end of modern business methods applied to evangelical religion. What MBI was to the age of large, single-branded corporations, the current welter of evangelical ministries is to the market-segmented present. Having pioneered the idea that religion was something to be consumed rather than practiced, MBI became lost in the shuffle of competing brands.

MBI's last great opportunity to retake the spotlight was through Jerry Jenkins, the coauthor of the wildly popular premillennial *Left Behind* series, published between the mid-1990s and the first decade of the new millennium. Though these books sold an astounding 63 million copies, few realize that Jenkins was the former editor of *Moody Magazine*, that he was vice president of its publishing division, or that he now serves as chairman of MBI's board of trustees. The benefits of this success accumulated in Jenkins's celebrity, while MBI was inadvertently left behind. This was not by Jenkins's design, as he prominently advertises his connections to MBI on his personal website.[22] But it speaks to a profound change in "respectable" middle-class Protestantism in the United States, which moved from compulsory denominational identity in the nineteenth century, to a transitional stage in which identification with a branded institution like MBI was required, to the present in which the brand alone is all that matters. Today, individuals, whether Jenkins or innumerable other celebrities with enough book sales or blog readers, can make it on their own without any institutional validation.

The future existence of the school that D. L. Moody founded does not appear to be in serious jeopardy; it continues to train students, publish books, and broadcast programs from the same corner of Chicago Avenue and Lasalle Boulevard in Chicago. But it seems unlikely that it would again become something more than the niche player it is. Having pioneered the techniques for establishing religious authority out of nothing, it is now a victim of its own success.

Notes

Abbreviations

Archival Collections

APF	Arthur P. Fitt Correspondence
BGC	Billy Graham Center Archives, Wheaton College, Wheaton, Ill.
BICA	Bible Institute Colportage Association Trustee Minutes
CES	Meeting Minutes of the Chicago Evangelization Society
DABI	Unprocessed files (box labeled "Departmental—Administration—Box 1")
DLM	Dwight L. Moody Correspondence
ECM	Executive Committee Meeting Minutes of the Moody Bible Institute
EDF	Emma Dryer Files
FC (1–5)	Unprocessed correspondence files for *The Fundamentals* Project. Numerical correspondence to folders named as follows: FC1—Fundamental Letters, beginning June 1, 1911; FC2—Fundamental Letters, 1911–1913; FC3—Fundamentals Letters, June 1, 1913, to August 1914; FC4—Fundamental Letters, June, 1 1913, to August 1914 (I); FC5—Fundamental Letters June 1, 1913, to August 1914 (II)
HPC	Henry Parsons Crowell Correspondence
JHH	J. H. Hunter Correspondence
JMG	James M. Gray Correspondence
LSP	Lyman Stewart Papers
MBI-BF	Moody Bible Institute Biographical Files
MBI-DF	Moody Bible Institute Departmental Files Collection
MBI-TM	Moody Bible Institute Trustee Minutes
MBIA	Moody Bible Institute Archives
RAT	Reuben A. Torrey Correspondence
TFP (1–14)	Torrey Family Papers, Montrose, Pennsylvania (fourteen folders)
WC (1–3)	Unprocessed Wooden File Cabinet (drawers 1–3)
WNC	William Norton Correspondence (including bound carbon copies)
WRM	William R. Moody Correspondence

Newspapers and Periodicals

AF	*Apostolic Faith*
BW	*Biblical World*
CDT	*Chicago Daily Tribune*
CIO	*Chicago Inter-Ocean*

CU	Christian Union
CWC	Proceedings of the Christian Worker's Convention (1886–1892)
CWM	Christian Workers Magazine
IT	Institute Tie
KB	King's Business
LH	Leaves of Healing
MBIM	Moody Bible Institute Monthly
NYT	New York Times
NYTr	New York Tribune
PP	St. Paul and Minneapolis Pioneer Press
RCW	Record of Christian Work

Introduction

1. *Salt Lake Herald*, October 13, 1907, 11.

2. H. R. 435, 26–27.

3. On the importance of metaphors, see Lakoff and Johnson, *Metaphors We Live By*.

4. McClay, *The Masterless*.

5. Pietsch, "Dispensational Modernism." See also Connolly, *Capitalism and Christianity, American Style*.

6. I explore this in more detail in Gloege, "The Problem of Christian History." See also, Butler, *Awash in a Sea of Faith*; Kidd, *The Great Awakening*.

7. Noll, *America's God*; Bozeman, *Protestants in an Age of Science*; Sehat, *The Myth of American Religious Freedom*.

8. Hatch, *The Democratization of American Christianity*; Schmidt, *Hearing Things*.

9. Bratt, "The Reorientation of American Protestantism"; Ryan, *Cradle of the Middle Class*; Taves, *Fits, Trances, and Visions*.

10. Carter, *The Spiritual Crisis of the Gilded Age*; Faust, *This Republic of Suffering*; Menand, *The Metaphysical Club*; Turner, *Without God, Without Creed*; Noll, *The Civil War as a Theological Crisis*.

11. Hart, *Deconstructing Evangelicalism*.

12. McCloud, *Divine Hierarchies*, has influenced my thinking on class and religion.

13. Particularly helpful in my understanding of this dynamic is Johnston, *Radical Middle Class*, and Beckert, *Monied Metropolis*.

14. I rely on the excellent work already done on the relationship of gender to fundamentalism in Bendroth, *Fundamentalism and Gender, 1875 to the Present*; DeBerg, *Ungodly Women*; and Hassey, *No Time for Silence*.

15. Peiss, *Hope in a Jar*; Manring, *Slave in a Box*; Weems, "The Revolution Will Be Marketed"; Lee and Sinitiere, *Holy Mavericks*.

16. Bebbington, *Evangelicalism in Modern Britain*, 3.

17. Lofton, *Oprah*; Schmidt, *Restless Souls*.

18. Lofton, "Commonly Modern"; Sutton, *American Apocalypse*. See also the forthcoming work by Brendan Pietsch and Seth Dowland.

Chapter 1

1. *CDT*, September 17, 1860, 1; Sims, Life of Rev. Thomas M. Eddy, esp. 264–66.

2. Moody and Fitt, *The Shorter Life of D. L. Moody*, 9–14.

3. Moody, *The Life of D. L. Moody*, 46; Sandage, *Born Losers*.

4. Halttunen, *Confidence Men and Painted Women*; Ryan, *Cradle of the Middle Class*.

5. Moody, *The Life of D. L. Moody*, 41.

6. Ibid., 44; Findlay, *Dwight L. Moody*, 49–51.

7. Friedman, *Birth of a Salesman*, 60.

8. Daniels, *D. L. Moody and His Work*, 78; Friedman, *Birth of a Salesman*, 56–57.

9. Moody, *The Life of Dwight L. Moody*, 50.

10. McLoughlin, *Modern Revivalism*, 172–73; Findlay, *Dwight L. Moody*, 53–63, 88. On income levels circa 1890, see Painter, *Standing at Armageddon*, xix.

11. Findlay, *Dwight L. Moody*, 74; *New York Observer and Chronicle*, March 14, 1872, 1.

12. Long, *The Revival of 1857–58*.

13. Dunn, "Formative Years of the Chicago Y.M.C.A."

14. Daniels, *D. L. Moody and His Work*, 36, 38.

15. Moody, *The Life of Dwight L. Moody*, 63–64.

16. Daniels, *D. L. Moody and His Work*, 47.

17. Ibid., 48.

18. Farwell, *Some Recollections of John V. Farwell*, 106; Findlay, *Dwight L. Moody*, 68–80.

19. Sunday School Share, in "D. L. M. Life Ministry Sunday School 2," Photograph Collection, MBIA.

20. Daniels, *D. L. Moody and His Work*, 81–82; "Lay-Preaching," *New Englander*, January 1876, 135, 137–38.

21. Daniels, *D. L. Moody and His Work*, 41–75; *Independent*, January 28, 1886, 14.

22. *New York Observer and Chronicle*, November 5, 1863, 1; June 18, 1863, 195.

23. *CDT*, April 22, 1862, 3; *CDT*, January 31, 1863, 4.

24. Dorsett, *A Passion for Souls*, 68–73; McLoughlin, *Modern Revivalism*, 174.

25. Daniels, *Moody and His Work*, 105; *United States Christian Commission Annual Reports*, 214. *CDT*, April 22, 1862, 3; *CDT*, January 31, 1863, 4.

26. Findlay, *Dwight L. Moody*, 108; Moody, *The Life of Dwight L. Moody*, 108. Dobschuetz, "Fundamentalism and American Urban Culture," 50–51, 57–58, reports disciplinary cases in the church that correlate to working-class culture, including "disorderly conduct" and saloon frequenting.

27. "Individual Obligation to Do Christian Work," *Missionary Magazine*, March 1863, 74.

28. *New York Observer and Chronicle*, December 27, 1866, 410; *Zion's Herald*, January 2, 1867, 1; *Independent*, December 12, 1867, 1.

29. *CDT*, June 22, 1869, 3.

30. *CDT*, July 14, 1870, 4.

31. *CDT*, June 8, 1866, 4.

32. *CDT*, April 25, 1869, 2; *CDT*, June 22, 1869, 3.

33. *CDT*, June 8, 1866, 4.

34. "Card from the Young Men's Christian Association," *CDT*, October 12, 1866, 4.

35. YMCA Proceedings (1869), 62–63.

36. Findlay, "Moody, 'Gapmen,' and the Gospel."

37. *Independent*, January 2, 1868, 2.

38. *CDT*, January 13, 1869, 4.

39. *CDT*, July 20, 1869, 3.

40. Moody, *The Life of Dwight L. Moody*, 63–64; Farwell, *Recollections*.

41. A similar connection to the early Social Gospel movement is made by Jackson, "What Would Jesus Do?," 641–61. Literary styles like realism relate both to the production of texts and how readers approach texts (even ancient texts like the Bible). Denning, *Mechanic Accents*, 259; Glazener, *Reading for Realism*, 373.

42. Bozeman, *Protestants in an Age of Science*; Noll, *America's God*.

43. Sandeen, *Roots of Fundamentalism*, 3–58.

44. Ibid., 93–99.

45. Ibid., 73–76; *Letters by J. N. D.*, 2:117, 2:162. Darby later grudgingly reassessed his opinion of Moody; ibid., 2:203.

46. Bundy, "Keswick and the Experience of Evangelical Piety"; Cooke, *Mildmay*; Dorsett, *Passion for Souls*, 134–35.

47. Findlay, *Dwight L. Moody*, 126, notes Moody's lack of public reaction to the sermons.

48. In *CDT*, April 6, 1885, 6, Moody's reference to ignoring Bible study dates to the late 1860s.

49. *CDT*, June 19, 1870, 2.

50. Dorsett, *A Passion for Souls*, 145–47.

51. *CDT*, December 21, 1869, 4; *CDT*, June 29, 1869, 4; *CDT*, August 6, 1871, 2; *CDT*, December 24, 1870, p. 4. *CDT*, April 19, 1869, 4.

52. *CDT*, June 22, 1869, 3.

53. [YMCA] Proceedings of the Fourteenth Annual Convention (July 1869), 61.

54. *CDT*, November 4, 1869, 1.

55. YMCA Proceedings, 49.

56. *CDT*, January 14, 1869, 2.

57. *CDT*, January 12, 1869, 4.

58. Findlay, *Dwight L. Moody*, 132.

59. Cuyler, *Recollections*, 90–91; "From Chicago," *CU*, November 13, 1872, 404.

60. *CDT*, December 1, 1872, 12; YMCA Proceedings (1872), 98.

61. Findlay, *Dwight L. Moody*, 120–24.

62. Evensen, *God's Man for the Gilded Age*.

63. Moody, *New Sermons, Addresses, and Prayers*, 294.

64. Marsden, *Fundamentalism and American Culture*, 32.

65. Quoted in McLoughlin, *Modern Revivalism*, 221, 244.

66. *Independent*, July 26, 1877, 1.

67. *NYTr*, January 30, 1879, 2.

68. Hillis, "The Last of the Great Group," *Interior*, January 4, 1900, 6.

69. *Zion's Herald*, January 28, 1875, 1.

70. Evensen, *God's Man for the Gilded Age*, 121.

71. "At Northfield," *CU*, August 20, 1885, 25.

72. *Zion's Herald*, November 25, 1875, 370.

73. *Independent*, January 28, 1886, 14.

74. Evensen, *God's Man for the Gilded Age*, quote 118.

75. D. L. Moody, *Addresses*, 1.

76. Moody, *New Sermons, Addresses, and Prayers*, 552.

77. Moody, "How to Read the Bible," in *Notes for Bible Readings*, 34; Moody, *Pleasure and Profit in Bible Study*, 50.

78. Moody, "The Gospel Awakening," 221.

79. Moody, *Anecdotes*, 114, 115–16, quote on 119.

80. Hilkey, *Character Is Capital*.

81. Moody, *Arrows and Anecdotes*, 71.

82. Moody, *Pleasure and Profit in Bible Study*, 47.

83. "At Northfield," *CU*, August 20, 1885, 25.

84. Quoted in "Fiftieth Annual Meeting" (1876), in *Christian Work in New York*, 68.

85. "Christian Work," *New York Evangelist*, April 6, 1876, 2.

86. Sandeen, *Roots of Fundamentalism*, 133; Needham, "Bible Conferences," *Watchword* 13 (1891): 60.

87. *NYTr*, November 20, 1868, 8.

88. Evensen, *God's Man for the Gilded Age*, 68–69.

89. *CDT*, November 28, 1875, 2; and November 27, 1875, 9.

90. Quoted in Evensen, *God's Man for the Gilded Age*, 144.

91. This and following based on Evensen, *God's Man for the Gilded Age*, 123–63, unless otherwise stated.

92. *CDT*, January 6, 1877, 7.

Chapter 2

1. Quotes from *CDT*, July 26, 1877, 3. Schneirov, "Chicago's Great Upheaval of 1877," 76–104; Currey, *Chicago*, 2:302; Avrich, *The Haymarket Tragedy*, 33; Green, *Death in the Haymarket*, 77–80.

2. Hounshell, *From the American System to Mass Production*; Nye, *Consuming Power*; Chandler, *The Visible Hand*.

3. Foner, *Free Soil, Free Labor, Free Men*; Montgomery, *Fall of the House of Labor*; Bledstein, *The Culture of Professionalism*.

4. Kazin, *The Populist Persuasion*, 13–15.

5. Black, "A Crime to Live without Work."

6. Schneirov, *Labor and Urban Politics*.

7. Marty, *Righteous Empire*, 67–77; Handy, *Christian America*, 24–56.

8. McLoughlin, *Modern Revivalism*, 198–99.

9. Quoted in ibid., 253.

10. Ibid., 198–205, 225–30, 248–56, 267–71.

11. Quotes in Evensen, *God's Man for the Gilded Age*, 107, 117, 120–21.

12. "Masks and Faces," *CDT*, January 30, 1877, 2.

13. Remlap, "The Gospel Awakening," 545.

14. Cooke, *Mildmay*, quote from 44.

86. Smith to "The Board of Managers," MBI-DF, 1, 6, 7–8.

87. *CDT*, February 22, 1889, 9.

88. CES, May 16, 1889, 77–79.

89. Moorehead to Moody, June 23, 1889, DLMC; Dorsett, *A Passion for Souls*, 307.

90. *CU*, July 1, 1886; Torrey, Autobiographical Notes, RAT; Waite, *Dr. Torrey*, MBI-BF.

91. Emma Dryer to Charles Blanchard, 29, EDF.

92. Findlay, *Dwight L. Moody*, 349–55.

Chapter 3

1. Torrey, Diary, 1889–1890, TFP.

2. Wacker, "The Holy Spirit and the Spirit of the Age."

3. Hatch, *Democratization of American Christianity*; Knox, *Enthusiasm*; Taves, *Fits, Trances, and Visions*; Johnson and Wilentz, *Kingdom of Matthias*.

4. Long, "Consecrated Respectability."

5. Daniels, *Moody*, 365–409.

6. Hilkey, *Character Is Capital*, 132; Moody, *Secret Power*.

7. *CDT*, January 18, 1886, 1.

8. Moody, *Secret Power*, 12, 13; Daniels, *Moody*, 367.

9. Quoted in Davis, *Torrey and Alexander*, 23–24.

10. Torrey, *The Holy Spirit*, 78; Roger Martin, *Reuben Torrey*, 27–37.

11. Torrey, "Autobiographical Notes," RAT. Torrey regularly equated this experience with his conversion. Torrey, *How to Pray*, 11; Torrey, *The Holy Spirit*, 36.

12. Torrey, "Autobiographical Notes," RAT. Gibbon, *History of the Decline and Fall of the Roman Empire*; Wacker, *Augustus H. Strong*.

13. Parker, "Discourse of the Transient," 358–59.

14. Emerson, "Self-Reliance."

15. Torrey, "Jesus the way, the truth, and the life" [handwritten manuscript], TFP, 15–16.

16. Davis, *Torrey and Alexander*, 29; Torrey, Diary 1, August 10, 1882, BGC.

17. Torrey, Diary 1, July 2, 1882, BGC.

18. Torrey, Diary 1, July 25, 1882, BGC. See also Hutchison, *Modernist Impulse*, 85; Torrey, Diary 1, August 15, 1882, and August 16, 1882, BGC.

19. Kloppenberg, *Uncertain Victory*.

20. Torrey, Diary 1, November 28, 1882, BGC.

21. Davis, "Critical Exposition."

22. Torrey, *How to Study the Bible*, 109.

23. Seeley, *Ecce Homo*, 2.

24. Ibid., 351. Hopkins, *The Rise of the Social Gospel*, 22–23; May, *Protestant Churches and Industrial America*, 150.

25. Wills, *Boosters, Hustlers, and Speculators*. On the wider regional context, see Cronin *Nature's Metropolis*.

26. In 1890, 51 percent of religious persons in Minnesota were Catholic, and 27.4 percent were Lutheran. Only 2.6 percent were Congregationalist. The population of Minneapolis and St. Paul were likewise Catholic dominated. Gaustad and Barlow, *New Historical*

Atlas of Religion in America, 360, 361, 376 (figures C.4, C.5, and C.17); see also Minnesota Population Center, National Historical Geographic Information System.

27. Shaw, "Cooperation in the Northwest," 238.

28. *Pilgrim*, February 1884, June 1885, March 1884, May 1884, October 1884, November 1885. For brief mention of Torrey's work, see "North East Neighborhood House," Collection P3, Box 1, Folder 3, Minnesota Historical Society.

29. Torrey, "How Shall We Invest?," *Pilgrim*, December 1885.

30. Sklansky, *The Soul's Economy*.

31. "Dr. Gladden on the Industrial Question," *CU*, January 20, 1887, 6.

32. "In and about Chicago," *CU*, January 7, 1886, 20.

33. *Northwestern Congregationalist*, January 1887.

34. *CWC* (1886), 74–77, 105.

35. Torrey, *The Holy Spirit*, 198–99.

36. Stanley, *From Bondage to Contract*.

37. Torrey, *Baptism with the Holy Spirit*, 32, 34–35.

38. Ibid., 15.

39. Ibid., 53–54.

40. Ibid., 27–29.

41. Ibid., 46–48, 50.

42. Ibid., 43.

43. Torrey, *How to Pray*, 65. Lears, "From Salvation to Self-Realization," describes this broader trend in consumer society.

44. Torrey, *How to Study the Bible*, 111.

45. Torrey, *Baptism with the Holy Spirit*, 70–72.

46. Ibid., 24.

47. Ibid., 74–76. See also Ostrander, "The Battery and the Windmill."

48. Torrey, *How to Study the Bible*, 111–12.

49. Ibid., 110–11.

50. Torrey, *How to Pray*, 49.

51. Ibid., 9.

52. Torrey, *How to Study the Bible*, 110–11.

53. Ibid., 109.

54. Torrey's Bible, Collection 107, Box 5, BGC.

55. *Southern Cross*, September 10, 1902, 12.

56. Torrey, *Difficulties*, 15, 29–31.

57. Torrey, *Divine Origin of the Bible*, 7.

58. *PP*, December 1, 1886, 6; *PP*, February 12, 1887, 6; *PP*, February 13, 1887, 6. National coverage included *The Philadelphia Inquirer*, February 14, 1887, 7; *Boston Daily Globe*, February 13, 1887, 2; *New York Times*, February 13, 1887, 7.

59. *Pilgrim*, February 1887–July 1887.

60. *CWC* (1888), 150–54.

61. *CU*, September 29, 1887, 294; *CWC* (1887).

62. *CU*, August 4, 1887, 112–13.

63. *CWC* (1888).

64. Torrey, *What I Believe*, 4.

65. Torrey, Diary, 1889–1890, 13, TFP.

66. Torrey, Diary, 1889–1890, 1–4, 8, 17, 20–21, TFP.

67. "How God Answered Prayer."

68. Torrey, Diary, 1889–1890, 21–22, TFP.

69. Torrey, *What I Believe*, 4.

70. *IT*, February 1901, 170.

71. Robinson, *Reporter at Moody's*, 72–73.

72. Nolt, "Avoid Provoking the Spirit of Controversy." Most lecturers are listed in the annual catalogs and bulletins at the MBI archives.

73. *IT*, October 30, 1892, 179.

74. "Men's Department of the Bible Institute," MBI-DF.

75. *CWC* (1890), 380.

76. Robinson, *Reporter at Moody's*, 99; Moody, *Life of Dwight L. Moody*, 344.

77. "Examination on John, Spring Term, 1899," CES Forms, MBI-DF.

78. *CWC* (1890), 373.

79. Torrey, *What the Bible Teaches*, 1–3, 5–12, 33–34. Marsden, *Fundamentalism and American Culture*, 60–61.

80. Torrey, *How to Study the Bible*, 54.

81. "Course of Study," (1891) MBI-DF.

82. Torrey, *How to Work for Christ*.

83. "Personal Work Examination," CES Forms, MBI-DF.

84. *CWC* (1890), 374–77.

85. "The Bible Institute Attendance Report Card" (1897); "Weekly Report Card," n.d. (circa 1892 based on marginalia), MBI-DF.

86. "Worker's Memorandum"; "Worker's Address Card"; "Women's Meeting Visitor's Report"; "Confidential" (1894) [for new converts] CES Forms, MBI-DF.

87. *CWC* (1890), 381.

88. *IT*, September 30, 1892, 171–72.

89. E. W. Wadsworth Interview, November 22, 1958, E. W. Wadsworth File, MBI-BF.

90. *IT*, November 24, 1891, 13.

91. *CWC* (1890), 374–77.

92. 02539M, Student Files, MBIA.

Chapter 4

1. Wharton, *Month with Moody*, 255–63.

2. Wacker, "Marching to Zion"; *LH*, August 31, 1894, 16.

3. *CWC* (1889–1891).

4. Torrey, *Power of Prayer*, 24.

5. Harlan, *Booker T. Washington Papers*, 3:371–73, 1:199–200, 1:323–24.

6. This is based on a case-insensitive search of these terms using Google's substantial American English ngram corpus at http://books.google.com/ngrams/, accessed May 1, 2014.

7. Findlay, *Dwight L. Moody*, 349–55.

8. Robinson, *A Reporter at Moody's*, 31–33.

9. MBI Catalog, 1890, MBIA.

10. "Personalia—Women's Department," *IT*, September 1900, 10.

11. *Student Register of the Moody Bible Institute of Chicago.*

12. 00014M, 02544M, 02549M, Student Records, MBIA.

13. Dobschuetz, "Fundamentalism and American Urban Culture," 178.

14. Hall, "The Power of One," 96–98.

15. Ibid.

16. Robinson, *A Reporter at Moody's*, 31–33.

17. Stelzle, *A Son of the Bowery*, 55–57.

18. Torrey to Fitt, September 19, 1908, RAT; Stelzle, "Jesus Christ as a Social Reformer," *IT*, July 1909, 906–8.

19. *CWC* (1890), 377.

20. Gilbert, *Perfect Cities*, 204.

21. Ibid., 192. Sea also Carter, "Union Made," 147–49.

22. Wharton, *Month with Moody*, 263, 259.

23. Baylen, "A Victorian's 'Crusade' in Chicago, 1893–1894"; CDT, November 13, 1893, 2; Stead, *If Christ Came to Chicago*, 270, 273, 465, 461–63.

24. CES, November 4, [1893], 87–89.

25. Stead, *If Christ Came to Chicago*, 144, 149.

26. Quoted in Smith, *Urban Disorder and the Shape of Belief*, 187.

27. Lindsey, *The Pullman Strike*; Painter, *Standing at Armageddon*, 122–28.

28. Lears, *Rebirth of a Nation*, 181.

29. Ibid., 170–74.

30. Cronon, *Nature's Metropolis*, 97–147.

31. Nugent, *Money and American Society*.

32. McGerr, *A Fierce Discontent*, 3–13.

33. Hicks, *The Populist Revolt*, 267.

34. Lears, *Rebirth*, 183–84.

35. Johnston, *The Radical Middle Class*, esp. 10–17.

36. Leonard, "More Merciful and Not Less Effective."

37. Nugent, *The Tolerant Populists*.

38. Horsman, *Race and Manifest Destiny*.

39. Painter, *Standing at Armageddon*, 103; Kazin, *The Populist Persuasion*, 28.

40. Creech, *Righteous Indignation*, xvii, 49.

41. Quoted in Lears, *Rebirth of a Nation*, 159.

42. Herron, "The Opportunity of the Church," *Arena*, December 1895, 42; Kazin, *The Populist Persuasion*, 32.

43. Carter, "Union Made," 160–65.

44. Schwantes, *Coxey's Army*.

45. Cook, *Zion City*, 10–11; Wacker, "Marching to Zion," 498–99. The last attack on Dowie at this time by the *Tribune* was "Dowie and the Spiritualists," *CDT*, June 24, 1891, 3.

46. Mullin, *Miracles and the Modern Religious Imagination*.

47. Cunningham, "From Holiness to Healing"; Marsh, *"Faith Healing"—A Defense*.

48. Dowie, *American First-Fruits*, appendix 1.

49. Duffy, "The Changing Image of the American Physician"; Numbers, "Do-It-Your-self the Sectarian Way"; *Annual Report of the Illinois State Board of Health* (1895), xii–xiii; *CDT*, April 30, 1894, 8; *Ibid.,* January 26, 1894, 8; Hansen, "New Images of a New Medicine."

50. Fessenden, *Culture and Redemption*; Sehat, *The Myth of American Religious Freedom*.

51. For examples of moral rhetoric in professional projects, see Bateman and Kapstein, "Between God and the Market"; Willett, *Permanent Waves*; and Hornstein, *A Nation of Realtors*. Contrast with Bledstein, *The Culture of Professionalism*, esp. 196–202.

52. I argue this point in more detail in Gloege, "Faith Healing, Medical Regulation, and Public Religion." See also Opp, *The Lord for the Body*, 14–15, 25–27; and Schoepflin, *Christian Science on Trial*.

53. *CIO*, November 8, 1895, 8; *CIO*, December 25, 1895, 8.

54. Carter, *"Faith Healing" Reviewed after Twenty Years.*

55. Quote in Dorsett, *A Passion for Souls* 334–35.

56. *Boston Daily Globe,* August 12, 1894, 20.

57. *Outlook*, October 2, 1897, 343.

58. Adams and Camp, *"I Cried, He Answered."*

59. Dobschuetz, "Fundamentalism and American Urban Culture," 169.

60. Torrey, Diary, 1889–1890, May 26, 1889, 17, TFP.

61. Hutchison, *Modernist Impulse*; Curtis, *Consuming Faith*; Bowman, "Sin, Spirituality, and Primitivism"; Lofton, "Methodology of the Modernists."

62. Marsden, *Fundamentalism and American Culture*, 51–55.

63. Pietsch, "Dispensational Modernism."

64. Rushing, "From Confederate Deserter to Decorated Veteran Bible Scholar."

65. "Defends the 'Higher Critics,'" *CDT*, February 23, 1893, 11.

66. Sketchy biographical information on Newell is found in "William R. Newell," MBI-BF.

67. Newell, *Romans*, 15.

68. The Pauline Epistles, according to dispensationalists, included all the New Testament Epistles except for the letters of Peter, James, John, and Jude.

69. Newell, *Romans*, 337–39, 15.

70. *RCW*, May 1898, 259–60.

71. Newell, *Romans*, 27. On sanctification, Newell explicitly encouraged the discarding of the "legal doctrine of sanctification, which has been, in another age, the sine qua non of orthodox belief." Newell, *Romans*, 364.

72. "Mr. Moody and the Churches," *RCW*, January 1897, 3.

73. Kazin, *A Godly Hero*, 45–79.

74. Quoted in Findlay, *Dwight L. Moody*, 277.

75. "Healed by Faith," *RCW*, March 1897.

76. *CDT*, December 16, 1895, 3; *CIO*, December 18, 1895, 10; *Independent*, February 27, 1896, 14; *Independent*, March 12, 1896, 11; *Independent*, March 25, 1897, 12; *Independent*, October 28, 1897, 11; *Independent*, December 30, 1897, 16; *New York Evangelist*, March 18, 1897, 11; *Congregationalist,* January 7, 1897, 10; *LH*, October 8, 1898, 975–77. Wacker, "Marching to Zion," 502–5.

77. *LH*, July 15, 1899, 737.

78. *Medical Standard*, April 1897, 111–12, and July 1897, 220–21.

79. *CDT*, March 30, 1899, 7.

80. Torrey to John H. Morgan, March 15, 1898, TFP-14.

81. Torrey, *The Holy Spirit*, 95.

82. Davis, *Torrey and Alexander*; Torrey, *The Holy Spirit*, 93–95; and Martin, *Reuben Torrey*, 125 (n. 13). Torrey's letter to Dowie reproduced in *LH*, April 8, 1899, 460.

83. Moody to Gaylord, May 20, 1898; W. R. Moody to the *Religious Telescope*, reprinted in *LH*, March 24, 1900, 699.

84. *LH*, May 28, 1898, 612–14.

85. Day, *Breakfast Table Autocrat*, 166. See also Runyan, *Dr. Gray at Moody Bible Institute*, 11–15. On Torrey at Chickamauga, see "News from the Front," Armed Services YMCA (Y.USA.4-4), Spanish American War undated, Kautz Family YMCA Archives; Moody to Gray, May 21, 1898, JMG; Moody to Gray, May 28, 1898, JMG.

86. *CDT*, November 4, 1898; Chicago YMCA Board of Managers Minutes, November 8, 1898, YMCA-C; Moody to Torrey, October 31, 1898, DLM; compare Findley *Dwight L. Moody*, 403–5.

87. Torrey to Morse, December 21, 1898, RAT; Reuben Torrey to Clara Torrey, October 13, 1899, TFP-14.

88. "Stands Up for Doctors" (unknown paper), D. L. Moody Clipping File, MBI.

89. *Leaves of Healing*, April 8, 1899, 457–62.

90. Moody to Torrey, March 14, 1899, DLM.

91. L. Wilbur Messer to Moody, June 24, 1899, and H. M. Moore to L. W. Messer, July 13, 1899, Box 88, Folder 12, YMCA-C.

92. *CDT*, July 30, 1899, 5.

93. The "proof" of Dowie's use of "means" was his incidental physical contact with the patient. *CDT*, August 29, 1899, 5; *CDT*, September 10, 1899, 32; *CDT*, September 10, 1899, 5.

94. "Medical Matters in Chicago," *Medical News*, September 9, 1899, 343.

95. *CIO*, October 2, 1899, 4.

96. *CDT*, September 9, 1899, 7; *CDT*, September 23, 1899, 9; *CDT*, September 28, 1899, 6.

97. *CDT*, October 3, 1899, 9; *Chicago Chronicle*, October 2, 1899; *Chicago Journal*, October 2, 1899, 1. National coverage included *Washington Post*, October 6, 1899, 6, and *Los Angeles Times*, October 17, 1899, 7.

98. *CDT*, October 6, 1899, 12.

99. Reuben Torrey to Clara Torrey, October 9, 1899, TFP-14.

100. *Medical News*, November 2, 1895, 496; Dorsett, *Passion for Souls*, 334–35; Dryer to Charles Blanchard, EDF, 8.

101. *Chicago Chronicle*, October 2, 1899, 2.

102. Compare *CDT*, October 26, 1899, 1, and *New York Times*, October 3, 1899, 4.

103. Fitt to Gaylord, December 23, 1899, APF; CES, January 25, 1900 (insert at page 94).

104. *LH*, January 20, 1900, 393–94.

105. Martin, *Reuben Torrey*, 129–30.

106. Torrey, *Divine Healing*, 37, 47, 50.

107. Torrey, "How Can I Know That I Am Led by the Holy Spirit," 102–6.

108. Buckley, "Faith-Healing and Kindred Phenomena," *Century Magazine*, March 1887, 781–87; Waldvogel, "The 'Overcoming Life,'" 110–16, 129–33.

109. The talk, originally given in 1899, is reprinted in Harper, *The Trend in Higher Education*, 207–33. Harper to Morgan, October 24, 1902, "G Campbell Morgan," MBI-BF.

110. Morgan to Harper, October 27, 1902, "G Campbell Morgan," MBI-BF.

Chapter 5

1. Day, *Breakfast Table Autocrat*, 35–59, quote on 59.

2. Ibid., 63–65, 80.

3. Ibid., 113–17.

4. Day, *Breakfast Table Autocrat*, 69–81, quote on 80.

5. Ibid., 5–6.

6. Marquette, *Brands Trademarks and Good Will*, 10–25.

7. Thornton, "History of Quaker Oats," 83.

8. The policy is reprinted in Day, *Breakfast Table Autocrat*, 124.

9. Thornton, "History of Quaker Oats," 33.

10. Marquette, *Brands, Trademarks, and Good Will*, 68.

11. Day, *Breakfast Table Autocrat*, 160–61.

12. Fitt to Gaylord, January 3, 1900, APF.

13. ECM, January 23, 1901, 23.

14. See "Moody Memorial Endowment," MBI-DF.

15. CES, February 2, 1900.

16. See "Large Contributor Research of 1938," MBI-DF.

17. See letters to Fitt from J. N. Field (September 25, 1901), John Dwight (November 15, 1901), and G. F. Swift (July 23, 1902), AFP.

18. *CDT*, April 14, 1900, 13.

19. "A Convention of Christian Workers," DAB1.

20. *CDT*, October 2, 1901, 5.

21. Fitt to Gaylord, December 24, 1900, APF.

22. Day, *Breakfast Table Autocrat*, 166–67; Runyan, *Dr. Gray at Moody Bible Institute*, 15.

23. Crowell to Fitt, May 11, 1901, HPC; Marquette, *Brands, Trademarks, and Good Will*, 77; MBI-TM, December 16, 1901, 25.

24. MBI-TM, February 3, 1903, 31.

25. Day, *Breakfast Table Autocrat*, 289.

26. Torrey, *Power of Prayer*, 94; Martin, *Apostle of Certainty*, 131–33; MBI-TM, December 16, 1901, 25.

27. Crowell to Gray, January 18, 1904, JMG.

28. Crowell to Gray, January 28, 1904, JMG.

29. ECM1; MBI-TM, September 27, 1904, 36.

30. Dixon to Stewart, November 20, 1909, FC1; Torrey to Dixon, September 15, 1909, WC3.

31. Gray to Henry W. Stough, September 23, 1921, Collection 106, Box 1, Folder 9, BGC; Gray, *Primers of Faith*, 238–39.

32. Day, *Breakfast Table Autocrat*, 193–200.

33. MBI-TM, July 14, 1905, 38. On Cleland, see *CDT*, September 11, 1907, 8; *CDT*, September 20, 1894, 7; and Norcross, "Criminal Law Reform," 386–93. On Osborne, see *CDT*, January 7, 1908, 9. On Bordon, see MBI-TM, September 16, 1909, 83; *CDT*, September 21, 1912, 1; and *CDT*, April 10, 1913, 8.

34. *IT*, May 1909, 735. See ECM for specific salaries. For wage comparisons, see Stricker, "American Professors in the Progressive Era."

35. CES, 6–9, 11.

36. MBI-CD, 41; Gray to Crowell, January 26, 1907, JMG.

37. ECM, September 15, 1905; Gray to Fitt, August 7, 1905, JMG.

38. Getz, *MBI*, 121–35.

39. Crowell to Gray, January 28, 1904, JMG; Crowell to Gray, May 10, 1904, JMG; Fitt to Gray, November 7, 1901, APF.

40. Calhoun to Fitt, July 29, 1905, JMG.

41. Gray, "Notes," July 7, 1905, JMG.

42. For example, Gray to Fitt, March 5, 1905, JMG.

43. Patton, "On Preaching," 36–37.

44. *Detroit Free Press*, March 20, 1903, 3.

45. *CDT*, June 14, 1903, 44.

46. McLoughlin, *Modern Revivalism*, 367–68. On Torrey in Britain, see Holmes, *Religious Revivals in Britain and Ireland*, 166–94.

47. Torrey to Fitt, November 29, 1904, RAT.

48. Letters from Calhoun to Gray dated August 9, 1905, and September 2, 1905, JMG.

49. Gray, "Notes," July 7, 1905, JMG; letters from Gray to Fitt dated July 7, 1905, July 25, 1905, and August 4, 1905, JMG.

50. *Aberdeen Daily News*, August 29, 1905, 2. Calhoun to Gray, September 2, 1905; Calhoun to Fitt, September 12, 1905; and Gray to Fitt, August 6, 1906, JMG.

51. Gray to Torrey, September 8, 1905, RAT; Torrey to Gray, September 20, 1905, RAT.

52. ECM, October 5, 1905; Torrey to Fitt, December 9, 1905, and December 19, 1905, RAT.

53. Rhondda, *The True Revival versus Torreyism*.

54. Marsden, *Fundamentalism and American Culture*, 94; Blumhofer, "Transatlantic Currents in North Atlantic Pentecostalism," esp. 353 and following.

55. Wacker, *Heaven Below*, 1; Blumhofer, *Restoring the Faith*, 11–34.

56. Hiss, "Shiloh"; Murray, *Sublimity of Faith*. See also, the semifictional, but immaculately sourced Nelson, *Fair, Clear, and Terrible*.

57. Anderson, *Vision of the Disinherited*, 47–49. Goff, *Fields White unto Harvest*.

58. Goff, *Fields White unto Harvest*, 57–64.

59. Creech, "Visions of Glory."

60. Wacker, *Heaven Below*, 44–51.

61. Torrey, *Is The Present "Tongues" Movement of God?*, 9.

62. Worrell, "An Open Letter," 16–18.

63. Anderson, *Vision of the Disinherited*, 111–12; Warner, *The Woman Evangelist*, 31 (n. 12). There are many other examples to be found in *Dictionary of Pentecostal and Charismatic Movements*.

64. Hollenweger, *The Pentecostals*, 221–23. See also Rennie, "Fundamentalism and the Varieties of North Atlantic Evangelicalism"; see Blumhofer, "Transatlantic Currents" for Torrey's role in global Pentecostalism.

65. Letters from Torrey to Fitt, July 4, 1906, and September 8, 1906, RAT; ECM, September 4, 1906.

66. *IT*, March 1906, 213–14.

67. Blumhofer, *Restoring the Faith*, 79–80; Riss, "William H. Durham"; Blumhofer, "William Hamner Piper"; *Latter Rain Evangel*, October 1908.

68. Torrey, Diary, 1906 –1907, Collection 107, Box 3, Folder 2, BGC.

69. *IT*, November 1906, 92.

70. Torrey to "Students and Faculty," November 28, 1906, RAT.

71. Gray to Fitt, October 26, 1906, JMG.

72. Gray to Fitt, January 26, 1907, JMG.

73. Fitt to Gaylord, May 22, [1907], APF.

74. "The Present Delusion Concerning the Gift of Tongues," *IT*, August 1907, 546; for source of article, see "Gospel Missionary Union" to Fitt, June 27, 1907, APF.

75. *AF*, 1:10 [October] 1907, 1.

76. Torrey to Gaylord, May 27, 1907, RAT.

77. Torrey to Fitt, April 10, 1906, RAT; Reuben Torrey to Clara Torrey, November 16, 1907, TFP-5.

78. *AF*, September 1907, 1.

79. ECM, August 19, 1908. Pierson, "The Passing of the Old Evangelism," *RCW*, December 1908, 925–28. Will Moody to Fitt, September 16, 1908, APF.

80. Cantwell, "The Bible Class Teacher," 185–91; *IT*, September 1910, 47–48.

Chapter 6

1. Woodruff to Gray, February 10, 1919, S. A. Woodruff, MBI-BF.

2. Scott, *Psychology of Advertising*, 106.

3. Lamoreaux, *The Great Merger Movement*, 2.

4. Sklar, *The Corporate Reconstruction of American Capitalism*.

5. Chandler, *The Visible Hand*.

6. Cohen, *Making a New Deal*; Glickman, *A Living Wage*.

7. Leach, *Land of Desire*; Lears, *No Place of Grace*.

8. Rieser, *The Chautauqua Moment*.

9. Marchand, *Advertising the American Dream*; Laird, *Advertising Progress*.

10. Agnew, "Coming Up for Air."

11. Ruse, *The Darwinian Revolution*.

12. Curtis, *A Consuming Faith*.

13. Marchand, *Advertising the American Dream*, xxi, xxii, 9.

14. Connerley, "Friendly Americans," especially 206–44.

15. Barabas, *So Great Salvation*; Bundy "Keswick and the Experience of Evangelical Piety"; Bebbington, *Evangelicalism in Modern Britain*, 151–80. For similar, but not identical, distinctions to mine, see Fea, "Power from on High in an Age of Ecclesiastical Impotence."

16. Scofield, "Plain Papers on the Holy Spirit," 573.

17. Torrey, *Why God Used D. L. Moody*; "D. L. Moody's Power," *CWM* 14 (February 1914): 373.

18. O'Meara, "God's Power to Usward and How to Obtain It," 406–8.

19. My interpretation deviates somewhat from the helpful treatment of the electrical metaphor in Ostrander, "The Battery and the Windmill," 42–62.

20. Gray, *"Have You Turned on the Button?"*

21. Newell [untitled manuscript beginning, "You remember that you saw God taught us . . ."], unpublished manuscript, W. R. Newell File, MBI-BF, 1.

22. Torrey, "Walking with God," 268–70.

23. Gray, *Salvation from Start to Finish*, 115.

24. Newell, "How to Live the Daily Life after Surrender," W. R. Newell File, MBI-BF, 1; Gray to Fitt, July 7, 1905, JMG.

25. Riebe "The Fruit of the Spirit Is Joy," 28, 7–9.

26. Radway, *A Feeling for Books*; Scanlon, *Inarticulate Longings*; Ohmann, *Selling Culture*; Hedstrom, *The Rise of Liberal Religion*.

27. The *Tie* was briefly published as a biweekly paper in the fall of 1891.

28. *IT*, September 1900, 26, 16; *IT*, February 1901, 169–72.

29. BICA, 1, 44–69.

30. BICA, February 5, 1905, 91; March 28, 1906, 102; ECM, November 15, 1905.

31. ECM, January 9, 1907.

32. *IT*, May 1907, middle insert.

33. *IT*, July 1907, 488, 496; Gray to Fitt, July 5, 1907, JMG.

34. Gray to Fitt, April 17, 1908, JMG.

35. Letters from Gray to Fitt, March 13, 1907; April 30, 1907; and July 7, 1907, JMG.

36. *IT*, July 1907, 471; Gray to Fitt, July 5, 1907, JMG.

37. Gray to Fitt, April 17, 1908, JMG.

38. *IT*, July 1907, 488, 496, 490.

39. *IT*, April 1907, 362–63; ECM, October 17, 1906, November 27, 1906.

40. Fitt to Torrey, July 17, 1907, APF; Torrey to Fitt, July 19, 1907, RAT; Fitt to Torrey, July 31, 1907, RAT; ECMi, July 31, 1907; August 30, 1907; and November 6, 1907.

41. This (and following) based on the two reports prepared for the executive committee, ECM, September 10, 1907, 57–59, and October 6, 1908, 88–94. See also ECM, June 23, 1908, July 19, 1909.

42. On new debt policy, see MBI-TM, December 9, 1908.

43. ECM, August 20, 1907; September 10, 1907; December 2, 1908, "Concerning the 25th Anniversary"; MBI-TM, September 10, 1907; ECM, October 25, 1905; Crowell to P. Webster Campbell, October 19, 1908, HPC; Fitt, Notes, March 30, 1908, APF. On puff pieces, see letters from John Offord to Fitt dated September 19, 1907; October 16, 1907; and October 21, 1907. Fitt to John Offord, October 23, 1907, APF; ECM, November 23, 1910.

44. O. A. Prince to Mrs. G. F. Swift, November 9, 1907, MBI History 1902–, MBI-DF; MBI-TM, September 10, 1907.

45. Torrey to Fitt, March 18, 1908, RAT.

46. ECM, November 6, 1907, and June 23, 1908; MBI-TM, November 10, 1908. Letters from Torrey to Fitt, April 23, 1908, and April 27, 1908, RAT; Letters from Fitt to Torrey, June 24, 1908, and July 22, 1908, APF. Fitt's research notes are misfiled in "MBI—History of 1899 July–December," MBI-DF.

47. Letters from Fitt to Torrey, July 22, 1908, and July 27, 1908, APF; Torrey to Gaylord, September 10, 1908, RAT. Torrey's grandson cites disagreements about the Baptism of the Holy Spirit as the primary reason for his resignation. "Oral History Interview Reuben Archer Torrey, III," Collection 331, Tape 1, BGC.

48. Fitt to Executive Committee, November 6, 1908, and Fitt to Norton, November 6, 1908, APF; Torrey to Fitt, December 14, 1908, RAT; William R. Moody to Fitt, November 27, 1908, WRM; ECM, December 15, 1908. As a legal formality, Fitt was reelected to the Executive Committee in September 1909, apparently without his knowledge. He was finally replaced by Edward K. Warren. MBI-TM, September 16, 1909, and September 13, 1910.

49. Fitt to Crowell, March 25, 1907; Crowell to Fitt, April 1, 1907; and Gray to Fitt, March 29, 1907, JHH. Compare Torrey's contrasting views in Torrey to Fitt, March 27, 1907, JHH.

50. MBI-TM, September 24, 1908.

51. See ECM entries from October 6, 1908–January 11, 1909 (with attached correspondence).

52. Crowell to Gray, April 13, 1909, HPC.

53. Fitt to Gaylord, April 20, 1909, APF.

54. See "Memorandum for the Executive Committee Regarding Our Missionary Instruction and Interest," in ECM, October 14, 1908; Fitt to Mrs. William Borden, November 27, 1908, APF.

55. Fitt to Mrs. William Borden, November 27, 1908, APF.

56. Martin, *Tongues of Fire*; Hollenweger, *The Pentecostals*.

57. Mrs. William Borden to Fitt, December 12, 1908, APF; Day, *Breakfast Table Autocrat*, 148.

58. *IT*, May 1909, 735.

59. MBI Catalog 1905, MBIA.

60. Day, *Breakfast Table Autocrat*, 174; Runyan, *Dr. Gray*, 147–51, 169.

61. Gray to "The Members of the Faculty," July 29, 1908, JMG.

62. MBI Catalog, 1910–11, 12; MBI Catalog, 1911, 10.

63. "Something to Cheer and Encourage" (1909 MBI Annual Meeting excerpts), MBIA, 5.

64. MBI Policy Manual, 14, 23, 23–a, 46, 72, 79, 81–b, 104, 108, MBIA.

65. Gray, *How to Master the English Bible*, 17.

66. MBI Policy Manual, 94, MBIA.

67. *IT*, January 1909, 377.

68. *IT*, April 1909, 687.

69. MBI Policy Manual, 97, MBIA.

70. *IT*, February 1909, 483.

71. Gosnell, "Prophecy and the Lord's Return," June 1917, *CWM*, 794.

Chapter 7

1. Frank H. Hagerty to Fitt, May 24, 1907, APF.

2. This and other Stewart biographical information taken from Krivoshey, "Going through the Eye of the Needle."

3. Ibid., 74.

4. Stewart to "Will, May and Fred" (Stewart's children), September 4, 1914, LSP. This document provides an overview of his early religious activities.

5. Ibid.; Stewart to George Carter, September 27, 1910, LSP.

6. On the timing of Biola's founding, see Stewart to M. M. Merriman, March 9, 1908; Stewart to Etta Rummey, March 12, 1908; Stewart to Blackstone, March 21, 1908; and Stewart to Kellogg, April 2, 1908, LSP.

7. Stewart to Fitt, May 20, 1908; and Stewart to Kellogg, April 24, 1907, LSP. Hadden to Fitt, February 12, 1908, APF.

8. Krivoshey, "Going through the Eye of the Needle," 163–76; Lyman Stewart to Milton Stewart, December 30, 1914, LSP.

9. Martin, "The Thought of Amzi Clarence Dixon," 216–22.

10. Dixon, *The Person and Ministry of the Holy Spirit*, 1.

11. See, for example *NYTr*, October 1, 1895, 7.

12. *CDT*, November 23, 1898, 1.

13. Dixon thus preceded J. Gresham Machen's argument in *Christianity and Liberalism* by a decade. See Hart, *Defending the Faith*, 67–78.

14. *Los Angeles Times*, August 16, 1909, 15; *IT*, August 1909, 980; Foster, *The Function of Religion*. On Foster, see Hutchison, *Modernist Impulse*, 215–19.

15. Stewart to Amy Saxton Fulton, June 22, 1908, LSP; *RCW*, August 1907, 660–61.

16. Stewart to Gaebelein, March 28, 1908, LSP.

17. Lyman Stewart to Milton Stewart, September 24, 1909, FC1; Stewart to "Will, May, and Fred," September 4, 1914, LSP.

18. *Detroit Free Press*, March 20, 1903, 3; *New York Observer and Chronicle*, January 26, 1905, 124; ECM, August 9, 1909.

19. Gray to Fitt, May 22, 1907, JMG.

20. ECM, July 19, 1909.

21. Lyman Stewart to Milton Stewart, September 24, 1909, FC1; Stewart to Dixon, December 18, 1909, FC1.

22. Stewart to Dixon, November 1, 1909, FC1.

23. Stewart to Meyer, July 3, 1911, FC2.

24. Stewart to Kellogg, September 24, 1909; and Stewart to Dixon, November 1, 1909, FC1.

25. Dixon to Stewart, September 8, 1909, FC1.

26. Ibid.

27. Draft Form Letter from Dixon, September 8, 1909, FC1.

28. Dixon to Stewart, November 25, 1909, FC1.

29. Dixon to Stewart, October 23, 1909, FC1.

30. Stewart to Dixon, November 1, 1909, FC1.

31. Ibid.

32. Dixon to Stewart, September 15, 1909; Stewart to Kellogg, September 24, 1909; and Stewart to Dixon, November 1, 1909, FC1.

33. Torrey to Stewart, January 13, 1914, FC4.

34. Stephens to Stewart, June 7, 1911, FC2.

35. Dixon to Stewart, November 9, 1909.

36. Stewart to Dixon, November 20, 1909, FC1.

37. Dixon to Stewart, September 15, 1909, and November 9, 1909; Stewart to Dixon, November 8, 1909, and November 20, 1909; Torrey to Dixon, November 10, 1909; and Torrey to Stewart, November 17, 1909, FC1.

38. Dixon to Kellogg, December 16, 1909, FC1.

39. "The Fundamentals" (report dating to around August 2, 1912), FC3.

40. Stewart to Dixon, November 1, 1909, FC1.

41. Ibid.

42. Stewart to Dixon, January 8, 1910, FC1.

43. Dixon to Fitt, April 18, 1910, APF; Stephens to Stewart, August 2, 1910, FC1; Stephens to Stewart, September 13, 1911, FC2.

44. Stewart to Dixon, December 18, 1909, FC1.

45. Lyman Stewart to Milton Stewart, July 26, 1911, LSP; Krivoshey, "Going through the Eye of the Needle," 219–20.

46. *Earth-Quaker*, May 1924, quoted in Thornton, *History of the Quaker Oats Company*, 110.

47. On the development of the modern market for branded consumer goods, see Strasser, *Satisfaction Guaranteed*. On Quaker Oats's use of promotions, see Thornton, *History of the Quaker Oats Company*, and Marquette, *Brands, Trademarks, and Good Will*.

48. *Daily Quaker*, March 24, 1911, quoted in Thornton, *History of the Quaker Oats Company*.

49. Young, *Pure Food*.

50. This and the following discussion of distribution networks is drawn primarily from Strasser, *Satisfaction Guaranteed*, esp. 58–88.

51. Lyman Stewart to Milton Stewart, September 24, 1909, FC1.

52. Dixon to Stewart, October 1, 1910, FC1.

53. Dixon to Stewart, November 9, 1909, FC1.

54. Dixon to Kellogg, December 4, 1909; and Dixon to Ralph D. Smith, January 14, 1910 (copy), FC1.

55. Stewart to Dixon, January 22, 1910; and Dixon to Kellogg, December 22, 1909, FC1.

56. Dixon to Stewart, December 17, 1909; and Dixon to Stewart, November 25, 1909, FC1.

57. Stewart to Dixon, December 18, 1909, FC1.

58. Dixon to Stewart, December 27, 1909, FC1.

59. Dixon to Fitt, April 18, 1910, APF. Letters from Dixon to Stewart dated October 11, 1910; February 28, 1910; March 19, 1910; and October 19, 1910. Stewart to Dixon, January 8, 1910, FC1.

60. Stewart to Dixon, November 1, 1909, FC1.

61. Stewart to Torrey, June 28, 1913, FC5.

62. Stephens to Stewart, July 16, 1910, FC1.

63. Stephens to Stewart, April 16, 1910; Dixon to Stewart, March 29, 1910; Stephens to Dixon, May 11, 1910; Stewart to Stephens, June 18, 1910; and Stephens to Stewart, November 29, 1910, FC1. Stephens to Stewart, June 21, 1911; and September 16, 1911, FC2. Stephens to Stewart, February 23, 1913, FC3. Stephens to Stewart, n.d. (June 1, 1915?), FC5.

64. Rev. James Robert Smith to Testimony Publishing Company, December 1, 1912, FC5.

65. [Unknown] to Rev. James Robert Smith, December 2, 1912, FC5.

66. "The Fundamentals," clipping from an unknown periodical in FC1.

67. "A Testimony to the Truth," *Christian*, May 26, 1910.

68. J. C. M. Floyd to Testimony Publishing Company, October 8, 1910, FC1.

69. E. J. Bulgin to Testimony Publishing Company, April 19, 1913, FC5.

70. Stephens to Stewart, February 25, 1911, FC1.

71. Lyman Stewart to Milton Stewart, September 19, 1910, LSP.

72. Reprinted in *Fundamentals*, 5:127.

73. *Fundamentals*, vols. 2, 3, and 4.

74. *New York Observer*, September 8, 1910, 309.

75. Stephens to Stewart, April 28, 1911, FC1.

76. Scofield to Dixon, January 5, 1910 (copy), LSP.

77. Dixon to Stewart, December 21, 1910, FC1.

78. Stewart to Stephens, November 15, 1910; and Stephens to Stewart, November 29, 1910, FC1.

79. Dixon to Stewart dated December 17, 1910; December 21, 1910; and February 2, 1911, FC1. Stewart to Dixon, January 7, 1911; and Stewart to Scofield, January 7, 1911, FC1.

80. Stewart to Meyer, May 31, 1911, FC1.

81. The other executive committee members were Arthur T. Pierson, L. W. Munhall, Charles Erdman, and William G. Moorehead. See Stewart to Dixon, May 10, 1911, FC1.

82. Meyer to Stewart, August 25, 1911, FC2.

83. Meyer to Stewart, September 6, 1911, FC2.

84. Meyer to Stewart, June 17, 1911; and Stewart to Meyer, August 1, 1911, FC2.

85. Stephens to Stewart, June 7, 1911, FC2. Dixon to Stewart, October 23, 1909; and Stephens to Stewart, August 2, 1910, FC1.

86. Notes of Thomas Horton dated May 6, 1911, FC1; Stewart to Meyer, May 11, 1911, FC1.

87. Meyer to Stewart, May 17, 1911, FC1.

88. Meyer to Stewart, August 2, 1911; and Stewart to Meyer, August 10, 1911, FC2.

89. Meyer to Stewart, February 3, 1913, FC3.

90. Stewart to Stephens, May 2, 1911, FC1.

91. McNicol, "The Hope of the Church," 123–27.

92. Erdman, "The Coming of Christ."

93. Moorehead, "Millennial Dawn," 106–27.

94. Wilson, "Eddyism," 111–27.

95. Pierson, "Our Lord's Teaching about Money."

96. Torrey to Stewart, May 29, 1914; and Stewart to Torrey, September 10, 1914, FC4.

97. Erdman, "The Church and Socialism."

98. Stewart to Meyer, February 1, 1913, FC3.

99. Meyer to Stewart, February 14, 1913, FC3.

100. Mrs. Louis Meyer to Stewart, June 2, 1913, FC3.

101. Stephens to Stewart, June 9, 1913, FC5; Stewart to Stephens, June 27, 1913, FC3.

102. Torrey to Stewart, July 21, 1913, FC3; Lofton, "Queering Fundamentalism."

103. Stephens to Stewart dated January 2, 1913; January 13, 1913; and January 17, 1913, FC3. Stewart to Stephens, January 6, 1913, FC3. Meyer to Stewart dated January 8, 1913; January 20, 1913; January 22, 1913; and January 28, 1913, FC3.

104. Stewart to Meyer, January 21, 1913, FC3.

105. Stewart to Meyer, February 14, 1913; Meyer to Stewart, February 15, 1913; Stewart to L. W. Munhall, March 12, 1913; Crowell to Stewart, March 20, 1913; Thomas Smith to Stewart, March 25, 1913; and Stewart to Stephens April 19, 1913, FC3.

106. Stewart to Stephens, July 30, 1913, FC3; "Annual Meeting of the Committee of 'The Fundamentals,'" August 8, 1913, FC4.

107. Torrey to Stewart, August 11, 1913, FC4.

108. Stewart to Torrey, December 12, 1913; Torrey to Stewart, January 7, 1914; Lyman Stewart to Milton Stewart, September 15, 1914; and Torrey to Stewart, September 15, 1914, FC4. Lyman Stewart to Milton Stewart, September 10, 1914, LSP.

109. Torrey to Stewart, January 13, 1914, FC4.

110. Stewart to Torrey, January 15, 1914, FC4.

111. Torrey to Stewart, December 23, 1914, FC3.

112. Stewart to Torrey, December 28, 1914, FC3.

113. Stewart to Torrey, January 5, 1915, FC3.

114. Torrey to Gray, March 13, 1915; and Gray to Torrey, March 30, 1915, RAT.

115. Stephens to Stewart, July 30, 1914, FC4.

116. On this phenomenon, see Radway, *A Feeling for Books*.

117. Manring, *Slave in a Box*.

118. Harding, *Book of Jerry Falwell*.

Chapter 8

1. Ellis, "A Cosmopolite," *Continent*, June 12, 1913, 821–22.

2. *Light on Prophecy*, 70–73.

3. Lyman Stewart to Milton Stewart, October 26, 1910, LSP; Krivoshey, "Going through the Eye of the Needle," 230–31.

4. Stewart to Stephens, January 6, 1913, FC5. Lyman Stewart to Milton Stewart, July 21, 1914; and Stewart to Torrey, September 18, 1914, LSP.

5. Stewart to Torrey, October 26, 1914; July 29, 1914; November 2, 1914; and December 21, 1914, LSP.

6. Stewart to Torrey, August 24, 1918, LSP.

7. ECM, June 17, 1914.

8. Sutton, *Aimee Semple McPherson*.

9. BICA I, 166, n.p. (189); BICA II, 29; ECM, January 5, 1909.

10. BICA I, 168, 171–73; BICA II, 166.

11. Gray to Torrey, March 23, 1910; and Torrey to Gray, March 28, 1910, RAT.

12. William R. Moody to Norton, February 18, 1911, and February 27, 1911, WRM; Fitt to Crowell, April 8, 1908, APF.

13. "A New Type of Christianity," *IT*, September 1910, 11–13.

14. *IT*, June 1907, 455. Gray to Fitt, July 7, 1907, JMG. Norton to Walter H. Hoyt, October 1, 1909; and Norton to Herbert D. Whitmore, November 17, 1909, WNF.

15. *CWM*, October 1910 (back cover), 73, 85.

16. ECM, June 3, 1914.

17. ECM, September 30, 1910.

18. ECM, October 18, 1916. It is not entirely clear if Chafer accepted their offer.

19. ECM, October 2, 1912; July 16, 1913; and November 19, 1913. MBI-TM, September 30, 1913.

20. Stewart to Dixon, November 16, 1910, FC1; ECM, November 26, 1913.

21. *The Coming and Kingdom of Christ*, 9.

22. Ibid., 9–10, 12–13, 241–49.

23. Ibid., 98, 103, 186–207, 65–79, 223–35, 236–38.

24. Ibid., 239–40.

25. Gray to Torrey, February 27, 1919, RAT.

26. *The Coming and Kingdom of Christ*, 239–40.

27. Ibid., 5–6.

28. Stephens to Stewart, February 28, 1914, FC4.

29. ECM, July 8, 1914; MBI-TM, July 15, 1914.

30. MBI Executive Committee to Palmer, Pettengill & Lange, July 28, 1914, "Scofield Course—1914. Correspondence," MBIA.

31. ECM, May 15, 1915, and May 26, 1915.

32. ECM, June 23, 1915; July 28, 1915; and August 26, 1914.

33. Lofton, "The Methodology of the Modernists," 378.

34. Federal Council of the Churches of Christ in America, *Report of the First Meeting*, 6. Note the difference between corporate governance among fundamentalists and church bureaucratization described by Primer, *Protestants and American Business Methods*.

35. "Introduction," *Constructive Quarterly*, March 1913, 1–4.

36. Mathews, "The Awakening of American Protestantism," *Constructive Quarterly*, March 1913, 102–7, 120.

37. Roosevelt, "The Constructive Quarterly," *Outlook*, March 13, 1913, 587–88.

38. Gray, "The Awakening of American Protestantism," 653, 661–63, 667–68.

39. "The By-Products of a Creative Age," *BW*, July 1914, 2.

40. Gladden, "A Dangerous Crusade," *BW*, July 1914, 3–14.

41. Erdman, "Premillennialism Defended against Assailants," *CWM*, August 1916, 914–17; Griffith Thomas, "Premillennialism and the Bible," *CWM*, August 1916, 918–21; *CWM* September 1916, 13–15, and October 1916, 101–5.

42. Woodruff to Gaylord, December 12, 1916, S. A. Woodruff, MBI-BF.

43. ECM, November 22, 1916; December 20, 1916; and January 17, 1917.

44. "Jesus Is Coming!," *Biblical World*, December 1916, 329.

45. "Propaganda of Reaction," *Biblical World*, April 1917, 201–2.

46. *CWM*, May 1918, 788–89; *KB*, January 1918, 3.

47. For example, see Buckham, "What Is Fundamental?," *BW*, April 1915, 211–16; and Strayer, "What Are the Christian Fundamentals?," *BW*, May 1916, 305–11.

48. Kennedy, *Over Here*, 153, 154.

49. BICA II, 184.

50. *CWM*, March 1917, 599.

51. *CWM*, April 1917, 680.

52. *CWM*, April 1917, 624.

53. MBI-TM, May 19, 1916, July 26, 191[6]; Getz, *MBI*, 190. Jenkins, "Chicago Christian Institute," *American Missionary*, March 1917, 644–46 (quote on 645).

54. ECM, January 17, 1915; *CWM*, September 1915, 9.

55. *CWM*, March 1917, 520.

56. *CWM*, September 1916, 105–8.

57. "The War as a Presage of the World's End," *Current Opinion*, February 1917, 117; Gosnell, "Prophecy and the Lord's Return," *CWM*, April 1917, 641.

58. *KB*, January 1918, 96.

59. Torrey, *Will Christ Come Again?*

60. Marsden, *Fundamentalism and American Culture*, 147.

61. [Editorial notes], *BW*, May 1918, 272.

62. Case, "The Premillennial Menace," *BW*, July 1918, 16–23.

63. Parker, "Premillenarianism: An Interpretation and an Evaluation," *BW*, January 1919, 37–40.

64. Leuchtenberg, *The Perils of Prosperity*, 12–47 (quote on 46).

65. *KB*, October 1917, 867–77, and November 1917, 963–66; Blackstone to Stewart, July 11, 1914, Blackstone Correspondence, LSP; ECM, November 7, 1917.

66. "Current Criticism of Premillennial Truth," *CWM*, March 1918, 548–50.

67. *CWM*, October 1918, 106; November 1918, 164–65; and December 1918, 228.

68. Woodruff, "'Billy' Sunday in Chicago," *CWM*, May 1918, 270–71.

69. *CWM*, March 1917, 557–58.

70. Newell (untitled speech given at First Methodist Episcopal Church, Chicago, Ill.], unpublished manuscript, W. R. Newell File, MBIA, 6.

71. Ibid., 11.

72. *Light on Prophecy*, 176–77.

73. Ruotsila, *Origins of Christian Anti-Internationalism*, 8–26.

74. See, for example, Gray, "The League of Nations and the Danger of Federation," *MBIM*, September 1920, 7.

75. Gray, "The Proposed World Church Union," *CWM*, May 1919, 633.

76. Ruotsila, *Origins of Christian Anti-Internationalism*, 27–52.

77. *CWM*, October 1919, 94.

78. Torrey to Gray, December 11, 1918, RAT; Sandeen, *The Roots of Fundamentalism*, 243–44.

79. Torrey to Gray, December 11, 1918, RAT.

80. *CWM*, January 1919, 328–29.

81. Ralston, "The Conference Considers Vital Questions," *CWM*, March 1919, 453–55.

82. Wollam, "Bible Institutes on the Offensive," *CWM*, April 1919, 533–35.

83. Gray to Torrey, February 27, 1919, RAT.

84. Torrey to Gray, December 11, 1918, and February 27, 1919, RAT; Gray to Torrey, January 2, 1919, RAT.

85. Bible Conference Committee, *God Hath Spoken*, 15.

86. *MBIM*, July 1921 (inside cover).

87. Bible Conference Committee, *God Hath Spoken*, 18–25; Torrey to Gray, November 13, 1919, RAT; Gray to Torrey, November 19, 1919, RAT; *CWM*, August 1920, 927–29.

88. "Another Milestone on Our Way," *CWM*, July 1920, 851–52.

89. *MBIM*, September 1920 (front cover).

90. *MBIM*, October 1920, 53.

91. Marsden, *Fundamentalism and American Culture*, 168–69.

92. Gray, "Stating the Fundamentals," *MBIM*, January 1921, 207–8.

93. *MBIM*, March 1921, 323.

94. *MBIM*, April 1921, 347.

95. *MBIM*, May 1922, 1003–4.

96. Fosdick, "Shall the Fundamentalists Win?," *Christian Work*, June 10, 1922, 716–22.

97. Gray, *The Deadline of Doctrine around the Church*.

98. Gray, "Bible Institute and Theological Seminaries," *MBIM*, April 1921, 249–51.

99. *MBIM*, August 1921, 508, 523.

100. Grossman, *Land of Hope*; Krist, *City of Scoundrels*.

101. Shuler, "Investigate the Ku Klux Klan," *MBIM*, December 1923, 182.

102. Little, "The Negro Problem in America," *MBIM*, September 1919, 32–37; *MBIM*, October 1919, 93.

103. Baker, *Gospel according to the Klan*.

104. *CWM*, June 1916, 776.

105. MBI bulletin, May 1919, MBIA.

106. Balibar and Wallerstein, *Race, Nation, Class*.

107. Toone, "Evangelicalism in Transition."

108. *MBIM*, February 1922, 797–802.

109. Will Moody to Fitt, October 20, 1920 (copy), Letters by Will Moody, MBI-BF.

110. *Christian Century*, October 6, 1921, 7.

111. Torrey to Gray, August 22, 1922, RAT.

112. *Christian Century*, July 12, 1923.

113. Gray to Torrey, July 14, 1923; Torrey to Gray, July 19, 1923; and Torrey to Gray, July 31, 1923, RAT.

114. *MBIM*, October 1923, 51.

115. *MBIM*, December 1923, 171–72.

116. *MBIM*, November 1923, 101–2; December 1923, 173–74; January 1924, 235–36.

117. Powell, "D. L. Moody and the Origin of Fundamentalism," *Christian Work*, April 19, 1924, 496–502.

118. "Correspondence," *Christian Work*, July 12, 1924, 60–61.

119. Torrey to Gray, February 18, 1925, RAT.

120. Crowell to Will Moody, June 29, 1925, MBI-TM.

121. Will Moody to Norton, December 30, 1926, Letters by Will Moody, MBI-BF.

122. Torrey to Gray, November 28, 1924; Gray to Torrey, December 26, 1924; and Torrey to Gray, January 5, 1925, RAT.

123. Quoted in Hannah, *An Uncommon Union*, 92.

124. Torrey to Gray, April 21, 1925, RAT.

125. *MBIM*, September 1925, 3, and April 1926, 364; Gray to Torrey, October 14, 1925, JMG.

126. *MBIM*, March 1922, 858; June 1922, 1053; and July 1922, 1103. See also *MBIM*, January 1922, 761–62.

127. "Special Minute" (loose), in BICA.

Epilogue

1. Carpenter, *Revive Us Again*, 133.

2. Gray to Edith Torrey, October 26, 1931 (copy); and Edith Torrey to Gray, November 9, 1931 (copy), TFP.

3. Carpenter, *Revive Us Again*, 144–45; Marsden, *Reforming Fundamentalism*; Getz, *MBI*, 243–45; Hangen, *Redeeming the Dial*.

4. WMBI, Box 2 (unprocessed), MBIA.

5. Getz, *MBI*, 300–301.

6. Ibid., 262; Flood and Jenkins, *Teaching the Word, Reaching the World*, 219.

7. Getz, *MBI*, 127–36.

8. ECM, October 20, 1909; MBI Policy Manual, 94-1, 94-2, MBIA.

9. WMBI, Box 2 (unprocessed), MBIA.

10. Sider-Rose, "Between Heaven and Earth."

11. Nelson, *The Last Year of the War*.

12. Cochran, *Evangelical Feminism*, 45–49.

13. Gilbert, *Redeeming Culture*, 121–45 (quotes on 125 and 135); Getz, *MBI*, 314–21; Smith, *A Watchman on the Wall*, 142–48.

14. Haas, "Early Links between the Moody Bible Institute and the ASA."

15. Flood and Jenkins, *Teaching the Word, Reaching the World*, 189–97.

16. Getz, *MBI*, 242.

17. Letter from Dale Carnegie to "Dr. Hitt," May 25, 1943, "B. I. Colportage Ass'n Chicago," MBI-DF.

18. Jacobsen and Trollinger, *Re-Forming the Center*.

19. Tedlow, *New and Improved*; Frank, *The Conquest of Cool*.

20. Bowler, *Blessed*. See also Daniel Vaca's forthcoming work on religious publishers.

21. Http://www.washingtonpost.com/local/education/virginias-liberty-transforms-into-evangelical-mega-university/2013/03/04/931cb116-7d09-11e2-9a75-dab0201670da_story.html; http://www.liberty.edu/news/index.cfm?PID=18495&MID=108250 (both accessed December 20, 2013).

22. Http://jerry-jenkins.com/about/ (accessed December 20, 2013).

Bibliography

Archival Sources

Chicago, Ill.
    Chicago Historical Society
        YMCA of Metropolitan Chicago Collection
    Moody Bible Institute Archives
        Biographical Collection
        A. F. Gaylord
        Armin Holzer
        Arthur P. Fitt Correspondence
        Charlotte Cary
        Dr. Francis L. Patton
        Dwight L. Moody Correspondence
        E. G. Keith
        Early Students Recollections
        Emily S. Strong
        Emma Dryer Files
        Frank Alvord Carpenter
        G. Campbell Morgan
        H. M. Ferguson
        Harry L. Carter
        Henry Parsons Crowell Correspondence
        J. B. Bowles
        J. H. Hunter Correspondence
        James M. Gray Correspondence
        John R. Riebe
        Mary Bethune
        Norman H. Camp
        O. E. Sandeen, *Why God Used R. A. Torrey*
        Paul Moody
        Reuben A. Torrey Correspondence
        Reverend H. K. Boyer
        Robert S. Scott
        S. A. Woodruff
        Sarah B. Capron
        Thomas C. Horton

Thomas S. Smith
W. E. Blackstone
W. H. Holden
W. R. Newell
W. S. Jacoby
William Evans
William Norton Correspondence (including bound carbon copies)
William R. Moody Correspondence
Corporate Files (Bound Meeting Minutes and Corporate Documents)
  Bible Institute Colportage Association Trustee Minutes (1900–1930)
  Corporate Records of the Moody Bible Institute [and CES] (1887–1930)
  Executive Committee Meeting Minutes of the Moody Bible Institute
    (1905–1930)
  Meeting Minutes of the Chicago Evangelization Society (1887–1900)
  Trustee Minutes of the Moody Bible Institute (1900–1930)
Departmental Files
  CES Annual Reports, 1887–1891
  CES Chicago Evangelization Society
  CES Constitution Bylaws First Annual Meeting
  CES Forms
  CES Incorporation Papers
  Historical Sketch of MBI
  MBI—History of, 1899 (July–December)
  MBI—History, 1889–1898
  MBI—History, 1902–
  Moody Memorial Endowment
Miscellaneous
  BICA Files—Reuben A. Torrey
  CES/MBI Catalog and Bulletin Collection (1874–1930)
  D. L. Moody Clippings Files
  MBI Student Files (1889–1910)
  MBI Policy Manual
  Photograph Collection
  Rules for the Guidance of the Faculty (1914, 1918)
  Scofield Course—1914 Correspondence
  Student Loan Board Minutes, August 1920–September 1931
  Unprocessed box, "Alumni Dept. Container [Box 88]"
  Unprocessed box, "Alumni Dept. Contents Box 2 [Box 89]"
  Unprocessed box, "Departmental—Administration—Box 1"
  Unprocessed box, "Departmental—Alumni—Box 1"
  Unprocessed box, "Departmental—Moody Publications—Box 1"
  Unprocessed box, "Departmental—Stewardship and Financial—Box 1 [Box 77]"
  Unprocessed box, "WMBI—Box 1 [Box 95]"
  Unprocessed box, "WMBI—Box 2 [Box 96]"
  Unprocessed box, "WMBI—Box 3 [Box 97]"

La Mirada, Calif.
  Biola University Archives
    Lyman Stewart Papers
    Unprocessed correspondence files for *The Fundamentals*
    Unprocessed wooden file cabinet (drawers 1–3)
Minneapolis, Minn.
  Kautz Family YMCA Archives
    Armed Services YMCA (Y.USA.4–4)
Montrose, Pa.
  Torrey Family Papers (private collection)
    Letters, diaries, ephemera of Reuben A. Torrey and Clara Smith Torrey
St. Paul, Minn.
  Minnesota Historical Society
    "North East Neighborhood House," Collection P3
Wheaton, Ill.
  Billy Graham Center Archives, Wheaton College
    Henry W. Stough Collection 106
    Reuben A. Torrey Sr. Collection 107
    Reuben Archer Torrey III Collection 331

Periodicals, Newspapers, and Serial Published Proceedings

Aberdeen (South Dakota) Daily News
American Missionary
Annual Report of the Illinois State Board of Health
Apostolic Faith
Arena
Atlanta Constitution
Biblical Repertory and Princeton Review
Biblical World
Boston Daily Globe
Century Magazine
Chicago Chronicle
Chicago Daily Tribune
Chicago Inter-Ocean
Chicago Journal
Christian
Christian Century
Christian Union
Christian Work
Christian Workers Magazine
Cleveland Gazette
Congregationalist
Constructive Quarterly
Continent

Current Opinion

Detroit Free Press

Evangelistic Record

Friends' Review

Independent

Institute Tie

Interior

King's Business

Knights of Labor

Latter Rain Evangel

Leaves of Healing

Los Angeles Times

Medical News

Medical Standard

Missionary Magazine

Moody Bible Institute Monthly

New Englander

New Haven Journal and Courier

New York Evangelist

New York Observer and Chronicle

New York Times

New York Tribune

Outlook

Philadelphia Inquirer

Pilgrim

Presbyterian and Reformed Review

Proceedings of the Christian Worker's Convention

Record of Christian Work

St. Paul and Minneapolis Pioneer Press

Southern Cross

United States Christian Commission Annual Reports

Washington Post

Watchword

YMCA Proceedings of the . . . Annual Convention

Zion's Herald

Essays and Journal Articles

Agnew, Jean-Christophe. "Coming Up for Air: Consumer Culture in Historical Perspective." In *Consumer Society in American History: A Reader*, edited by Lawrence B. Glickman. Ithaca and London: Cornell University Press, 1999: 373–97.

Bademan, R. Bryan. "'Monkeying with the Bible': Edgar J. Goodspeed's 'American Translation.'" *Religion and American Culture* 16, no. 1 (Winter 2006): 55–93.

Baer, Jonathan R. "Redeemed Bodies: The Functions of Divine Healing in Incipient Pentecostalism." *Church History* 70, no. 4 (2001): 735–71.

Bateman, Bradley W., and Ethan B. Kapstein. "Between God and the Market: The Religious Roots of the American Economic Association." *Journal of Economic Perspectives* 13, no. 4 (Autumn 1999): 249–58.

Baylen, Joseph O. "A Victorian's 'Crusade' in Chicago, 1893–1894." *Journal of American History* 51, no. 3 (1964): 418–34.

Bernstein, Michael A. "American Economists and the 'Marginalist Revolution': Notes on the Intellectual and Social Contexts of Professionalization." *Journal of Historical Sociology* (Great Britain) 16, no. 1 (2003): 135–80.

Black, Joel E. "A Crime to Live without Work: Free Labor and Marginal Workers in Industrial Chicago, 1870 to 1920." *Michigan Historical Review* 36, no. 2 (Fall 2010): 63–93.

Blumhofer, Edith L. "Restoration as Revival: Early American Pentecostalism." In *Modern Christian Revivals*, edited by Edith L. Blumhofer and Randall Balmer, 118–44. Urbana: University of Illinois Press, 1993.

———. "Transatlantic Currents in North Atlantic Pentecostalism." In *Evangelicalism: Comparative Studies of Popular Protestantism in North America, the British Isles, and Beyond, 1700–1990*, edited by Mark A. Noll, David Bebbington, and George A. Rawlyk. New York: Oxford University Press, 1994.

Bowman, Matthew. "Sin, Spirituality, and Primitivism: The Theologies of the American Social Gospel, 1885–1917." *Religion and American Culture* 17, no. 1 (2007): 95–126.

Boyer, Paul S. "In His Steps: A Reappraisal." *American Quarterly* 23, no. 1 (1971): 60–78.

Bratt, James D. "The Reorientation of American Protestantism, 1835–1845." *Church History* 67, no. 1 (March 1998): 52–82.

Bundy, David. "Keswick and the Experience of Evangelical Piety." In *Modern Christian Revivals*, edited by Edith L. Blumhofer and Randall Balmer, 118–44. Urbana: University of Illinois Press, 1993.

Butler, Jon. "Disquieted History in a Secular Age." In *Varieties of Secularism in a Secular Age*, edited by Michael Warner, Jonathan VanAntwerpen, and Craig Calhoun, 193–216. Cambridge, Mass.: Harvard University Press, 2013.

———. "Jack-in-the-Box Faith: The Religion Problem in Modern American History." *Journal of American History* 90, no. 4 (2004): 1357–78.

Callahan, R. J., Kathryn Lofton, and C. E. Seales. "Allegories of Progress: Industrial Religion in the United States." *Journal of the American Academy of Religion* 78, no. 1 (January 2010): 1–39.

Creech, Joseph W. "Visions of Glory: The Place of the Azusa Street Revival in Pentecostal History." *Church History* (September 1996): 405–25.

Cunningham, Raymond J. "From Holiness to Healing: The Faith Cure in America." *Church History* 43, no. 4 (December 1974): 499–513.

Curtis, Heather D. "Houses of Healing: Sacred Space, Spiritual Practice, and the Transformation of Female Suffering in the Faith Cure Movement, 1870–90." *Church History* 75, no. 3 (2006): 598–611.

Czaplicki, Alan. "'Pure Milk Is Better than Purified Milk': Pasteurization and Milk Purity in Chicago, 1908–1916." *Social Science History* 31, no. 3 (September 21, 2007): 411–33.

Dobschuetz, Barbara. "Emma Dryer and the Moody Church: The Role of Gender and Proto-Fundamentalist Identity, 1864–1900." *Fides et Historia* 33, no. 2 (Summer 2001): 41–52.

Doherty, William T. "The Impact of Business on Protestantism, 1900–29." *Business History Review* 28, no. 2 (June 1954): 141–53.

Duffy, John "The Changing Image of the American Physician." In *Sickness and Health in America: Readings in the History of Medicine and Public Health*, edited by Judith Walzer Leavitt and Ronald L. Numbers, 131–37. Madison: University of Wisconsin Press, 1978.

Dunn, F. Roger. "Formative Years of the Chicago Y.M.C.A.: A Study in Urban History." *Journal of the Illinois State Historical Society (1908–1984)* 37, no. 4 (December 1, 1944): 329–50.

Elfenbein, Jessica. "'An Aggressive Christian Enterprise': The Baltimore YMCA's Journey to Institutional Credibility and Religious Legitimacy, 1852–1882." In *Men and Women Adrift: The YMCA and the YWCA in the City*, edited by Nina Mjagkij and Margaret Ann Spratt, 22–39. New York: New York University Press, 1997.

Emerson, Ralph Waldo. "Self-Reliance." In *Ralph Waldo Emerson*, edited by Richard Poirier, 131–51. New York: Oxford University Press, 1990.

Erdman, Charles R. "The Church and Socialism." In *The Fundamentals: A Testimony*, vol. 12, 108–19. Chicago: Testimony Publishing Company, 1910–1915.

———. "The Coming of Christ." In *The Fundamentals: A Testimony*, vol. 11, 87–99. Chicago: Testimony Publishing Company, 1910–1915.

Fea, John. "Power from on High in an Age of Ecclesiastical Impotence: The Enduement of the Holy Spirit in American Fundamentalist Thought, 1880–1936." *Fides Et Historia* 26 (Summer 1994): 23–35.

Findlay, James, Jr. "Moody, 'Gapmen,' and the Gospel: The Early Days of Moody Bible Institute." *Church History* 31, no. 3 (1962): 322–35.

Fox, Richard Wightman. "The Culture of Liberal Protestant Progressivism, 1875–1925." *Journal of Interdisciplinary History* 23, no. 3 (January 1, 1993): 639–60.

Gitre, Edward J. "The 1904–05 Welsh Revival: Modernization, Technologies, and Techniques of the Self." *Church History* 73, no. 4 (2004): 792–827.

Gloege, Timothy E. W. "Faith Healing, Medical Regulation, and Public Religion in Gilded Age Chicago." *Journal of Religion and American Culture* 23, no. 2 (Summer 2013): 185–231.

———. "The Trouble with Christian History: Thomas Prince's Failed 'Great Awakening.'" *Church History* 82, no. 1 (March 2013): 125–65.

Goff, Philip. "Fighting Like the Devil in the City of Angels: The Rise of Fundamentalist Charles E. Fuller." In *Metropolis Rising: Los Angeles in the 1920s*, edited by Tom Sitton and William Francis Deverell, 220–51. Berkeley: University of California Press, 2001.

Griffith, R. Marie, and Melani McAlister. "Introduction: Is the Public Square Still Naked?" *American Quarterly* 59, no. 3 (2007): 527–63.

Gutman, Herbert G. "Protestantism and the American Labor Movement: The Christian Spirit in the Gilded Age." *American Historical Review* 72, no. 1 (October 1, 1966): 74–101.

Haas, John W., Jr. "Early Links between the Moody Bible Institute and the ASA." *Perspectives on Science and Christian Faith* 43, no. 4 (December 1991): 249–57.

Hackett, David G., Laurie F. Maffly-Kipp, R. Laurence Moore, and Leslie Woodcock Tentler. "Forum: American Religion and Class." *Religion and American Culture* 15, no. 1 (2005): 1–29.

Hansen, Bert. "America's First Medical Breakthrough: How Popular Excitement about a French Rabies Cure in 1885 Raised New Expectations for Medical Progress." *American Historical Review* 103, no. 2 (April 1998): 373–418.

———. "New Images of a New Medicine: Visual Evidence for the Widespread Popularity of Therapeutic Discoveries in America after 1885." *Bulletin of the History of Medicine* 73, no. 4 (Winter 1999): 629–78.

Hart, D. G. "The Failure of American Religious History." *Journal of the Historical Society* 1, no. 1 (2000): 1–31.

Hatch, Nathan O. "Sola Scriptura and Novus Ordo Seclorum." In *The Bible in America: Essays in Cultural History*, edited by Nathan Hatch and Mark Noll, 59–78. New York: Oxford University Press, 1982.

Heath, Alden R. "Apostle in Zion." *Journal of the Illinois State Historical Society* 70, no. 2 (1977): 98–113.

Hollinger, David A. "After Cloven Tongues of Fire: Ecumenical Protestantism and the Modern American Encounter with Diversity." *Journal of American History* 98, no. 1 (June 2011): 21–48.

Jackson, Gregory S. "'What Would Jesus Do?': Practical Christianity, Social Gospel Realism, and the Homiletic Novel." *PMLA* 121, no. 3 (May 2006): 641–61.

Johnson, James E. "Charles G. Finney and a Theology of Revivalism." *Church History* 38, no. 3 (1969): 338–58.

Kidd, Thomas S. "Daniel Rogers' Egalitarian Great Awakening." *Journal of the Historical Society* 7, no. 1 (2007): 111–35.

Knoth, Donna Quaife. "John Alexander Dowie: White Lake's Healing Evangelist." *Michigan History* 74, no. 3 (1990): 36–38.

Leavitt, Judith Walzer. "Medicine in Context: A Review Essay of the History of Medicine." *American Historical Review* 95, no. 5 (December 1990): 1471–84.

LeBeau, Bryan F. "Why Upstarts Win in America: Religion in the Market Place." *American Studies* (Lawrence, Kan.) 36, no. 2 (1995): 111–17.

Leonard, Thomas C. "'More Merciful and Not Less Effective': Eugenics and American Economics in the Progressive Era." *History of Political Economy* 35, no. 4 (2003): 687–712.

———. "Protecting Family and Race." *American Journal of Economics and Sociology* 64, no. 3 (July 2005): 757–91.

Lofton, Kathryn. "Commonly Modern: Rethinking the Modernist-Fundamentalist Controversies." *Church History* 83, no. 1 (March 2014): 137–44.

———. "The Methodology of the Modernists: Process in American Protestantism." *Church History* 75, no. 2 (June 2006): 374–402.

———. "Queering Fundamentalism: John Balcom Shaw and the Sexuality of a Protestant Orthodoxy." *Journal of the History of Sexuality* 17, no. 3 (2008): 439–68.

Long, Kathryn. "Consecrated Respectability: Phoebe Palmer and the Refinement of American Methodism." In *Methodism and the Shaping of American Culture*, edited by John H. Wigger and Nathan O. Hatch, 281–307. Nashville, Tenn.: Abingdon Press, 2001.

Lundén, Rolf. "The Protestant Churches and the Business Spirit of the Twenties." *European Contributions to American Studies* 10 (1986): 47–62.

Luskey, Brian P. "Riot and Respectability: The Shifting Terrain of Class Language and Status in Baltimore during the Great Strike of 1877." *American Nineteenth-Century History* 4, no. 3 (2003): 61–96.

Mahoney, Timothy R. "Middle-Class Experience in the United States in the Gilded Age, 1865–1900." *Journal of Urban History* 31, no. 3 (March 1, 2005): 355–66.

Mathisen, James A. "Thomas O'dea's Dilemmas of Institutionalization: A Case Study and Re-Evaluation after Twenty-Five Years." *Sociological Analysis* 47, no. 4 (1987): 302–18.

May, Henry F. "The Recovery of American Religious History." *American Historical Review* 70, no. 1 (1964): 79–92.

McCloskey, Dierdre. "Why Economic Historians Should Stop Relying on Statistical Tests of Significance, and Lead Economists and Historians into the Promised Land." *Newsletter of the Cliometrics Society* 2, no. 2 (December 1986): 5–7.

McCloud, Sean. "Putting Some Class into Religious Studies: Resurrecting an Important Concept." *Journal of the American Academy of Religion* 75, no. 4 (2007): 840–62.

McFadden, Margaret. "The Ironies of Pentecost: Phoebe Palmer, World Evangelism, and Female Networks." *Methodist History* 31, no. 1 (January 1993): 63–75.

McNicol, John. "The Hope of the Church." In *The Fundamentals: A Testimony*, vol. 6, 114–27. Chicago: Testimony Publishing Company, 1910–1915.

Meyer, D. H. "American Intellectuals and the Victorian Crisis of Faith." *American Quarterly* 27, no. 5 (1975): 585–603.

Moody, Dwight Lyman. "How to Read the Bible." In *Notes for Bible Readings*, edited by S. R. Briggs and J. H. Elliott, 33–34. Toronto: Toronto Willard Tract Society, 1877.

Moorehead, William G. "Millennial Dawn: A Counterfeit of Christianity." In *The Fundamentals: A Testimony*, vol. 7, 106–27. Chicago: Testimony Publishing Company, 1910–1915.

Mullin, Robert Bruce. "The Debate over Religion and Healing in the Episcopal Church: 1870–1930." *Anglican and Episcopal History* 60, no. 2 (1991): 213–34.

Noll, Mark A. "The American Revolution and Protestant Evangelicalism." *Journal of Interdisciplinary History* 23, no. 3 (January 1, 1993): 615–38.

———. "Common Sense Traditions and American Evangelical Thought." *American Quarterly* 37, no. 2 (Summer 1985): 216–38.

Nolt, Steven M. "'Avoid Provoking the Spirit of Controversy': The Irenic Evangelical Legacy of the Biblical Seminary in New York." In *Re-Forming the Center: American Protestantism, 1900 to the Present*, edited by Douglas Jacobsen and William Vance Trollinger, 318–40. Grand Rapids, Mich.: Wm. B. Eerdmans, 1998.

Norcross, Frank H. "Criminal Law Reform." *Journal of the American Institute of Criminal Law and Criminology* 3 (September 1910): 386–93.

Nord, David Paul. "The Paradox of Municipal Reform in the Nineteenth Century." *Wisconsin Magazine of History* 66, no. 2 (Winter 1982): 128–42.

———. "The Public Community: The Urbanization of Journalism in Chicago." *Journal of Urban History* 11, no. 4 (1985): 411–41.

———. "Reading the Newspaper: Strategies and Politics of Reader Response, Chicago, 1912–1917." *Journal of Communication* 45, no. 3 (1995): 66–93.

Numbers, Ronald L. "Do-It-Yourself the Sectarian Way." In *Sickness and Health in America: Readings in the History of Medicine and Public Health*, edited by Judith Walzer Leavitt and Ronald L. Numbers, 87–95. Madison: University of Wisconsin Press, 1978.

O'Meara, T. R. "God's Power to Usward and How to Obtain It," *MBIM* 27 (May 1928): 406–8.

Ostrander, Richard. "The Battery and the Windmill: Two Models of Protestant Devotionalism in Early Twentieth-Century America." *Church History* 65, no. 1 (March 1996): 42–61.

———. "Proving the Living God: Answered Prayer as a Modern Fundamentalist Apologetic." *Fides et Historia* 28, no. 3 (Winter 1996): 69–89.

Parker, Theodore. "A Discourse of the Transient and Permanent in Christianity." In *Transcendentalism: A Reader*, edited by Joel Myerson, 340–65. New York: Oxford University Press, 2000.

Phelps, William Lynon. "When Yale Was Given to Sumnerology." *Literary Digest International Book Review* (September 1925): 661–63.

Pierson, Arthur T. "Our Lord's Teachings about Money." In *The Fundamentals: A Testimony*, vol. 10, 39–47. Chicago: Testimony Publishing Company, 1910–1915.

Pietsch, Brendan. "Lyman Stewart and Early Fundamentalism." *Church History: Studies in Christianity and Culture* 82, no. 3 (2013): 617–46.

Pratt, Douglas. "Terrorism and Religious Fundamentalism: Prospects for a Predictive Paradigm." *Marburg Journal of Religion* 11, no. 1 (2006): 1–16.

Priest, Gerald L. "A. C. Dixon, Chicago Liberals, and *The Fundamentals*." *Detroit Baptist Seminary Journal* 1 (Spring 1996): 113–34.

Reinders, Robert C. "Training for a Prophet: The West Coast Missions of John Alexander Dowie, 1888–1890." *Pacific Historian* 30, no. 1 (1986): 2–14.

Rennie, Ian S. "Fundamentalism and the Varieties of North Atlantic Evangelicalism." In *Evangelicalism: Comparative Studies of Popular Protestantism in North America, the British Isles, and Beyond, 1700–1990*, edited by Mark A. Noll, David Bebbington, and George A. Rawlyk, 333–50. New York: Oxford University Press, 1994.

Ribuffo, Leo P. "Jesus Christ as Business Statesman: Bruce Barton and the Selling of Corporate Capitalism." *American Quarterly* 33, no. 2 (1981): 206–31.

Roosevelt, Theodore. "The Constructive Quarterly." *Outlook* 103 (March 13, 1913): 587–88.

Rubin, Joan Shelley. "Self, Culture, and Self-Culture in Modern America: The Early History of the Book-of-the-Month Club." *Journal of American History* 71, no. 4 (March 1985): 782–806.

Schneirov, Richard. "Chicago's Great Upheaval of 1877: Class Polarization and Democratic Politics." In *The Great Strikes of 1877*, edited by David O. Stowell, 76–104. Urbana: University of Illinois Press, 2008.

Scholnick, Robert J. "J. G. Holland and the 'Religion of Civilization' in Mid-Nineteenth-Century America." *American Studies* 27, no. 1 (1986): 55–79.

Schorman, Rob. "Claude Hopkins, Earnest Calkins, Bissell Carpet Sweepers, and the Birth of Modern Advertising." *Journal of the Gilded Age and Progressive Era* 7, no. 2 (April 2008): 181–219.

Schultz, K. M., and P. Harvey. "Everywhere and Nowhere: Recent Trends in American Religious History and Historiography." *Journal of the American Academy of Religion* 78, no. 1 (February 2010): 129–62.

Scroop, Daniel. "The Anti-Chain Store Movement and the Politics of Consumption." *American Quarterly* 60, no. 4 (December 2008): 925–49.

Shaw, Albert. "Cooperation in the Northwest." In *History of Cooperation in the United States*, edited by Herbert Adams, 199–366. Vol. 6. of *Johns Hopkins University Studies in Historical and Political Science*. Baltimore: Johns Hopkins University Press, 1888.

Sheehan, Jonathan. "When Was Disenchantment? History and the Secular Age." In *Varieties of Secularism in a Secular Age*, edited by Michael Warner, Jonathan VanAntwerpen, and Craig Calhoun, 217–42. Cambridge, Mass.: Harvard University Press, 2013.

Smith, Timothy L. "Protestant Schooling and American Nationality, 1800–1850." *Journal of American History* 53, no. 4 (March 1, 1967): 679–95.

Steigerwald, David, T. H. Breen, and Lizabeth Cohen. "Exchange: American Consumerism." *Journal of American History* 93, no. 2 (September 2006): 385–413.

Stricker, Frank. "American Professors in the Progressive Era: Incomes, Aspirations, and Professionalism." *Journal of Interdisciplinary History* 19, no. 2 (Autumn 1988): 231–57.

Tarr, Joel A. "The Chicago Anti-Department Store Crusade of 1897: A Case Study in Urban Commercial Development." *Journal of the Illinois State Historical Society* 64, no. 2 (July 1, 1971): 161–72.

Tobin, James. "Neoclassical Theory in America: J. B. Clark and Fisher." *American Economic Review* 75, no. 6 (1985): 28–38.

Torrey, Reuben A. "How Can I Know That I Am Led by the Holy Spirit?" In *Traits and Tracts of Torrey: A Fresh Appreciation of a Great Man and Teacher*. Edited by Louis T. Talbot. Los Angeles: Bible Institute of Los Angeles, n.d.

Wacker, Grant. "The Holy Spirit and the Spirit of the Age in American Protestantism, 1880–1910." *Journal of American History* 72, no. 1 (1985): 45–62.

———. "Marching to Zion: Religion in a Modern Utopian Community." *Church History* 54, no. 4 (December 1985): 496–511.

Weems, Robert E., Jr. "The Revolution Will Be Marketed: American Corporations and Black Consumers during the 1960s." In *Consumer Society in American History: A Reader*, edited by Lawrence B. Glickman, 316–25. Ithaca and London: Cornell University Press, 1999.

Wilson, Maurice E. "Eddyism: Commonly Called Christian Science." In *The Fundamentals: A Testimony*, vol. 9, 111–27. Chicago: Testimony Publishing Company, 1910–1915.

Woodman, Harold D. "Economic History and Economic Theory: The New Economic History in America." *Journal of Interdisciplinary History* 3, no. 2 (October 1, 1972): 323–50.

Worrell, A. S. "An Open Letter to the Opposers of the Pentecostal Movement." Reprinted in *Assemblies of God Heritage* 12, no. 1 (Spring 1992): 16–18.

Wyllie, Irvin G. "Social Darwinism and the Businessman." *Proceedings, American Philosophical Society* 103, no. 5 (1959): 629–35.

Digital Sources

Minnesota Population Center. National Historical Geographic Information System: Version 2.0. Minneapolis: University of Minnesota, 2011.

Books and Other Publications

Abell, Aaron. *Urban Impact on American Protestantism, 1865–1900*. Cambridge, Mass: Harvard University Press, 1943.

Abelson, Elaine S. *When Ladies Go A-Thieving: Middle-Class Shoplifters in the Victorian Department Store*. New York: Oxford University Press, 1992.

Abrams, M. *Natural Supernaturalism: Tradition and Revolution in Romantic Literature.* New York: Norton, 1973.

Abzug, Robert. *Cosmos Crumbling: American Reform and the Religious Imagination.* New York: Oxford University Press, 1994.

Adams, Henry W., and Norman Harvey Camp. *"I Cried, He Answered": A Faithful Record of Remarkable Answers to Prayer.* Chicago and London: Bible Institute Colportage Association, 1918.

Ahlstrom, Sydney. *A Religious History of the American People.* New Haven, Conn.: Yale University Press, 2004.

Allen, Frederick Lewis. *Only Yesterday: An Informal History of the 1920s.* New York: Perennial Modern Classics, 2000.

Ames, Edward Scribner. *The New Orthodoxy.* Chicago: University of Chicago Press, ca. 1918.

Anderson, Robert Mapes. *Vision of the Disinherited: The Making of American Pentecostalism.* New York: Oxford University Press, 1979.

Asad, Talal. *Formations of the Secular: Christianity, Islam, Modernity.* Stanford, Calif.: Stanford University Press, 2003.

———. *Genealogies of Religion: Discipline and Reasons of Power in Christianity and Islam.* Baltimore: Johns Hopkins University Press, 1993.

Ault, James M. *Spirit and Flesh: Life in a Fundamentalist Baptist Church.* New York: Knopf, 2004.

Avrich, Paul. *The Haymarket Tragedy.* Princeton, N.J.: Princeton University Press, 1984.

Bademan, R. Bryan. "Contesting the Evangelical Age: Protestant Challenges to Religious Subjectivity in Antebellum America." Ph.D. diss., University of Notre Dame, 2004.

Baer, Jonathan R. "Perfectly Empowered Bodies: Divine Healing in Modernizing America." Ph.D. diss., Yale University, 2002.

Baird, Robert. *Religion in America: Or an Account of the Origin, Relation to the State, and Present Condition of the Evangelical Churches in the United States: With Notices of the Unevangelical Denominations.* New York: Harper & Brothers, 1844.

Baker, Kelly. *Gospel According to the Klan: The KKK's Appeal to Protestant America, 1915–1930.* Lawrence: University Press of Kansas, 2011.

Baldasty, Gerald J. *The Commercialization of News in the Nineteenth Century.* Madison: University of Wisconsin Press, 1992.

Balibar, Étienne, and Immanuel Maurice Wallerstein. *Race, Nation, Class: Ambiguous Identities.* London and New York: Verso, 1991.

Barabas, Steven. *So Great Salvation: The History and Message of the Keswick Convention.* London: Marshall, Morgan & Scott, 1953.

Beaman, Warren Jay. "From Sect to Cult to Sect: The Christian Catholic Church in Zion." Ph.D. diss., Iowa State University, 1990.

Bebbington, David W. *Evangelicalism in Modern Britain: A History from the 1730s to the 1980s.* New York: Routledge, 1989.

Beckert, Sven. *The Monied Metropolis: New York City and the Consolidation of the American Bourgeoisie, 1850–1896.* Cambridge, UK, and New York: Cambridge University Press, 2003.

Bederman, Gail. *Manliness and Civilization: A Cultural History of Gender and Race in the United States, 1880–1917.* Chicago: University of Chicago Press, 1996.

Bendroth, Margaret Lamberts. *Fundamentalism and Gender, 1875 to the Present*. New Haven, Conn.: Yale University Press, 1996.

Bible Conference Committee. *God Hath Spoken . . .* N.p., Bible conference committee, 1919.

The Biographical Dictionary and Portrait Gallery of Representative Men of Chicago, Minnesota Cities, and the World's Columbian Exposition: With Illustrations on Steel. Chicago: American Biographical Publishing Company, 1892.

Biographical Sketches of the Leading Men of Chicago. Chicago: Wilson & St. Clair, 1868.

Blackstone, William E. *Jesus Is Coming*. New York and Chicago: Fleming H. Revell, 1908.

Bledstein, Burton J., and Robert D. Johnston. *The Middling Sorts: Explorations in the History of the American Middle Class*. New York: Routledge, 2001.

Bledstein, Burton J. *The Culture of Professionalism: The Middle Class and the Development of Higher Education in America*. New York: Norton, 1976.

Blum, Edward J. *Reforging the White Republic: Race, Religion, and American Nationalism, 1865–1898*. Baton Rouge: Louisiana State University Press, 2007.

Blumhofer, Edith L. *Aimee Semple McPherson: Everybody's Sister*. Grand Rapids, Mich.: Wm. B. Eerdmans, 1993.

———. *Restoring the Faith: The Assemblies of God, Pentecostalism, and American Culture*. Urbana: University of Illinois Press, 1993.

Blumhofer, Edith L., and Randall Balmer, eds. *Modern Christian Revivals*. Urbana: University of Illinois Press, 1993.

Blumin, Stuart Mack. *The Emergence of the Middle Class: Social Experience in the American City, 1760–1900*. Cambridge, UK, and New York: Cambridge University Press, 1989.

Bowler, Kate. *Blessed: A History of the American Prosperity Gospel*. New York: Oxford University Press, 2013.

Boydston, Jeanne. *Home and Work: Housework, Wages, and the Ideology of Labor in the Early Republic*. New York: Oxford University Press, 1994.

Boyer, Paul S. *Urban Masses and Moral Order in America, 1820–1920*. Cambridge, Mass.: Harvard University Press, 1978.

Bozeman, Theodore Dwight. *Protestants in an Age of Science: The Baconian Ideal and Ante-Bellum American Religious Thought*. Chapel Hill: University of North Carolina Press, 1977.

———. *To Live Ancient Lives: The Primitivist Dimension in Puritanism*. Chapel Hill: University of North Carolina Press, 1988.

Breen, T. H. *The Marketplace of Revolution: How Consumer Politics Shaped American Independence*. Oxford, UK, and New York: Oxford University Press, 2005.

Brekus, Catherine A. *Strangers and Pilgrims: Female Preaching in America, 1740–1845*. Chapel Hill: University of North Carolina Press, 1998.

Brereton, Virginia Lieson. *Training God's Army: The American Bible School, 1880–1940*. Bloomington: Indiana University Press, 1990.

Briggs, S. R., and J. H. Elliott, eds. *Notes for Bible Readings*. Toronto: Toronto Willard Tract Society, 1877.

Burgess, Stanley M., Gary B. McGee, and Patrick H. Alexander. *Dictionary of Pentecostal and Charismatic Movements*. Grand Rapids, Mich.: Zondervan, 1988.

Butler, Jon. *Awash in a Sea of Faith: Christianizing the American People*. Cambridge, Mass: Harvard University Press, 1992.

Butler, Jonathan M. *Softly and Tenderly Jesus Is Calling: Heaven and Hell in American Revivalism, 1870–1920.* Brooklyn, N.Y.: Carlson Pub., 1991.

Calder, Lendol. *Financing the American Dream: A Cultural History of Consumer Credit.* Princeton, N.J.: Princeton University Press, 1999.

Cantwell, Christopher Daniel. "The Bible Class Teacher: Piety and Politics in the Age of Fundamentalism." Ph.D. diss., Cornell University, 2012.

Carpenter, Joel. *Revive Us Again: The Reawakening of American Fundamentalism.* New York: Oxford University Press, 1997.

Carroll, Edward Perry. "Daniel Brink Towner (1850–1919): Educator, Church Musician, Composer, and Editor-Compiler." Thesis, New Orleans Baptist Theological Seminary, 1979.

Carter, Heath. "Union Made: Working People and the Rise of Social Christianity in Chicago." Ph.D. diss., University of Notre Dame, 2012.

Carter, Paul Allen. *The Decline and Revival of the Social Gospel: Social and Political Liberalism in American Protestant Churches, 1920–1940.* Hamden, Conn: Archon Books, 1971.

———. *The Spiritual Crisis of the Gilded Age.* DeKalb: Northern Illinois University Press, 1971.

Carter, Russell Kelso. *"Faith Healing" Reviewed after Twenty Years.* Boston and Chicago: Christian Witness Co., 1897.

Cashdollar, Charles D. *The Transformation of Theology, 1830–1890: Positivism and Protestant Thought in Britain and America.* Princeton, N.J.: Princeton University Press, 1989.

Chandler, Alfred D. *The Visible Hand: The Managerial Revolution in American Business.* Cambridge, Mass.: Belknap Press of Harvard University Press, 1993.

Chartier, Myron Raymond. *The Social Views of Dwight L. Moody and Their Relation to the Workingman of 1860–1900.* Hays, Kan.: Fort Hays Kansas State College, 1969.

Cochran, Pamela. *Evangelical Feminism: A History.* New York: New York University Press, 2005.

Cochran, Thomas C. *Business in American Life: A History.* New York: McGraw-Hill, 1976.

Cohen, Lizabeth. *A Consumers' Republic: The Politics of Mass Consumption in Postwar America.* New York: Vintage Books, 2003.

———. *Making a New Deal: Industrial Workers in Chicago, 1919–1939.* Cambridge, UK, and New York: Cambridge University Press, 1990.

The Coming and Kingdom of Christ. Chicago: Bible Institute Colportage Association, 1914.

Committee of the Young Men's Christian Associations International. *Proceedings . . . International Convention.* N.p.: Association Press, 1870.

Connerley, Jennifer. "Friendly Americans: Representing Quakers in the United States, 1850–1920," Ph.D. diss., University of North Carolina at Chapel Hill, 2006.

Connolly, William. *Capitalism and Christianity, American Style.* Durham, N.C.: Duke University Press, 2008.

Convention of the Young Men's Christian Associations of the United States and British Provinces. *Journal of Proceedings of the . . . Annual Convention of Young Men's Christian Associations of the United States and British Provinces.* N.p.: The Associations, 1869.

Cook, Philip L. *Zion City, Illinois: Twentieth-Century Utopia.* Syracuse, N.Y.: Syracuse University Press, 1996.

Cooke, Harriette J. *Mildmay; or, The Story of the First Deaconess Institution*. London: Elliot Stock, 1893.

Corrigan, John. *Business of the Heart: Religion and Emotion in the Nineteenth Century*. Berkeley: University of California Press, 2001.

Cox, Harvey. *Fire from Heaven: The Rise of Pentecostal Spirituality and the Reshaping of Religion in the Twenty-First Century*. New York: Perseus Books, 1994.

Crapanzano, Vincent. *Serving the Word: Literalism in America from the Pulpit to the Bench*. New York: New Press, 2000.

Creech, Joe. *Righteous Indignation: Religion and the Populist Revolution*. Urbana: University of Illinois Press, 2006.

Cronon, William. *Nature's Metropolis: Chicago and the Great West*. New York: W. W. Norton & Company, 1992.

Cross, Gary. *An All-Consuming Century: Why Commercialism Won in Modern America*. New York: Columbia University Press, 2002.

Currey, J. Seymour. *Chicago: Its History and Its Builders, a Century of Marvelous Growth*. Chicago: S. J. Clarke Publishing Co., 1912.

Curtis, Heather D. *Faith in the Great Physician: Suffering and Divine Healing in American Culture, 1860–1900*. Baltimore: Johns Hopkins University Press, 2007.

Curtis, Susan. *A Consuming Faith: The Social Gospel and Modern American Culture*. Columbia: University of Missouri Press, 2001.

Cuyler, Theodore Ledyard. *Recollections of a Long Life: An Autobiography by Theodore Ledyard Cuyler*. New York: Baker & Taylor Co., 1902.

Daniels, William Haven. *D. L. Moody and His Work*. London: Hodder and Stoughton, 1875.

———, ed. *Moody: His Words, Work, and Workers: Comprising His Bible Portraits; His Outlines of Doctrine, as Given in His Most Popular and Effective Sermons, Bible Readings, and Addresses . . .* New York: Nelson & Phillips, 1877.

Darby, John Nelson. *Letters by J. N. D., 1849–1875*. London: G. Morrish, 1881.

Davenport, Stewart. *Friends of the Unrighteous Mammon: Northern Christians and Market Capitalism, 1815–1860*. Chicago: University of Chicago Press, 2008.

Dávila, Arlene. *Latinos, Inc.: The Marketing and Making of a People*. Berkeley: University of California Press, 2001.

Davis, Gary W. "A Critical Exposition of F. H. R. Von Frank's System of Christian Certainty." Ph.D. diss., University of Iowa, 1972.

Davis, George T. B. *Torrey and Alexander, the Story of a World-Wide Revival; a Record and Study of the Work and Personality of the Evangelists R. A. Torrey and Charles M. Alexander*. New York and Chicago: Fleming H. Revell, 1905.

Day, Richard Ellsworth. *Breakfast Table Autocrat: The Life Story of Henry Parsons Crowell*. Chicago: Moody Press, 1946.

Dayton, Donald W. *The Theological Roots of Pentecostalism*. Peabody, Mass.: Hendrickson Publishers, 1987.

Dayton, Donald W., and Robert K. Johnston, eds. *The Variety of American Evangelicalism*. Knoxville: University of Tennessee Press, 2001.

DeBerg, Betty A. *Ungodly Women: Gender and the First Wave of American Fundamentalism*. Macon, Ga.: Mercer University Press, 2000.

Deems, Charles Force, John Bancroft Devins, and Amory Howe Bradford. *Christian Thought*. New York: W. B. Ketcham, 1913.

Denning, Michael. *Mechanic Accents: Dime Novels and Working-Class Culture in America*. London and New York: Verso, 1987.

Dixon, A. C. *The Person and Ministry of the Holy Spirit*. Baltimore: Wharton, Barron, 1890.

Dobschuetz, Barbara. "Fundamentalism and American Urban Culture: Community and Religious Identity in Dwight L. Moody's Chicago, 1864–1914," Ph.D. diss., University of Illinois at Chicago, 2002.

Dochuk, Darren. *From Bible Belt to Sunbelt: Plain-Folk Religion, Grassroots Politics, and the Rise of Evangelical Conservatism*. New York: W. W. Norton & Company, 2010.

Dorrien, Gary. *Soul in Society: The Making and Renewal of Social Christianity*. Minneapolis: Fortress Press, 1995.

Dorsett, Lyle. *A Passion for Souls: The Life of D. L. Moody*. Chicago: Moody Publishers, 1997.

Douglas, Ann. *The Feminization of American Culture*. New York: Knopf, 1977.

Dowie, John Alexander. *American First-Fruits: Being a Brief Record of Eight Months' Divine Healing . . .* 2nd ed. San Francisco: Leaves of Healing, 1889.

———. *Zion's Holy War against the Hosts of Hell in Chicago: A Series of Addresses*. Chicago: Zion Publishing House, 1900.

Enstad, Nan. *Ladies of Labor, Girls of Adventure: Working Women, Popular Culture, and Labor Politics at the Turn of the Twentieth Century*. New York: Columbia University Press, 1999.

Evans, Christopher Hodge. *Social Gospel Liberalism and the Ministry of Ernest Fremont Tittle: A Theology for the Middle Class*. Lewiston, N.Y.: Edward Mellen Press, 1996.

Evensen, Bruce J. *God's Man for the Gilded Age: D. L. Moody and the Rise of Modern Mass Evangelism*. New York: Oxford University Press, 2003.

Farwell, John Villiers, Jr. *Some Recollections of John V. Farwell: A Brief Description of His Early Life and Business Reminiscences*. Chicago: R. R. Donnelley & Sons Company, 1911.

Federal Council of the Churches of Christ in America. *Report of the First Meeting of the Federal Council, Philadelphia, 1908*. New York and Chicago: Fleming H. Revell, 1909.

Fessenden, Tracy. *Culture and Redemption: Religion, the Secular, and American Literature*. Princeton, N.J.: Princeton University Press, 2006.

Fifty-Five Years: The Young Men's Christian Association of Chicago, 1858–1913. Chicago: Board of Managers, 1913.

Findlay, James F., Jr. *Dwight L. Moody: American Evangelist, 1837–1899*. Chicago: University of Chicago Press, 1969.

Finke, Roger. *The Churching of America, 1776–2005: Winners and Losers in Our Religious Economy*. Revised ed. New Brunswick, N.J.: Rutgers University Press, 2005.

Flood, Robert G., and Jerry B. Jenkins. *Teaching the Word, Reaching the World*. Chicago: Moody Press, 1985.

Foner, Eric. *Free Soil, Free Labor, Free Men: The Ideology of the Republican Party before the Civil War*. New York: Oxford University Press, 1995.

Foster, Gaines M. *Moral Reconstruction: Christian Lobbyists and the Federal Legislation of Morality, 1865–1920*. Chapel Hill: University of North Carolina Press, 2002.

Foster, George Burman. *The Function of Religion in Man's Struggle for Existence*. Chicago: University of Chicago Press, 1909.

Foucault, Michel. *Discipline and Punish: The Birth of the Prison*. New York: Penguin Books, 1991.

Frank, Thomas. *The Conquest of Cool: Business Culture, Counterculture, and the Rise of Hip Consumerism*. Chicago: University of Chicago Press, 1998.

———. *What's the Matter with Kansas? How Conservatives Won the Heart of America*. New York: Macmillan, 2005.

Fraser, Steve. *Wall Street: America's Dream Palace*. New Haven, Conn.: Yale University Press, 2008.

Friedman, Walter A. *Birth of a Salesman: The Transformation of Selling in America*. Cambridge, Mass: Harvard University Press, 2004.

The Fundamentals: A Testimony to the Truth. 12 vols. Chicago: Testimony Publishing Co., 1910–1915.

Gaustad, Edwin S., Philip L. Barlow, Richard W. Dishno, and Edwin S. Gaustad. *New Historical Atlas of Religion in America*. New York: Oxford University Press, 2001.

Getz, Gene A. *MBI: The Story of Moody Bible Institute*. Chicago: Moody Press, 1969.

Gibbon, Edward. *The History of the Decline and Fall of the Roman Empire*. 7 vols. Edited by J. B. Bury. New York: Macmillan, 1914.

Giddens, Anthony. *Capitalism and Modern Social Theory: An Analysis of the Writings of Marx, Durkheim, and Max Weber*. Cambridge, UK, and New York: Cambridge University Press, 1971.

Gilbert, James Burkhart. *Perfect Cities: Chicago's Utopias of 1893*. Chicago: University of Chicago Press, 1991.

———. *Redeeming Culture: American Religion in an Age of Science*. Chicago: University of Chicago Press, 1997.

Gladden, Washington. *Recollections*. New York: Houghton Mifflin Company, 1909.

Glazener, Nancy. *Reading for Realism: The History of a U.S. Literary Institution, 1850–1910*. Durham, N.C.: Duke University Press, 1997.

Glickman, Lawrence B. *A Living Wage: American Workers and the Making of Consumer Society*. Ithaca, N.Y.: Cornell University Press, 1999.

Goff, James R., Jr. *Fields White unto Harvest: Charles F. Parham and the Missionary Origins of Pentecostalism*. Fayetteville: University of Arkansas Press, 1989.

Goodspeed, Edgar Johnson. *A Full History of the Wonderful Career of Moody and Sankey, in Great Britain and America . . .* New York: H. S. Goodspeed, 1876.

Goodwyn, Lawrence. *The Populist Moment: A Short History of the Agrarian Revolt in America*. Abridged ed. New York: Oxford University Press, 1978.

Gordon, Sarah Barringer. *The Mormon Question: Polygamy and Constitutional Conflict in Nineteenth-Century America*. Chapel Hill: University of North Carolina Press, 2002.

Gray, James M. *The Deadline of Doctrine around the Church: A Reply to Dr. Harry Emerson Fosdick's Sermon Entitled "Shall the Fundamentalists Win?"* Chicago: Moody Bible Institute of Chicago, 1922.

———. *Great Epochs of Sacred History and the Shadows They Cast*. New York and Chicago: Fleming H. Revell, 1910.

———. *"Have You Turned on the Button?"* Chicago: Bible Institute Colportage Association, n.d.

———. *How to Master the English Bible*. Edinburgh and London: Oliphant, Anderson & Ferrier, 1907.

———. *Primers of the Faith*. New York and Chicago: Fleming H. Revell, 1906.

———. *Salvation from Start to Finish: Bible Expositions Covering the New Life of the Believer from Its Inception in Faith to Its Consummation in Glory*. New York and Chicago: Fleming H. Revell, 1911.

Green, James. *Death in the Haymarket: A Story of Chicago, the First Labor Movement, and the Bombing That Divided Gilded Age America*. New York: Pantheon Books, 2006.

Grem, Darren Elliott. "The Blessings of Business: Corporate America and Conservative Evangelicalism in the Sunbelt Age, 1945–2000." Ph.D. diss., University of Georgia, 2010.

Grossman, James R. *Land of Hope: Chicago, Black Southerners, and the Great Migration*. Chicago: University Of Chicago Press, 1991.

Gustav-Wrathall, John Donald. *Take the Young Stranger by the Hand: Same-Sex Relations and the YMCA*. Chicago: University of Chicago Press, 1998.

Hall, David D. *Worlds of Wonder, Days of Judgment: Popular Religious Belief in Early New England*. New York: Knopf, 1989.

Hall, Eve M. "The Power of One: Mary McLeod Bethune's Legacy in Leadership, Learning, and Service." Ph.D. diss., Cardinal Stritch University, 2009.

Halttunen, Karen. *Confidence Men and Painted Women: A Study of Middle Class Culture in America, 1830–70*. New Haven, Conn.: Yale University Press, 1986.

Hammond, Sarah Ruth. "'God's Business Men': Entrepreneurial Evangelicals in Depression and War," 2010.

Handy, Robert T. *A Christian America: Protestant Hopes and Historical Realities*. New York: Oxford University Press, 1984.

———. *The Social Gospel in America, 1870–1920*. New York: Oxford University Press, 1966.

Hangen, Tona J. *Redeeming the Dial: Radio, Religion and Popular Culture in America*. Chapel Hill: University of North Carolina Press, 2002.

Hannah, John D. *An Uncommon Union: Dallas Theological Seminary and American Evangelicalism*. Grand Rapids, Mich.: Zondervan, 2009.

Hanson, Joyce Ann. *Mary McLeod Bethune and Black Women's Political Activism*. Columbia: University of Missouri Press, 2003.

Harding, Susan Friend. *The Book of Jerry Falwell: Fundamentalist Language and Politics*. Princeton, N.J.: Princeton University Press, 2000.

Harlan, Rolvix. *John Alexander Dowie and the Christian Apostolic Church*. Evansville, Ind.: Antes, 1906.

Harper, William Rainey. *The Trend in Higher Education*. Chicago: University of Chicago Press, 1905.

Hart, D. G. *Deconstructing Evangelicalism: Conservative Protestantism in the Age of Billy Graham*. Baker Publishing, 2005.

———. *Defending the Faith: J. Gresham Machen and the Crisis of Conservative Protestantism in Modern America*. Grand Rapids, Mich.: Baker Publishing, 1995.

Haskell, Thomas L. *The Emergence of Professional Social Science: The American Social Science Association and the Nineteenth-Century Crisis of Authority*. Urbana: University of Illinois Press, 1977.

Hassey, Janette. *No Time for Silence: Evangelical Women in Public Ministry around the Turn of the Century*. Grand Rapids, Mich.: Academie Books, 1986.

Hatch, Nathan O. *The Democratization of American Christianity*. New Haven: Yale University Press, 1989.

Hatch, Nathan O., and Mark Noll, eds. *The Bible in America: Essays in Cultural History*. New York: Oxford University Press, 1982.

Hedstrom, Matthew S. *The Rise of Liberal Religion: Book Culture and American Spirituality in the Twentieth Century*. New York: Oxford University Press, 2012.

Hicks, John Donald. *The Populist Revolt: A History of the Farmers' Alliance and the People's Party*. Minneapolis: University of Minnesota Press, 1931.

Hilkey, Judy. *Character Is Capital: Success Manuals and Manhood in Gilded Age America*. Chapel Hill: University of North Carolina Press, 1997.

Hiss, William Charles. "Shiloh: Frank W. Sandford and the Kingdom, 1893-1948." Ph.D. diss., Tufts University, 1978.

Hofstadter, Richard. *Social Darwinism in American Thought*. Boston: Beacon Press, 1944.

Holifield, E. Brooks. *Theology in America: Christian Thought from the Age of the Puritans to the Civil War*. New Haven, Conn.: Yale University Press, 2003.

Hollenweger, Walter J. *The Pentecostals*. Hendrickson Pub., 1988.

Holmes, Janice Evelyn. *Religious Revivals in Britain and Ireland, 1859-1905*. Dublin: Irish Academic Press, 2000.

Hopkins, Charles Howard. *The Rise of the Social Gospel in American Protestantism, 1865-1915*. New Haven: Yale University Press; London: H. Milford; New York: Oxford University Press, 1940.

Hornstein, Jeffrey M. *A Nation of Realtors: A Cultural History of the Twentieth-Century American Middle Class*. Durham, N.C.: Duke University Press, 2005.

Horowitz, Daniel. *The Morality of Spending: Attitudes toward the Consumer Society in America, 1875-1940*. Chicago: Ivan R. Dee, 1992.

Horsman, Reginald. *Race and Manifest Destiny: Origins of American Racial Anglo-Saxonism*. Cambridge, Mass.: Harvard University Press, 1986.

Hounshell, David. *From the American System to Mass Production, 1800-1932: The Development of Manufacturing Technology in the United States*. Baltimore: Johns Hopkins University Press, 1985.

Howe, Daniel Walker. *Making the American Self: Jonathan Edwards to Abraham Lincoln*. New York: Oxford University Press, 2009.

"How God Answered Prayer: From the Diary of Rev. R. A. Torrey, D.D." Chicago: Bible Institute Colportage Association, n.d.

Hudnut-Beumler, James. *In Pursuit of the Almighty's Dollar: A History of Money and American Protestantism*. Chapel Hill: University of North Carolina Press, 2007.

Hughes, Richard T., ed. *The American Quest for the Primitive Church*. Urbana: University of Illinois Press, 1988.

Hughes, Richard T., and Leonard Allen. *Illusions of Innocence: Protestant Primitivism in America, 1630-1875*. Chicago: University of Chicago Press, 1988.

Hunter, Tera W. *To 'Joy My Freedom: Southern Black Women's Lives and Labors after the Civil War*. Cambridge, Mass: Harvard University Press, 1997.

Hutchison, William R. *The Modernist Impulse in American Protestantism*. Cambridge, Mass.: Harvard University Press, 1976.

Igo, Sarah E. *The Averaged American: Surveys, Citizens, and the Making of a Mass Public*. Cambridge, Mass: Harvard University Press, 2007.

Jacobsen, Douglas, and William Vance Trollinger, eds. *Re-Forming the Center: American Protestantism, 1900 to the Present*. Grand Rapids, Mich.: Wm. B. Eerdmans, 1998.

Johnson, Paul E. *A Shopkeeper's Millennium: Society and Revivals in Rochester, New York, 1815–1837*. New York: Hill and Wang, 2004.

Johnson, Paul E., and Sean Wilentz. *The Kingdom of Matthias: A Story of Sex and Salvation in 19th-Century America*. New York: Oxford University Press, 1994.

Johnston, Robert D. *The Politics of Healing: Histories of Alternative Medicine in Twentieth-Century North America*. New York: Routledge, 2004.

———. *The Radical Middle Class: Populist Democracy and the Question of Capitalism in Progressive Era Portland, Oregon*. Princeton, N.J.: Princeton University Press, 2003.

Joiner, Thekla Ellen. *Sin in the City: Chicago and Revivalism, 1880–1920*. Columbia: University of Missouri Press, 2007.

Kazin, Michael. *A Godly Hero: The Life of William Jennings Bryan*. New York: Anchor, 2007.

———. *The Populist Persuasion: An American History*. New York: Basic Books, 1995.

Keane, Webb. *Christian Moderns: Freedom and Fetish in the Mission Encounter*. Berkeley: University of California Press, 2007.

Kennedy, David M. *Over Here: The First World War and American Society*. New York: Oxford University Press, 2004.

Kidd, Thomas S. *The Great Awakening: The Roots of Evangelical Christianity in Colonial America*. New Haven, Conn.: Yale University Press, 2009.

Kimball, Caleb. *The Young Christian Directed*. Boston: B. Perkins & Co., 1847.

Kloppenberg, James T. *Uncertain Victory: Social Democracy and Progressivism in European and American Thought, 1870–1920*. New York: Oxford University Press, 1988.

Knox, Ronald A. *Enthusiasm: A Chapter in the History of Religion*. Notre Dame, Ind.: University of Notre Dame Press, 1994.

Kostlevy, William. *Holy Jumpers: Evangelicals and Radicals in Progressive Era America*. New York: Oxford University Press, 2010.

Krist, Gary. *City of Scoundrels: The 12 Days of Disaster That Gave Birth to Modern Chicago*. New York: Broadway Books, 2013.

Krivoshey, Robert M. "'Going through the Eye of the Needle': The Life of Oilman Fundamentalist Lyman Stewart, 1840–1923." Ph.D. Diss., University of Chicago, 1973.

Laird, Pamela Walker. *Advertising Progress: American Business and the Rise of Consumer Marketing*. Baltimore: Johns Hopkins University Press, 2001.

Lakoff, George, and Mark Johnson. *Metaphors We Live By*. Chicago: University of Chicago Press, 1980.

Lambert, Frank. *"Pedlar in Divinity": George Whitefield and the Transatlantic Revivals, 1737–1770*. Princeton, N.J.: Princeton University Press, 2002.

Lamoreaux, Naomi R. *The Great Merger Movement in American Business, 1895–1904*. Cambridge, UK, and New York: Cambridge University Press, 1988.

Larson, Edward J. *Summer for the Gods: The Scopes Trial and America's Continuing Debate over Science and Religion*. New York: Basic Books, 1997.

Leach, William R. *Land of Desire: Merchants, Power, and the Rise of a New American Culture*. New York: Pantheon, 1993.

Lears, T. J. Jackson. *Fables of Abundance: A Cultural History of Advertising in America*. New York: Basic Books, 1995.

———. *No Place of Grace: Antimodernism and the Transformation of American Culture, 1880–1920*. New York: Pantheon Books, 1981.

———. *Rebirth of a Nation: The Making of Modern America, 1877–1920*. New York: Harper Perennial, 2010.

Leuchtenberg, William E. *The Perils of Prosperity: 1914–1932*. Chicago: University of Chicago Press, 1958.

Lienesch, Michael. *In the Beginning: Fundamentalism, the Scopes Trial, and the Making of the Antievolution Movement*. Chapel Hill: University of North Carolina Press, 2007.

Light on Prophecy: A Coordinated, Constructive Teaching; Being the Proceedings and Addresses at the Philadelphia Prophetic Conference, May 28–30, 1918. New York: Bible House, Christian Herald, 1918.

Lindsey, Almont. *The Pullman Strike: The Story of a Unique Experiment and of a Great Labor Upheaval*. Chicago: University of Chicago Press, 1943.

Livingstone, David N. *Darwin's Forgotten Defenders: The Encounter between Evangelical Theology and Evolutionary Thought*. Grand Rapids, Mich.: Wm. B. Eerdmans, 1987.

Livingstone, David N., D. G. Hart, and Mark A. Noll. *Evangelicals and Science in Historical Perspective*. New York: Oxford University Press, 1999.

Lofton, Kathryn. *Oprah: The Gospel of an Icon*. Berkeley: University of California Press, 2011.

Long, Kathryn Teresa. *The Revival of 1857–58: Interpreting an American Religious Awakening*. New York: Oxford University Press, 1998.

Longfield, Bradley J. *The Presbyterian Controversy: Fundamentalists, Modernists, and Moderates*. New York: Oxford University Press, 1991.

Machen, J. Gresham. *Christianity and Liberalism*. New York: Macmillan Company, 1923.

MacIntyre, Alasdair. *After Virtue: A Study in Moral Theory*. 2nd ed. Notre Dame, Ind.: University of Notre Dame Press, 1984.

Manring, Maurice M. *Slave in a Box: The Strange Career of Aunt Jemima*. Charlottesville: University Press of Virginia, 1998.

Marchand, Roland. *Advertising the American Dream: Making Way for Modernity, 1920–1940*. Berkeley: University of California Press, 1986.

Marquette, Arthur F. *Brands, Trademarks, and Good Will: The Story of the Quaker Oats Company*. New York: McGraw-Hill, 1967.

Marsden, George M. *The Evangelical Mind and the New School Presbyterian Experience: A Case Study of Thought and Theology in Nineteenth-Century America*. New Haven: Yale University Press, 1970.

———. *Fundamentalism and American Culture: The Shaping of Twentieth-Century Evangelism, 1870–1925*. New York: Oxford University Press, 1980.

———. *Reforming Fundamentalism: Fuller Seminary and the New Evangelicalism*. Grand Rapids, Mich.: Wm. B. Eerdmans, 1988.

———. *The Soul of the American University: From Protestant Establishment to Established Nonbelief*. New York: Oxford University Press, 1996.

Marsh, R. L. *"Faith Healing"—A Defense; or, The Lord Thy Healer*. New York and Chicago: Fleming H. Revell, 1889.

Martin, David. *Tongues of Fire: The Explosion of Protestantism in Latin America*. Cambridge, Mass.: Wiley-Blackwell, 1993.

Martin, Donald Lewis, Jr. "The Thought of Amzi Clarence Dixon," Ph.D. diss., Baylor University, 1989.

Martin, Roger. *R. A. Torrey: Apostle of Certainty*. Murfreesboro, Tenn.: Sword of the Lord Publishers, 1976.

Marty, Martin E. *Righteous Empire: The Protestant Experience in America*. New York: Dial Press, 1970.

Marty, Martin E., and R. Scott Appleby, eds. *The Fundamentalism Project*. 5 vols. Chicago: University of Chicago Press, 1991.

May, Henry F. *Protestant Churches and Industrial America*. New York: Harper, 1949.

McClay, Wilfred M. *The Masterless: Self and Society in Modern America*. Chapel Hill: University of North Carolina Press, 1994.

McCloud, Sean. *Divine Hierarchies: Class in American Religion and Religious Studies*. Chapel Hill: University of North Carolina Press, 2007.

McGerr, Michael E. *A Fierce Discontent: The Rise and Fall of the Progressive Movement in America, 1870–1920*. New York: Oxford University Press, 2005.

McLoughlin, William G. *Modern Revivalism: Charles Grandison Finney to Billy Graham*. New York: Ronald Press Company, 1959.

Menand, Louis. *The Metaphysical Club: A Story of Ideas in America*. New York: Farrar, Straus and Giroux, 2001.

Mihm, Stephen. *A Nation of Counterfeiters: Capitalists, Con Men, and the Making of the United States*. Cambridge, Mass.: Harvard University Press, 2009.

Montgomery, David. *The Fall of the House of Labor: The Workplace, the State, and American Labor Activism, 1865–1925*. Cambridge, UK, and New York: Cambridge University Press, 1987.

Moody and Sankey: The New Evangelists, Their Lives and Labours. London: Ward, Lock, & Tyler, 1875.

Moody Bible Institute. *Student Register of the Moody Bible Institute of Chicago: Revised to February, 1920*. Chicago: n.p., 1920.

Moody, Dwight Lyman. *Addresses*. London: Morgan and Scott, 1900.

———. *Glad Tidings: Comprising Sermons and Prayer-Meeting Talks Delivered at the N.Y. Hippodrome . . .* New York: E. B. Treat, 1876.

———. *New Sermons, Addresses, and Prayers*. New York: Henry S. Goodspeed & Co., 1877.

———. *Pleasure and Profit in Bible Study: And Anecdotes, Incidents and Illustrations*. N.p.: Marshall, Morgan & Scott, 1911.

———. *Secret Power; or, The Secret of Success in Christian Life and Christian Work*. New York and Chicago: Fleming H. Revell, 1881.

Moody, Dwight Lyman, and J. B. McClure. *Anecdotes and Illustrations of D. L. Moody*. Chicago: Rhodes & McClure, 1877.

Moody, Dwight Lyman, and John Lobb. *Arrows and Anecdotes*. New York: H. Gurley, 1877.

Moody, Dwight Lyman, and L. T. Palmer. *The Gospel Awakening*. Chicago: Fairbanks, Palmer & Co., 1883.

Moody, Paul Dwight, and Arthur Percy Fitt. *The Shorter Life of D. L. Moody*. Chicago: Bible Institute Colportage Association, 1900.

Moody, William R. *The Life of Dwight L. Moody, by His Son*. New York and Chicago: Fleming H. Revell, 1900.

Moore, Robert Laurence. *Religious Outsiders and the Making of Americans.* New York: Oxford University Press, 1987.

———. *Selling God: American Religion in the Marketplace of Culture.* New York: Oxford University Press, 1995.

Moorhead, Jonathan David. "Jesus Is Coming: The Life and Work of William E. Blackstone (1841–1935)." Ph.D. diss., Dallas Theological Seminary, 2008.

Moreton, Bethany. *To Serve God and Wal-Mart: The Making of Christian Free Enterprise.* Cambridge, Mass: Harvard University Press, 2009.

Moskowitz, Marina. *Standard of Living: The Measure of the Middle Class in Modern America.* Baltimore: Johns Hopkins University Press, 2004.

Mott, Frank Luther. *A History of American Magazines.* New York and London: D. Appleton and Company, 1930.

Mullin, Robert Bruce. *Miracles and the Modern Religious Imagination.* New Haven, Conn.: Yale University Press, 1996.

Murray, Frank S. *The Sublimity of Faith: The Life and Work of Frank W. Sandford.* Amherst, N.H.: Kingdom Press, 1981.

Nelson, Shirley. *Fair, Clear, and Terrible: The Story of Shiloh, Maine.* Eugene, Ore.: Wipf and Stock Publishers, 2005.

———. *The Last Year of the War.* New York: Harper & Row, 1978.

Newell, William R. *Lessons on the Epistle of Paul to the Romans.* Toronto, Ontario, Canada: J. I. C. Wilcox, 1925.

New York City Mission and Tract Society. *Christian Work in New York.* New York: Bible House, 1877.

Noll, Mark A. *America's God: From Jonathan Edwards to Abraham Lincoln.* New York: Oxford University Press, 2002.

———. *Between Faith and Criticism: Evangelicals, Scholarship, and the Bible in America.* Grand Rapids, Mich.: Baker Pub. Group, 1991.

———. *The Civil War as a Theological Crisis.* Chapel Hill: University of North Carolina Press, 2006.

———. *God and Mammon: Protestants, Money, and the Market, 1790–1860.* New York: Oxford University Press, 2002.

Noll, Mark A., David Bebbington, and George A. Rawlyk, eds. *Evangelicalism: Comparative Studies of Popular Protestantism in North America, the British Isles, and Beyond, 1700–1990.* New York: Oxford University Press, 1994.

Nord, David Paul. *Faith in Reading: Religious Publishing and the Birth of Mass Media in America.* New York: Oxford University Press, 2004.

Nugent, Walter T. K. *Money and American Society, 1865–1880.* New York: Free Press, 1968.

———. *The Tolerant Populists: Kansas, Populism and Nativism.* Chicago: University of Chicago Press, 1963.

Numbers, Ronald L. *Antievolutionism before World War I.* Vol. 1. New York: Garland Publishers, 1995.

———. *The Creationists.* Berkeley: University of California Press, 1992.

Numbers, Ronald L., and Darrel W. Amundsen. *Caring and Curing: Health and Medicine in the Western Religious Traditions.* New York.: Macmillan, 1986.

Nye, David E. *Consuming Power: A Social History of American Energies*. Cambridge, Mass.: MIT Press, 1998.

Ohmann, Richard M. *Selling Culture: Magazines, Markets, and the Class at the Turn of the Century*. New York: Verso, 1998.

Olsen, Margaret Hook. *Patriarch of the Rockies: The Life Story of Joshua Gravett*. Denver, Colo.: Golden Bell Press, 1960.

Opp, James William. *The Lord for the Body: Religion, Medicine, and Protestant Faith Healing in Canada, 1880–1930*. Montreal and Ithaca, N.Y.: McGill-Queen's University Press, 2005.

Ostrander, Rick. *The Life of Prayer in a World of Science: Protestants, Prayer, and American Culture, 1870–1930*. New York: Oxford University Press, 2000.

Painter, Nell Irvin. *Standing at Armageddon: United States, 1877–1919*. New York: W. W. Norton & Co., 1988.

Palmer, Phoebe. *The Way of Holiness: With Notes by the Way . . .* New York: Piercy and Reed, 1843.

Peck, William Farley. *History of Rochester and Monroe County, New York*. New York and Chicago: Pioneer Publishing Company, 1908.

Peiss, Kathy. *Hope in a Jar: The Making of America's Beauty Culture*. Philadelphia: University of Pennsylvania Press, 2011.

Pettegrew, Justin H. "Onward Christian Soldiers: The Transformation of Religion, Masculinity, and Class in the Chicago YMCA, 1857–1933." Chicago: Loyola University Chicago, 2006.

Pietsch, Brendan. "Dispensational Modernism." Ph.D. diss., Duke University, 2011.

Poovey, Mary. *A History of the Modern Fact: Problems of Knowledge in the Sciences of Wealth and Society*. Chicago: University of Chicago Press, 1998.

Pope, Daniel. *The Making of Modern Advertising*. New York: Basic Books, 1983.

Primer, Ben. *Protestants and American Business Methods*. Ann Arbor, Mich.: UMI Research Press, 1978.

The Prophetic Conference: New-York, October 30, 31, and November 1, 1878: Christ's Second Coming. New York: New York Tribune, 1878.

Prophetic Studies of the International Prophetic Conference. New York and Chicago: Fleming H. Revell, 1886.

Rack, Henry D. *Reasonable Enthusiast: John Wesley and the Rise of Methodism*. New York: Trinity Press Intl., 1989.

Radway, Janice A. *A Feeling for Books: The Book-of-the-Month Club, Literary Taste, and Middle-Class Desire*. Chapel Hill: University of North Carolina Press, 1997.

Rall, Harris Franklin. *Modern Premillennialism and the Christian Hope*. Nashville, Tenn.: Abingdon Press, 1920.

Riebe, John R. *The Fruit of the Spirit Is Joy*. Chicago: Moody Press, 1928.

Remlap, L. T., ed. *"The Gospel Awakening": Comprising the Sermons and Addresses, Prayer-Meeting Talks and Bible Readings of the Great Revival Meetings Conducted by Moody and Sankey . . .* Chicago: Fairbanks and Palmer Publishers Co., 1885.

Rhees, Rush. *The Life of Jesus of Nazareth: A Study*. New York: C. Scribner's Sons, 1902.

Robins, R. G. *A. J. Tomlinson: Plainfolk Modernist*. New York: Oxford University Press, 2004.

Robinson, Margaret Blake. *A Reporter at Moody's*. Chicago: Bible Institute Colportage Association, 1900.

Rodgers, Daniel T. *Atlantic Crossings: Social Politics in a Progressive Age*. Cambridge, Mass.: Belknap Press of Harvard University Press, 1998.

———. *The Work Ethic in Industrial America, 1850–1920*. Chicago: University of Chicago Press, 1979.

Runyan, William M. *Dr. Gray at Moody Bible Institute*. New York: Oxford University Press, 1935.

Ruotsila, Markku. *The Origins of Christian Anti-Internationalism: Conservative Evangelicals and the League of Nations*. Washington, D.C.: Georgetown University Press, 2007.

Ruse, Michael. *The Darwinian Revolution: Science Red in Tooth and Claw*. Chicago: University of Chicago Press, 1999.

Rushing, D. Jean. "From Confederate Deserter to Decorated Veteran Bible Scholar: Exploring the Enigmatic Life of C. I. Scofield, 1861–1921," M.A. thesis, East Tennessee State University, 2011.

Ryan, Mary P. *Cradle of the Middle Class: The Family in Oneida County, New York, 1790–1865*. Cambridge, UK, and New York: Cambridge University Press, 1983.

Sandage, Scott A. *Born Losers: A History of Failure in America*. Cambridge, Mass: Harvard University Press, 2005.

Sandeen, Ernest R. *The Roots of Fundamentalism: British and American Millenarianism, 1800–1930*. Chicago: University of Chicago Press, 1970.

Sanders, Elizabeth. *Roots of Reform: Farmers, Workers, and the American State, 1877–1917*. Chicago: University of Chicago Press, 1999.

Scanlon, Jennifer. *Inarticulate Longings: The "Ladies' Home Journal," Gender, and the Promise of Consumer Culture*. New York: Routledge, 1995.

Schaack, Michael J. *Anarchy and Anarchists*. F. J. Schulte & Company, 1889.

Schmidt, Jean Miller. *Souls or the Social Order: The Two-Party System in American Protestantism*. Brooklyn, N.Y.: Carlson, 1991.

Schmidt, Leigh Eric. *Consumer Rites: The Buying and Selling of American Holidays*. Princeton, N.J.: Princeton University Press, 1997.

———. *Hearing Things: Religion, Illusion, and the American Enlightenment*. Cambridge, Mass: Harvard University Press, 2000.

———. *Holy Fairs: Scotland and the Making of American Revivalism*. 2nd ed. Grand Rapids, Mich.: Wm. B. Eerdmans, 2001.

———. *Restless Souls: The Making of American Spirituality from Emerson to Oprah*. San Francisco: HarperSanFrancisco, 2005.

Schneirov, Richard. *Labor and Urban Politics: Class Conflict and the Origins of Modern Liberalism in Chicago, 1864–97*. Urbana: University of Illinois Press, 1998.

Schoepflin, Rennie. *Christian Science on Trial: Religious Healing in America*. Baltimore: Johns Hopkins University Press, 2003.

Schwantes, Carlos Arnaldo. *Coxey's Army: An American Odyssey*. Caldwell, Idaho: Caxton Press, 1985.

Scofield, Cyrus I. *Rightly Dividing the Word of Truth: Ten Outline Studies of the More Important Divisions of Scripture*. 4th ed. Philadelphia: Philadelphia School of the Bible, 1928.

———, ed. *Scofield Reference Bible*. New York: Oxford University Press, American Branch, 1909.

Scott, Walter Dill. *The Psychology of Advertising: A Simple Exposition of the Principles of Psychology in Their Relation to Successful Advertising*. Boston: Small, Maynard & Company, 1910.

Sears, Robert E. "MBI and the Fundamentalist Movement 1886–1930." Ph.D. thesis, Trinity Evangelical Divinity School, 1986.

Seeley, John Robert. *Ecce Homo: A Survey of the Life and Work of Jesus Christ*. London: Macmillan and Co., 1866.

Sehat, David. *The Myth of American Religious Freedom*. New York: Oxford University Press, 2011.

Sellers, Charles. *The Market Revolution: Jacksonian America, 1815–1846*. New York: Oxford University Press, 1992.

Sider-Rose, Michael Jay. "Between Heaven and Earth: Moody Bible Institute and the Politics of the Moderate Christian Right, 1945–1985." Ph.D., diss., University of Pittsburgh, 2001.

Sims, Charles N. *The Life of Rev. Thomas M. Eddy, D.D.* New York: Phillips & Hunt, 1880.

Sklansky, Jeffrey P. *The Soul's Economy: Market Society and Selfhood in American Thought, 1820–1920*. Chapel Hill: University of North Carolina Press, 2002.

Sklar, Martin J. *The Corporate Reconstruction of American Capitalism, 1890–1916: The Market, the Law, and Politics*. Cambridge and New York: Cambridge University Press, 1988.

Smith, Carl. *Urban Disorder and the Shape of Belief: The Great Chicago Fire, the Haymarket Bomb, and the Model Town of Pullman*. Chicago: University of Chicago Press, 2007.

Smith, Christian. *American Evangelicalism: Embattled and Thriving*. Chicago: University of Chicago Press, 1998.

———. *The Bible Made Impossible: Why Biblicism Is Not a Truly Evangelical Reading of Scripture*. Ada, Mich.: Brazos Press, 2011.

Smith, Wilbur M. *A Watchman on the Wall: The Life Story of Will H. Houghton,.* Grand Rapids, Mich.: Wm. B. Eerdmans, 1951.

Spalding, John Augustus. *Illustrated Popular Biography of Connecticut*. Accessed online September 28, 2009.

Stanley, Amy Dru. *From Bondage to Contract: Wage Labor, Marriage, and the Market in the Age of Slave Emancipation*. Cambridge, UK, and New York: Cambridge University Press, 1998.

Stansell, Christine. *City of Women: Sex and Class in New York, 1789–1860*. New York: Knopf, 1986.

Starr, Paul. *The Social Transformation of American Medicine*. New York: Basic Books, 1982.

Stead, W. T. *If Christ Came to Chicago! A Plea for the Union of All Who Love in the Service of All Who Suffer . . .* Chicago: Laird & Lee, 1894.

Stelzle, Charles. *A Son of the Bowery: The Life Story of an East Side American*. North Stratford, N.H.: Ayer Publishing, 1926.

Stephens, Randall J. *The Fire Spreads: Holiness and Pentecostalism in the American South*. Cambridge, Mass: Harvard University Press, 2010.

Stewart G. Cole. *The History of Fundamentalism*. Westport, Conn.: Greenwood Press, 1971.

Stoltzfus, Duane C. S. *Freedom from Advertising: E. W. Scripps's Chicago Experiment.* Urbana: University of Illinois Press, 2007.

Stowell, David Omar, ed. *The Great Strikes of 1877.* Urbana: University of Illinois Press, 2008.

Strasser, Susan. *Satisfaction Guaranteed: The Making of the American Mass Market.* Washington, D.C.: Smithsonian Books, 2004.

Strong, Josiah. *Our Country: Its Possible Future and Its Present Crisis.* New York: Baker & Taylor for the American Home Missionary Society, 1885.

Sutton, Matthew Avery. *Aimee Semple McPherson and the Resurrection of Christian America.* Cambridge, Mass.: Harvard University Press, 2007.

———. *American Apocalypse: A History of Modern Evangelicalism.* Cambridge, Mass.: Belknap Press of Harvard University Press, 2014.

Szasz, Ferenc. *Divided Mind of Protestant America, 1880–1930.* Tuscaloosa: University of Alabama Press, 1982.

Taves, Ann. *Fits, Trances, and Visions: Experiencing Religion and Explaining Experience from Wesley to James.* Princeton, N.J.: Princeton University Press, 1999.

Taylor, Charles. *A Secular Age.* Cambridge, Mass.: Belknap Press of Harvard University Press, 2007.

Tedlow, Richard S. *New and Improved: The Story of Mass Marketing in America.* Cambridge, Mass.: Harvard Business School Press, 1996.

Thompson, Edward Palmer. *The Making of the English Working Class.* New York: Pantheon Books, 1964.

Thornton, Harrison John. *The History of the Quaker Oats Company.* Chicago: University of Chicago Press, 1933.

———. "The History of the Quaker Oats Company." Ph.D. diss., University of Chicago, 1929.

Toone, Mark James. "Evangelicalism in Transition: A Comparative Analysis of the Work and Theology of D. L. Moody and His Protégés, Henry Drummond and R. A. Torrey." M.A. thesis, University of St. Andrews, 1988.

To Prohibit the Use of the Name of Any Religious Denomination, Society, or Association for the Purposes of Trade and Commerce. H. R. 435, Serial 30, February 3, 1916. Washington, D.C.: Government Printing Office, 1916.

Torrey, Reuben A. *Anecdotes and Illustrations.* New York and Chicago: Fleming H. Revell, 1907.

———. *The Baptism with the Holy Spirit.* New York and Chicago: Fleming H. Revell, 1895.

———. *The Bible and Its Christ: Being Noonday Talks with Business Men on Faith and Unbelief.* New York and Chicago: Fleming H. Revell, 1906.

———. *The Christ of the Bible.* New York: George H. Doren Co., 1924.

———. *Death Defeated and Defied: A Message of Comfort, Consolation and Cheer.* Los Angeles: Biola Book Room, 1923.

———. *Difficulties and Alleged Errors and Contradictions in the Bible.* New York and Chicago: Fleming H. Revell, 1907.

———. *Divine Healing: Does God Perform Miracles Today?* Grand Rapids, Mich.: Baker Book House, 1924.

———. *The Divine Origin of the Bible: Its Authority and Power Demonstrated and Difficulties Solved.* New York and Chicago: Fleming H. Revell, 1899.

——. *The Fundamental Doctrines of the Christian Faith*. New York: George H. Doran, 1918.

——. *Getting the Gold out of the Word of God; or, How to Study the Bible*. New York and Chicago: Fleming H. Revell, 1925.

——. *The God of the Bible; the God of the Bible as Distinguished from the God of "Christian Science"*... New York: George H. Doran Co., 1923.

——. *The Gospel for To-Day: New Evangelistic Sermons for a New Day*. New York and Chicago: Fleming H. Revell, 1922.

——. *The Higher Criticism and the New Theology : Unscientific, Unscriptural, and Unwholesome*. New York: Gospel Publishers House, 1911.

——. *The Holy Spirit: Who He Is and What He Does, and How to Know Him in All the Fulness of His Gracious and Glorious Ministry*. New York and Chicago: Fleming H. Revell, 1927.

——. *How to Bring Men to Christ*. New York and Chicago: Fleming H. Revell, 1893.

——. *How to Obtain Fullness of Power in Christian Life and Service*. New York and Chicago: Fleming H. Revell, 1897.

——. *How to Pray*. New York and Chicago: Fleming H. Revell, 1900.

——. *How to Study the Bible for the Greatest Profit*. New York and Chicago: Fleming H. Revell, 1896.

——. *How to Succeed in the Christian Life*. New York and Chicago: Fleming H. Revell, 1906.

——. *How to Work for Christ: A Compendium of Effective Methods*. New York and Chicago: Fleming H. Revell, 1901.

——. *The Importance and Value of Proper Bible Study; How Properly to Study and Interpret the Bible*. New York: George H. Doran Co., 1921.

——. *Individual Soul-Winning: Its Obligation and Its Methods*. Los Angeles: Biola Book Room, 1917.

——. *Is the Bible the Inerrant Word of God, and Was the Body of Jesus Raised from the Dead?* New York: George H. Doran Co., 1922.

——. *Is the Present "Tongues" Movement of God?* Los Angeles: Biola Book Room, 1913.

——. *The New Topical Textbook*. Minneapolis: World Wide, 1960.

——. *Peanut Patriotism and Pure Patriotism*. Los Angeles: Biola Book Room, 1918.

——. *The Person and Work of the Holy Spirit as Revealed in the Scriptures and in Personal Experience*. New York and Chicago: Fleming H. Revell, 1910.

——. *The Power of Prayer and the Prayer of Power*. New York and Chicago: Fleming H. Revell, 1924.

——. *Practical and Perplexing Questions Answered*. Chicago: Moody Press, 1909.

——. *The Real Christ: The Christ of Actual Historic Fact, as Distinguished from the Christ of Man's Dreams and Fancies and Imaginings*... New York: George H. Doran, 1920.

——. *Real Salvation and Whole-Hearted Service*. New York and Chicago: Fleming H. Revell, 1905.

——. *The Resurrection of the Lord Jesus*. Los Angeles: Bible Institute of Los Angeles, n.d.

——. *The Return of the Lord Jesus: The Key to the Scripture and Solution of All Our Political and Social Problems*. Los Angeles: Bible Institute of Los Angeles, 1913.

——. *Revival Addresses*. New York and Chicago: Fleming H. Revell, 1903.

——. *Soul-Winning Sermons*. Westwood, N.J.: Fleming H. Revell, 1956.

———. *Talks to Men about the Bible and the Christ of the Bible*. New York and Chicago: Fleming H. Revell, 1904.

———. *Traits and Tracts of Torrey: A Fresh Appreciation of a Great Man and Teacher*. Edited by Louis T. Talbot. Los Angeles.: Bible Institute of Los Angeles, n.d.

———. *Vest Pocket Companion for Christian Workers: The Best Texts for Personal Work Classified for Practical Use, Printed in Full and Arranged for Ready Reference*. New York and Chicago: Fleming H. Revell, 1895.

———. *The Voice of God in the Present Hour*. New York and Chicago: Fleming H. Revell, 1917.

———. *What the Bible Teaches: A Thorough and Comprehensive Study of What the Bible Has to Say Concerning the Great Doctrines of Which It Treats*. New York and Chicago: Fleming H. Revell, 1898.

———. *What I Believe*. London and Glasgow: R. L. Allan & Son, n.d. [1904?].

———. *Why God Used D. L. Moody*. Chicago: Bible Institute Colportage Association, 1923.

———. *Will Christ Come Again? An Exposure of the Foolishness, Fallacies, and Falsehoods of Shailer Mathews*. Los Angeles: Bible Institute of Los Angeles, 1918.

Trollinger, William Vance. *God's Empire: William Bell Riley and Midwestern Fundamentalism*. Madison: University of Wisconsin Press, 1990.

Turner, James. *Without God, Without Creed: The Origins of Unbelief in America*. Baltimore: Johns Hopkins University Press, 1985.

Turner, John G. *Bill Bright and Campus Crusade for Christ: The Renewal of Evangelicalism in Postwar America*. Chapel Hill: University of North Carolina Press, 2008.

Tweed, Thomas A., ed. *Retelling U.S. Religious History*. Berkeley: University of California Press, 1997.

Umansky, Ellen M. *From Christian Science to Jewish Science: Spiritual Healing and American Jews*. New York: Oxford University Press, 2005.

United States Bureau of the Census. *Historical Statistics of the United States: Colonial Times to 1970*. Washington, D.C.: Government Printing Office, 1975.

United States Christian Commission, for the Army and Navy. Work and Incidents. First-[fourth] Annual Report. 1863.

Vincent, James M. *The MBI Story: The Vision and Worldwide Impact of the Moody Bible Institute*. Chicago: Moody Publishers, 2011.

Vogel, Morris J., and Charles E. Rosenberg, eds. *The Therapeutic Revolution: Essays in the Social History of American Medicine*. Philadelphia: University of Pennsylvania Press, 1979.

Wacker, Grant. *Augustus H. Strong and the Dilemma of Historical Consciousness*. Macon, Ga.: Mercer University Press, 1985.

———. *Heaven Below: Early Pentecostals and American Culture*. Cambridge, Mass.: Harvard University Press, 2001.

Waldvogel, Edith L. "The 'Overcoming Life': A Study in the Reformed Evangelical Origins of Pentecostalism." Ph.D. diss., Harvard University, 1977.

Warfield, Benjamin Breckinridge. *Counterfeit Miracles*. New York: Charles Scribner's Sons, 1918.

Warner, Michael, Jonathan VanAntwerpen, and Craig Calhoun, eds. *Varieties of Secularism in a Secular Age*. Cambridge, Mass.: Harvard University Press, 2013.

Warner, Wayne E. *The Woman Evangelist: The Life and Times of Charismatic Evangelist Maria B. Woodworth-Etter*. Metuchen, N.J.: Scarecrow Press, 1986.

Washington, Booker Taliaferro, and Louis R. Harlan. *The Booker T. Washington Papers*. 14
vols. Urbana: University of Illinois Press, 1984.

Weber, Timothy P. *Living in the Shadow of the Second Coming: American Premillennialism,
1875–1925*. New York: Oxford University Press, 1979.

West, Nathaniel. *Premillennial Essays of the Prophetic Conference: Second Coming of Christ
with an Appendix of Critical Testimonies*. New York and Chicago: Fleming H. Revell,
1879.

Wharton, Henry Marvin. *A Month with Moody in Chicago: His Work and Workers*. Wharton
& Barron Pub. Co., 1894.

White, Christopher G. *Unsettled Minds: Psychology and the American Search for Spiritual
Assurance, 1830–1940*. Berkeley: University of California Press, 2008.

White, Ronald C., and Charles Howard Hopkins. *The Social Gospel: Religion and Reform in
Changing America*. Philadelphia: Temple University Press, 1976.

Wiebe, Robert H. *The Search for Order, 1877–1920*. New York: Hill and Wang, 1967.

Wigger, John H., and Nathan O. Hatch, eds. *Methodism and the Shaping of American
Culture*. Nashville, Tenn.: Abingdon Press, 2001.

Willard, Frances Elizabeth. *Glimpses of Fifty Years*. Evanston, Ill.: National Woman's
Christian Temperance Union, 1904.

Willett, Julie A. *Permanent Waves: The Making of the American Beauty Shop*. New York: New
York University Press, 2000.

Williams, Thomas Rhondda, ed. *The True Revival versus Torreyism*. London: Percy Lund,
Humphries, 1904.

Wills, Jocelyn. *Boosters, Hustlers, and Speculators: Entrepreneurial Culture and the Rise of
Minneapolis and St. Paul, 1849–1883*. St. Paul: Minnesota Historical Society Press, 2005.

Winston, Diane. *Red-Hot and Righteous: The Urban Religion of the Salvation Army*.
Cambridge, Mass: Harvard University Press, 1999.

Winston, Diane, and John M. Giggie, eds. *Faith in the Market: Religion and the Rise of Urban
Commercial Culture*. New Brunswick, N.J.: Rutgers University Press, 2002.

Winter, Alison. *Mesmerized: Powers of Mind in Victorian Britain*. Chicago: University of
Chicago Press, 2000.

Winter, Thomas. *Making Men, Making Class: The YMCA and Workingmen, 1877–1920*.
Chicago: University of Chicago Press, 2002.

Wosh, Peter J. *Spreading the Word*. Ithaca, N.Y.: Cornell University Press, 1994.

Wuthnow, Robert. *After Heaven: Spirituality in America since the 1950s*. Berkeley: University
of California Press, 1998.

Young, James Harvey. *Pure Food: Securing the Federal Food and Drugs Act of 1906*.
Princeton, N.J.: Princeton University Press, 1989.

Index

Bible conferences, 38, 129, 150, 165, 195, 212

Bible Institute Colportage Association (BICA), 149–50, 195, 230

Bible Institute of Chicago. *See* Moody Bible Institute

Bible Institute of Los Angeles (Biola), 166, 168, 179, 183–84, 186, 188–89, 194–95, 208, 212, 227, 229

Bible institutes: coordination among, 189, 194, 210–13; critiques of, 202, 213, 216; defense of, 202; role of, 211

Bible readers, 46, 48

Biblical World, 196, 202, 207

BICA. *See* Bible Institute Colportage Association

Binary thinking, 184, 203, 211, 214–16

Biola. *See* Bible Institute of Los Angeles

Blackstone, William, 49–50, 61, 166, 168, 204

Blanchard, Charles, 190

Bliss, Phillip, 39–40

Boardman, William E., 100

Bob Jones University, 196, 233

Booth, Herbert, 206

Borden, Mary, 157

Borden, William Whiting, 125

Bouton, Nathaniel S., 26, 60

Brand: in religion, 11, 13, 179, 195, 213, 232–33; in business, 120, 142–43, 174–75, 179, 192, 195, 213, 232–33. *See also* Trademark

Brookes, James, 104, 165

Brooks, Phillips, 36

Brothels, 17, 94–95

Bryan, William Jennings, 106–7, 222, 224

Buckley, J. M., 112–13

Buddhism, 71

Bureaucracy, 32, 87–88, 122, 125, 127–28, 153, 157, 166, 172, 202, 205, 232, 257 (n. 34). *See also* Management

Burgess, Marie, 133

Bushnell, Horace, 61, 100

Business: religion and, 3–4, 22, 36, 37, 76, 118, 121–22, 128, 130, 136–37, 138–39, 143, 163, 174, 176–77, 191–92, 199, 202, 206,

208–9, 218–19, 222, 231–33; ideology of, 5, 10, 19, 43, 142, 164, 206; reform and, 17–18, 49; strategies of, 19, 21, 117, 120–21, 138–42, 164–65, 174–76, 191–92, 231; influence on MBI, 125–30, 139, 150, 151–56, 158–61, 195, 200, 231, 233; influence on *The Fundamentals*, 167, 168, 172–74, 176–77; liberal Protestant complaints against, 202, 204. *See also* Elites

Businessman's revival. *See* Revival of 1857–58

Cabrini Green Housing Project, 229

Cadburys, 130

Calhoun, Joseph, 129–30

Calvinism, 23, 36, 146, 182, 202, 232

Capital, 23, 42, 53–54, 96, 99, 157, 164, 187, 201. *See also* Finances; Money; Stock; Wealth

Capitalists, 43, 120

Carnegie, Andrew, 120

Carnegie, Dale, 230

Carson Pirie, Scott & Co., 125

Cary, Charlotte, 155

Case, Shirley Jackson, 207

Catholicism, 12, 43, 67, 73, 82, 104, 165, 167, 168, 173, 188, 242 (n. 26)

Celebrity, 33, 39, 48, 56, 61, 69, 91, 128–29, 136, 195, 208, 233

Certitude, 4, 71–72, 84, 89, 103, 112

Cessationism, 100

Chafer, Louis Sperry, 197, 223, 257 (n. 18)

Channing, William Ellery, 71

Chapman, J. Wilbur, 129

Chicago Ave. Church. *See* Moody Church

Chicago Bible Work, 46–48, 54–55

Chicago Christian Institute, 205

Chicago Civic Commission, 95

Chicago Evangelization Society (CES), 62–64, 125. *See also* Moody Bible Institute

Chicago Fire (1871), 32–33, 43, 46, 49, 68

Chicago Relief and Aid Society, 43

Chicago Times, 39

Consumer culture, 14, 117, 138–39, 141–42, 145, 147, 207

Consumer goods, 21, 34, 117, 137, 139, 176–77, 218

Consumer identity, 11, 14, 139–43, 191–92, 205, 218–19, 232–34

Consumers, 9, 139, 140–43, 145, 159, 160, 164, 174–77, 205, 218–19, 224–25, 232–34

Consumer society, 117, 243 (n. 43)

Consumption (disease), 118

Contract, 77, 84, 85, 97–98, 140, 174; in religion, 78–80, 82, 145

Conversion, 20, 24, 36, 64, 75, 87, 88, 94, 104, 124–25, 126–27, 230, 242 (n. 11)

Cook, Edward F., 204

Cooperatives, 73–74, 97, 120. *See also* Communalism

Copyright, 149, 150, 227

Corporate Evangelicalism: as ideology, 2; defined, 2–5; realist beginnings of, 8, 18, 21, 24, 27–28, 34, 36, 40; social disorder and, 9, 42, 44–45, 54, 112–13, 162, 176–77; modernity and, 10, 121; "orthodoxy" and, 10, 176–78, 182, 184–85, 186, 191–92; disseminated by MBI, 137; consumer capitalism and, 138–39, 141–43, 146–47, 231–34; directed at professionals, 159–61. *See also* Evangelicalism; Evangelical Realism

Corporations: influence on religion, 3, 5, 14, 125–28, 136–37, 143, 145, 148, 155–56, 158–60, 196, 201, 231–33; relationship to consumers, 9, 140, 142–43, 145, 148, 196; structure of, 117, 120–21, 139–40, 164, 201; legal personhood of, 140, 143

Coverture, 68, 77

Coxey, Jacob, 99

Credit, 96, 175. *See also* Debt

Creeds, 8, 19, 81, 85, 163, 177, 178, 185, 185, 192, 200, 201, 210, 212, 216, 217, 222–23, 230. *See also* Theology

Creel, George, 207

Crittenton, Charles, 82

Crowell, Henry P., 1, 2, 3, 9; business practices of, 117, 119–22, 142–43, 174–76;

need for control, 117, 120, 123, 125–26, 128, 136, 153, 154–56, 163; leadership at MBI, 118, 123–30, 136–37, 145, 148–50, 151–59; background on, 118–19; other religious activities of, 121, 136–37; Torrey and, 129–30, 154–55, 227; involvement with *The Fundamentals*, 163, 168, 170–71, 173–74, 176–77, 183–84, 188–90; conflicts with Stewart, 188–90. See also *Fundamentals, The*; Moody Bible Institute; Quaker Oats

Crowell, Lillie (Wick), 119

Crowell, Susan (Coleman), 121, 157

Cruden's Concordance, 149

Cullis, Charles, 100

Culture, evangelicalism and, 4, 10

Cuyler, Theodore, 25, 33

Dallas Theological Seminary, 197, 233

Darby, John Nelson, 29–30, 31, 103–4

Darwin, Charles, 4, 23, 71, 162–63

Davenport, James, 67

Debt, 18, 82–83, 104

Delitzsch, Franz, 72

Demand: in economy, 53, 120, 143, 174–76; in religion, 177

Democracy, 5, 48, 98, 101, 107, 201, 202, 207–9

Democratic Party, 39, 106

Denominations, 42, 100, 113, 131; evangelicalism and, 4, 5, 7, 44, 161, 233; liberal Protestantism and, 8, 162–63, 166–67, 201–4, 216–17; Moody and, 19, 21–22, 24, 36, 38–40, 51, 62–64; premillennialism and, 29, 31, 49, 61, 185, 198–200; MBI and, 42, 46–47, 59, 62–65, 87, 92, 94, 127–30, 157–58, 195–96, 198, 202, 204, 205, 211, 212, 214, 216–17, 223; *The Fundamentals* and, 163, 168–69, 171, 173, 176–79, 181, 191–92; fundamentalist movement and, 198, 200–202, 203–4, 210–12, 216. See also Churchly Protestantism; Religious authority

Devil, 86, 100, 109, 111, 112, 135, 170, 184, 210, 221–22, 225

Diphtheria, 107–8, 111

Dispensationalism, 12–13, 197–98, 208–9, 220, 233; professional middle classes and, 9, 121, 124, 145, 147–48, 160–61, 186, 206; miracles and, 103, 105, 108, 113; development of, 103–4; radical evangelicalism and, 103–8, 113; Moody and, 104, 106, 107; MBI and, 104–5, 108, 145, 148, 151–52, 154, 157, 166, 194, 200, 204, 206, 211, 217, 227; Biola and, 166, 194; Pentecostalism and, 132–33, 227; Stewart and, 165, 166, 168, 179, 182, 184, 194; *The Fundamentals* and, 178, 179, 183–84, 188, 192. *See also* Bible; Keswick Holiness; Premillennialism; Synthetic method

Dixon, Azmi C., 90, 166–67, 206, 222, 253 (n. 13); *The Fundamentals* and, 168–72, 177, 179–80, 182–84, 197–98

Dixon, Thomas, 166

Doctrine. *See* Theology

Dodge, Grace, 82

Dowie, John Alexander, 11, 90, 112–13, 202; background of, 99–101; medical professionals and, 101–2, 107, 109–11, 247 (n. 93); Torrey and, 108–11, 122–23, 135–36; influence on Pentecostalism, 130–31, 134, 136

Drake, Edwin, 163–64

Dryer, Emma, 46–49, 52–53, 54, 61, 62–64, 76, 111, 125–26

Durant, Henry F., 25

Durham, William, 134

Duty, 37, 141, 156, 213

Dwight, John, 122

Ecce Homo, 72–73

Economy: moral theories of, 11, 53, 68, 83, 96–98, 186–87; panics in, 18, 21, 69, 70, 95–96; ideas about, 54, 76, 117; depressions in, 95–97, 139

Eddy, Mary Baker, 186

Eddy, Sherwood, 91

Eddy, Thomas M., 17–18

Education, college: MBI leadership and, 46, 70, 104, 152, 206, 213; MBI's relation

to, 84, 92, 152, 159, 213, 229, 231; liberal Protestantism and, 91, 162–63, 210, 220; Pentecostalism and, 99, 131, 133; Stewart's relationship to, 164, 166; *The Fundamentals* and, 167, 173, 179–80; fundamentalist movement and, 212–13

Edwards, Jonathan, 67, 232

Efficiency, 34, 54, 69, 96, 119–20, 152, 156, 195, 211

Eight-hour workday, 43, 53, 54, 59

Electricity, 78, 146, 161, 206, 229, 251 (n. 19)

Elites, 27, 42, 48–49, 51, 69–70, 72, 107, 118; evangelicalism and, 6–8, 34, 65, 160–61, 187; professionals and, 12, 97–98, 101; critiques of, 43–45, 54, 58, 74–75, 97–99, 208; labor unrest and, 53, 57, 96; MBI and, 55, 57–58, 60, 153–54, 229; fundamentalist movement and, 193, 203–4. *See also* Class; "Respectable" Protestantism

Emerson, Ralph Waldo, 71

Empiricism, 6, 27, 89; evangelicalism and, 7, 8, 12, 28, 38, 67, 84

Employee, 19, 25, 41, 42, 77–78, 99, 137, 140, 142, 187, 220, 228, 231; MBI policies for, 125, 155–56, 158–59, 222

Employer, 21, 23, 31–32, 77–78, 84, 128, 145–46, 149

Endowment, 63, 122, 153, 166

Enduement of power. *See* Baptism of the Holy Spirit

Engineering, 2, 4, 5, 9, 42, 92, 97, 104, 120, 147, 206, 229, 230

Enlightenment, 6, 100

Enthusiasm, 67, 132

Episcopals, 9, 70, 100, 123, 201

Equality, 52, 75, 77, 142, 167, 186

Erdman, Charles, 185, 187, 203, 255 (n. 81)

Erdman, William J., 38, 169

Eugenics, 98, 218

Evangelicalism, 2, 66, 71, 137, 141, 195; as orientation, 6, 12–13, 20, 163, 216; before the Civil War, 6–7, 20–24; as label, 10, 206, 216, 220, 227. *See also* Conservative Evangelicalism;

Corporate evangelicalism; Evangelical realism; Fundamentalism; Radical evangelicalism

Evangelical realism, 8, 11, 27–28, 32, 36–38, 47–48, 75, 95, 99, 103, 105–6, 112–13, 139, 143, 146, 161, 208–9. *See also* Corporate evangelicalism; Realism

Evangelism, 13, 46, 49, 50, 62, 75, 76, 91, 94, 112, 136, 151, 187, 190, 203, 210, 229–30; relationship to sales, 8, 34, 36, 76, 86, 136, 139; Moody and, 32, 33, 90–92, 112; as a personal act, 56, 139, 147, 190; Torrey and, 81–82, 86–87, 102. *See also* Revivals

Evangelistic Record, 52

Evans, William, 210

Evolution, 80, 167, 184, 194, 202, 206, 209–10, 213, 214, 217, 223–24, 230

Faith: as act of believing, 30, 37, 72, 73, 80–81, 84, 89, 90, 93, 100, 108, 131, 182, 211, 231; judging authenticity of, 5–7, 8, 18, 19, 20, 28, 36, 38, 139, 141, 218, 220

Faith healing, 8, 119, 146, 186; evangelical realism and, 80–81, 100, 112; medical professionalization and, 101–2, 107–11; MBI and, 108–11, 122, 127, 152; Pentecostalism and, 130–32

Faith work, 30, 66, 82–84, 131–33

Family, 7, 67, 77, 81, 88, 111, 141, 147, 152, 165, 205

Farm Implement News, 138

Farming. *See* Agriculture

Farwell, John V., 21–22, 24, 39, 41–42, 60, 76, 95

Farwell Hall, 26, 31–32, 60

Federal Communications Commission, 228

Federal Council of Churches (FCC), 1–2, 201, 209

Federation of Ministers, 95

Field, Marshall, 39, 95

Filling of the Holy Spirit, 145, 158, 199. *See also* Baptism of the Holy Spirit; Holy Spirit

Finances, 33, 48, 51, 57, 58, 70, 82–83, 87, 88, 95, 98, 122, 125, 127–28, 134, 149, 163–65, 172, 177, 182, 183, 189, 198, 200, 220, 231. *See also* Capital; Money; Stock; Wealth

First Congregational Church (Chicago), 31

Fitt, Arthur P., 95, 111, 122–24, 126, 129, 134–35, 149–50, 152, 154–55, 156, 166, 252 (n. 48)

Fosdick, Harry Emerson, 216–17, 220, 221

Foster, George Burman, 167

"Founder's week," 211

Frame, Esther, 76

Frank, F. H. R., 72, 79

Freedom: personal, 22, 98, 141, 178; religious, 22, 145–46; political, 42; economic, 42–43, 77, 140–41; academic, 166. *See also* Autonomy; Choice

French Revolution, 28

Fuller Theological Seminary, 228

Full gospel, 76, 90, 100. *See also* Faith healing; Pentecostalism; Tongues, speaking in

Function of Religion, 167

Fundamentalism, 2, 8, 10, 145, 231; related to corporate evangelicalism, 3; perception as traditional, 11; defined, 13. *See also* Evangelicalism

Fundamentalist-modernist controversies, 196, 198, 201–4, 207, 209–10, 216–17, 225, 227

Fundamentalist movement: formation of, 178, 191, 194; MBI's involvement in, 194, 195–201, 204, 213, 224–225; perceived as elite, 203; World War 1 and, 206–9; WCFA and, 210–16, 223; evolution and, 223–24

Fundamentals, The, 2, 9–10, 163; inception, 167–68; MBI's involvement in, 168, 169–70, 171–74, 183–84, 189–90, 222; Stewart's influence on, 168, 169–70, 172–73, 179, 184, 187–88, 190; envisioned as magazine, 168–69, 173, 188–89; reputation of, 169, 172, 179–81; content of, 169–70, 178–88, 190, 191, 194, 222; contributors to, 169–70, 179, 184, 191,

Holiness, 67–68, 145–46, 227. *See also*
    Keswick Holiness
Holy Ghost and Us Bible School, 131
Holy Roller, 202, 231. *See also* Enthusiasm;
    Pentecostalism
Holy Spirit, 81, 84, 199, 200; as God's
    envoy, 32, 88, 105, 161; theories about,
    66–69, 75, 76, 145, 147, 155, 158, 167, 178;
    Pentecostalism and, 130, 131, 134, 135. *See
    also* Baptism of the Holy Spirit
Horton, Thomas, 165–66, 183–84, 223
Houghteling, James, 26
Houghton, Will, 229–30
Howard, Oliver O., 90
Howland, W. H., 82
How to Study the Bible for Greatest Profit, 86
Hull House, 46, 97
Hunter, John, 155–56

Identity: religious, 7, 10–11, 76, 132, 185,
    191, 230, 232, 233; class-based, 10, 43,
    97, 98, 140–41, 148, 213; legal, 68, 77;
    organizational, 221. *See also* Consumer
    identity
Illinois Street Church. *See* Moody Church
Independence. *See* Autonomy; Freedom
Individualism: evangelicalism and, 2, 4–7,
    12–13, 20, 187, 192, 199, 207, 210, 218,
    228, 231, 233–34; economy and, 4–5,
    74–75, 83–84, 89, 96–97, 139–42, 187; the
    Enlightenment and, 6; Moody's views
    on, 37, 38, 42, 50–51, 56, 66; Torrey's shift
    to, 67, 72, 83–84; social reform and, 75,
    205; Crowell and, 118; race and, 218, 228
Industrial capitalism, 8, 75; development
    of, 42; work relations and, 43, 53, 73–74,
    96. *See also* Wage labor; Work
Influenza, 210
Insanity, 32, 159
Institute Tie, 134, 135, 150–51, 157–58,
    162, 189. See also *Christian Workers
    Magazine*; *Moody Bible Institute Monthly*
International Harvester, 21, 54
International Workers of the World
    (IWW), 207

Intuition, 71, 80
Investment, 21, 31, 49, 53–54, 74, 83, 89,
    118, 120, 121, 164, 169, 187. *See also*
    Speculator; Stock
Israel, 50

Jefferson Street Church (Minneapolis), 74
Jehovah's Witnesses (Millennial Dawn),
    186, 202
Jenkins, Jerry, 233–34
Jesus, 12, 20, 23, 36, 66, 72–73, 98–99,
    185; ethics of, 9, 51, 60, 74–75, 99,
    103, 186–87, 196, 199, 208, 217;
    premillennialism and, 28–29, 31, 38,
    40, 49, 185; miracles and, 90, 100, 103;
    dispensationalism and, 104–5; deity
    of, 167, 182, 185–86
Jesus Is Coming, 49–50, 168
Jews, 81, 133, 170, 190, 204. *See also* Anti-
    Semitism; Judaism
Jones, Bob, 196
Jones, Jenkin Lloyd, 95
Judaism, 71, 202

Keith, Elbridge G., 26, 60
Kellogg, Giles, 170
Keswick Holiness, 145–48, 155, 160–61, 165,
    178, 199, 227, 229
King's Business, 188–89, 190, 194
Knights of Labor, 53
Knights of Labor (newspaper), 60
Ku Klux Klan, 218

Labor activists, 99, 140. *See also*
    Working class
Laborers. *See* Workers
Labor ladder, 43, 140
Labor unrest, 3, 8, 25, 41–44, 47, 48, 49–50,
    53–54, 57, 59–60, 96, 99, 210, 218–19. *See
    also* Populism; Working class
Laity, 25, 27, 38, 40, 48, 55, 58–59, 62, 72,
    136–37, 150, 165, 167, 169, 171, 173, 177,
    181, 191, 193, 204, 229
Latter rain, 132, 133, 134
Latter Rain Evangel, 135

Middlebury College, 220

Middle class, 33, 52; identity of, 10, 24,
   97–98; conflict within, 12, 96–99;
   reproduction of, 19; cultural norms
   of, 27, 67–68, 89, 131, 158–59, 217–19,
   225, 228; the social order and, 41, 43,
   57, 59–60; respectability and, 43, 103,
   196, 217; consumption and, 139–43;
   corporate evangelicalism and, 143–48;
   MBI targeting, 148–53, 155–56, 158, 160,
   161, 205, 213, 216. *See also* Professional
   middle class; Radical middle class;
   "Respectable" Protestantism

Middle-class Protestantism. *See*
   "Respectable" Protestantism

Mildmay, 30, 45–46, 48, 62, 68, 145

Military, 24, 41, 99, 205, 207–8, 211, 230;
   imagery in religion, 85–86, 205

Millennial Dawn, 186, 202

Miller, William, 29, 49

Milton, John, 198

Mind cure, 80

Ministers, 2, 70, 74, 82, 107, 146, 160, 202–4,
   207, 210, 232–33; the *Fundamentals*
   and, 10, 163, 165, 169, 173, 177, 180–81,
   183–84, 191; traditional role of, 19, 25,
   28, 30, 55, 67, 75; Moody and, 22, 24–25,
   34, 38, 45, 51, 57–58; MBI and, 85, 91–93,
   95, 113, 205, 229; social order and, 101;
   professional medicine and, 101–2,
   109–11, authority of, 121

Minneapolis, 73–74

Minneapolis City Mission, 81–82

Miracles, 6, 8, 9, 66, 71, 73, 76, 100, 103–5,
   112–13, 124–25, 133, 162, 202. *See also*
   Faith healing; Faith work; Prayer

Missionary, 55, 56, 92–93, 125, 134, 157–58,
   160, 168, 173, 183, 204, 205, 230

Missionary Training Home for Young
   Women, 45–46. *See also* Mildmay

Missions, overseas, 132, 173, 213, 230. *See
   also* Missionary

Modernism, theological. *See* Liberal
   Protestantism

Modernity, 5, 162, 163, 206

Mohammedanism (Islam), 71

Monetary policy, 96, 97

Money, 32, 74, 95, 99, 118, 120, 121, 140, 147,
   153, 165, 166, 167, 169, 183, 186–87, 194,
   202, 204, 207. *See also* Capital; Finances;
   Stock; Wealth

Montgomery, Carrie Judd, 100

Montgomery Ward, 205

Moody, Betsey, 18–19

Moody, Dwight L., 3, 8, 42, 167; early
   life, 18–24; as man of business, 21–22,
   24, 34; YMCA and, 25–27, 31–32, 109;
   premillennialism and, 30–31, 38–39,
   49–50, 61, 109; revival ministry of,
   33–34, 39–40, 44–45, 49–50, 55–56, 59,
   69, 90–92, 94–95, 111, 118, 167; religious
   message of, 35–38, 143; the "masses"
   and, 44–46, 54–62, 94, 99; the Chicago
   Bible Work and, 48; social views of,
   51–52; at Northfield, 52–53, 65; the CES
   and, 62–64; MBI and, 64–65, 84–85, 110,
   111, 125–26, 213, 219–23; views on Holy
   Spirit, 66, 68–69; faith healing and,
   102–3, 108–11, 229; dispensationalism
   and, 104, 106, 107, 208; death of, 111–12;
   use of by others, 118, 122, 128, 129,
   136, 153–54, 162, 194, 196, 211, 219–23;
   connections to Keswick Holiness, 145

Moody, Edwin, 18

Moody, Emma (Revell), 24, 63, 149

Moody, Paul, 52, 167, 220–21

Moody, William R., 52, 136, 149, 155, 162,
   195–96, 220–21, 222–23

Moody Bible Institute (MBI), 2, 3;
   beginnings of, 8, 55, 56, 64–65; disorder
   and, 9, 42; elites and, 58, 60, 61, 87,
   95, 125, 153–54, 157–58; trustees of, 60,
   62–64, 122, 123–26, 149, 158, 170, 190,
   194, 196–97, 200, 205, 222, 232, 233;
   donors to, 60, 64, 122, 125, 149, 153, 162,
   172, 196, 222; premillennialism and,
   61, 64–65, 194, 197–99, 203–4, 207, 211,
   217–18, 220–22, 227, 233–34; gender and,
   62, 92–94, 125–26, 152, 155, 159–60, 205,
   229; publications of, 83–84, 88, 130, 135,

138, 148–51, 156, 162, 195–96, 200, 205, 213–14, 230, 233; Torrey's development of, 84–89, 102; evangelism and, 86–87, 90, 94–95, 136–37; students at, 87–88, 92–94, 102, 108, 129, 131, 133, 135, 136, 152, 154, 157, 158–60, 196–97, 205–6, 213, 218–19, 222, 228, 229, 234; race and, 93, 159–60, 196–97, 217–19, 228–29; faculty of, 94, 124, 158–59, 195, 198, 205, 206, 214, 225, 227, 228, 229; faith healing and, 102, 108, 110–11; dispensationalism and, 105; Moody's death and, 111–13; Crowell's development of, 118, 123–27, 151–60, 204–6; crisis at, 122–23, 127, 137; executive committee of, 123, 126, 127, 130, 149, 155–57, 196–97, 220, 251 (n. 41); Business department of, 127; Educational department of, 127, 151–53; Correspondence department of, 127, 206, 220, 227, 228; Extension department of, 127–30, 136, 148, 150, 152, 157, 196–97, 205, 227, 228, 230; Pentecostalism and, 132–35, 225, 227, 231; shift to Keswick Holiness theology, 145, 148, 158; relation to Moody family, 149, 155, 219–23; relation to Moody Church, 153, 155–56, 168, 213; as supplier of "pure religion," 153, 162–63, 168, 213–19; founding date controversy, 153–54; promotional techniques of, 153–54, 158–59, 195–96, 199–200, 203–4, 205–7, 213–14, 218–20, 222–23; corporate policies of, 155–56, 158–60; foreign mission department of, 156–58, 204; involvement in *The Fundamentals*, 163, 168, 170–72, 173–74, 176–77, 180, 181–83, 189, 190; influence on other organizations, 166, 196–97, 200, 210, 212–13, 223, 225, 227–33; as fundamentalist headquarters, 194, 195–201, 204, 213, 224–25; continuing *The Fundamentals*, 195–201; battles with liberals and, 202–4, 207–8, 209–10, 216–17, 220–23; WFCA and, 210–13, 216; aviation department of, 230; declining

profile of, 231–34. *See also* Bible Institute Colportage Association; Chicago Bible Work; Chicago Evangelization Society; *Institute Tie*; Moody Institute of Science
Moody Bible Institute Monthly, 213–16, 223, 228. See also *Christian Workers Magazine*; *Institute Tie*
Moody Church, 24, 30, 46, 61, 63, 93, 125, 153, 155–56, 167, 169, 170, 171, 213
Moody Institute of Science (MIS), 229–30
Moody Press, 230. *See also* Bible Institute Colportage Association
Moody Tabernacle (Chicago), 39, 41–42
Moon, Irwin, 229–30
Moorehead, William G., 64–65, 186, 255 (n. 81)
Moorehouse, Henry, 30, 33
Morgan, G. Campbell, 113
Moses, 104, 106, 112
Mott, John, 91, 193
Moule, Handley C. G., 179–80
Mount Vernon Congregational Church, 19
Muckraking, 91, 163, 169, 171, 178, 179, 188
Mueller, George, 30, 82
Music, 33, 87, 120, 130, 156, 233

National Association of Evangelicals, 228
National Religious Broadcasters, 228
Needham, George, 61
Nelson, Shirley, 229
Neoclassical economics, 141
Newell, William, 104–5, 107, 121, 124, 145, 146–47, 208–9, 246 (n. 71)
Newton, Isaac, 198
New York Tribune, 56
Niagara Bible Conference, 38, 165. *See also* Bible conferences
Norris, J. Frank, 223, 225
North Avenue Mission (Chicago), 134
Northern Baptist Convention, 216
Northfield, Mass., 18, 52, 59, 65, 88, 104; Moody's ministries at, 52, 122–23, 162, 165, 167–68, 220–23
Northfield Bible Conference, 52, 165
Norton, William, 149, 195

Power: social, 5–7, 11–12, 42, 75, 99, 101, 176–77, 191, 205; spiritual, 33, 65, 66–69, 75, 76–79, 84–85, 88, 123, 130, 132, 135, 145–48, 200, 221, 232; physical, 42, 73, 146; institutional, 123–26, 183, 221; market, 173–76, 232. *See also* Religious authority

Pragmatism, 27, 52, 53, 61, 76, 91, 93, 94

Prayer, 40, 51; devotional, 20, 68, 76–77, 78; corporate, 21–22, 25, 52, 56, 88, 93–94, 131, 218; for miraculous intervention, 30, 61, 66, 79–84, 87, 102–3, 107–11, 132, 186. *See also* Faith healing; Faith work

Premillennialism: development of, 28–31, 38, 49–50, 60–61; Moody and, 32, 38–40, 50, 91; Dryer and, 46–48; MBI and, 61, 64–65, 194, 197–99, 203–4, 207, 211, 217–18, 220–22, 227, 233–34; Torrey and, 80, 207, 227; dispensationalism and, 103–5, 211, 227; Stewart and, 165, 168; Biola and, 166; *The Fundamentals* and, 169, 170, 183–86, 188, 192, 198; fundamentalist movement and, 193–94, 197–99, 202–4, 206–9, 211, 217–18, 232; World War I and, 206–9. *See also* Biblical prophecy; Dispensationalism; Latter Rain; Rapture

Premiums, 143, 153. *See also* Promotion

Presbyterian Evangelistic Committee, 129

Presbyterians, 36, 39, 58, 69, 118, 125, 128, 129–30, 163, 165, 169, 170, 188, 193, 198, 210, 214

Press, the, 81, 83, 97, 101, 110, 153–54, 173; Moody and, 27, 31, 33–34, 39–40, 44, 57, 62; Torrey and, 81, 83, 110–11, 122, 129

Princeton Seminary, 92, 104, 112, 128, 168, 179, 185, 202, 203, 205

Princeton University, 54

Print culture, 148

Private property, 98

Producerism, 43, 45, 47, 97, 117, 119, 120

Production, 42, 117, 120, 142, 164, 174–75, 238 (n. 41). *See also* Industrial

Capitalism; Manufacturing; Overproduction

Professional medicine. *See* Medical profession

Professionalization, 9, 100–102, 126, 133, 152, 187, 230; influence on religion, 51, 137, 147, 153, 209

Professional middle class, 2–5, 10, 42–43, 217; expertise and, 9, 147; ideology of, 12, 14, 97–98, 104, 126; evangelical realism and, 18, 25, 57, 112, 139; MBI and, 92, 94, 127–30, 136–37, 153, 156, 158–60, 205, 206; dispensationalism and, 104, 124, 145, 147; religious influence on, 109–10, 138–39; Pentecostalism and, 131–33; fundamentalist movement and, 213, 216. *See also* Legal profession; Medical profession; Middle class; Professionalization

Profit: in business, 54, 57, 61, 96, 119–21, 140, 142, 164, 174–76; as idea in religion, 74, 86

Promotion, 1, 9–10, 117, 120–21, 141–43, 173–76; used in religion, 14, 23, 153–54, 158, 163, 177. *See also* Advertising

Propaganda, 203, 204, 207, 208

Prophecy: in Bible, 28–29, 49–50, 85, 104, 134, 179, 182, 183, 184, 187, 188, 190, 194, 206, 207, 209

Prophecy Conferences: 1878 in New York, 49–50; 1886 in Chicago, 60–61; 1914 at MBI, 197–200, 203, 212; 1918 in Philadelphia, 193–94. *See also* Bible conferences; Premillennialism

Proprietors, small, 42, 96, 121, 140. *See also* Populism; Radical middle class

Prostitution, 17, 94–95

Protestant establishment, 7, 58, 101, 111. *See also* "Respectable" Protestantism

Protestant work ethic, 68

Psychology, 103, 138–39, 142, 151. *See also* Social science

Psychology of Advertising, 138–39

Pullman, George, 96

Pullman Strike, 96–97

Sandford, Frank, 131
"Sands, The," 22
Sankey, Ira, 33, 40, 45
Satan. *See* Devil
Schumacher, Ferdinand, 119, 121–22, 124
Science, 4, 9, 80, 101, 103, 141–42, 161, 167,
    193, 194, 198, 206, 210, 229–30, 231. *See
    also* Social science
Scofield, Cyrus I., 90, 104–5, 107, 133,
    145–46, 152, 168, 182, 183, 187, 188, 190,
    198, 212, 220
Scofield Correspondence Course, 105, 200,
    203, 205
Scofield Reference Bible, 105, 147–48, 200
Scopes Trial, 224
Scott, Robert, 26, 60
Scott, Robert L., Jr., 125
Scott, Walter Dill, 138–39
Scudder, Vida D., 206
Secret Power, 68
Secret societies, 70, 165, 187–88, 190, 192
Sects: social disorder and, 28–29, 31, 49,
    67, 107, 109, 110; MBI and, 59, 61, 64,
    85, 151–52, 153, 159, 161, 198, 200, 204,
    225, 228, 231–32; *The Fundamentals* and,
    179, 185, 186; fundamentalist movement
    and, 202, 212–13
Secular, 1, 8, 10, 75, 100–101, 136, 138–39,
    187, 193, 208–9, 217–18, 231–32
Seeley, John, 72–73
Seminary, 2, 25, 46, 52, 55, 56, 61, 64, 65,
    70–71, 84, 92, 94, 123, 127, 133, 152, 159,
    160, 173, 177, 180, 198, 202, 210, 211–12,
    222
Sermon on the Mount, 105, 133, 217
Sermons from Science, 230
Service, 205
Seymour, William, 132, 134
Shaw, John Balcom, 188
Sherman Antitrust Act, 120
Shoe industry, 19, 21, 118
Simpson, Albert B., 100, 102, 105, 107
Smith, George Adam, 221, 222
Smith, Merton, 63–64
Smith, Sydney T., 196

Smith, Thomas S., 125, 170–71, 183, 189–90,
    195, 222, 223, 228
Smith, Wilbur, 228
Social Darwinism, 27, 75
Social disorder. *See* Social order
Social gospel, 75, 82, 84, 91, 92, 141, 167, 187,
    201, 203, 208, 238 (n. 41)
Socialism, 60, 187. *See also* Communism
Social order, 3, 17–18, 41–43, 65, 98, 109,
    165; evangelicalism and, 6–8, 25, 49–50,
    66, 81, 112–13, 133, 137; Holy Spirit and,
    32, 67–68, 145; MBI and, 55–60, 62, 127;
    critique of, 131–33
Social reform, 6–7, 13, 25–26 (benevolence),
    42, 51, 66, 74–76, 94–95, 148, 161, 169,
    201
Social science, 4–5, 8, 75, 141
Social unrest. *See* Social order
Society, ideas of, 4, 6, 51, 73, 75, 83–84, 98,
    141
Society of Friends (Quakers), 1, 76
Sodomy, trial for, 188
Soldiers. *See* Military
Southern whites, 43, 48–49, 51–52, 90, 97,
    133, 160, 168, 196–97, 198, 204, 212, 214,
    216, 233
Spanish-American War, 108
Speculator, 18, 43, 75, 96. *See also*
    Investment; Stock
Speer, Robert, 91
Spiritualism, 188
Standard Oil, 164, 169, 182
Statistics, 87–88
Stead, William, 94–95
Stelzle, Charles, 92–94, 241 (n. 51)
Stephens, Thomas, 170, 172, 180–81, 182,
    184, 188, 189, 191, 200
Stewart, Lyman, 9, 163, 227; desire for
    control, 16, 172, 194; business and
    religious background, 163–66; concerns
    with secret societies, 165, 187–88, 190;
    philanthropic work, 165–66; Biola and,
    166, 184, 188–89, 194–95; MBI and, 166,
    188–90, 194, 200; concerns with liberal
    theology, 166–69, 179; interest in biblical

Made in the USA
Columbia, SC
25 August 2024

41122662R00195